An Introduction to the Kabbalah

SUNY Series in Judaica: Hermeneutics, Mysticism, and Religion
Michael Fishbane, Robert Goldenberg, and Elliot Wolfson, Editors

AN INTRODUCTION TO THE KABBALAH

MOSHE HALLAMISH

Translated by

Ruth Bar-Ilan and Ora Wiskind-Elper

STATE UNIVERSITY OF NEW YORK PRESS

Published by
State University of New York Press, Albany

Printed in the United States of America

For information, address the State University of New York Press,
State University Plaza, Albany, NY 12246

Production by Bernadine Dawes • Marketing by Patrick Durocher

Library of Congress Cataloging-in-Publication Data

Ḥalamish, Mosheh.
[Mavo la-Kabalah. English]
An introduction to the Kabbalah / Moshe Hallamish ; translated by
Ruth Bar-Ilan and Ora Wiskind-Elper.
p. cm. — (SUNY series in Judaica)
Includes bibliographical references and index.
ISBN 0-7914-4011-7 (alk. paper). — ISBN 0-7914-4012-5 (pbk.: alk.
paper)
1. Cabala—History. 2. Mysticism—Judaism—History. I. Title.
II. Series.
BM526.H3413 1999
296.1'6—dc21 98-7527
CIP

1 2 3 4 5 6 7 8 9 10

CONTENTS

PREFACE

> In our generation, whoever has a general soul must occupy himself with Introductions, providing the keys for every lofty matter.
>
> —Rabbi Kook, *Orot ha-Kodesh*

In this day and age, when a variety of outlooks and lifestyles vie for our attention, and the mass media, along with modern sophisticated technology, allow for a relatively smooth transition from one area of interest to another, the widespread fascination with the world of mysticism and the yearning to get to know it more intimately are quite remarkable. Unfortunately, these pursuits have produced some side effects that are inherently dangerous or smell of pure charlatanism.

My purpose in writing this book is to enlighten the educated public about Jewish mysticism, namely the Kabbalah, by presenting its major concepts through the filter of scientific evaluation. Thus, my approach in handling the subject matter is to describe things objectively, as far as possible, without any missionary attempts at indoctrination or practical guidance. Naturally, whoever wishes to go beyond the basics provided in this book, in order to pursue in depth some particular direction, is welcome to do so.

This book, then, seeks to open the gates of the Kabbalah to the educated reader, inviting him to peer into the world of the Kabbalist and contemplate the outlook of the Kabbalah as an ideology. Clearly, as an introductory text, this book is not meant to exhaust these two major aspects of the Kabbalah; rather, it outlines the essential processes, problems, developments, and ramifications that are related to them. Differences of opinion are pointed out only insofar as they are called for in the context of some specific discussion. But there is room for other views, as the history of kabbalistic literature itself shows. Consequently, the references in the notes draw attention to sources and critical works that dwell on other points of interest. In presenting the kabbalistic themes, I am not concerned with tracing their historical development; I have taken the license to skip across historical periods. I tried to include as many kabbalistic terms and concepts as possible in order to acquaint the reader with their exact meaning. Many quotations of passages from kabbalistic texts are given to introduce readers to the atmosphere and literature of the Kabbalah and to acquaint them with its somewhat obscure language.

In deciding upon the selection, arrangement, and presentation of the material, I have been guided by didactic considerations. These dictated what weight to give to each subject. Depending upon reader response, other topics may be incorporated in a future, enlarged edition. At any rate, I did not have in mind to write an all-inclusive encyclopedic work. The book is as suggested by its title—an introduction designed to make the worlds of the Kabbalah and the Kabbalist more accessible to the educated reader.

It is a pleasant duty for me to express my thanks to Dr. Meir Ayali and Ephraim Ben Ḥayyim, who sponsored the original Hebrew version of this book. I am grateful to my friend, Dr. Abraham Shapira, who assisted me with sound advice. Special thanks are due to the translators: Ms. Ruth Bar-Ilan (who translated the first part of this book), and Ms. Ora Wiskind-Elper (who translated the second part). I am deeply grateful for the financial support I received from the following at Bar-Ilan University: Prof. M. E. Rackman, the chancellor; the Department of Philosophy; and Rabbi Dr. Alexandre Safran, Chair of Research into Kabbalah. Last but not least, I wish to express my thanks to the editorial board of State University of New York Press for adding my book to the list of its distinguished publications.

Moshe Hallamish

Part I

The Kabbalah and its Attainment

1 • Mysticism and the Kabbalah

At the turn of the first millennium, philosophical questions engaged the attention of many Jews. It is beyond the scope of this book to explore what motivated them to immerse themselves in philosophical pursuits in preference to other intellectual currents of the cultural world. Suffice is to say that they did so by taking several different routes. Some attached themselves to the Aristotelian framework, while others were affiliated with the Neoplatonic one; some emerged as original thinkers, while others simply responded to current philosophical themes in an attempt to adjust the intellectual Jewish world to philosophical thinking. Questions concerning the Godhead, the Creation, the World, Man, and so on, aroused intellectual curiosity. The Kabbalah, which surfaced at the end of the twelfth century,[1] provided its own answers to such philosophical questions. The uniqueness of the Kabbalah lies in the nature of its response, as well as in the method of its explorations. While the nature of the response often meets philosophical criteria and reflects an awareness of, and inspiration from, the realm of philosophy, what binds up these quests with the world of mysticism is the method of obtaining the answers.

Though the new, kabbalistic current relates to philosophical questions, a considerable portion of its speculative thought is devoted to the religious world of man, especially that of the Jewish person, and in this respect too, this current differs from its philosophical counterpart.[2] Thus Kabbalah stands out as *Jewish* mysticism; it is imprinted by the seal of the Jewish religion, along with its values and particular way of life.

The total unity of the contents, means, and objectives at least distinguishes the Kabbalah of the second millennium, which manifests itself as a mystical *current,* from its counterpart in the first millennium (particularly during its first half), which is more inclined toward mystical *experience*. To a large extent, the later stage of the Kabbalah is our primary concern in the next chapters of this book.

These chapters introduce the major themes of the Kabbalah, without going into detail about the sources of individual concepts and values in Kabbalah, or of how they unfolded. My main goal is to provide an overview that focuses on the common denominator while acknowledging and clarifying some opposite views that also struck root among the Kabbalists. In this presentation, special attention is given to the very phenomenon of mysticism and its human complexity.

The Kabbalah is marked by numerous philosophical trends and a variety of different, and sometimes contrary, views. Despite this divergence, certain shared elements—the common spiritual basis, the attitude toward the sources of knowledge, the particular manner of attaining mystical knowledge, the underlying conceptual-symbolic system, and particularly the sense of inner continuity that distinguishes the kabbalistic figures—allow us to assign these wide-ranging currents of thought to a single comprehensive outlook. Nonetheless, one must bear in mind that the Kabbalah is much more than a mere outlook, however profound in perception and singular in its mythical and anthropomorphic mode of presentation. Essentially, the Kabbalah is a way of life and a culture in itself. Symbolic thinking and ecstatic experiences require man's total devotion. They lead toward the achievement of lofty goals, and, under their guidance, all aspects of the religious way of life are illuminated with the light of the mystical world.

WHAT IS KABBALAH?

Historically, the term "Kabbalah" denotes a comprehensive religious movement of various methods and directions, which is rooted in the tannaitic tradition as crystallized at the end of the Second Temple period. In the course of time, the Kabbalah shaped the life of many Jews and exerted a strong influence on Jewish culture. Segments of Jewish prayers, much of the liturgical procedure, various religious customs, and popular sayings, all of which became part and parcel of Judaism, however obscure their origin seems to be, can actually be traced down to the teaching of Kabbalah. The great talmudic scholars were affiliated with the kabbalistic school of thought. Among them are the Rabad (R. Abraham ben David of Posquières), the Ramban (Naḥmanides), the Rashba (R. Solomon ben Abraham ibn Adret), R. Joseph Karo, R. Moses Cordovero, R. Ḥayyim Joseph Azulay, R. Elijah, the Gaon of Vilna, R. Ḥayyim of Volozhin, and Rabbi Shneur Zalman of Lyady. These luminaries in the field of Halakhah also played a crucial role in the development of the Kabbalah.

Every form of mysticism is connected with a particular religion, and this is particularly true with the Kabbalah. A somewhat parallel current of thought, namely Jewish philosophy, never attained the status of the Kabbalah, probably because the Kabbalah was deeply rooted in the Jewish spiritual heritage without estranging itself from any of its branches. Whereas the talmudic Halakhah was almost outside the philosopher's scope of discussion and the Aggadah often proved to be problematic for him in its formulations and ideas, the Kabbalah based itself on both the Halakhah and the Aggadah while providing its own interpretations, which were at times both daring and far-reaching, to phenomena or concepts drawn from the long-standing tradition. Philosophy somewhat disregarded the practical commandments. It imparted the light of reason to a few individuals while confusing many others, who turned away from the old without reaching out to the new. It thus opened the way to the "emancipation" of the Jews, but also led to a loss of Jewish identity and even to assimilation (as happened at the time of the expulsion of the Jews from Spain and during the period of the Enlightenment). The Kabbalah, on the other hand, contributed a good deal to the strengthening of religious awareness in daily practice.

But what is the nature of the Kabbalah? It is difficult to formulate an inclusive definition that will exhaust the whole range of phenomena and currents populating the world of Kabbalah. To adopt a partial, though important, definition,[3] the Kabbalah adopts a religio-mystical point of view that impinges on every area of existence and seeks solutions to the mysteries of the world and the vicissitudes of life. At the very core of Kabbalah lies the mystery of the knowledge of the Godhead, *raza dimehemanuta* (the secret of faith), from which all the other subjects of speculative investigation branch out. Kabbalah deals with the hidden realms of the life of the Godhead and the life of man as an individual person and the relationship between them.

In rabbinic literature, the term Kabbalah is used in two senses. The first refers to the words of the prophets and the Hagiographa, as differentiated from the Pentateuch; the second denotes the tradition of the oral Torah, as distinguished from the written Torah. These meanings of "Kabbalah" are interrelated, for essentially both of them convey the difference between the written Torah, which has to be followed to the letter, without adding or subtracting anything, and the oral teaching, which is expandable.

In the beginning of the thirteenth century, individual sages used the word Kabbalah in reference to particular secrets of tradition that are divulged in private or transmitted by whispering "from mouth to mouth," or rather from mouth to ear, so that they reach only the elect. The things that are communicated in this way are things that by their very nature cannot be understood by everyone.

In order to conceal them from the masses, or from those individuals who are not worthy of them, they are told in secret. That is to say, Kabbalah means the "receiving" of secret contents. The question that obviously arises is why these things should be kept secret. In order to explain this, let me first clarify some related phenomena.

WHAT IS MYSTICISM?

"As all faces of people are unlike, so too their opinions."[4] Human beings, just like the elements of the cosmos, are defined within a hierarchical order.[5] On a much smaller scale, every human society, however superficially homogeneous, is many-sided. Similarly, any religious system is characterized by diversity because the individual members who belong to it differ in their religious level. To give an analogy, an army is composed of several different corps, each consisting of numerous individuals of various ranks. Within the military hierarchy, all of these individuals, from the private and up to the chief of staff, fall under the category of "soldiers." When a general command is issued, each soldier takes part in executing it, but does so in his own manner and according to his given character. In the Sinai revelation, said Rabbi Ḥayyim Vital (sixteenth century), sixty myriads Israelites heard the Torah, and consequently there are sixty myriads of interpretations of the Torah—each individual produced a unique interpretation that derived from the very root of his soul (*Sha'ar Ma'amrey Razal,* fol. 19a). Speaking along the same lines, a Hasidic rabbi once said: "On the third Sabbath meal, when I deliver a sermon in front of three hundred persons, it is as though I deliver three hundred sermons."

It follows that natural stratification is the hallmark of every human society, and the same must be true of the religious society. Whether gentiles or Jews, people differ in terms of their level of religious affinity. In every community, there are those who attempt to get much closer to God. Under certain circumstances, this attempt is qualified as "mysticism." According to the *Hebrew Encyclopedia,* mysticism is

> A term denoting a category of religious phenomena (experiences and doctrines) that does not lend itself to a precise definition and is related—despite numerous significant differences—to an array of phenomena that are found in most religions. Generally speaking, the term "mysticism" conveys an intensive inner experience of the supreme religious reality, as distinguished from strict observance of the "exteriority" of the forms of objective religion (such as the cultic system, the organizational-ecclesiastic system, the conceptual-dogmatic system). . . . Most of the personalities in the history of religion who are designated as "mystics" sought to penetrate the core of inner spirituality in their religion.

It is important to add that, generally speaking, the mystic's quest leads him to explore in depth both poles of religion, namely God who commands, on the one hand, and man who obeys, on the other.

The mystic adheres to some specific religion and accepts the principles of this religion unquestioningly. Hence there is no clear-cut definition of mysticism,[6] just as there is no clear-cut definition of religion. Generally speaking, mysticism can be regarded as a sort of religion that emphasizes the direct consciousness and intimate experience of divine presence. Such is the brief definition[7] formulated by Thomas Aquinas (1225–74), the Christian theologian and philosopher. Mysticism, says Aquinas, is *cognitio dei experimentalis,* knowledge of God obtained through living experience. Aquinas interprets the words of the Psalmist, "Oh taste and see that the Lord is good" (Ps. 34:9), as meaning a direct and immediate contact. The word "taste" conveys a personal experience that must be perceived with the senses. Whatever is grasped by the intellect can be communicated to another person if he too uses his intellect to decode the message. Taste, on the other hand, is uncommunicable by words. To get the sense of what something tastes like, you have to taste it yourself. Similarly, the mystic, who seeks to establish a direct contact with the Primary Source, cannot rely upon intermediaries. As Gershom Scholem observed, one of the first teachers of Hasidism intuitively used the same imagery of eating in reference to the mystical experience. This is what he said:

> *Nistar* is the name given to a matter which one cannot transmit to another person; just as the taste of [a particular] food cannot be described to a person who has ever tasted this taste, [so] is it impossible to explain in words how it is and what it is; such a thing is called *seter* [hidden]. Thus is the love and fear of God, blessed be He—it is impossible to explain to another person the love [of God] in one's heart; [therefore], it is called *nistar*.[8]

That is to say, some things must be felt directly. This is what the ancients must have meant when they pointed out the difference between the poet and the person who knows the rules of poetry. What comes from inside you is not the same as what is imposed on you from the outside, even if you believe that you know it very well. The difference between the two is profoundly significant. The Kabbalist Rabbi Moses Cordovero explained the relationship between the philosopher and the Kabbalist along the same lines. The Kabbalist is comparable to a man who is carrying a sack on his shoulder and is well aware of its contents. The philosopher observes the sack from the outside and attempts to make inferences about its contents on the basis of various external data (*Eilimah* 6c–d).

Let us now turn to another "definition." Rabbi Levi Isaac of Berdichev writes:

> There are those who sense God with their human intellect and others whose gaze is fixed on Nothing. . . . He who is granted this supreme experience loses the reality of his intellect, but when he returns from such contemplation to the intellect, he finds it full of divine and inflowing splendor.[9]

It should be noted that the act of contemplation suggested in the above excerpt presupposes a certain distance between the viewer and the object, regardless of the emphasis it places on experiencing the presence of this object. Nevertheless, this goes beyond rational knowledge, which presupposes that the viewer and the object are absolutely far apart. Aristotle, who defined God as "pure thought thinking itself," deeply influenced the way of thinking of many philosophers. In his opinion, cognition is man's greatest perfection and bliss. Indeed, according to the Aristotelian philosophers, cognition reaches its peak in the fusion of consciousness with God. The Neoplatonic philosophers, however, placed emphasis on the fusion of the soul with the Divine. Both the Aristotelian and Neoplatonic formulations of God refer to a supernal being in its absolute purity. In contrast, in Judaism, God is "alive," a living God, and maintains contact with the world and with man alike. In mysticism God does not generally appear as the commanding God, but in Judaism mysticism adjusts itself to the concept of the personal, commanding God. Without this element, the commandments would have no place in Judaism. Until the period of the Enlightenment, the observance of the divine commandments was supposed to go hand in hand with the great principle of "Torah from heaven."[10] Once again, each form of mysticism feeds on the conceptual framework of its own religion.

The mystics want to "lift the veil" that separates between man and God; they want to attain a more profound spiritual closeness with the divine entity, perhaps "through nourishment, rather than through knowledge," as suggested by the Kabbalist Rabbi Isaac the Blind (circa 1200) in reference to contemplation. It is important to pay attention to the positive and negative aspects of this experience. Apparently, R. Isaac wanted to emphasize that in the course of the mystical experience, the very act of contemplation produces a direct and intimate connection with the Source and the Root, almost to the point of identification. When a baby or a tree feed on Mother Earth, it becomes, as it were, an integral part of the nourishing source.[11] In any case, one can see that it is difficult to give an accurate definition of this phenomenon, which involves both the attempt to reach rational understanding and the spiritual elation[12] aroused by the extraordinary encounter.

Maimonides began his codex of the Law, *Mishneh Torah,* with a discussion of the commandment to know God. He postulates that man's observation of nature and its complexities reveals to him the wisdom and greatness of the creator, thus inducing him to love God. This love is explicitly bound up with the acquired intellectual knowledge of God ("according to that knowledge will that love be"—*Hilkhot Teshuvah* X, 6). Obviously, this approach is meant only for the few who belong to the intellectual elite. In contrast, *Sefer Ḥasidim* (sec. 5) tells about a shepherd who used to express the stirrings of his heart in utmost sincerity, saying each day: "Master of the world, it is well known to you that if you had beasts and asked me to keep them, I would not charge you anything for keeping them for you because I love You." The shepherd expresses in a simple, yet profound, way the pure love that he feels for his Maker—the kind of love that is not provoked by any philosophical considerations. It is quite clear that both of these instances of the love of God imply some distance between man and God and convey the sense of human insignificance in the face of divine power and greatness.

The encounter between man and God gives rise to yet another kind of feelings. In his important book, *Das Heilige,* which is devoted to the concept of the Holy, Rudolph Otto dwells on three major elements: the numinous, the *mysterium tremendum,* and the *fascinorum*—namely, He who terrifies and is awe-inspiring also attracts us, so that we are fascinated by Him. Otto underscores man's ambivalence toward "the mystery which causes trembling and fascination" and toward this completely different (*das ganz andere,* the Wholly Other) reality. This ambivalence finds its expression in love and fear, cleaving (attachment to God) and recoiling (fear of excessive proximity), and standing before God, the merciful Father.

In Jewish religious literature, we find similar verbal expressions of the relationship with God. Though God is "He that dwells in the secret place of the most High," he is also "My [!] God; in Him will I trust" (Ps. 91:1-2). The prophet Isaiah (45:15) realized that "thou art a God who hidest thyself" and so did the liturgical poet Benjamin ben Rabbi Samuel in the opening of his liturgical hymn. On the basis of these verses, the poets named God "A Hidden God" (as in the popular poem by Rabbi Abraham Maimin). Precisely this nature of God stimulates in man the thirst to meet him, the yearning for the ineffable and the hidden. "My soul thirsts for thee," says the Psalmist (Ps. 63:2), and Rabbi Abraham ibn 'Ezra draws on this verse in his well-known poem, "My Soul Thirsts for Thee." In "An'eim zemirot ve-shirim e'erog" [I Shall Sing Joyful Songs], one of the most famous poems of the *Yiḥud,* the "Unification" of God, which was composed by the Ashkenazi Hasidim, the phrasing, "my soul pants after thee," is found in the opening and concluding verses.[13] In the sixteenth century, R. Eleazar Azikri borrowed the first part of the same verse ("As the hart pants after the water brooks," Ps. 42:2) and sang: "Bosom Friend, merciful Father, thy servant shall run like a hart." This poem was introduced into the circle of spiritualists who gathered together to sing "Songs of Friendship and Love [of God]"—they were like amorous lovers whose soul yearned for their bride, the object of their passion: God.

A presumably authentic historical evidence reinforces this point: "It was told about a woman of valor that her two beloved and pleasant sons were slaughtered in her presence by some heartless gentiles in 1492, which was 'a time of trouble unto Jacob' [i.e., the expulsion from Spain]." She was brave enough to say: "Oh Lord, my God, I have always loved you. True, as long as my beloved and pleasant offspring inhabited the earth, I did not love you totally, with all my heart, because I also found room in my heart for the love of my sons. But now that my sons are gone I transformed all my heart into a dwelling place for your love. Now I can fulfill the scriptural verse: 'Thou shalt love the Lord Your God with all your heart and all your soul.'"[14]

But are these yearnings sufficient to denote a mystical relationship? The deeper the sense of being close to God, and the more intense the attempt to get to know him, perhaps even in preparation for any religious practice, the nearer one gets to the mystical level. In other words, the mystical experience is not just an aspect of some "hidden wisdom," or a demonstration of love on the part of the believer; it is also spiritual elation that springs from the very encounter with the divine presence.

Thus the Kabbalah is a historical Jewish phenomenon that phenomenologically can be compared to general mysticism.[15] The essence of mysticism is a direct and intimate contact between the two poles: man and God. The mystic strives to get a direct sense of the divine presence. This involves not only some sort of rational knowledge, but also a psychospiritual experience.

One might add that from a psychological point of view, the mystic's aspiration to establish a direct contact with the source of his physical and spiritual life must provide him with a sense of security and makes him recognize the value and purpose of his life. Even if the intermediate stages of mystical transcendence are accompanied by deep psychological wrestling, the very groping for a clear destination can relieve the tension. The words of the Psalmist: "Whom have I in heaven but thee? and there is none upon earth that I desire beside thee" (Ps. 73:25), must be interpreted, in this light, as a recognition of the redeeming exclusivity of God that inspires boundless tranquility. Let us now recapitulate the discussion of the term 'mysticism' and its importance for the Kabbalah.

The word mysticism originates in the Greek word *muein,* which means "to close one's eyes." From this derives the word *mysterion,* which refers to the cult of mysteries. The closure suggested by this word finds its expression in two ways:

1. Closure of the mouth. The subject matter of mystical speculation is esoteric (which means in Greek: internal, namely what can be expressed in words, but cannot be disclosed in public). For this reason, the closure is in the social sense.[16] Since the mystics deal with unusual phenomena, which they do not wish to communicate indiscriminately, because not everyone is capable of truly understanding them, they discuss these things in secret, among exclusive circles, or *mysteries.* The parallel Jewish term is *sod* (secret). *Sod,* however, has two meanings: (a) Information one wishes to hide from most people for various utilitarian considerations. (b) Information that by its very nature is uncommunicable. This concerns first and foremost the concept of God. What does the Bible say about God himself? Hardly anything. Whatever we are told about God, beginning with the first verse of Genesis, refers to his relations with others: with the world, with the people of Israel, with certain individuals. As a matter of fact, human beings can say nothing about the divine sphere, because it is not part of human experience or human language. The body of knowledge we possess derives from experience and inquiry. The science of physics, for instance, conducts experiments on existing phenomena and attempts to establish the laws that govern the totality of these phenomena and their parallels. Yet it is not possible for us to form an adequate laboratory where God can be explored. There is no entity that is analogous to him: "To whom then will you liken me, that I should be his equal, says the Holy one" (Isa. 40:25). God is beyond our grasp and any statement about him is necessarily lacking. Nor are there any proper language tools that can capture this exceptional divine being. Though the Psalmist enthusiastically defines the superiority of man by saying "yet thou hast made him a little lower than the divine" (Ps. 8:6), the gap is not merely quantitative but actually absolute. From the point of view

of God, it is not at all possible to bridge this gap: "Hitherto shalt thou come, but no further" (Job 38:11). From the point of view of man, the desire to know the Ineffable is unquenchable. As already mentioned, man is fascinated by and attracted to the hidden God whom he wishes to know. The experience of spiritual elation or the contemplation of a realm that by definition is uncommunicable, transcendental, finds its expression, for instance, in the words of the *Zohar:*[17] "'And the perceivers *[maskilim]* shall shine' (Dan. 12:3)—who are the perceivers? It is the wise man who, of himself, looks upon things that cannot be expressed orally." This tension is the foundation of mystical life.

2. Closure of the senses to this world and opening up the soul to spiritual matters and to the supernal world. Man's entire world is oriented toward the world on high. From this follow two characteristic features: (a) Withdrawal from this world, to the extent of asceticism. A case in point is Baḥya ibn Pakuda (eleventh century), who under the influence of the Moslem mystics, the Sufis, postulated the cultivation of asceticism as a necessary preparation for the love of God. But he was against extreme forms of asceticism, and the same holds true of the Kabbalists. In ancient Greece, however, the mysteries of the Dionysian cult required complete withdrawal from this world. (b) Since the mystic closes himself to the materialism of this world, he opens up his soul in one single direction: toward the divine object. Hence the sense of unity, or unification, that strikes him and occasionally brings him to the state of *unio mystica.* The Moslem philosopher Abunaṣer Alfarabi entertained the possibility of the union of the human intellect with the active intellect, though at the end of his life he dismissed this notion as one of the vanities of old age. This image of vanities of old age was widespread in medieval Jewish literature, as for instance in the works of Isaac ibn Latif of the thirteenth century. But in *Maḥberet ha-Tofet* Immanuel of Rome was highly critical of this image. The Sufi Galal al Din Romi (thirteenth century) describes the man who attains the mystical state of self-obliteration by using an interesting image: "The essence of his being continues to exist but his qualities blend with those of God, just as the candle flame exists in the presence of the sun—for if you insert a piece of cotton in it, it will burn. Yet the flame does not exist because it does not give you light. The light of the sun has overshadowed it."[18] Indeed, Kabbalah concerns communion with God, but not total merging with him. It is rather a

communion of thought, of the will. Of itself, the identification with the divine will does not entail identification with the divine immanence. Even when Kabbalah discusses the obligation to erase corporeality and annihilate the self, so that the *ani* (ego) is transformed into *ayin* (naught), it does not mean total fusion with the divine being. Nonetheless, several kabbalistic formulations explicitly convey such total identification.

The notion of unity with God gave rise to the widespread tendency in various mystical traditions to use erotic symbolism.[19] God is depicted as a desirable female and the attachment to him is presented in terms of male-female sexual relations. This accounts for the introduction of love poems into some kabbalistic circles.

From the foregoing exposition it emerges that the mystic cannot easily communicate to his fellow men either his experiences or the thoughts resulting from his awareness and speculative study. Yet, paradoxically, the mystic feels the urge to tell of his "findings" and of his experiences. In fact, many of the non-Jewish mystics presented such revelations in their autobiographies, which stand out as literary gems. Jewish mysticism treats the transmission of mystical contents in a dialectical manner. The obligation of knowledge (as Rabbi 'Azriel says: "Whoever does not know Him, cannot worship Him") goes hand in hand with the obligation of maintaining nonknowledge, or concealing. In the words of *Sefer Yeṣirah,* "Restrain your mouth from speaking, and your heart from thinking, and if your heart runs let it return to its place."[20]

When speaking of consciousness and knowledge in relation to mysticism, we must bear in mind that they are not restricted to the functioning of the cognitive faculties. Generally speaking, the human sources of knowledge are the senses and the intellect. The intellect processes the data perceived by the senses. The mystic believes that there are other sources of knowledge, which manifest themselves mainly through the soul. Perceived as "a sparkle of the divine source,"[21] the soul is inextricably connected to its source. This leads to an important conclusion: the intellect, being a physical entity, is limited in terms of its physical existence and its spiritual accomplishments alike; the soul, being of a divine essence, is eternal, independent of the reality of the body, and has access to reliable sources of knowledge. Since a direct contact with the divine cannot take place in the world of nature, the arena of the encounter between man and God is the human soul.

THE WORLD OF SYMBOLS

Because the hidden and transcendental divine reality is not perceived by our senses or known to our intellect, as they are far too inadequate for this purpose, but rather is perceived by the soul, an important question arises: In what language does the soul express itself? In other words, what is the nature of the discourse between the souls? The answer to this question was well expressed by a Taoist: "The rabbit chase owes its existence to the rabbit. Once you catch the rabbit, you can forget about the chase. Similarly, words owe their existence to their meaning. Once you grasp the meaning, you can forget about the words. Now where can I find a man who has already forgotten the words so that I can exchange a word with him?"[22]

The mystic does not want to dispense with words, but rather wants to improve upon them by expanding their meaning. The additional meanings he is looking for, which are somehow inherent in the ordinary sense of the words, are supposed to intimate divine truths that cannot be captured and conveyed by the ordinary, simplistic language, which relates to a lower layer of reality. For this purpose, the Kabbalist uses several methods of word manipulation. The most common ones are *gimatria, notrikon,* and *temurah.* In *gimatria,* every letter of the alphabet and their combinations have numerical value, and a word or a phrase can be replaced by another one of the same numerical value. *Notrikon* treats a word as an acronym concealing a meaningful statement within itself. *Temurah* means permutation: each letter can be exchanged with another one according to a certain code, such as Aleph = Tav; Bet = Shin; and so forth.[23]

The use of *gimatria* was a common practice among the Hasidim of Ashkenaz. In order to caution against the misuse of *gimatria,* one of the Kabbalists of the sixteenth century wrote the following: "They based their kabbalistic knowledge on *gimatria* so that the latter will serve as proof and evidence of the kabbalistic knowledge they possessed, because Kabbalah is the essence and *gimatria* is but the aftercourse of wisdom."[24] The method of letter combinations was adopted mainly by Barukh Togarmi, by his eminent disciple Abraham Abulafia, and by the members of their circle.[25] Other similar methods consist of combinations of words and *gimatriyot* that evoke additional meanings and statements.

Another method of expanding the meaning of words is the symbolic one (to be distinguished from the allegorical one, used by the philosophers, which was not acceptable to the Kabbalists),[26] which views every being as a reflection of a higher reality. In the symbolic approach, words and objects are matched to each other in order to express to the fullest what cannot be captured by ordinary words. The symbols function as codes through which one is supposed to grasp what lies behind the symbol. Indeed, the philosophers coined terms, while the mystics and the Kabbalists created symbols.

When the word is used as a symbol,[27] it assumes a higher value, because it is loaded with multiple meanings. In itself, the word delimits meaning; as a symbol, it opens up diverse possibilities. For instance, a piece of red cloth has one meaning in Spain, another in Russia, and still another when it sticks out in the back of a truck in Israel or in the United States. Symbols can also be paradoxical. For instance, one may say about God that he is *ayin* (naught), which actually means that he is beyond apprehension, or that his being is distinguishable and separable from any physical entity known to us. As one of the Kabbalists says: "This *ayin* is more substantive than all the substances in the world."[28] This brings to mind the sun in its moments of full intensity, when its light is so powerful that if we look at the sun, we see nothing at all. In short,

1. The symbol is an approximation—it is as close as we can get to convey the meaning of that which in itself is indescribable.

2. The symbol is a remote echo of some essence that is unapprehensible and uncommunicable, partly because of the inadequacy of human perception. As one Kabbalist of North Africa said in the seventeenth century: "And you, son, take in the essence of things, not their material aspects. For matter is but an analogy to the spirit. Having been created of matter, we have no recourse to comprehend the divine, the spiritual, except by means of a metaphor."[29]

3. Hence the abundant, and sometimes contradictory, use of symbols, and the benefit derived from it: "Even when profound matters are communicated in public, only those who are meant to understand them, will do so."[30]

4. The symbols themselves were revealed, so to speak, by God himself through his Torah and his creation.

5. The symbol serves not only a vehicle of expression but also as a means of exerting influence on the supernal world.

In using symbolic language, every word assumes a deeper, and therefore a more truthful, meaning. Words are used not in their literal sense, but as a symbol of something else. For example, the metaphor of corporeality as the garb of the human soul suggests that what is exterior is transient, while what is interior and hidden is the real thing. In fact, this is one of the basic ideas of Kabbalah and mysticism in general, for the reality of this world is but a reflection of the divine, supernal reality, which is the true reality.

Since in essence the mystical symbol seeks to express that which is beyond words, the symbol itself does not exhaust meaning. Therefore the mystics and the Kabbalists use a wide range of symbols to express a single idea. Naturally, familiarity with this symbolic system is indispensable for encoding and decoding kabbalistic texts.

From whence does the Kabbalist draw his symbols? First and foremost, from the Scriptures, but also from the rabbinic tradition, the world at large, and human reality. Man, who was created "in the image of God,"[31] the structure of the universe, and human history consist of an array of facts that symbolize higher values. The kabbalistic quest makes reality as whole transparent and uncovers, stage by stage, its various layers, until it reaches the very root of the universe: divine unity. This outlook allows the Kabbalist to use an anthropomorphic form of expression. As Gershom Scholem says: "The Kabbalists were not deterred from using bold language that referred to very subtle matters in extremely corporeal terms."[32] Nonetheless, the Kabbalist warns against simplistic interpretation or understanding. For instance, the *Idra,* the part of the *Zohar* that displays the strongest tendency to speak of divine matters in corporeal terms, opens with a warning based on the verse: "Cursed be the man that makes any carved or molten idol" (Deut. 27:15). Rabbi Meir ben Simeon of Narbonne (thirteenth century), who attacked the Kabbalists, adopted such a simplistic approach. By dwelling on the literal meaning of the kabbalistic text, he inferred that it was heretical and unacceptable to the faithful of Israel. The truth of the matter is that the Kabbalist took the license to express his ideas in the most extreme fashion.[33]

The symbolistic approach is what brings the Kabbalists together, for the Kabbalah is not a speculative-philosophical system in the full sense of the word. It deals with various subjects related to divine life, the world, man, and religion, but not necessarily as a coherent system. It has a wide range of views and contains conflicting ideas even about basic matters. Yet there is a common denominator that unites all Kabbalists and it is manifest particularly in their basic attitude toward the symbol. True, contemporary science distinguishes between various types of symbols in terms of their meanings and their relationship to the thing symbolized, such as the descriptive symbol, the creative symbol, and so on. However, the approach that lies at the center of Kabbalah and that most characterizes kabbalistic thinking is that things are transparent and lend themselves to profound investigation that uncovers their inner layers. The symbol is not merely a vehicle of expression that addresses an elusive reality that cannot be adequately conveyed by human language—such as the divine realm, which is essentially different from human experience. Rather, the symbol is an instrument of profound knowledge. It captures the whole world—the physical world and the spiritual one, the physical reality and the spiritual Torah—and uses it as a basis for widening human horizons and deepening the scope of man's understanding.

2 • The Kabbalist and His Kabbalah

THE WAYS OF TRANSMISSION

With the emergence of the mystical outlook on life, it was only natural that new elements were to manifest themselves in the Jewish world, necessarily causing inevitable friction with rabbinical tradition—which lays claim to the continuity of halakhic authority, along with its dictates of normative life. Granted, in Judaism the tension between institutionalized religion and the mystical outlook was less pronounced than in other religions, for Kabbalah leaned heavily on religious tradition. Nonetheless, the progress of Kabbalah met with opposition on the part of rabbinical leaders, who considered the teachings of the Kabbalah as a foreign element that does not feed on rabbinical tradition. The Kabbalists themselves rejected this view. For them Kabbalah meant the "receiving" of an ancient tradition that goes back to Adam, the first man, if not far beyond him. From this point of view, Kabbalah is the same old wine—poured into a new jar. In other words, Kabbalah offers a new interpretation of Jewish life, drawn directly from scripture, but it does so by employing different, unconventional hermeneutic rules. It was also argued that the mystical approach did not seek to undermine the ordinary spiritual world. On the contrary, it fed on it, preserved it, and even legitimated the expanded application of relatively new laws and customs. Some of the greatest masters of Kabbalah were also outstanding figures in the field of

Halakhah, which ruled out the possibility of dismissing the Kabbalah or relegating it to the sidelines of Judaism. If Kabbalah, at least in the first half of the second millennium, was confined to small circles, this was a matter of choice, motivated by the conviction that its contents are not suitable for everyone. According to Abraham Abulafia, even the rabbis fell into this category: "For this Kabbalah is unknown to the multitude of rabbis who occupy themselves with the wisdom of the Talmud."[1]

The Kabbalists believe that what is revealed to them is not a new teaching, but rather notions that existed under the surface.[2] According to the Talmud, the patriarch Abraham literally fulfilled the entire Torah. By the same token, say the Kabbalists, one must acknowledge that Abraham was versed in the hidden wisdom as well. (Indeed, *Sefer Yeṣirah* is attributed to him). In fact, Abraham himself was just a link in the long chain of the Kabbalah. The Kabbalist believes that what is revealed to him in any given moment is not new invention, but rather a "find." He uncovers something that was already known long before him, but was hidden by the ancients. This notion opens the way to pseudepigraphic literature, namely books that are composed in a later period and are attributed to some ancient figure (e.g., *Sefer ha-Bahir* is attributed to R. Neḥuniya ben ha-Kanah and *Sefer ha-Temunah* to Rabbi Yishmael).

Even if the words of Kabbalah are not communicated as a direct tradition taught by a rabbi to his disciples, importance must be attached to those who were privileged to gain insight of the "mystery" by consulting the Scripture.[3] Thus, for instance, *Sefer ha-Temunah* (fol. 25a) states that "everything is found in the reception *[kabbalah]* through the perceptive Kabbalists, who understood everything with the help of prophets, by consulting texts that instruct the given matters through biblical verses whose meaning is known to those who understand." Moreover, says the same source, "all these ways are mysterious and known from Scripture to the perceptive Kabbalists. And all this emerges from the purity of the soul, which had passed through the supernal worlds before it came into contact with the lower worlds" (fol. 66b).

In this context, it is appropriate to repeat a fundamental question that was asked about the Kabbalists: Why is it that they do not behave like the philosophers, who provide logical proofs of their teaching, but, instead, support their views by drawing on the Scriptures? The answer is twofold. First of all, because of "the weak perception of the masses as far as matters of logic are concerned"— namely, the public at large cannot be convinced by philosophical arguments. This is quite an interesting argument, in that it takes into account the common man, whereas in general we are used to such statements as: "This is a great and astounding mystery, which every *maskil* [Kabbalist] should hide from the masses and even from the privileged individuals."[4] Secondly, the public was already used to the notion that "all the prophetic secrets are implicit in the Torah," so that the Kabbalists follow a well-trodden path.[5]

Thus, according to a certain kabbalistic orientation, study of the Torah, in the particular way known only to the Kabbalists, reveals various meanings and mysteries. For instance, "In that moment when he was occupying himself with the Torah by cleaving his thought to the Divine, from that emanation and that thought other things expanded and multiplied, and in this state of rapture they were revealed to him. In this way, there was a drawing down of prophecy, namely the prophet, being in solitary meditation, directed his heart and fixed his thought on high, and proportionally to the degree of immediate communion with God he would foresee by divine inspiration what was going to happen."[6] This is actually one of the important sources of kabbalistic knowledge and it leads us to another area.

One does not necessarily "receive" from another living person, a creature of flesh and blood in whose company one is studying. It is also possible to receive revelation from Elijah the prophet *(gillui Eliyahu).* If the kabbalistic contents are divine in nature, the channels of transmission are not only corporeal but also tied in with the world on high. While this kind of revelation[7] is not very common, when it does occur it signifies historical continuity, authenticity, and certitude in the truth of the revelations.

In the beginning of the Kabbalah, there were quite a few admissions that the plethora that is emanated from heaven[8] does not always descend on one's initiative; at times it is one's humbleness that draws it down. For instance, in *Sefer Tashak,* attributed to Joseph of Hamadan, the author announces that he writes not out of his own wisdom, but thanks to divine inspiration: "I am revealing that which I learned with the help that came to me from heaven."[9]

This relates to the literal meaning of Kabbalah as "receiving." However, the receiving associated with *kabbalah* does not signify merely absorption and transmission of the same thing; it also involves creative elaboration. Therefore the Kabbalists also pursued further questions, thus expanding and developing the Kabbalah.

Now, creativity also operates in the field of Halakhah, but the Halakhah is not independent—the masters of the Halakhah interpret the law according to given rules of interpretation just as a contemporary judge bases himself on the laws of the state: when he pronounces judgment he is subject to the written law, which he interprets and applies, but he does not create anything new. Even in the case of a difference of opinion, the final decision is made according to the principles of ruling. In contrast, when the Kabbalists disagree with each other, no resolution is needed. Sometimes a difference of opinion reflects different levels of attainment. This can be demonstrated by what is told about R. Isaac Luria, who refused to include in his circle of students such known personalities as Rabbi Joseph Karo, his in-law, or Rabbi Moses Alshekh. In his opinion they belonged to a different psychic and intellectual world. Similarly, in the name of the ARI was cited a fundamental distinction between his teaching and that of Rabbi Moses Cordovero, who was his teacher for a certain period of time. Rabbi Kook aptly expressed[10] the difference between Kabbalah and Halakhah while drawing attention to the distinction between the terms "Halakhah" and "dallying in the Pardes" (which refers to kabbalistic pursuits). "Halakhah" is related by its root to *halikhah* (going), which presupposes a well-defined destination and practical results. In contrast, when one dallies in the Pardes (garden), he aimlessly walks to and fro. The walking itself is of interest to him. As much as one studies and meditates, one cannot penetrate the mystery of the Godhead and the mystery of the world. There are many paths in the Pardes and just as many walkers. No one can congratulate himself by saying: I have reached my destination. Much is beyond reach and there is always room for expansion and revelation, or further clarification. This is what makes the walk so attractive.

This means that Kabbalah is not only something that is received from the outside, with the Kabbalists functioning merely as a channel of transmitting knowledge to another meritorious individual. By its very nature, the mystical vitality cannot be stopped. The Kabbalist must keep developing the revelations that are passed on to him. This duty can also serve as a self-test that establishes whether indeed one's soul belongs to the world of mysteries and can therefore be perfected by one's endeavors. It may also happen that one keeps one's revelations to oneself, in an attempt to keep the matter in secret, and transmits only the "heading of chapters," as suggested in the Talmud (*Ḥagigah* 13a).

Divulging secrets face-to-face is one of the basic methods in every esoterics. Rabbi Isaac the Blind, for example, addressed a letter to Rabbi Jonah and Naḥmanides in Gerona, and passed on other secrets to his nephew, so that he would transmit them orally.[11]

In sum, though we know of conservative Kabbalists who were hardly innovative (such as Rabbi 'Ezra of Gerona),[12] it was generally accepted that the Kabbalist had to elaborate on what was communicated to him.

A document dating from the beginning of the Kabbalah lists several persons who "all received by way of kabbalah, [namely], without getting any definitive proofs [about what they were told], just as he who tells a secret to his friend does not need to prove it."[13] Commenting on *Yebamot* 61a–b, Rabbi Todros Abulafia writes along the same lines in his book *Oṣar ha-Kavod:* "Now take my advice and God be with you. Choose yourself a rabbi and acquire a friend and he will tell you the mysteries of wisdom. Do not be tempted to believe that you can thoroughly understand these mysteries with the help of this commentary before you are shown the way through some opening. For the meaning is not to be taken in the literal sense. And be cautious not to impose on the text your subjective interpretation, for your our own reasoning will not be helpful to you, as such a rational method has already destroyed too many people."[14] Rabbi Isaac ibn Latif also alludes to a living mystical tradition of secrets that are transmitted by "whispering" [a conventional term in esoteric tradition]. He states that in Toledo, he presides over a circle of colleagues whom he teaches "secrets," and he claims to have experienced prophetic "illuminations" and mystical "revelations."[15]

Let us turn to more testimonies. Rabbi Isaac Mor Ḥayyim, an Italian Kabbalist (end of the fifteenth century), concludes his kabbalistic epistle with the words: "Keep them in a storehouse[;] they should not fall into the hands of anyone who is unworthy of them, nor be disclosed to anyone unless you know that he is a trustworthy person who conceals secrets and loves truth."[16] Another Italian Kabbalist, Rabbi Joseph Ergas (eighteenth century), warns in his book *Shomer Emunim* (par. 11) "not to read the kabbalist books, but to receive the words of Kabbalah from a *maskil* [Kabbalist] who himself had received them by oral transmission, for this science, as suggested by its name, is *kabbalah* [i.e., "receiving" through oral communication]." In the beginning of the seventeenth century, Rabbi Yehudah Aryeh of Modena refers to the transmission of Kabbalah by using the same terms: "Kabbalah is exactly as suggested by its name— one must receive it from a master who, in turn, had received it [from another master]" (*Responsa,* par. 77). R. Meir Poppers shares this opinion: "As far as the science of Kabbalah is concerned, one should not verbalize anything unless he heard it from a trustworthy person."[17]

In this way, it was possible to control the transmission of Kabbalah. Thus, in his letter dated 1582, Rabbi Shimshon Baek relates that Rabbi Joseph ibn Tabul, who used to teach only orally, adjured the recipients not to reveal anything without permission.[18] Indeed, in his famous letter, Rabbi Isaac the Blind warns not to write down anything, because "A book which is written cannot be hidden in a cupboard"[19]—it cannot be hidden in a safe place and is therefore accessible to everybody. Apparently, this view was shared by Baḥya ben Asher, a Spanish Kabbalist of the end of the thirteenth century. Though his commentary on the Pentateuch was designed to disseminate the ideas of the Kabbalah, in his book *Kad ha-Kemaḥ,* which is basically a collection of homilies, he kept them to a minimum, fearing that printed the oral discourses might lead to misunderstanding.[20] A somewhat peculiar approach is introduced by a well-known Hasidic rabbi, R. Ṣadok ha-Kohen of Lublin: "Though he who writes in a book is comparable to one who expounds to thousands of people, this practice is allowed in the latter generations." He explains his statement by saying that what is forbidden is only the "expounding" (see Mishnah, *Ḥagigah* II,1) of profound matters, which might lead to the higher spheres. But there is nothing wrong in listening to a homily or reading a book, because such activities do not exceed the bounds of the presentation itself.

Some Kabbalists expressed qualms about committing their revelations to writings. In the beginning of the thirteenth century, Rabbi Barukh Togarmi writes: "I want to write it down and I am not allowed to do it, I do not want to write it down and cannot entirely desist; so I write and I pause, and I allude to it again in later passages, and this is my procedure."[21] This suggests that in order to grasp the full meaning of his work, one has to consider carefully his scattered thoughts and then piece them together. R. Joseph Gikatilla, who was younger than Rabbi Barukh Togarmi but apparently maintained contacts with him, writes in the same vein: "I want to write it down and I am not allowed to do it, I do not want to write it down and cannot entirely desist; so I go back and forth, like 'running and returning,' and the *maskil* shall keep silent."[22] *Zohar Ḥadash* provides us with an effective parable on this: "Whoever discloses secrets [of the Torah] to the wicked is comparable to one who 'uncovers nakedness' in proscribed sexual relations."[23] In itself, the disclosure of mystical secrets is advisable, and even obligatory in the case of the zaddik, because it is an integral part of him. Yet whoever discloses secrets to those who are not worthy of them commits a serious transgression and is considered as if he had intercourse with a married woman, who is forbidden to him. The introduction of the *Zohar* (fol. 5a) presents this matter from a different point of view: whoever discloses secrets improperly strengthens the power of the *sitra aḥra* (the other side) and other evil spirits.

However, there was also an approach of deepening on the part of the initiated. In tractate *Ḥagigah,* the second chapter begins as follows: "One should not expound . . . unless he be a sage and comprehends by his own knowledge." Ephraim Urbach observes that this qualification "does not appear in any other context and suggests the power of understanding as inherent in the expounder himself, independent of received teaching or some conventional studying. What R. Yoḥanan ben Zakkai means by this statement is that in the matter of the Chariot, the rabbi plays no effective role if the student himself is incapable of attaining by himself the correct understanding."[24] Joseph Gikatilla expresses a similar notion: "[The Blessed One] ordered man not to make up fictional teaching [by imagining things], not to make of himself a dry well, but rather to receive teaching from his masters so that his wisdom [will] be based on the solid foundation of divine wisdom. And after receiving the secrets of the Torah, if he is a sage he will comprehend by his own knowledge and will establish himself as a fountain [that regenerates] the matters he had received. Then he will experience pure and total devotion."[25]

Indeed, many sources provide supporting arguments in favor of the Kabbalist's obligation to elaborate the teachings that were transmitted to him. For example, Naḥmanides introduces his commentary on the Torah by making the following statement: "Now behold I bring into a faithful covenant and give proper counsel to all who look into this book not to reason or entertain any thought concerning any of the mystic hints which I write regarding the hidden matters of the Torah, for I do hereby firmly make known to him [the reader] that my words will not be comprehended nor known at all by any reasoning or contemplation, excepting [if received] from the mouth of a *mekubbal ḥakham* [the wise Kabbalist who, having already received the Kabbalah, is thoroughly steeped in it] into the ear of a *mekabbel mevin* [the recipient who grasps it by his own intelligence]."[26] Significantly, Naḥmanides is not content with the familiar terminology "from mouth into ear" and adds to it the relationship between the *ḥakham,* the perceptive master, and the *mevin,* the disciple who possess the cognitive power of making inferences (as in the talmudic sense of *mevin davar mitokh davar,* infers one thing from the other).

This means that the Kabbalist receives hints and elaborates on them. When he is given a hint, his task is to strive to grasp its full meaning. Rabbi Isaac ibn Abu Sahulah, a Kabbalist from Spain (thirteenth century), writes in his commentary to the Song of Songs 7:6: "I heard from my masters that this verse contains an inconceivable secret and a secret of the Most High, which could not be captured by any thought or idea. Nonetheless, I will give you some clue for its solution, and I will proceed slowly in reference to it." In this way, the esoteric character of kabbalistic matters was maintained, and, at the same time, the ability of the listener to comprehend secrets was tested. "You should know that when you enter the Pardes of the marvels of wisdom, you will be able to get hold of its contents with the help of a few hints at the great and lofty things, and with the help of a subtle hint you will be able to infer one thing from the other."[27] Rabbi Jacob ben Sheshet, who was affiliated with Naḥmanides' circle in Gerona, stated unequivocally: "Know that the pronouncements of our Rabbis, may their memories be blessed, are words of the living God and one should never contradict them. But it is also the religious duty of each wise man to *make innovations* in the Torah according to his own ability."[28] Displaying a sense of self-satisfaction, R. Jacob ben Sheshet also observes: "You should not consider this a remote possibility, for were it not that I arrived at this new interpretation of my own mind, I would have to say that this was ancient tradition attributed to Moses."[29] In the same vein he writes elsewhere: "I am explaining this matter to the best of my ability, and concerning what was handed down to me, as well as what I attained by toiling and arguing about these secrets and by adding and expanding then, I shall not conceal any holy words from those who comprehend."[30] At about the same time, another Kabbalist writes: "I will interpret what I can and I will make innovations in the Torah through investigation."[31] Let us conclude with another example dating from the seventeenth century:

> "Haven ba-ḥokhmah va-ḥakham ba-binah." The meaning of this teaching as it was passed on to me by my masters is that a minor scholar as I am today will grasp what he received from his masters and will make inferences from the words of Wisdom that he received, instead of behaving like a barren intellect that bears no fruit. . . . But he should be cautious to grow wise through understanding, namely that the wisdom he has received from his masters would agree with the understanding he has gained from their wisdom . . . like the branches that stem out of the tree.[32]

It is true that this creative process, which was viewed as the complementary aspect of traditional learning, sometimes led to extreme innovations (Lurianic teaching), antinomies (*Sefer Ha-Kanah,* or *Tikkuney Zohar*) or highly controversial issues (such as the doctrine of the *shemittot*). On the one hand, perhaps this is the price one has to pay in order to keep Kabbalah tradition from becoming fossilized and handed down in a fixed manner from generation to generation. The *Sefer Yeṣirah*'s statement "haven ba-ḥokhmah" [grasp the wisdom] was interpreted by various Kabbalists as an obligation to expand and elaborate in depth that which was transmitted to them. On the other hand, the Kabbalists were perhaps somewhat naive in thinking that they only uncovered existing truths, and that the most profound and supreme truth was latent in the depths of the language, the symbols, and the Scriptures, namely, in the innermost recesses of things, just as the real essence of man—his soul—is concealed deep inside the body, so that it is completely invisible. "You will find out that the mystery is hidden beneath the shell . . . just as the fruit of the nut is found in the inside, where it is surrounded by the shell."[33] One must crack the shell to penetrate the core.

Thus we find secrets of which it is explicitly said that they did not emerge from the chain of transmission, but rather originated in self-study and speculation. These secrets, perhaps because they emerged from the Kabbalists' purity of soul, have the same validity as the secrets that are revealed from heaven. For instance, Rabbi Menaḥem Recanati, an Italian Kabbalist (end of the thirteenth century), writes that "mi-pi ha-sevara nashiv" [we will find answers by logical reflection].[34] And the anonymous book *Ma'arekhet ha-Elohut* states: "Some of them [i.e., the names of the Sefirot] they perceived themselves, by considering the occurrences in the world below; others they acquired from the mysteries of the Pentateuch, the Prophets, and the Hagiographa; still others were derived from the mysteries of the Aggadah and the Midrash."[35] In the fifteenth century, it is a philosopher who defines the Kabbalist as "the person to whom the divine mysteries were thoroughly revealed, for he received them either from his predecessor or from the light of the Plethora. And what he received is that which is called the wisdom of the Kabbalah."[36]

Nonetheless, one senses that some things are entirely uncommunicable, while others are potentially transmissible, but need to be kept secret. The Kabbalist who was privileged to receive a revelation of profound matters is bound to conceal part of them. For instance, "Of the little that we have drawn . . . we give our perceptive companions a slight hint, a taste of the essence of things."[37] According to R. Moses Cordovero, this is by the nature of things: "No one who studies the books of the Wisdom of the Kabbalah should think that it is possible for a kabbalist sage to write down in a book whatever is known to him, for an inevitable reduction occurs on the way from thought to speech and from speech to writing. Therefore, no one who possesses any knowledge of the Kabbalah should imagine that he [has] delved down into the depth of the books of this wisdom" (*Shi'ur Komah,* par. 11). Therefore the RaMaK posited: "It is improper to reveal it even orally [lit., from mouth to mouth]. If he merits it, he will explore the divine secret by himself. And whoever is privileged to do so should not verbalize it."[38] Furthermore, the *Zohar* makes several references to the great occasion of transmitting special secrets to the privileged. For example: "These things are not to be revealed but to the most holy persons" (III, fol. 290a; also cf. I, fol. 64a; II, fol. 200b).

Against the view that only a small portion of the words of Kabbalah is transmissible, there is the view of Abraham Abulafia (thirteenth century) who writes: "And if he proves to be a reliable person, his master ought to communicate to him everything he knows as far as he can understand. He will not conceal from him even the ultimate, most profound point, as long as he is capable of grasping it. At times he will write them down by providing enough clues for him to understand; at other times, he will transmit them to him exactly as he understands them; and at still other times, he will transmit them in the form of 'chapter heading' or explain them to him."[39]

Sometimes what the Kabbalists said was so daring that it seems that their reliance on tradition was but a cover-up for their bold intellectual outburst. Oftentimes they begin or conclude their discourse with the biblical verse "the counsel of the Lord is with those who fear him," thereby suggesting that the secrets concern only God-fearing people. Indeed, what is hidden in such secrets may be quite overwhelming to the layman.

Sometimes the Kabbalists say that the reader has misunderstood their words and is unable to fathom their depth. At other times they seem to have drawn their ideas from external currents of thoughts, though they ascribe them to an underlying Jewish root. For example, according to a medieval tradition, Plato received words of Wisdom from Jeremiah. Human wisdom is not created ex nihilo: it emanates from the Source of Wisdom, and this divine source can reveal it also to non-Jews. A similar idea emerged among the Hasidim concerning the *niggun* (melody). In Hasidism, a melody is "redeemed" when it is reconstructed and reintroduced into the Jewish congregations.

The problem of tradition and authority is intricate, even though the Kabbalists insist on the chain of transmission as governing the Kabbalah. To ensure the progress of Kabbalah, those who wish to study it must meet certain rigorous criteria and participate in special rituals.

THE QUESTION OF RELIABILITY

As already mentioned, mysticism constitutes an attempt to "taste" the divine world, to get to know it closely. The ultimately subjective nature of such pursuit may find its expression in a variety of heterogeneous accounts. In the realm of philosophy, things are subjected to the test of logic and can therefore be evaluated objectively. But what are the criteria for validity in the realm of experience and mysticism? (The same problem applies to the visions of the false prophets who declared: "I have dreamt, I have dreamt"—see Jeremiah 23.) This, among other things, is why the element of *kabbalah* (in the sense of "receiving and transmission") is crucial. One transmits only what he received by direct communication. Some of the Kabbalists articulate this notion by citing the biblical verse "hear it, and know it" (Job 5:27). R. Isaac of Acre, a Kabbalist who settled down in Spain at the end of the thirteenth century, denounced a Kabbalist "who made a serious mistake." "Because he made such a mistake," R. Isaac said, "it is unlikely that he received it, but rather he wrote so by drawing on his own speculations. And since he presented his own speculations as if he received them from a pious Kabbalist, his iniquity is greater than he can bear."[40] However, although *kabbalah* means tradition, the term is somewhat paradoxical. On the whole, Kabbalah was confined to restricted circles of the spiritually exalted, the *ṣenu'im* (the humble and pious). Kabbalistic teaching was regarded as esoteric. Nonetheless, it is also believed that Kabbalah is "wisdom of the Truth," the ultimate truth, which is passed on from the master to his student as a traditional body of knowledge and not as something that can be grasped by one's intellect.[41] It is also emphasized that Kabbalah is a tradition that is handed down from generation to generation, going back to Moses,[42] or even as far back as Adam[43] (who, among other things, transmitted the secrets found in the *Book of Razi'el,* which had been revealed to him by the angel). The notion that the chain of Kabbalah begins with Moses suggests that Kabbalah forms an integral part of Halakhah. In other words, there is an intimate connection between the exoteric, the teaching of visible things, and esoteric, the teaching of hidden things. This is supported by talmudic and midrashic literature, according to which both the written Torah and the oral Torah were simultaneously revealed to Moses on Mount Sinai. As to the second notion (that kabbalistic transmission begins with Adam), it views Kabbalah as the foundation of Creation. This corresponds to the midrash that God created the world by contemplating the ancient Torah. According to this notion, Kabbalah is an integral part of the spiritual-ideational aspect of Creation. As such it gives expression to something that is fundamental yet beyond human reach, which is why Kabbalah addresses itself only to the elect.

The Kabbalists' insistence on the divine source of their revelations seems to be contradicted by their differences of opinion concerning major issues.[44] Since the truth that is revealed from heaven is necessarily the absolute truth, one would expect it to be the same for all of its bearers. The Kabbalists themselves grappled with this paradox and attempted to resolve it. The Kabbalist Rabbi Joseph Ergas attributed this state of affairs to external causes. He explained that in the past, the Kabbalists communicated their revelations by way of allusion. In later generations, the hints they had made became subject to different clarifications and interpretations, some of which were based on misunderstanding. It is this mediating factor which produced the given confusions and inner contradictions. However, these difficulties were smoothed out with the emergence of Rabbi Moses Cordovero and Rabbi Isaac Luria in Safed:

> Indeed, I found no differences of opinions in *Sefer Yeṣirah, Sefer ha-Bahir, Pirkey Heikhalot,* and the *Book of the Zohar,* whether in essential matters or in any other thing . . . I will tell you the reason for the controversies. . . . From the time of the Ge'onim up to Naḥmanides, the concerns of this Wisdom were not written in books, but were passed on by way of chapter headings and allusions, so that only those receiving the keys [of understanding] by oral communication would be able to comprehend these matters. . . . But after the time of Naḥmanides, when oral transmission of Kabbalah diminished in scope, they were confused in their understanding of the ancients and each one wrote down whatever was caught in his speculative net. Their views turned to be inconsistent and hence the controversy among the last Kabbalists. . . . The holy person R. Moses Cordovero, of blessed memory, balanced things out and investigated and amended in order to reduce the controversies and separate the food from the waste.[45]

Historically, some of the details are questionable, but the essence of the above description is noteworthy: secrets are, indeed, revealed and to the extent that they are written down, they are conveyed by hints. The problem is not the source (which is divine), but rather the channel and method of communication, which are part of the human realm. And "to err is human."

Moreover, one must bear in mind that the entire history of human thought, including mysticism and Jewish mysticism, is the fruit of human effort. God revealed himself only once, in public, in the Sinaitic revelation. As R. Yehudah Halevi said, no one ever denied this tradition, and therefore it is indisputable. On the other hand, Moses' question to Joshua, his disciple and successor, "What did the Shekhinah tell you?," was left unanswered. We do not know for sure what secret the Shekhinah revealed to the elect individuals, nor what of it they understood thoroughly and what of it was grasped by those to whom they communicated these revelations. As the author of *Gle Razaya* admits, "This is what I attained by my limited comprehension and if any one offers better, plausible answers, I am willing to accept them 'to magnify the Law and make it honorable' [cf. *Avot* VI,11]" (fol. 29d). Even with respect to Kabbalistic matters, things are judged by a "rational" criterion, so that various answers are possible to any given problem.

Furthermore, as has already been demonstrated, the Kabbalist does not serve as a mere channel of transmission; he has to elaborate on what he receives. At this stage of expansion, there might certainly occur differences of opinion and different ways of understanding the issues. This is the nature of the long and winding route to the peak. As one proceeds, coming to grips with the issues is no less important than the final accomplishment. Indeed, there are numerous ways to reach the Omnipresent.

Finally, it should be noted that though in general women refrained from intellectual activities because of their domestic roles, there were some outstanding exceptions. Just as there were women who gave a talmudic lesson in the yeshivah, so were there women who took part in the study of Kabbalah. R. Aaron Berakhiah of Modena mentions his grandmother, "the virtuous and pious Mrs. Fiorita who is called Bath-Sheba." She was versed in the Scripture, the Mishnah and the literature of the codifiers, "and she also meditated on the *Zohar* according to her mental capability."[46] Rabbi Joseph Ḥayyim of Baghdad tells about women who study "Petiḥat Eliyahu" (from *Tikkuney Zohar*), even though for mystical-theurgical reasons he objected to their reciting of *tikkun ḥaṣot* (midnight prayer).[47] Some women taught the *Zohar* and hidden mysteries, and one of them was a contemporary of R. Elijah, the Gaon of Vilna.[48] In the Hasidic world, there were women who served as rabbis. In particular it is Hanna Rahel, known as the Maiden of Ludmir, who is fondly remembered. Also known is Devorah, the daughter of Rabbi Shneur Zalman of Lyady, who wrote epistles conveying the teaching of Hasidism. And so on.

3 • Prerequisites

Since the Kabbalah addresses itself to the elect, it is worthwhile to explore the conditions, criteria, and restrictions posited by the sources in order to ensure the suitability of those who wish to study Kabbalah. Abulafia asks, "How is it possible that the disciple who receives this divine wisdom will not be tested by the divine teacher and the human teacher in all the ways of testing, when by its very nature, the splendor of supernal wisdom is withheld from the Kabbalist who did not attempt to experience the divine ways."[1] As it turns out, the sources are quite rich and diversified[2] in their listing of all the necessary requirements for the study of Kabbalah. In the discussion below, I will refer to several categories of requirements, while singling out significant details.

By way of introduction, let's begin with a beautiful and thought-provoking story, which may be subject to different interpretations:

> It happened that R. Ḥanina b. Dosa went to study Torah with R. Yoḥanan ben Zakkai. The son of R. Yoḥanan be Zakkai fell ill. He said to him: Ḥanina, my son, pray for him that he may live. He put his head between his knees and prayed for him and he lived. Said R. Yoḥanan ben Zakkai: If ben Zakkai had stuck his head between his knees all day long, no notice would have been taken of him. Said his wife to him: Is Ḥanina greater than you are? He replied to her: No, but he is like a servant before the king, while I am like a prince before a king. (*Berakhot* 34b)

Basically the story concerns a clash between two personalities: Rabban Yoḥanan ben Zakkai and Rabbi Ḥanina ben Dosa. R. Yoḥanan ben Zakkai was a high-ranking sage, but R. Ḥanina ben Dosa had supernatural powers. Unlike R. Yoḥanan ben Zakkai, the "prince" of God, he was a "servant" of God and as such was able to perform miracles. R. Ḥanina's mystical tendencies were acknowledged by the Kabbalists. Thus, for instance, R. Isaac the Blind was praised for being "as powerful in prayer as was Rabbi Ḥanina ben Dosa when it came to curing the sick."[3]

The recognition that Halakhah and Kabbalah attract different types of personality is also implicit in a kabbalistic text of the sixteenth century. It is well known that one of the prerequisites for studying Kabbalah was the study of the Talmud and the codifiers, as will be clarified below. Now, R. Ḥayyim Vital suggests that "if this person finds the study of the Talmud too burdensome and difficult, it would be better for him to desist and after trying his luck [and succeeding] in this wisdom [= Kabbalah], to occupy himself with the wisdom of the Truth."[4] Though Vital implies that Kabbalah requires a different mental capacity than does the Halakhah, so that one may master the former without mastering the latter, he does not specify the nature of this capacity. A similar failure to define the qualifications of the Kabbalist is manifest in Cordovero's works. In reference to the traditional limitations of age and marital status, he states: "Do not argue that some have studied earlier than this age, because intellectual capacity differs. . . . And many acted in conformity with our opinion and did well. At any event, all of this is a matter of one's purity of heart and sound judgment."[5] In the mid-eighteenth century, an author of a kabbalistic book warned the reader not to study his work unless he was capable of thoroughly understanding the matters discussed therein. As the author says in his introduction, he wanted to hide his book, but "perhaps contrary to my intention and desire, this holy book has fallen into your hands. Therefore I adjure you by the great Name and the decree of the ban to make sure that its secrets be not revealed and that no one reaches out his hand to read it, even in privacy, unless he has already read and filled himself with Scripture so that he knows that his mind can tolerate this stuff . . . but he should not reveal its secret to any other person."[6] Five hundred years before him, Rabbi 'Azriel had said: "Not all periods of time are the same. Everything depends on the merit of man's heart, his conduct, and his inner recognition that his thoughts contain the truth so that he needs no other proof."[7] This is indeed a high level of personality.

The notion that each case must be judged on its own merits was also embraced by Rabbi Yehudah Ḥayyat, a Spanish Kabbalist who lived during the period of the expulsion from Spain. According to him, all depends on the root of one's soul, as defined by its origin in the Supernal Man.[8] At about the same time, R. Meir ibn Gabbay wrote that the Holy One, blessed be He, was revealed in the fire, and the Torah was given in seven voices; according to the Sages, "from this result the differences of opinions."[9] As if to confirm his statement, the Geonim of Babylonia concluded their responsa by saying: "But we pray mercy for you. May whoever is meritorious be enlightened from heaven."[10] This suggests that only in heaven is it known for sure who is worthy of these revelations. Nonetheless, in order to prevent chaos and protect the majority, the masters of Kabbalah saw the need to impose conditions and restrictions on the study of Kabbalah.

Because the phenomenon of mysticism was known during the time of the masters of the Mishnah and the Talmud, they saw fit to establish formal criteria. The school of Hillel had said: "One ought to teach every man, for there were many sinners in Israel who were drawn to the study of Torah, and from them descended righteous, pious, and worthy folk."[11] In contrast, the target population of esoterics is quite restricted. The second chapter of *Ḥagigah* contains a detailed discussion of the subject. Some of the recommendations mentioned in this text reappear in later sources, while others were rejected in practice. The text is as follows:

> R. Zera said: The Headings of Chapters may be transmitted only to the head of a court and to one whose heart is anxious within him. . . . R. Ammi said: The mysteries of the Torah may be transmitted only to one who possesses five attributes, [namely], The captain of fifty, and the man of rank, and the counselor, and the cunning charmer, and the skillful enchanter.[12]

In addition, the Sages clarify the meaning of "Headings of Chapters." It turns out that in the initial stages of the exposure to the Kabbalah, things are taught in some detail, but at a more advanced stage, only the

"Headings of Chapters" are taught. "Henceforward, if he is a sage and comprehends of his own knowledge," he is capable of absorbing what he is taught and making progress. If not, he has to stop at this stage. This suggests that one of the mystic's qualifications is the ability to develop things on his own on the basis of what he was taught.

The *Heikhalot* literature, which goes back to the talmudic period, offers important, though scattered, material on the subject. To give one example: "He stood up and disclosed the mystery of the world . . . to one who was worthy of gazing at the king . . . one who has cleansed himself and has shaken off idolatry and incest and bloodshed and profanity and blasphemy and unmotivated hostility, and who observes all the positive and negative commandments."[13] While the Talmud points out mainly intellectual conditions and age restrictions (e.g., "when man reached half his years"), *Heikhalot Rabbati* lays emphasis on moral and religious virtues. Here is another excerpt from this source (chap. 21):

> No one descends from the chariot unless he possesses these two virtues: he has read Torah and the prophets and the Hagiographa and studied Mishnah, and the Midrash of halakhot and aggadot, and the resolution of the laws concerning what is permitted and what is forbidden; and he who has fulfilled everything that is written in the Torah and observed all warnings of the laws and the statutes and the teachings that Moses was told in Sinai.

From the third or fourth century, distinctions based on physiognomy and palmistry[14] were applied as well. In reference to a long Hebrew text named *Hakkarat Panim shel Rabbi Yishmael,* Naḥmanides (relying on the words of R. Sherira Gaon), wrote: "The secrets and mysteries of the Torah are transmitted only to those in whom we see signs indicating that they are worthy of them" (commentary on Gen. 5:1).

PHYSIOGNOMY AND CHIROMANCY

The science of *sirtutin* (which in our literature is also called *ḥariṣim, shevilim, shurot,* etc.), purports to describe one's character and destiny according to *sidrey sirtutin*—the arrangement of lines and undulations of the palm of the hand, the feet, the fingers and toes, the shoulder, the forehead, the face, and so forth. This science was widespread among the Jewish people and the nations of the world (as early as the Hellenistic period). Historically, the facial features were investigated first and gradually other parts of the body were subject to investigation (the *Zohar* itself lists six or seven organs but mainly discusses the hand and the forehead). Eventually the scope of investigation expanded to include other shapes and features, such as color, thin or thick hair, and so on.[15] In some sources, this science serves to predict one's destiny, but in others it helps to decide whether a certain individual is worthy of being initiated into a certain science (such as magic, or the mysteries of the Torah). The *Zohar* contains a treatise entitled *Raza de-Razin,*[16] which mainly discusses the features of the forehead and their meaning. Because this science is "affiliated with the Holy Spirit," its secrets are imparted only to those who have reached an appropriate moral-religious level. In later generations, it was argued that the Gentiles borrowed from the Jews the science of palmistry and geomancy *(goral ha-ḥol).*[17]

GENERAL CONSIDERATIONS

Let us now consider whether there are additional primary factors that may interfere with the apprehension of Kabbalah. Rabbi Moses Cordovero discussed this issue in several places. The following is an excerpt from *Shi'ur Komah* (end of par. 58):

> Furthermore, I fear that you might come into harm and that the power of the shell that is attached to it might carry you to a place where you would fall into the pit of destructive beliefs, as did many who preceded you, for they wanted to be initiated into the wisdom of the Pardes before the appropriate time. . . . Some were bothered and confused for a number of reasons, while others imagined it as a high and steep mountain, or a very deep hole, and still others felt that this wisdom has no substance at all. There were also those ashamed of learning from other people, for this desire reached them at the end of their life; and those who felt they had no need for this matter . . . because they wanted to attain this wisdom before they trained themselves by serving their masters sufficiently, which led them to believe in corporeality and other inconceivable beliefs and, furthermore, they caused those who heard their inferior reasoning

> to attribute it to all those who occupy themselves with this wisdom. ... Therefore you, my brother, enter the Pardes step by step, guided by a well-versed master, and train yourself on the books of R. Simeon of blessed memory [= the *Zohar*], in which you will find pleasance for your pure intellect, if you are one of the meritorious individuals. And do not rush to peer through the lattice of your scarce knowledge, lest your eyes be obscured by false reasonings, so that you would be hurt. Rather, stand and contemplate until the gates of science open before you, and you would be . . . of the family of those who gather unto it in peace and enter in peace.

This text suggests that some people are afraid of the very preoccupation with the Kabbalah, while others think they have no need for it, either because it has no substance or because it exerted a pernicious influence on them in terms of their religious-speculative conception. Therefore R. Moses Cordovero advises the person who is one of the "meritorious individuals" to proceed slowly, step by step, and learn from a knowledgeable master, until he reaches the stage in which he feels worthy enough "to peer through the lattice."

In some kabbalistic works there is an enumeration of conducive and adverse qualities. Such works include *Badey Ha-Aron* by Rabbi Shem Tov ibn Gaon;[18] Azharat ha-ARI in the introduction to *Eṣ Ḥayyim* (and other works), which lists ten positive commandments ("Do good") and ten negative commandment ("turn away from evil") as preconditions for attaining wisdom; *Sha'ar ha-Yiḥudim* by Rabbi Ḥayyim Vital; *Shomer Emunim* by R. Joseph Ergas, fol. 28d–29a; and, in particular, *Sur me-Ra va-'Aseh Tov* by R. Ṣevi Hirsch of Zhidachov. There are other short lists of requirements. For instance, in the thirteenth century, an interesting description is provided by Rabbi Abraham Abulafia:

> The rabbi has to discern in his disciple the human ways that are called virtues, such as integrity, and love of wisdom for its own sake, and little anger and much patience, and compassion for every man, including his enemies as long as they are not the enemies of God, as well as generosity and a broken spirit and humility and joy of heart and restraint of the Evil Urge in most things under his control; and contempt of the lust for power and falsehood and possessions; and contempt of gluttony; and contempt of the desire for other women; and propensity toward seeking the truth; and hatred

> of lies and hypocrisy; and paying respect to the sages and honoring the secrets of wisdom; and love of hearing about the rudiments of wisdom, which are indispensable for acquiring wisdom and serve as the foundations upon which one can erect high buildings; and love and pursuit of much learning while returning what he has received once, twice and thrice, until things are arranged in his heart as they are in a book.[19]

The above excerpt lists a variety of interesting requirements, some of which seem to be irrelevant to the study of Kabbalah, and places emphasis on the need for moral and didactic perfection. At about the same time, R. Jonah Gerondi (in his commentary on Prov. 1:8) presents "four introductions on how to succeed in the service of God," which purport "to reveal to you the ways of the worship and fear of God, their order and their secrets." They are: choosing a good teacher, distancing oneself from bad company, fear of God, and extensive preoccupation with the desired wisdom.

INTELLECTUAL LEVEL

Though in many cases, there is a fuzzy distinction between moral and religious qualities, the virtues may gravitate toward one or the other direction. I have already mentioned the list found in *Pirkey Heikhalot* concerning proficiency in the sacred books. But in addition to the study of their intellectual aspect, the sources also insist on practice. In other words, whoever wishes to contemplate the secrets of the Kabbalah must practice what he preaches. As stated in *Zohar Ḥadash:* "One does not reveal the mysteries of the Torah but to a wise man who reads and studies, and practices what he has learnt and has the fear of heaven and is well versed in all things."[20]

Rabbi Moses Cordovero too insists on the importance of study, which he details as follows: "Third, he should devotedly fill himself with the laws of the Talmud and the explanation of the divine Commandments in the literal sense, as explained by Maimonides in his Code of Law *[Ha-Yad ha-ḥazakah].* Fourth, he should guide himself in Scripture, whether much or only a little, so that he will have full knowledge of Scripture and Mishnah and will have correct knowledge, and will not err."[21] Indeed, this detail, that the Kabbalist must "fill himself" with the Talmud and the codifiers, is frequently mentioned by the Kabbalists. Here is a small sample, drawn from several spheres of life:

The field of Halakhah

R. Moses Isserles in *hagahah* to *Shulḥan Arukh, Yore De'ah* 246:4 writes: "One may not dally in Pardes till he has first filled himself with meat and wine; by which I mean knowledge of what is permitted and what is forbidden and *diney ha-miṣvot* [literally, laws of the Commandments]."[22]

The realm of community leadership

The Brody ban of 1755 against the Frankist movement states the following: "Even at the age of forty, not everyone who wants to take the Name may come and get it, only he who has filled himself with Talmud and the codifiers."[23] In the Brody ban of 1772 against the Hasidic movement it was stressed that only "the greatest in the Talmud and the codifiers, those who are God-fearing and preoccupy themselves with the Torah and its commandments" are entitled to use the ARI prayer book.[24]

Kabbalists

"And the Great Assembly agreed that they [the secrets of Kabbalah] should not be transmitted except to one who has reached the age of forty and has filled himself with bread and wine. And whoever has understanding will comprehend this secret. Then he will enter the Pardes."[25] Similarly, R. Isaiah Horowitz states: "After he filled himself with Scripture, the Mishnah and the Talmud, he will preoccupy himself, with fright and fear, holiness and purity, in the wisdom of the Kabbalah, in the *Zohar* and the *Tikkunim* and their commentators."[26] His son, Rabbi Sheftel Horowitz, the author of *Vavei ha-'Amudim,* expressed the same things in his spiritual will: "And see after you have filled yourself with Talmud and the codifiers you will study the science of Kabbalah because no man with the fear of heaven shuns from studying this science." At about the same time, R. Meir Poppers (who had emigrated from Cracow to Jerusalem, where he died in 1662), expressed the same idea in a more extreme formulation: "One should not study the books of the Kabbalah if one is empty of the codifiers' writings."[27]

Apparently, the idea behind these requirements is that the scholar should be rooted in the mainstream of Jewish tradition, along with its major sources. This will ensure that he does not deviate from the traditional path or be led astray and succumb to heresy. In addition, the method of the *pilpul* (legalistic dialectics), which requires a high level of thinking, might train the learner in abstract thinking. As articulated by R. Moses Botarel: "This wisdom is attainable only by one who possesses pure intellect and lucid reasoning [namely, a rationalist]."[28] This is a very important element, for in Kabbalah, which expresses its ideas in a symbolic manner, one has to penetrate the language of its symbols in order to extricate their underlying meaning. As Moses Cordovero says: "He must be proficient in *pilpul* so that he can extract the statements of the parables and penetrate into the intended meaning of this science."[29]

MORAL PERFECTION

On the whole, it is believed that "whoever enters the interior wisdom without repentance and good deeds, will never penetrate into the core of widsom."[30] The insistence on moral perfection is sometimes translated into specific qualities. For instance, the Kabbalists recommend asceticism and strongly disapprove of pride and anger.

At times, these moral requirements are encapsulated in the phrase "fear of God." For example, the author of *Masekhet Aṣilut* quotes a biblical verse as proof that fear of God is indispensable:

> It is written, "The counsel of the Lord is with them that fear him and He will reveal to them his Covenant" (Ps. 25:14). From this we learn that the Holy One, blessed be He, reveals his secrets only to those who fear him. So much so, that even if one of Israel studies Scripture, Mishnah, Talmud, Haggadah and Tosefta, but does not have the fear of God in him, in vain did he plunge deep, and all his toil was for nothing. And whoever fears heaven and pursues hidden things and the Account of the Divine Chariot, which is the essence of wisdom and knowledge . . . fear is like a copper shield and a sword of steel, and he is not afraid of anything . . . for the Shekhinah straightens him out and guards him and reveals to him hidden secrets.[31]

Also: "Inner fear serves as a preparation for attaining wisdom."[32] Even a symbolic act is involved in this requirement: "One must have great fear of God to attain this wisdom, and love of God as well. And I heard that the ancient masters used to sit on the ground while teaching this wisdom to their students in order to subdue and intimidate them."[33] An Italian Kabbalist of the seventeenth century conveys the same idea: "And purity of heart is important to the Blessed One more than any wisdom and science that are not pursued for their own sake, heaven forbid. But one should remove pride and arrogance and the evil way [cf. Prov. 8:13] from his heart, and should minister to the masters and consult with those who know it [= the Kabbalah]."[34] And in a much stronger language: "And since they [the homiletic interpretations of *Shemen Mishḥat Kodesh*] originate in a high place, not everyone who wishes to take the Name may come and get it, so as to meditate upon them without much preparation and great purity of heart. Rather, he must cleanse himself of the windy storm and the tempest [cf. Ps. 55:9], the husk of pride, and let him be holy in abstinence, and be content with what he has and with the purity of his body as best as he can."[35] The same Kabbalist says elsewhere: "But it is necessary to experience purity and asceticism and fear of heaven and to serve God with love; and whoever has a defect should not draw near, and one should not walk on burning coals without purity and holiness, lest, heaven forbid, he finds the poison of vipers in what he expounds. And 'blessed is he who comes hither with his learning in his hand' [cf. *Pesaḥim* 50a], after he has already filled himself with meat and wine, and acquired proficiency in the Scripture, and the Mishnah and Talmud, and all his words and deeds are for the sake of heaven and to give joy to his Maker."[36] I have quoted here from three texts by R. Aaron Berakhiah of Modena, an Italian Kabbalist of the seventeenth century, whose concern with the Kabbalist's qualifications speaks for itself.

It should be added that some sources indicate the positive influence of the study of Kabbalah on the purification of matter and the development of one's spiritual powers. It is as if a closed circuit is formed. For instance, the introduction to *Arb'a Meot Shekel Kesef* by R. Ḥayyim Vital says: "And whoever has not seen the light of this wisdom has never seen any lights in his life, because it [this wisdom] gives life to those who study it, to attain the true intelligibles and to strengthen the intellect over matter, so that it will be devoid of any impurity and adjust to the intensity and strength of the supernal influence from which all the emanated beings draw."[37]

PRIDE AND ANGER

Significantly, several sources link moral and religious preparations with acquiring extensive talmudic knowledge. *Avot* 2:8 says, "If thou hast learnt much Torah, do not claim credit unto thyself, because for such [purpose] wast thou created." Since such knowledge is taken for granted, one should not boast of it; rather, he should stick to the virtue of humility (as advocated by R. Isaiah Horowitz in the above quotation). The more a man's soul is exalted, the more he should nullify himself. Pride and anger are among the basest traits, and whoever possesses them is unworthy of attaining secrets. "This book which is called 'The Secrets of Raziel' is to be handed only to one who is humble and has reached half of his years and does not get angry or drunk and acts with forbearance."[38] One must "attach himself to the attribute of modesty" and "be humble."[39]

The strong insistence on these virtues is made clear in the following story, which is contained in the epistle of Rabbi Samson Bacchi, written in 1584: "This meek person [Rabbi Joseph ibn Tabul] told us, his companions, that he felt we were so irascible that he hardly wanted to study in our company; for the quality of anger removes the spirit of purity. And everyone was searching his own acts. Then I said to him: 'Master, you know that I am not quick-tempered. Granted, today I scolded some woman for her insolence, but I did so for the sake of heaven.' He responded: 'This is the counsel of the Evil Urge, who makes it seem to the person that his anger is for the sake of heaven.'"[40] This strict approach originates in the teaching of the ARI, who even gave an interesting reason for this: "The attribute of anger . . . entirely prevents [one] from attaining comprehension. . . . Now, my teacher, may his memory be blessed, was more strict about anger than about any other transgression, even when one gets angry on behalf of a commandment. And he would explain this by saying that each of the other transgressions damages a particular part of the body, while the attribute of anger spoils the entire soul and replaces it with another soul, which originates from the husk."[41] It was further quoted in the name of the ARI (*Sha'ar ha-Yiḥudim,* chap. 5) that "mostly he should take care not to be angry with his wife, even for a [justified] reason."

LOVE AND UNITY

The rejection of anger and the insistence on humility produce not only inner balance but, to some extent, also a sense of unity. Perhaps this is the meaning of the statement: "The very essence of attaining wisdom depends on two conditions: humility and absence of mockery."[42] At any rate, this attribute is more discernible in the requirement of "love of companions," which is considered to be extremely important. It must be borne in mind that precisely among the "professionals," among individuals involved in the same intellectual sphere, a hidden envy is natural. For some people, "when scholars vie, wisdom mounts." For others, jealousy is a devouring fire. Perhaps this is what lies behind the statement made by R. Simeon bar Yoḥai in the name of Rabbi Abba: "All those companions who did not love one another departed from this world before their time."[43] The word "companions" suggests that this reproach was directed at the circle of Kabbalists. Perhaps it was jealousy that prevented them from observing this principle. Similarly, we are told about a strife among the Safedian Kabbalists, who all lived with their families in one courtyard. The close contact, together with some hidden jealousy, was bound to result in some friction: "After five months, a quarrel broke out among the wives. They told about it to their husbands and this went on until the companions were dragged into the feud. Now the rabbi [ha-ARI] used to caution them about the need for brotherhood and love, saying that peace, love, and brotherhood should prevail among them. Yet on that day, they disobeyed him. He went out with the companions to welcome the Sabbath and returned to the house of study sullen and displeased. And during the entire service he was in mourning, for the decree [of death] was already sealed because of our manifold iniquities, as a result of the quarrel that occurred today among the companions."[44] Indeed, this is what Rabbi Ḥayyim Vital tells about the teaching of the ARI: "Especially important is the love of companions who study Torah together; each of them must regard himself as though he were one part of the body of the group of his companions. . . . And if one of them is in trouble, they must all share his sorrow, or if it is a matter of sickness or of his sons, they must pray for him. . . . And my rabbi of blessed memory greatly cautioned me about the need for love to prevail among the companions in our group."[45] In short, "The wisdom of the Kabbalah is worthy only of those companions that are bonded together with love."[46] To give a concrete form to this love and to institutionalize it in a binding framework, *shitrey hitkasherut* (deeds of alliance) were signed.

As an example, let me quote from such an agreement, as signed by the students of Beth El Yeshivah in Jerusalem in the eighteenth century. It is interesting to note the various conditions specified in this document in reference to this world and the world to come. One's duty is to admonish the transgressor (without any intent to offend him by doing so)[47]—as a correcting measure, designed to raise the overall spritual level—and to forgive him:[48]

> All of us, the undersigned, twelve men, corresponding in number to the tribes of the Lord, shall be all loving one another with great love, in body and soul, and all of this in order to give satisfaction to our Maker . . . that all of us, the twelve men, shall be like one single, magnificent soul. And each one will relate to his companion as if he were actually an integral part of him, with all his soul and his whole being. . . . And, in principle, each should admonish his companion if, heaven forbid, he hears of any sin committed by him. . . . And we undertake from now on that for endless days and years in the world to come, each one shall toil . . . to redeem and restore and raise the soul of each member of our fraternity in whatever he can. . . . In sum, that from now on, we have convened and associated and affiliated and united as one man, companions in all respects, to assist and help and strengthen and encourage each other to repent and to reprimand and share each other's troubles, whether in this world or in the world to come. . . . And we have undertaken that none of us shall praise his companion, even if he is greater than he is . . . that we conduct ourselves as one man, with none of us deemed superior to the others. . . . We have further committed ourselves to not be angry with each other, whether concerning the admonition or concerning any other matter. And should one person sin against another, he will be immediately forgiven with all one's heart and soul.

AGE

The age factor is mentioned time and again in considering one's readiness to study Kabbalah. Naturally, preoccupation with mysticism requires psychological maturity, as well as physical and spiritual ripeness. R. David Messer Leon, an Italian Kabbalist (ca. 1470–ca. 1535), relates in his introduction to *Magen David* that his father, Rabbi Yehudah, did not let him study Kabbalah because he was too young to do so. Now, one of the views of the Talmud posits the minimum age as fifty, and in the same context we are told about a *tinok* (infant) who used to "expound the mysteries of Ḥashmal" and another one who "apprehended [or: gazed at] the secrets of Ḥashmal" (Ḥagigah 13a). Though older than an infant, this *tinok,* or rather *tinok shel bet rabban,* a schoolchild,[49] is of a very young age. Similarly, *Gle Razaya* (14d) states: "And all of this I understood from the words of this *tinoket,* as written in a certain book *[Kaf ha-Ketoret],* for as soon as she was born, she began to discuss those things." Various personal accounts attest to the insight of children. The author of *Ha-Peliah* writes in his introduction to it that his father took him to a mountain "when [he] was four years old and had some schooling."[50] Well known is the story "The Child's Prophecy" about Naḥman Katofa (or Ḥatofa), who as a child revealed wondrous secrets. Rabbi Isaac Judah Yeḥiel Safrin of Komarno relates, "From the day I was two years old till I was five years old, I saw marvelous visions and attained divine inspiration and spoke words of prophecy."[51] And in *Heikhal ha-Berakhah* he states: "From the age of five until the age of twenty, the soul is nourished by the Sefirah of Binah [Reason]."[52] Especially known are the Zoharic stories (in particular in the portion of Balak), about the *yenuka*—a child prodigy who surprisingly proves to possess mystical revelations. However these are extraordinary cases; as a rule, the age limit is well justified.

But what is it? There is a difference of opinion as to the right age, not only because there are no suitable parameters but also because this is an entirely individual matter. Above[53] we mentioned Cordovero's argument in favor of the age of twenty that "many who followed our view did well." This is acceptable to his disciple, R. Menaḥem 'Azariah of Fano, who adds that "from now on, their comprehension does not depend on years [chronological age], as they are subject to influences that operate beyond the order of time *[seder zemanim].*"[54] Rabbi Meir Poppers is of the same view: "Whoever is unmarried is forbidden regardless of age, and the married one—precisely at the age of twenty."[55] Nathan of Gaza, the prophet of Sabbatai Ṣevi, attests, "When I was twenty years old, I began to study the *Zohar* and some of the writings of the ARI, of blessed memory."[56] According to Gershom Scholem, "this was the custom of the Sephardic Jews in those days, as introduced by the Safedian Kabbalists in the mid-sixteenth century."[57] In fact, further testimonies, of a somewhat later period, suggest that this age was acceptable even among the Ashkenazi communities. For example, ten years before the Brody ban, R. Moshe of Satanow discussed this age.[58] And one of the eminent Kabbalists among the Hasidim, R. Ṣevi Hirsch of Zhidatchov, testified: "When I was about twenty years old, I began to study this wisdom."[59]

An ancient text, *Ma'aseh Merkavah,* reads: "R. Yishmael said: I was thirteen years old." A testimony to the same effect is provided by R. Meir Poppers, one of the pillars of seventeenth-century mysticism. "From the day I was thirteen years old," he said, "it was like a consuming fire. What could I do, when my soul was yearning for the teaching of the wisdom of the Kabbalah? And my soul was like a flame of fire in its burning desire for the wisdom of the Kabbalah, until the King brought me inside the halls of his palace, and I was privileged to taste of it in the house of the distinguished pious and humble rabbi and perfect sage, the physician Rabbi Jacob Ṣemaḥ. I studied his books and found favor in his eyes, and he made me taste of the ARI's honeycomb."[60]

Rabbi Moshe Ḥayyim Luzzatto, too, was introduced into Kabbalah when he was still a young boy. According to Rabbi Yekuthiel Gordon, at the age of fourteen the Ramḥal was already well versed in the writings of the ARI.[61]

The most widespread view was in favor of a more advanced age. It is noteworthy that a similar restriction applied to the study of philosophy. The Barcelona ban of 1305, which was issued by some rabbis headed by R. Solomon ben Abraham ibn Adret, declared philosophy as out of bounds for every Jew below the age of twenty-five.[62]

Testimonies dating from an earlier period say the Kabbalah should not be studied before the age of thirty. In his introduction to the book of Ezekiel, Hieronymus says one was not allowed to read the biblical text about the Divine Chariot before he reached the age of thirty.[63] R. Ḥayyim Vital too admits that he began to study Kabbalah when he reached his thirtieth birthday.[64]

The majority of the Sages set the age limit at forty.[65] According to a commentary on the secrets of Naḥmanides, "The Great Assembly agreed that they should be transmitted only to an individual who was past the age of forty . . . and it is forbidden to communicate any of these secrets to any one who is forty years old or younger, because they are frivolous and pursue the vanities of the world by indulging themselves in adultery, drunkenness, gluttony, lust, warfare."[66] Granted that this is an exaggerated description, the principle itself is clear enough.

Rabbi Simeon ibn Lavi's commentary on the *Zohar* (I, fol. 191a), posits that the soul does not descend into one's body before one is forty. This is indicated by the correspondence between the Hebrew letters of *neshamah* נשמה (soul) and *mem shanah* מ שנה (forty years). R. Moses Cordovero refers to this view by saying "some commented"[67] and R. Aaron Berakhiah of Modena mentions it several times in his writings.[68] This view was reinforced by the famous Brody ban of 1755 against the Frankist movement.[69] This ban included an important provision: "We hereby decree that *Shomer Emunim* and *Pardes Rimmonim* by Rabbi Moses Cordovero of blessed memory are subject to the same law, namely that from the age of thirty onwards, it is allowed to study them, provided that they are in print and not handwritten."[70] We see, then, that two age limits were set, but in the course of time the more advanced age was preferred.

In 1764, nine years later, *Darkhey No'am* by Rabbi Shmuel ben Eleazar of Kalvarija indicates the age of forty.[71] Gershom Scholem observes that "it is doubtful that it [the ban] had any practical significance. At all times, even after the great ban of 1757, a large number of people devoted themselves from their youth to kabbalistic study."[72] Though Scholem's evaluation seems to be somewhat exaggerated, it must contain more than a little truth. This discrepancy between theory and practice is echoed in *Torah ve-Ḥayyim* by R. Ḥayyim Palache, one of the renowned sages of Smyrna in the nineteenth century: at one place he sets the age limit at forty,[73] while elsewhere he settles for the age of twenty, but adds the condition of being married.[74]

FIXED TIMES OF STUDY

While age restriction is understandable, time restriction (in the sense of setting fixed times for study) is not that obvious. As is well known, the study of Torah is recommended at all times: "Thou shalt meditate therein day and night" (Josh. 1:8). As for Kabbalah, "Surely one may study every day. However, the times that lend themselves to in-depth study are the long nights, from midnight onwards, or the Sabbath day, for it is a unique day. . . . Also on Friday from midday onwards, and the festivals, and Shavu'ot—for I have tried this out many times and found it ['Azeret] to be a day of miraculous success. And the same is true of the days of Sukkot, inside the *sukkah*—for there, one meets with great success. And these specified times are well-tested and proven by me, for I am speaking from experience."[75] So, on the one hand we are told that any hour is suitable, but on the other hand, special times are most favorable. Cordovero lists several such occasions and strongly recommends, on the basis of his own experience, the festival of Sukkot. However, mystical experience depends on many individual factors, so that in the final analysis, the right time is a matter of personal preference. This is why other suggestions are made. For example, Rabbi Shem Tov ibn Gaon, a Spanish Kabbalist of the fourteenth century who settled down in Safed, recommends "from midnight until morning, as it is said, 'I shall arise at midnight.'"[76] Rabbi Aaron Berakhiah of Modena recommends Friday afternoon and the Holy Sabbath.[77] Rabbi and Kabbalist Moses Isserles, who lived in Poland in the sixteenth century, relates that he studies Kabbalah "only on Saturday and the festivals and on the intermediate days of festivals while other people are taking a walk," whereas on weekdays he deals with the various aspects of the Halakhah.[78] For Rabbi Meir Poppers, "engaging in the wisdom of the Kabbalah and succeeding in doing so—on Friday after midday, and inside the *sukkah* on the festival of Sukkot. In my own experience with the Kabbalah, it is advisable [to engage in this study] on the eve of the festival of Shavu'ot."[79] We are presented with a wide range of views, all of which subscribe to the notion that "all times are not equal." The cycle of the year is not a mere mechanical sequence of identical days. As stated in *'Eṣ Hayyim,*[80] "Hour by hour the world changes and no hour is [exactly] like this one."

Certain occasions, especially the Sabbath day, were considered suitable for the teaching of Kabbalah. Rabbi Joseph ibn Tabul "used to pronounce homiletic interpretations whose majestic greatness could be appreciated only by those who heard them, especially when delivered on Saturday, for on that day the rabbi acquired 'an additional soul' and was like a perennial spring."[81]

PLACE

In the study of Kabbalah, significance is also attached to where it takes place. "And mostly if he lives in the Land of Israel, because the air of the Land of Israel most wisens in this wisdom."[82] A story about the Ari, who is highly praised for his wisdom, concludes with the statement: "And all this he was privileged to accomplish in the Holy Land after he emigrated from Egypt."[83] And Rabbi Shneur Zalman of Lyady defines the land of Israel as "a place ready for the revelation of the unification on high."[84] Rabbi Kook, too, attaches great importance to the holy wisdom that is to be found in the Land of Israel.[85]

4 • Early Preparations

In addition to meeting certain criteria, the individual who wishes to be initiated into the mysteries of the hidden wisdom, or is already adept in exploring them, has to engage in special preparations designed to ensure the success of his pursuit. If not for these preliminary procedures, it is doubtful whether the mystic, who time and again experiences a "fall,"[1] an inevitable regression, could regain the receptive state of mind he is constantly and strenuously striving to sustain. The present chapter discusses some of the "techniques" that are practiced in order to counteract the psychic setbacks to mystical ascent. Granted that the distinction between "preparations" and "requirements" is not always clear-cut—the dynamic in the mystic's life goes beyond so-called scientific taxonomies and rigid dividing lines—it is still valid and instructive where applicable.

SOLITUDE

It has been noted by the scholars that on the whole, membership in Kabbalist circles did not manifest itself in outward appearance, such as special attire. Nor were the Kabbalists required to abstain from family life and adopt a monastic lifestyle. In this respect, the Kabbalists differed from their Christian and Muslim counterparts.[2] Kabbalistic writings nonetheless tend to make references to mystical seclusion. The question whether solitude is a common kabbalistic practice, or even a technique specifically designed for attaining secrets, is crucial.

First of all, it should be noted that even in the writings of those close to the world of Kabbalah, the word *hitbodedut,* in the sense of "solitude with God," is suggestive of moralistic manuals rather than of strictly kabbalistic works. For instance, in his *Sefer Ḥaredim,* R. Eleazar Azikri states in the name of *Beit Middot* that a scholar who devotes his life to the Torah should refrain from tormenting himself, but, instead, "should withdraw from the company of people once a week to be alone with God, binding his thought to Him as if he were standing before Him on the Day of Judgment."[3] In another well-known moralistic manual, which is much influenced by the Kabbalah, "a counsel is offered to anyone who is called by the name of 'Israel' to subdue his hardened heart and make time to seclude oneself in some hidden place . . . and meditate upon the bygone days and years of his life."[4] Similarly, *'Alim li-Terufah* cites a letter that Rabbi Nathan of Bratslav addressed to his son, R. Isaac, in 1831. Among other things, this letter makes the following exhortation: "Do not lose even one single day by forgoing solitary meditation, and ponder on your purpose in life every day. . . ."

Sometimes one's seclusion in a special room or a "house of solitary retreat" is instrumental for employing a technique of mental concentration. This state involves other concomitant practices, such as wearing special clothes, sitting in a particular position, breathing scented air, and singing melodies while pronouncing or writing down the Names of God. This technique was elaborated in the kabbalistic circle presided over by Abraham Abulafia, which thrived in Spain in the thirteenth century. Some contemporary books provide full or partial descriptions of this technique. Written testimonies of these practices, some of which have parallels with Sufi writings of the fourteenth century.

At other times, solitude lends itself to communication with the higher spheres. Occasionally, the purpose of solitude is to enable the Kabbalist to devote himself to the study of Kabbalah without environmental disturbances. For example, R. Ḥiyya recounts that on his way to Rabbi Simeon bar Yoḥai, he noticed some fissures in a mountain rock, through which he overheard two tradesmen (!) debating about R. Simeon bar Yoḥai's words. These individuals used to go into retreat two days a week.[5] Elsewhere in the *Zohar* it is told about some men who used to spend the weekdays in the mountains, where they occupied themselves with the

Torah while surviving on nothing but a few herbs, and returned home just before Sabbath eve.[6] Similarly, Rabbi Naḥman of Bratslav says: "Whoever wishes to taste of the Hidden Light, namely the secrets of the Torah that will be revealed in the future to come, must often practice solitude with God."[7]

Whoever wishes to climb the mystical ladder must withdraw from the world and detach himself from its physical manifestations. "The root of everything is solitude, for it is a lofty and exalted matter to experience the sequence of sanctity. . . . When one isolates himself, he cleaves to God even as far as his bodily needs are concerned."[8] It is told about the ARI (in the beginning of *Shivḥey ha-ARI*) that after he got married, for seven years he practiced solitary meditation together with R. Beṣal'el Ashkenazi and then continued doing so on his own for the next six years. "Then he led the life of a recluse, sanctifying himself exceedingly for two years in some house on the Nile, where he stayed all by himself, with no one around . . . and there he was gifted with the Holy Spirit." One generation after the ARI, R. Eleazar Azikri "projected" this situation on Noaḥ: "It is written (Gen. 6:9) 'And Noah walked with God.' This signifies that he secluded himself with his Maker and avoided human company. Or else, it may signify that he was advanced in the practice of solitude so that even when he was among men, these did not distract him, for they were as nonexistent in his eyes."[9]

It should be noted that Azikri raises two possibilities: (1) seclusion as a deliberate act of retreat, as indicated above; (2) a higher state, in which an individual lives in society, but mentally detaches himself from it. Whether by physical or social isolation, then, he psychologically manages to transcend the bounds of time and place.

In this context, it is appropriate to cite what is written in *Sefer Ma'aseh Ḥasidim:* "[A] certain Hasid was one of the recluses who withdrew from the affairs of the world, for he was always cleaving to the Blessed One. In the course of time, this Hasid came back to his town, and, not being recognized for what he was, he was appointed as the beadle of the synagogue. Now, when he poured the oil for the candles, he would spill it, because his intense devotion made him miss the candles. . . ."[10] This Hasid was so absorbed in binding himself to God that his hands were shaking, making the oil spill out. The Hasid's solitary meditation raised him to the exalted state of *devekut,* communion with God. The famous Maggid, R. Simḥah of Zalozhtsy (also known by his description of his journey to the Land of Israel in 1765, which he documented in his treatise, *Ahavat Ziyyon*), used the above story as supporting evidence when he wrote: "And though we were concerned with corporeal matters, nonetheless our heart was set on our Father in heaven."[11] The isolation characterizing the *devekut* was already described five hundred years earlier by Naḥmanides, in his commentary on the biblical phrase *u-le-dovkah bo* (and cleave to Him) (Deut. 11:22): "It is possible that the term 'cleaving' includes the obligation that you remember God and His love always, that your thought should never be separated from Him 'when thou walkest by the way, and when thou liest down, and when thou risest up' to such a degree that during his conversation with people by mouth and tongue, [a person's entire] heart will not be with them, but instead be directed towards God."[12]

The trembling of the above-mentioned Hasid is not accidental. As *Sefer Ḥaredim* instructs us, "[W]e find in the ascetic writings of the ancients that the pious used to practice ascetic solitude and *devekut,* which means that when they were alone they withdrew their minds from all worldly things and bound their thoughts on the Lord of all. And so my master, R. Isaac the Kabbalist [= the ARI], taught that this is seven times more efficacious for the soul than studying. And according to one's strength and ability, one should withdraw from the world and seclude himself one day a week or once in fifteen days or once a month, but no less frequently." The author proceeds to explain in the Mishnah (*Berakhot* V,1] that "the early Hasidim used to wait [i.e., prepare themselves] one hour before praying [and one hour afterwards] in order to concentrate their mind on God" as follows: "They daily took off nine hours from the study of Torah and devoted this time to solitary contemplation and *devekut*. Then they would imagine the light of the Shekhinah above their heads as though it were flowing all around them and they were sitting in the midst of the light. . . . And while in that state of meditation, they are all trembling as a natural effect but rejoicing in trembling."[13]

Another important passage is found in the conclusion of his book, where Azikri lists various remedies for mental ailments: "The fifth condition [for the attainment of the state of *devekut*] is the practice of solitary contemplation as described above. . . . At the appropriate times one should withdraw to a secluded place where one cannot be seen by others, lift up one's eyes on high to the one King . . . ; 'as in water face answereth to face, so the heart of man to man' (Prov. 27:19), and similarly, as man turns his face to his God so also will He turn to him and they will cleave together [in mystical communion]. This I have heard from my master and teacher, the holy and pious Rabbi Joseph Sagis, and this was also his practice. Similarly I have found in the writings of Rabbi Isaac of Acre that this was the practice of some pious men in his time."[14] The beginning of this paragraph is anchored in moralistic literature, but the text proceeds in the direction of mystical practice, dwelling on the reciprocal relationship between man and God.[15]

It should be added that solitary meditation involves various physiological phenomena and frequently entails a special psychic phenomenon, generally known in Jewish literature as *hishtavut* (equanimity).

EQUANIMITY

The practice of equanimity originated in Greek culture, and the form it takes in Jewish mysticism differs in some respects from the original concept. Equanimity is mentioned in Baḥya ibn Pakuda's *Ḥovot ha-Levavot,* which displays Sufi influence, as well as in the literature of the Ashkenazi Hasidim and in the kabbalistic works of Rabbi Isaac of Acre and others. I will not go into detail about the specific differences between the authors in approaching this phenomenon (while some maintain that equanimity must precede solitude with God, others subscribe to the opposite view). At any rate, the essence of equanimity is absolute impartiality and indifference to the mockery or admiration of others. The individual is so attached to the world on high that the way he is treated by people has no impact on him.

The element of impartiality stands out in an early Hasidic exhortation to embrace equanimity. In *Ṣava'at ha- RiBaSH*—a work that is attributed to the Besht (R. Israel Ba'al-Shem-Tov), but clearly belongs to the school of his disciple, Rabbi Dov Baer of Mezhirech—the following passage appears in the beginning of the text: "'Shiviti ha-Shem le-Negdi Tamid [I have set the Lord always before me]' (Ps. 16:8)—*shiviti* derives from *hishtavut,* 'equanimity'. Whatever happens, all is equal to him, whether people praise him, or are contemptuous of him. And the same is true of other things, including the food he eats—whether it is delicacies or plain food—all is equal in his eyes, since the Evil Urge is completely removed from him. And he reacts to everything that happens to him by saying, 'this comes from Him, the Blessed One, and if He finds it proper,' etc. And his intention is purely and wholly for the sake of heaven, without any questioning on his part. Now this is a very high [spiritual] level."[16]

In various works, indifference assumes an extreme form. Though these works concern not equanimity, but solitude and communion with God (*hitbodedut* and *devekut*), these states entail forsaking one's family members and failure to support them. Such measures may seem to us too drastic, perhaps even somewhat cruel, but it is the price paid by many mystics. For example, Rabbi Shem Tov ibn Gaon writes: "The essence of [the mystic's] life essentially consists in ascending from earthly dwelling to celestial dwelling, to be sustained by the splendor of the Divine Presence and not to feel for his sons and other members of his family, out of his exceedingly strong devotion to God."[17] Similarly, Rabbi Menaḥem Mendel of Vitebsk, the great Hasidic leader of the second half of the eighteenth century, recommends the Hasidic Jew "to further the enquiry of divine Wisdom . . . to treat himself as if he were non-existent, in total renunciation of his body and soul . . . and wherever he is, to desire nothing but Him, may His name be blessed . . . for he has nothing to do with himself in terms of how and what he is . . . once he has completely annihilated his self by contemplating the greatness of the Creator."[18] Rabbi Shneur Zalman of Lyady, the disciple and companion of Rabbi Menaḥem Mendel, followed along the same lines when he preached "to let alone and abandon everything one has, from things of the soul to things of the flesh, and to renounce everything in order to attach oneself to the Blessed One with devotion, ardent desire and exalted delight. And there should be nothing to prevent this either from the inside or from the outside—whether physical or spiritual, whether money matters or family concerns."[19]

SILENCE

Another form of mystical preparation that is repeatedly mentioned in kabbalistic literature is the many-sided[20] state of silence. The disciples of the ARI state in his name that "whoever sat for forty days in a row without verbalizing any mundane thought, will attain wisdom and comprehension."[21] Indeed, R. Ḥayyim Vital lists silence as the first condition for attaining wisdom.[22] In this connection it must be noted, without going into details, that the very fact that silence is specified as one of the conditions—sometimes in association with midnight as the propitious time for gaining comprehension—attests to the importance of solitude.

This calls to mind the stand taken by Rabbi Isaac of Acre, according to which the prophet's public calling interferes with the process of his *devekut*. Hence, if the prophet wishes to resume the prophetic state, he ought to "stand before God in solitude, divesting his soul of the sensibility with which it clothed itself." Occasionally, Rabbi Isaac stretches this point to the extreme by advocating the mortification of the flesh.[23]

Among the Bratslav Hasidim, the notion of *hitbodedut,* "solitude with God," led to an intricate practice. Rather than discussing it in detail, let me introduce two passages taken from a Bratslav manual of *hanhagot. Likkutey 'Eiṣot,* s.v. "hitbodedut," par. 13 (and, in parallel, *Likkutey Moharan,* part 2, par. 25), reads as follows: "Solitude is a great virtue and a proper and very straight way by which to draw nearer to God, blessed be He. And every one ought to set aside a few hours a day, during which he will pour out his heart to God in the vernacular, such as Yiddish, which is spoken in these countries. . . . For it is easier to converse well in the spoken language. And whatever he feels at heart, he will communicate to God, blessed be He, such as complaints and excuses and placating words and supplications, so that he will be able to approach Him. And every one should do so to the extent of his awareness of the flaws of his heart and how much he is distant from God. . . . It is only by conducting themselves in this fashion that the greatest of the zaddikim [the Hasidic rabbis] attained their spiritual level." In par. 20, the author proceeds along the same lines: "When God, blessed be He, helps the individual to practice solitude, he can converse with Him as one does with a friend. And one must train oneself to converse with God as one does with his rabbi or his friend, for God is everywhere."

In conclusion, it is appropriate to cite the words of Rabbi Kook: "The greater the individual, the more he must search within himself . . . so that he must devote himself to solitary meditation, to the elevation of ideas, the deepening of thought, and the liberation of knowledge, so that eventually his soul will reveal itself to him. . . . Then he will find bliss, will rise above all base things, and transcend all things, by reaching the state of equanimity and unity with all things . . . to the point of annihilating the *yesh,* the 'substantially', in the innermost recesses of his self. . . .

Then will he know every glimmer of truth and every glitter of honesty wherever it flashes."[24]

ASCETICISM AND FASTING

In the eleventh and twelfth centuries, asceticism was widespread among the Jews in France. Various sages were known by semantically related appellations that were indicative of this trend, such as Rabbi Isaac ha-Parush, "the Pious Ascetic"; R. Jacob ha-Nazir, "the Nazirite"; 'Ezra ha-Navi, "the Prophet" of Moncontour; and so forth. A striking testimony that reflects this ethos is the Rules and Regulations entitled *Ḥukkey ha-Torah,* as recorded by M. Guedemann.[25] Apparently, these circles were the social nucleus to which the Kabbalah originally attached itself.[26] Gershom Scholem demonstrated the profound links that bound together the *perushim* and the *nezirim,* those occupying themselves with philosophy and the circle of the Rabad (R. Abraham ben David of Posquières) in Provence. In the mid-thirteenth century, R. Isaac ha-Kohen associates asceticism with the Kabbalists: "*Anshey ha-Shem,* 'the men of God' [or: the persons of distinction], are marked by wisdom, asceticism, and sanctity."[27] In other words, preoccupation with mysticism requires one to ignore and transcend the materialistic aspects of life. As explained by R. Elijah de Vidas, a Safed Kabbalist of the sixteenth century, "[L]et them choose a special house, set apart from the house in which they live with their wives, while earning a living one day a week to support themselves and their families. In this way, they should observe the sanctity of speech and other sanctities. . . . For as long as one conducts business in the marketplace, he cannot avoid gossip, anger, or feasting his eyes indecently. Retreating into a separate house saves man from all of this. This is the straight way to be followed by anyone who wishes to sanctify himself."[28] He also says, "[W]hen a man desires human company, he cannot cleave [to God]."[29] The difference between solitude and abstinence is that the latter implies a more ascetic approach and at times involves fasting.

Fasting is not merely a matter of asceticism, or the mortification of the flesh. On the one hand, it serves as a way of purifying the individual from mundane concerns; on the other hand, it exalts him to the spiritual rung of the angels, who are not constrained by bodily needs.[30] In his address to the people of Israel (Deut. 9:9), Moses our master points out that for forty days and forty nights he "neither did eat bread nor drink water" before he experienced the most sublime moment of his life—receiving the Tablets of the Law from God. This seems to be the underlying meaning of the story of Elijah the prophet: sustained by the nourishment of some food ("in the strength of that meal"), he was able to walk for forty days as far as Horeb, "the Mountain of God" (1 Kings 19:8).

One of the Kabbalists explains the meaning of fasting as follows: "When we sanctify ourselves by abstaining from eating and drinking, which give strength to the body, we bind ourselves to Him, and to those holy and separate beings that minister to Him by abstaining from eating and drinking. Then he responds to us, because we cleave to Him. But by eating and drinking we are set apart from Him."[31]

It is no wonder, then, that kabbalistic literature recommends fasting, preferably for forty days, as a means to attain secrets. The *Zohar* tells about R. Abba, who fasted for forty days in order that he might envisage the splendor of R. Simeon and learn from him. When he was told that he was not yet permitted to behold his deceased master, he fasted another forty days.[32] And this is not the only story of its kind.

In the mystical preparations, the Kabbalists' approach to sexual intercourse plays an important role. The following excerpt from Tishby's discussion of the *Zohar* encapsulates the overriding principle: "The specifically Jewish character of the *Zohar*'s doctrine of love, which distinguishes it from the idea of love in non-Jewish mystical systems . . . [is that] whereas Christian, and to some extent Muslim, mysticism connects the love of God with sexual abstinence and celibacy, or at least with restraint in bodily sexual contact, the *Zohar* sees man's intercourse with his wife, when practiced with holy intentions, as a stage in the mystical love of God, and they form together a harmonious whole."[33]

Yet what is required of the Kabbalist is not only fasting, namely abstaining from eating and from the gratification of basic physical needs, but rather a total retreat from the world. This phenomenon of abstinence and asceticism has always characterized those who wish to sanctify themselves, whether they are Jews or Gentiles. Rabbi Abraham, Maimonides' son, attests to the existence of this phenomenon among the neighbors of the Jews,[34] while Baḥya ibn Pakuda writes in his philosophical book about the recluse in Spain.[35] In the beginning of the fourteenth century, kabbalistic books mention houses for solitary retreat, and the Hasidic moralistic literature of the eighteenth century advises every devout person to set apart a special room for solitary retreat.[36] This amounts to a sort of institute frequented by those who seek solitary meditation.[37] The same phenomenon marks out the Jews of Ashkenaz and Provence at the end of the twelfth century. For instance, *Sefer ha-Bahir* states: "Whoever turns his heart away from the affairs of the world and contemplates the Works of the Chariot, this is considered by the Holy One, blessed be He, as if he were praying all day long" (par. 68), and further: "The one whose heart makes him willing to withdraw from this world—honor him, for in him I rejoice for knowing My name" (par. 97).[38]

There is a reason why the background stories in the *Zohar,* which precede the disclosure of secrets, take place in isolated locations: on the way, on a cape in the sea, in the desert plain of Lod, along the coast of the Sea of Galilee, inside caves, or around graves.[39] In his introduction to *Sefer ha-Peliah,* the author recounts: "One day, my father took me, and led me to some mountain, where we sat in fear and great awe and recited this prayer. And when I was four years old, having had some schooling, my father led me to a mountain where no mortal was to be found, and he made me stay there for forty days. And my father was standing there in prayer with . . . some bread and a flask of water. There we occupied ourselves with the Commandments, striving to explore their meaning."[40]

The references of Rabbi Jonah of Gerona to the act of praying are reminiscent of the above quotation. (Rabbi Jonah was affiliated with the Gerona Kabbalist circle of the thirteenth century, as confirmed by the research literature.) He interprets the talmudic statement that "the worshipper should fix his eyes downwards and his heart upwards" as follows: "He should imagine and picture himself as if he were standing in heaven and should banish from his heart all the pleasures of the world and all the enjoyments of the body, as the ancient said: '[W]hen you wish to concentrate your mind and will [in prayer], divest your soul of your body.'"[41]

Sometimes, withdrawal from the world is regarded not as a means but rather as the end result. In other words, one who is bent on the study of Torah, or is yearning for proximity with God, necessarily banishes from his mind all other thoughts, "just as the person who desires some woman obliterates all his thoughts because of his great desire, which consumes his heart like a burning fire, to the extent that when he eats and when he drinks and when he sleeps, his mind is focused on the object of his desire."[42] Thus, necessarily, the more one strives to cleave to God, the more one renounces this world. This notion stands out at the end of the chapter, where R. Elijah de Vidas adds: "And he need not mortify his flesh or torment himself by fasting, for *devekut* depends on nothing but ardent desire [for God]." In other words, fasts and self-flagellation are considered artificial means, while desire, or spiritual yearning, functions as a natural and active concentration of one's mental faculties. De Vidas illustrates this by a detailed story taken from *Ma'asiyyot ha-Perushim* by R. Isaac of Acre.[43] The conclusion he draws from this story is that "whoever loves no woman is comparable to an ass, if not lower than that. For the emotive must lead him to the fervent service of God."[44] In other words, through love for a woman one is trained to experience intense love of God, which requires utmost devotion. As he puts it, "[W]hoever loves two women does not experience total love, for they are rivals. A woman's love is well rooted in her husband when she sees that he loves no other woman in the world but her alone. Then she forms a bond of love with him. In the same way, the Shekhinah will not extend her love to a man who is deeply involved in worldly concerns."[45]

However, seclusion is not posited as an absolute imperative. "Solitude is fine," says Baḥya ibn Pakuda, "when you acquire a friend."[46] And according to the introduction to *Sefer ha-Peliah,* "it would be better for him to be in the company of a good friend, so that they can sit together and teach each other, without being led astray." This implies that when two friends share the same goal, it is easier for them to reach it. It is also said: "Study in the company of others, 'for the Torah cannot be learned save in company . . .' and a sound way of acquiring wisdom is to study together with the disciples."[47] Presumably, these two requirements are complementary. On the one hand, importance was attached to shared study by individuals who have common interests, and hence the emergence of the "houses of solitary retreat" (known as *batey-mitbodedim,* or *hesger* or *cloyz*), and Kabbalist communes whose members were bound to each other by a written agreement *(shetar hitkasherut).* On the other hand, in many cases isolation is essential because Kabbalists differ from each other not only in character traits, but also in spiritual level and mystical accomplishments.

This kind of bonding, which the Mishnah defines as *dibbuk ḥaverim* (attachment to colleagues)[48] and posits as one of the conditions for learning Torah, is also typical of non-Jewish religious groups among other nations. For instance, Galal al-din Romi, the great Sufi poet, was so impressed by the unity of the dervishes that he described it in the following laudatory terms: "The dervishes are in a state of one single body. If one part of this body is ailing, all the others follow suit: the eye ceases to see; the ear ceases to hear; the tongue ceases to talk. All converge at one and the same place. The state of true friendship means that you sacrifice yourself for your friend, you risk your life for him. For all set their hearts on one and the same thing. They are all in the same boat."[49] It is on the basis of this perception that this Sufi mystic stated: "If you find fault with your brother, the flaw you perceive in him is [actually] inside you . . . redeem yourself of this flaw of yours, because what bothers you about it in your brother, bothers you in yourself."[50] Five hundred years later, the same approach is found in Hasidism. In the name of the Besht, who knew nothing about this Sufi, the Hasidim interpret the Mishnaic saying "kol nega'im adam ro'eh ḥuṣ mi-nig'ey aṣmo" [one sees the faults of others but not one's own] (*Nega'im* II,5), as "kol nega'im [she-]adam ro'eh [ba-]ḥuṣ [hem] mi-nig'ey aṣmo" [The faults one sees outside {oneself} are one's own].

The Kabbalists also joined forces to form exclusive and cohesive groups. Testimonies of the thirteenth century make numerous references to the *ḥaverim* (companions). For instance, in one of his epistles, Rabbi 'Ezra of Gerona uses the term *kat ha-ḥaverim* (group of companions),[51] and in reference to him Naḥmanides (on Lev. 19:19) writes: "And one of our companions adds. . . ."[52] Also, at the end of his introduction to *Torat ha-Adam,* once more Naḥmanides refers to this *kat ha-ḥaverim:* "And God . . . will soon show us the Temple and fulfill in us and in the entire *ḥavurah* [band of companions] the scriptural verse. . . ."[53] In the fourteenth century, R. Joseph Angelino observes: "and I heard from the *ḥaver* [companion], R. Isaac."[54] Especially in the *Zohar,* the Kabbalists are called *ḥavrayah* (companions)—or, as in *Zohar* III, fol. 10a, *ḥaverana yatvey deroma* (companions who dwell in the South), for the South signifies the place of wisdom.[55] Let me illustrate this point by quoting a passage from the *Zohar:* "When the Companions came before R. Simeon, he at once saw from their faces that something was troubling them. He said to them: Enter, my holy children! Come, O ye, beloved sons of the King! Come, my cherished and dearly loved ones, ye who love one another! For R. Abba once said that Companions who do not love one another pass away from the world before their time. All the Companions in the time of R. Simeon loved one another in soul and spirit and therefore in his generation [the secrets of the Torah] were revealed."[56] Even the yeshivah, in the Garden of Eden was called *metivta de-reḥimuta* (the academy of love.)[57] Later on, among the Kabbalists circles of Safed in the sixteenth century, this term was in current use. For instance, we are told about R. Joseph ibn Tabul: "He said to us, the companions. . . ."[58] R. Ḥayyim Vital too tended to use this term frequently.[59]

Another symbol of group cohesion is the *idra.* This well-known term comes from Greek, where it literally means sitting in a semicircle.[60] One of the most important units in the *Zohar* is titled "Idra," calling to mind the typical sitting arrangement of the companions, which enabled them to see each other's faces while studying together. In the fourteenth century, R. David ben Yehudah he-Ḥasid named the companions *beney idra* (members of *idra*).[61] By tradition, the Safed Kabbalists identified a small structure with a white dome (located very close to the road from Meron to Safed) as the meeting place of the *idra.* It is also said that the ARI used to occupy the regular seat of R. Simeon bar Yoḥai.[62]

The group cohesion that characterizes the Kabbalist circles points at the need to counteract the inevitable stresses inherent in their pursuit by strengthening group support. The practice of singing also helped to lessen psychological pressures (see, for example, *Reshit Ḥokhmah,* II,10), though it had other functions as well: triggering spiritual awakening, glorifying God and expressing love to him, and communicating whatever cannot be adequately expressed by normal speech.

CONFESSIONS

Within this framework of "love of the companions," confession played a significant role. Particularly on Friday afternoons, the Safedian Kabbalists used to make confessions to one another about the sins they had inadvertently committed during the week. This custom suggests mutual trust and social esteem, as well as an aspiration to sustain intense religious tension, for the duty to confess involves self-awareness, with every failure to conform to the group norms resulting in remorse and repentance. Naturally, underlying this practice is the conviction that moral-religious perfection is a crucial condition for attaining secrets.

The practice of confession did not last long. The opponents, such as

R. Ḥayyim Vital, came from amongst the Kabbalists themselves. Sometimes they argued that the companions dare not reveal their hidden secrets. At other times they raised the objection that the practice of confession was reminiscent of Christianity. Indeed, in the course of time, the practice of confession died out, and even the subsequent resurgence of confession in Hasidism was short-lived. When R. Menaḥem Mendel of Vitebsk sojourned in the Land of Israel, he wrote to his followers abroad: "Every one has to make sure that he has *dibbuk ḥaverim* [attachment to the companions], in the sense of receiving the loving support of his fellows in accordance with their intellectual level, for they all seek the truth and want to rid themselves of the snares of evil: lusts, hypocrisy, and lies. Therefore, every day he must talk to them for half an hour and denigrate his vices, as he perceives them. And his companion should do the same. And when he trains himself in this practice, whenever any of his companions displays some flaw of character or misconduct, he should admonish him for this. By the same token, he should not be ashamed of his companion and should confess to him the truth about himself. Thus, of itself, falsehood will be shed and truth will begin to glitter."[63] Among the Bratslav Hasidim, it was customary to confess to the zaddik, the Hasidic rabbi. Since for them the real zaddik is Rabbi Naḥman of Bratslav, who is still alive in the consciousness of his followers, in this Hasidic sect the practice of confession has continued to this day. This, however, is not a common practice in other Hasidic courts.

PURIFICATION

For the Kabbalist, the need to purify oneself is taken for granted. Purification applies to one's body as well as to his possessions and clothes. Outward cleanliness leads to an awareness of the cleanliness of the soul. Related to this is the practice of immersion in water. The immersion is supposed to purge and purify the soul. In addition, the posture that is required much resembles sitting with the head between one's knees, the position of the embryo inside the womb. So, on the one hand, the immersion signifies nullification and fusion with the Source; and on the other hand, it leads to a state of renewal and purification. Sometimes it goes hand in hand with ascetic behavior, as when the mystic immerses himself in freezing water. For example, it is told that in the winter, the ARI used to immerse himself in cold water although he was not supposed to do so, because of some disease from which he suffered. Indeed, one winter, his mother forbade him to immerse himself and, respecting her wishes, he refrained from doing so.[64] As a rule, said R. Jonathan Sagis in the name of the ARI, "as far as attaining [mystical knowledge and experience] is concerned, there is nothing more necessary and needful for man than to immerse himself in water."[65] On the basis of the instruction issued in the name of the ARI, R. Aaron Berakhiah of Modena says the following: "And several times I cautioned my companions and disciples to accustom themselves" to immersion.[66] Similarly, it is told about the disciples of Sabbatai Ṣevi that whenever they wanted to learn from him, they would immerse themselves in the sea just as he did.[67] Of special interest is the tradition concerning Miriam's well, which is located at the Sea of Galilee—whoever immerses himself in it, or drinks of its water, experiences mystical exaltation and attains the wisdom of the Kabbalah. Thus, for instance, Rabbi Ḥayyim Vital relates:

> When I came to my master ZLHH to learn this wisdom from him, my teacher went to Tiberias and led me into the sea in a small vessel right opposite the pillars of the old synagogue. Then he took a plate and filled it with water, which he took from between the pillars, and made me drink it. And he said to me: Now you will attain this wisdom, because this water which you have drunk is from Miriam's well. It is then that I began to plunge into the depth of this wisdom.[68]

PERSEVERANCE AND MUCH TOIL

This requirement, or condition, is not related to one's physical makeup or intellectual or moral-religious perfection as discussed earlier, but rather concerns the very process of mystical life. The kabbalistic sources attach great importance to this factor, and therefore it will be presented here, though in brief.

By their very nature, lofty things are not easily attained. The principle of "le-fum ṣa'ara agra" [according to the suffering {i.e., toil} is the reward] (*Avot* V,22), which has been associated with learning Torah, is all the more applicable to the pursuit of the hidden wisdom. The mystic's determination is judged by his strong desire to attain secrets and draw nearer to God, by his industriousness, and by the intensity of his concentration. The Kabbalist's perseverance and the pains he takes in his explorations are often acknowledged. For instance, using a florid language, replete with biblical embeddings, Rabbi Todros Abulafia (thirteenth century) expresses his strong desire to attain wisdom and describes the efforts he made to reach his goal:

> And since my heart and yours know my honest wish and true desire to climb to the top of the stairs of wisdom and reason . . . and my soul thirsted . . . and I yearned for your teaching, which drops down like rain, and for your speech, which distills as the dew . . . but I did not drink my fill to quench the fire of passionate desire . . . I had neither repose nor rest and I did not despair nor did I tarry to seek and search out wisdom and pursue those who are knowledgeable in it. . . . Attaining to wise counsel, I increased learning and through a great deal of effort on my part, the eyes of my heart opened. Indeed, I am confident that with the help of the Creator, I shall rise to the top of the ladder to capture the essence of the hidden matter.[69]

The same insistence on perseverance also stands out in *Ḥemdat Yamim,* a seminal book of the eighteenth century. The author observes that "the essence of the Torah, its mysteries and hidden and profound secrets, is unknown to all in the initial stages of the enquiry, so that whoever has reason must bend his shoulder to the toil and burden of studying day after day until he uncovers that which he seeks."[70] According to kabbalistic testimonies, this approach was typically adopted by the ARI:

> I asked my master ZLHH what made him attain this wondrous wisdom. He told me that after toiling on the language of the *Zohar* for a week or two, he was informed that he had not yet attained, and then he would delve deeper. And I asked him: R. Moses Cordovero and I also took pains, why then did we not attain it? And he said that indeed we did take pains, but not that much.[71]

And R. Elijah, the Gaon of Vilna, used to say, "[I]t is impossible to thoroughly understand the *Zohar* and the *Tikkunim* unless one takes pains to study each matter and every text for several weeks."[72]

Probably the most interesting description appears in a famous Zoharic parable that was subject to several literary adaptations.[73] The parable is as follows:

> What can be compared to this? It is like a girl, beautiful and gracious, and much loved, and she is kept closely confined in her palace. She has a special lover, unrecognized by anyone and concealed. This lover, because of the love that he feels for her, passes by the door of her house and looks on every side, and she knows that her lover is constantly walking to and fro by the door of her house. What does she do? She opens a tiny door in the secret palace where she lives and shows her face to her love. Then she withdraws at once and is gone. None of those in her lover's vicinity sees or understands, but her lover alone knows, and his heart and soul and inner being yearn for her, and he knows that it is because of the love that she bears him that she showed herself to him for a moment, in order to awaken love in him. . . . This is the way of the Torah. At first, when she begins to reveal herself to a man, she gives him a sign. If he understands, good. If he does not understand, she sends to him . . . and she begins to speak with him through the curtain that she has spread before him, in the way that best suits him, so that he can understand little by little. . . . Then she talks with him through a very fine veil and discusses enigmatic things. . . . And then when he has become accustomed to her, she reveals herself to him face to face, and speaks to him about all her hidden mysteries . . . and she has neither hidden or withheld anything from him.[74]

Whoever is not discouraged by the hardship involved in pursuing the secret, then, is likely to get hold of it eventually.

To conclude, let me quote two long paragraphs that incorporate a number of elements we have mentioned. The first text, taken from a book composed at the end of the thirteenth century, reads as follows:

> We must inform you of some great principles. Know that before man is initiated into the secret of God, blessed be He, he must cross several fords and encounter a number of supernal multitudes, and there are ten rungs, one above the other. . . . This is comparable to a minister who went to see the king. This king dwells in his palace, where there are eleven rooms, each facing the next one. Now, the

> king stationed outside, in the outermost room, some efficient guards. He said to them: "Inspect whoever wishes to enter your room; do not admit anyone whose clothes are dirty." He then ordered those in the second and the third room: "Whoever enters and shifts his eyes to the left or to the right, do not admit him." . . . To those in the tenth room he said: "Do not admit anyone who does not bear your image." . . . After this introduction, know that before the prophets are initiated to the influx of prophecy, they go through fords and passages where the celestial angels encounter them and check them, inspecting them in each gate in a different manner. . . . If the prophets prove to be worthy of entering, the angels let them in, and if not, they leave them outside. . . . And the living creatures that are called *ḥashmal* inspect the prophets when they reach the gate through which one enters to behold the mirror, which is not a clear crystal, and the *ḥashmal* rushes in its swift manner and ease of speech to talk with the prophet who enters in order to behold. And if the prophet is able to comprehend the words of the *ḥashmal* instantly and to give answers to each and every discourse, then it is established that he is worthy of entering and beholding the glory of the king. . . . Now, the *ḥashmal* inspects all those who have reached the rung of prophecy. If they answer to the point and ask properly, promptly, and instantly like the *ḥashmal*, they are allowed to enter. Otherwise, they are rejected and pushed outside.[75]

From the second work,[76] dating from the sixteenth century, I would like to quote a longer passage. The text is as follows:

> In clarifying the ways of solitude and *devekut* and the appropriate preparation required of the recluse, suffice it [to state] that he should reach the essence of devotional intention and actually attach his soul to the Intellect, so that the holy spirit rests upon him. Know that the proper preparations required of the recluse in order for him to find precious things by divesting his intellect of corporeality are diverse and numerous. First of all, as far as the body is concerned, he ought to diminish his corporeal desires. Eating must be restricted to food of little quantity and high quality, including small intakes of cooked portions and wine. . . . This is not meant to inflict upon him sorrows. On the contrary, this [state of mind] is bound to keep him from attaining perfection. What is proposed here is that even if he possesses great wealth, he should enjoy it only for the purpose

of maintaining the soul in his body. And he should aggravate his beastly powers, depriving them of what they desire, for by enfeebling them the soul is strengthened and the intellect is set free from the imprisonment of the instinctual powers and cleaves to its Maker. The same holds true of sexual intercourse. . . . He should observe his conjugal duties on Friday nights, doing so in great cleanliness and purity, focusing his thought on the worship of his Maker and attaching himself to the supernal communion. . . . To maintain the purity of the body he must also immerse himself in the waters of the ritual bath. . . . And when he conducts his body and his physical powers in this way and thus perseveres for a long time, not just a day or a couple of days or a month, but really a very long time, until he reaches the point where his physical powers no longer distress him by demanding of him what was previously in their power, then he will also turn to make some restoration concerning his soul and the perfection of his virtues, especially to remove from himself anger and worries and the pursuit of luxuries, as these stand in the way of attaining a higher level of being. In this way he will reach the level of equanimity . . . [which] brings him to the solitude of the soul, and solitude leads to the Holy spirit, which in turn leads to prophecy, which is the highest rung. Thus, one of the principles that the recluse needs to follow is that first he must attain the level of equanimity, namely not to be impressed by anything. On the contrary, he must experience spiritual joy and be content with his lot and consider himself the sole ruler of this base world, having no one, near or far, to either care for him or pay him homage or do him any good. For all of the world's prosperity and abundance is in his hands. So that there is nothing that he needs. . . . And he must choose for himself a house where he will live all by himself. . . . He must furnish this house with fine vessels, the best ones he has, and with all sorts of scents and spices—if there are plants and herbs in the house, it is very good for him to savor all of these things, thus refining his vegetative soul and his vital soul. He will also play musical instruments or sing in his own voice . . . to refine the vital soul, which overlaps with the speaking soul and the intellectual soul. If he does so during the day, this is fine as long as the house is somewhat dark. But it is much better to do this at night, with many candles lit up. And he should wear nice, clean, and preferably white clothes. For all of this is efficacious to the intention of Fear and Love [of God]. . . . And after having made all these preparations, then, while you prepare yourself to talk with your Maker, make sure you empty your thoughts of all the vanities of the world, wrap yourself in your prayer shawl and place the phylacteries on your arm and around your head so as to be awestruck and fearful of the Shekhinah, which keeps you company at that time. Then sit down and take ink and pen and paper and start combining letters quickly and zestfully . . . in order to separate the soul and purify it of all material forms and things that preceded it and to divest yourself of them so as to focus your heart and thought and intellect and soul on the mental image. . . . And in this state he [the mystic] should prepare his true thought to imagine in his heart and intellect that he is sitting above in heaven before God, amidst the splendor and glory of His divine presence and that the Holy One, blessed be He, is sitting on His throne like an exalted king and the hosts of heaven are all standing before Him in awe and fear and trembling and he too is amongst them. . . . And precisely in this state, he will firmly close his eyes and in fear and trembling will shake his entire body and will take deep breaths as far as possible for him, until all the parts of his body, the external and the internal ones alike, will weaken. Then he will ascend, attaching and cleaving his soul and thought from one rung to another in those spiritual matters as far as it is possible for him to bring it up . . . to the hidden supernal world of emanation, so that he will be almost like a virtual intellect without any sensation of the material things, for he has emerged from the human realm . . . and entered the divine realm. It is then that his soul expands and is refined by cleaving to the root of the Source from which it was hewn. . . . But know that permission is not given to every man—though it is worthwhile to draw everyone nearer to the holy labor of uttering the holy name—unless he is well accustomed and experienced in this practice . . . and know that the matter of *devekut,* which is mentioned in this chapter, is a wonderful thing, serving as a ladder to the rung of prophecy. When the pious and pure man attaches his soul to the supernal world and meditates and brings up his soul and intellect, divesting his thought of material things . . . then, know that every thing and every matter upon which he concentrates his mind and soul at that moment immediately comes true as he willed, for better or worse. . . . And comprehend this matter because it requires subtle consideration. For it is impossible to write about it in a precise manner that conveys the depth of the matter—this must be imparted orally.

5 • The Dangers Facing the Mystic

In the Bible, the revelation of God coincides with dangerous phenomena such as fire, smoke, and lightning. Fire illuminates, but also consumes. Just before the Sinaitic revelation, Moses was warned to restrain the Israelites: "But let not the priests and the people break through to come up to the Lord" (Exod. 19:24). An ecstatic outburst was well anticipated. On the Day of Atonement, when the High Priest entered the sanctuary, the congregation was likely to be swept away by the same ecstatic exaltation, and they all rejoiced when he came out safely from the Holy of Holiness. Indeed, the strong impact of the mystical experience causes the souls of some people to take flight then and there, being in a state of *yeṣiah me-ha-keilim* (separation from the corporeal vessels that contain their souls). This "tasting" of the Divine is not meant for everyone—"not everyone who wants to take the Name may come and get it."[1]

Sometimes the Kabbalist writes: "I am not permitted to explain, because my heart does not pass on [the hidden things] to my mouth"[2]—namely, the secret is sealed in the mystic's mind and cannot be verbalized at all. In this case, he must be content in possessing it himself, without communicating it to someone else. However, talmudic and kabbalistic literature also contains warnings about the potential dangers involved in penetrating the hidden mysteries. In a play on words taken in earnest (for nothing in the world, and particularly in the holy language, is accidental), the Kabbalists suggest that Pardes (orchard grove, garden) can be either a delightful and pleasurable site, or *shemad* (a destructive and fatal place), as both words have the numerical value of 344.[3]

Generally speaking, the talmudic sages (*Ḥagigah* 13a) and their successors caution about the investigation of hidden meanings by citing an injunction that originates in the Book of Ben Sira (3:22): "Do not explore that which is concealed from you; do not expound that which is hidden from you. Think about that which is permitted to you, but do not occupy yourself with mysteries."[4] This injunction is formulated in general terms and a lot was written in an attempt to clarify the meaning of its details.

A well known *baraitha,* which has numerous parallels, concerns four men who "entered the Pardes," of whom only one *nikhnas ve-yaṣa be-shalom* (entered and came out in peace), namely, emerged unhurt. This *baraitha* lends itself to many questions, which were dealt with at length by Yehuda Liebes.[5] Though these interpretations are beyond the scope of the present discussion, I would like to call attention to a significant detail found in the text. Of Ben Azzai who "cast a look and died," the *baraitha* adds that "of him Scripture says, 'Precious in the sight of the Lord is the death of his pious ones'" (Ps. 116:15). What does this mean? It is not plausible that the text is meant to extol this venerated sage. The very next sentence refers to the other person who entered the Pardes: Ben Zoma, who "cast a look and was hurt *[nifg'a].* Of him Scripture says: 'Hast thou found honey? Eat as much as sufficient for thee, lest thou be sated with it, and vomit it up'" (Prov. 25:15). What does this verse teach us? It seems that Ben Zoma deserved some measure of knowledge but tried to go beyond the limit or, perhaps, beyond his mental capability. This suggests that the mystics, those who are subject to direct revelations, are in as much danger as those who experience them vicariously by way of oral transmission. That the mystics must have been aware of this danger is implicit, for example, in the following statement:

> He [Ben Zoma] used to say: Do not look into a man's orchard. If you have looked, do not go down into it. If you have gone in, do not stare [at the fruit]. If you stared, do not touch. If you touched, do not eat. If a man eats, he removes his soul from the life of this world and the life of the world to come.[6]

A more succinct formulation of the same principle is found in *Heikhalot Zutarti:*[7]

> Be careful about the glory of your creator and do not descend to it. When you [however] have descended to it, do not enjoy anything of it. Your end would then be to be banished from the world.

Similarly, medieval Kabbalists express the opinion that certain individuals were actually punished by heaven for their excessive explorations of the unknown. For example, Abel, Cain's brother, was punished by death even though "we found no iniquity with him," because "in offering his sacrifice he peered more than was appropriate."[8] Moreover, the ARI explained to R. Ḥayyim Vital, his disciple, that because he had looked at his master's face while concentrating on the Shema and on similar occasions, his eyes were bothering him.[9]

The danger inherent in one's preoccupation with the mysteries of the hidden meanings is repeatedly emphasized. The Talmud cautions that "there was once a child who expounded [the mysteries of] Ḥashmal, and a fire went forth and consumed him."[10] A later testimony, by R. Hai Gaon, confirms this: "Several books that were handed down to us indicate some of the [divine] names and the angels' names. . . . When the Elders and the pious men saw these, they were frightened."[11] The Kabbalists themselves warned of the dangers inherent in kabbalistic pursuits.

Rabbi Abraham Abulafia writes: "And whoever approaches the Unification more than is worthy of him, is bound to die for [by doing so] he sheds his own blood."[12] In another book he makes the same point: "He who combines [the holy letters] must take heed to protect himself from His fear and in His honor, lest his blood escapes from him so that he should die by his own doing."[13] Both cases, so it seems, do not concern the layman, but rather the initiate who seeks to expand his mystical activities by occupying himself with the science of letter combinations. For there is a limit to man's attempts to transcend the physical world. While the direct causes of danger are not always specified, presumably each stage of the spiritual process requires a greater spiritual readiness, or a higher intellectual level.

Pirkey Heikhalot Rabbati describes the gates of the celestial palaces, through which the "descenders into the Chariot" enter, and the gatekeepers who closely watch these gates. The text conveys the following warning: "I testify and caution that no one may descend into the Chariot unless he possesses these two virtues: he has read and studied the Pentateuch, the Prophets and the Hagiographa, as well as the Mishnah, the halakhic discussions and the Aggadot, and the rulings concerning the laws of what is forbidden and permitted. And he has fulfilled the entire Torah, obeying all the warnings and observing all the laws and statutes and the teachings that were given to Moses in Sinai."[14] In the thirteenth century it was stated:

> Before one is initiated into the secrets of God, blessed be He, one must go through a number of fords and encounter several supernal multitudes [just like the prophets, who used to "cleanse themselves in seclusion and prepare their mind for the attainment of prophecy"]. . . . And the angels would check them, subjecting them to a different inspection at each and every gate.[15]

A well-known anonymous text of the fourteenth century describes the mystical quest in the following terms:

> And these hidden, interior things are awesome and wondrous, pure and illuminating in the mind's eye and give light to the soul. For this is the light of the image envisioned by the beholders. Amongst them, some faces lit up, and others were darkened, while still others were drawn to it like one precious thing to another. Yet one should not pursue them at all times, but only on a *clear day,* and with a *pure soul* and *lucid reason,* and with a good intention—pure, clean, and refined—to ascend higher and higher toward the light of brightness, to go up to the mountain of the Lord and to His place of holiness with clean hands and a pure heart, in order to perceive and comprehend great, awesome things. And one should not delve deeply into religion and knowledge unless he follows a straight way and not [that which leads to] death, as was the case of Elisha Aḥer. And you should understand this, because everything is displayed before you as on a set table; should one eat, he may live forever [cf. Gen. 3:22]. For this is the table set before God, in which the angels of the Living God take delight. And beware how you approach these things or else keep away from them. And tightly seal these things, and to the frame attach a golden wreath—a seal upon a seal. For it is the glory of God to conceal a thing; but the honor of kings is to search out a matter.[16]

R. Ḥayyim Vital relates that he entreated his master, Rabbi Isaac Luria (the ARI) to teach him a *yiḥud* (act of Unification), namely, a mystical formula,

> so that I could attain some perception. But the ARI said to me: "You are as yet unable to do so." Yet I kept entreating him and he gave me a brief [formula of] Unification. In the middle of the night, I got up and recited this Unification. And I felt my body shaking and my head feeling heavy, and my mind became demented and my mouth twisted to one side. So I ceased [to recite] the Unification. In the morning, my master of blessed memory said to me: "I told you that you would go through the same experience as Ben Zoma, who 'was hurt' *[nifg'a]*."[17]

The dangers confronting the mystic are indicated by various images. The given *baraitha* about the four men who entered the Pardes mentions the likelihood of *kiṣuṣ ba-neti'ot* (mutilating the shoots), namely heresy, which is punishable by death, and *heṣiṣ ve-nifg'a* (cast a look and was hurt), the meaning of which is obscure. The *Heikhalot* literature specifies jets of water and *pulsey de-nura* (rods of fire). The last two images appear also in later works. Moshe Idel observed that Sufi literature, as well as some kabbalistic works of the thirteenth century, introduce the motif of sinking in water, while other works warn of great fire.[18] Much later works caution against mental derangement. Indeed, in his responsum, R. Ḥai Gaon explained the meaning of *heṣiṣ ve-nifg'a* as "someone who lost his mind after being exposed to frightening sights, which his mind could not tolerate."[19]

True, there is a danger that man would not be able to contain the intensity of the light and the majestic sublimity of the revelation; nonetheless, the mystic believes that he has the power to uplift his soul, and he even employs certain techniques to make his wish come true. Let us now survey these techniques and find out what they can accomplish.

6 • Techniques of Exploring Mysteries

The chapters of prophecy in the Scripture give the impression that the prophet was passive while receiving the divine words of prophecy. The notion that the spirit of prophecy was bestowed upon the prophet irrespective of his own wishes or efforts is in line with the fundamental nature of biblical prophecy as a mission assigned to the individual from above. Nonetheless, the phenomenon of *beney nevi'im* (2 Kings 2:3) is generally interpreted as a circle of "disciples" preparing themselves to receive inspiration. This suggests that prophetic inspiration is also a matter of labor, of taking some active part in the process. When, many generations later, Maimonides considered the prophet's role, he associated it with some strict requirements, even as he recognized that the inspiration of prophecy depended on God's choice and his absolute will. If this is the state of affairs in the world of prophecy, then what happens in the world of hidden mysteries? Does the individual who is worthy of perceiving these mysteries depend on the use of a certain technique to get inspiration, or does inspiration come to him naturally?

Since Kabbalah is an esoteric doctrine that is passed on by oral and personal transmission, by "whispering," to the *ṣenu'im,* the few humble and virtuous men who study it in *ṣin'ah,* in privacy, within confined circles, it is understandable why the Kabbalists are reluctant to disclose their techniques for attaining divine secrets. In this respect, Kabbalah differs from mysticism. While the mystics dwelled on their experiences and the stages necessary for their attainment, the Kabbalists wrote as little as possible about their personal experiences. Yet one can glean from their writings some of the methods that were used for attaining secrets. A considerable number of these ways and means are also common to non-Jewish forms of mysticism, which makes it easier to grasp the nature of their Jewish correlates.

Various sources suggest that, with no special preparations on his part, a man may be endowed with mystical tendencies that qualify him to reach heights at any moment. Other sources explicitly mention specific techniques. Let me introduce some of the techniques that were widespread among the Kabbalists.

In his responsum, Rav Hai Gaon testifies:

> Many scholars thought that when one who is distinguished by many qualities described in the books seeks to behold the *merkavah,* the "divine Chariot," and the palaces of the angels on high, he must fast a number of days and place his head between his knees and whisper downward many hymns and songs of praise whose texts are known from tradition.[1]

The first technique, that of fasting, aims at self-nullification. It is designed to counteract the influence exerted by one's body, thus cleansing and purifying his soul. This is a superhuman condition into which man enters with full consciousness. Something of this sort was conveyed by Moses our master when he stated: "Forty days and forty nights I neither did eat bread nor drink water" (Deut. 9:9). The forty days of fasting (probably implicit in R. Hai Gaon's responsum) also symbolize the time it takes for the formation of the embryo, as stated in the Talmud. This suggests that after a continuous fast, the person is reborn in a renewed state of purity. Perhaps, too, it signifies the obliteration of individuality by being fused with, and integrated into, the universal soul.

Significantly, fasting is associated with a well-defined posture of the body: sitting with one's head between one's knees. This technique is already mentioned in the biblical stories of Elijah the prophet (1 Kings 18:42) and in the striking talmudic story of the repentant (Eleazar ben Dordia) who in contrition adopted this posture and wept, whereupon his soul departed from his body (*'Avodah Zarah* 17a, and see also *Berakhot* 34b). This practice signified a return to the embryonic state, the position of the embryo in its mother's womb (see *Nidah* 30b). By the analogy to the embryo, this posture indicates that a new man is about to be born, a pure man, who is therefore worthy of perceiving divine mysteries.

The motif of pure renewal also underlies the legal procedure of *seder malkot* (punishment by lashing) as implemented in the city of Hebron in the sixteenth century. At the first stage, the repentant is "crouching" submissively. At the second stage, when the *dayyanim,* (religious judges) absolve him of his vow, he "sits with his head between his knees." The difference in the descriptive terms is intentional. The second posture is reminiscent of the embryonic state, thus suggesting that after repentance, a newborn person, cleansed and pure, faces the world (*Sheney Luḥot ha-Berit,* fol. 227b).

Let us turn to a dramatic description that appears in the *Zohar* (III, fol. 166b):

> [Rabbi Simeon] began his discourse by saying: ". . . Torah, Torah, what should I say about you? You are *ayelet ahavim* [a lovely doe] and *ya'alat ḥen* [a graceful gazelle], above and below. Who amongst your lovers would merit to be properly nourished by you? Torah, Torah, the delight of your Master. Who could uncover and disclose your secrets and hidden treasures?" He wept and placed his head between his knees and kissed the dust, whereupon he saw several of the companions standing around him. They said to him: "Do not fear, ben Yoḥai; do not fear, the Holy Luminary. Write and rejoice in the happiness of your Lord." He then wrote down all he had heard that night and meditated upon it without forgetting anything. And that [hidden] light was shining for him all through the night. When the day had dawned, he lifted his eyes and saw a vision of light illuminating the firmament. He cast down his eyes, and, lifting them up again, he saw a light illuminating the whole firmament and the contours of the Temple appeared in that light in several images. R. Simeon rejoiced, whereupon that light vanished from his sight and was concealed. Meanwhile, those two celestial messengers arrived. They found him with his head between his knees and said to him: "Peace be with you, our master; peace to he whom the upper and the lower worlds wish to welcome. Stand up." R. Simeon stood up and rejoiced with them.

According to the above excerpt, while sitting in the given posture Rabbi Simeon saw certain visions. This technique is mentioned later on, for example in *Eben ha- Shoham* (1538) by R. Joseph ibn Sayaḥ. Among other things, the author advises the reader "to isolate himself and meditate in solitude on matters known to us in this wisdom, and to bend his head like a reed between his knees until all his senses are numb. Then he shall see the supernal lights manifestly, and not just suggestively."[2]

In the seventeenth century, R. Aaron Berakhyah of Modena recommended the same technique: "Behold how good it is to place one's head between one's knees."[3] He also offered a symbolic explanation for this posture.

According to the above excerpt, R. Simeon bar Yoḥai was sitting on the ground. Perhaps this detail is implicit in the wording of R. Hai Gaon's responsum "and whispers downward," to which I will soon return. As a rule, it can be assumed that every case of sitting with one's head between one's knees entails sitting on the ground. Sitting on the ground is significant in itself, regardless of whether or not it involves the given posture.

Sitting on the ground, amidst the dust, usually symbolizes humility. This is also the opinion of R. Moses Cordovero: "And I heard that the ancients used to sit on the ground when they taught this wisdom to their disciples, in order to subdue them and frighten them."[4] Presumably, they adopted this posture not only in the presence of their masters and teachers. But sitting on the ground may also signify reestablishing contact with the earth by returning to the source—in the sense of "for thou art dust and to dust shalt thou return" (Gen. 3:19). Contrarily, those practising yoga make sure they sit on some sort of a mattress that would separate them from the ground proper.

As for "and [he must] whisper downward many hymns and songs of praise," even this detail is found in non-Jewish forms of mysticism. Singing puts the mystic in a certain trance. Sometimes the mystics chant a certain word (such as *ram-ram*) faster and faster. At other times, a more elaborate recitation of poetry is involved. We know of some hymns that the "descenders into the Chariot" used to hear during contemplation and perhaps these urged them to take part in the spiritually uplifting panegyrics. A parallel to the excerpt from R. Hai Gaon's responsum reads as follows:

> It is specified in the *Heikhalot* [literature] that the sages who were worthy of this, prayed and cleaned themselves of all impurity, and fasted and bathed themselves and became pure and they used the Names and gazed at the *Heikhalot*.[5]

This text lists prayer as one of the components of mystical preparation. In this context, praying is self- evident, and perhaps the prayer included a personal request for divine assistance. At any event, in later generations we find "a prayer to be recited before studying the Kabbalah." This prayer finds expression in various formulations, most of which repeat the Psalmist's wish: "Open thou my eyes, that I may behold wondrous things out of thy Torah" (Ps. 119:18).

At times, these prayers involved uttering the holy Names, as indicated in the above excerpt: "and they used the Names." This practice, which is reminiscent of the Indian mantra, functioned like the chanting of a magic word. It was supposed to establish contact with the appropriate supernal powers that could be of help in the given case. Presumably, it is against such an attempt on the part of unworthy persons that the Tanna mentioned in *Avot* (I, 13) and its parallels warns that "u-de-ishtamash be-taga ḥalaf," namely, he who exploits the crown (of the Name) for his personal benefit shall pass away before his time.

A strong criticism, which provides an interesting description of current kabbalistic practices, is also voiced by Rabbi Moshe Taku of the thirteenth century. This Ashkenazi *ḥakham* complains about the *ḥaserey da'at* (those lacking knowledge) who believe that they are able to transform themselves into prophets and train themselves to utter the holy names. Sometimes they are so focused on uttering the names that their soul takes fright and their body drops down in exhaustion, as if nothing separates the body from the soul; the soul then becomes the essential and is far-sighted. Yet, after a while, when the power of the name they uttered is removed from them, they resume their former state, while their mind is overwhelmed.[6]

Finally, let me quote a concluding warning of Rabbi Moses Ḥayyim Luzzatto: "After he proved himself to possess the virtues we mentioned so far, beginning with watchfulness and up to fear of sin, he will sanctify himself and will prosper. For if the former are missing, he is like a common man and a cripple."[7] Apparently, it is no coincidence that Luzzatto used the terms a "common man" and a "cripple." It is as if he wished to convey that this practice is holy labor, which corresponds to the service of the priest in the Temple. Just as no one is allowed to administer the sacrifices in the Temple save the priest, who must be intact, without any flaw, so also the Kabbalist's labor is a holy service performed by a holy man.

Since this book is not devoted exclusively to the description of the diverse techniques and the necessary preparations for receiving revelations—though such exploration is advisable—I will just allude to a number of additional details.

An ancient text recommends the following: "And he who seeks Torah must wear new garments and cover himself with a new mantle, made of wool . . . and in the evening he should eat bread made by his own hands and on that day he should not come and go."[8] It is noteworthy that the writer not only mentions new garments, which symbolize renewal and purification, but refers specifically to a woolen mantle, which calls to mind Elijah the prophet.[9] As indicated in Zekhariah's prophecy (13:4), the "hairy mantle" was the typical garment of the prophets, a sort of a class symbol. Elijah also used to wear "a girdle of leather about his loins" (2 Kings 1:8), which probably was not an expensive accessory. Woolen garments also characterized the Sufis (who were named after them). But for the Sufis, these were a symbol of simplicity, while the given text specifies new woolen mantles, thus emphasizing the element of renewal. Attention should also be drawn to the personal baking of bread—designed to ensure that it would not be touched by an unclean (i.e., menstruating) woman.[10]

With regard to articles of clothing, it is sometimes stated that "as far as possible, all of them should be white, because this is very efficacious to one's concentration on his fear and love [of God].[11] White symbolizes cleansing and purity, as well as the clean and pure tabula rasa, which stands for the Godhead. (As discussed in the second part of this book, the highest Sefirah is depicted in terms of the whiteness of the snow.) At any event, it seems that the special combination of simplicity and purity, which is reflected in the white garments, removes man from the world of material needs and draws him nearer to his spiritual source.

Of special interest in this context is an ancient technique associated with drinking water or revelations that take place near water. In the traditional sources, drinking water[12] or pouring it[13] are associated with the relationship between a disciple and his teacher. Drinking water is also part of the ritual act of sanctification in one of the Gnostic sects,[14] and similar practices are mentioned in the Jewish sources as well. For example, according to tradition, Rabbi Menaḥem Recanati, a distinguished

Kabbalist, experienced a turning point early in his mystical career as a result of drinking pure water: "One day, when he was praying and fasting in the synagogue, he fell asleep. A man holding a flask of water woke him up and said to him: 'Drink this.' He woke up and drank it, but before he finished drinking, the man went away. The rabbi went to the house of study as usual and found his mind to be lucid and perceptive because had just been transformed into a different person."[15] Rabbi Ḥayyim Vital recounts a similar incident:

> When I came to my master [ha-ARI] ZLHH to learn this wisdom from him, my teacher went to Tiberias and led me . . . right opposite the pillars of the old synagogue. And he took a plate and filled it with water, which he took from between the pillars, and made me drink it. And he said to me: "Now you will attain this wisdom, because this water which you have drunk is from Miriam's well." It is then that I began to plunge into the depth of this wisdom.[16]

A vivid description of a quite unusual ritual of sanctification by the water is found in the testimony of R. Eleazar of Worms, one of the outstanding personalities in Ashkenazi Hasidism at the beginning of the thirteenth century:

> The name is transmitted only to the *ṣenu'im* [the initiates], who are not prone to anger, who are humble and God-fearing, and carry out the commandments of their Creator. And it is transmitted only over water. Before the master teaches it to his pupil, they must both immerse themselves and bathe in forty measures of flowing water, then put on white garments and fast on the day of instruction. Then both must stand up to their ankles in the water, and the master must say a prayer ending with the words: "The voice of God is over the waters! [Ps. 29:2] Praised be Thou, O Lord, who revealest Thy secret to those who fear Thee, He who knoweth the mysteries." Then both must turn their eyes toward the water and recite verses from the Psalms, praising God over the waters. . . . [At this time, the master transmits one of the secret names of God that the adept is permitted to hear, whereupon] they return to the synagogue or schoolhouse, holding water in a pure vessel and the rabbi says: "Blessed art thou, the Lord, our God, King of the Universe, who has sanctified us by His commandments and has distinguished us from all the nations and revealed to us His mysteries."[17]

Sometimes the revelation itself takes place by the water. As articulated by R. Baḥya ben Asher, a Spanish Kabbalist who wrote his commentary on the Pentateuch in 1291: "It is a tradition among the sages of the Truth that the Name is not passed on save by the water."[18] In fact, Ezekiel and Daniel received revelation by the river: "Now it came to pass in the thirtieth year . . . as I was among the exiles by the river Kevar, that the heavens were opened, and I saw visions of God" (Ezek. 1:1).[19] And the same applies to the Apocalyptic literature. For example, "And I went thence and sat in the valley of Cedron in a cave of the earth, and I sanctified my soul there. . . . And afterwards I came to that place where He had spoken with me . . . and I began to speak in the presence of the Mighty One, and said. . . ."[20] Of special importance is *Re'uyot Yeḥezkel,* a mystical midrash from the Cahiro Genizah on the first verse of the book of Ezekiel, which according to Gershom Scholem dates no later than the fifth century. This text connects water to revelation in the following way:

> While Ezekiel was looking, the Holy One, blessed be He, opened up for him seven firmaments and he saw the Almighty. A parable. To what is it like? To a man who went to a barber and the barber cut his hair and handed him a mirror in which he saw his reflection. . . . So also Ezekiel was standing by the river Kevar and was looking at the water. And seven firmaments were opened to him and he saw the glory of God, as well as the beasts and ministering angels and the troops *[gedudim]* and the Seraphim and those with sparkling wings that were all joined together in the Chariot—they were passing in heaven while Ezekiel saw them in the water. Therefore it is written, 'by the river Kevar.'"[21]

From this we learn that water was used as a mirror, reflecting various events that take place in heaven.[22]

PROSTRATION ON THE GRAVES OF THE ZADDIKIM

This, too, is a well-accepted practice for attaining secrets. By prostrating oneself on the grave of the zaddik, one performs an act of *hitkasherut* (bonding) with his spirit, which in turn serves as a channel that passes on the hidden secrets to the living person. This act of bonding is not simple and requires preparations in the form of *yiḥudim* (mystical formulae that serve as acts of Unification). According to the ARI, not every hour is propitious for performing these Unifications, nor is every Kabbalist allowed to do so, and certainly not indiscriminately. In order for the bonding to be properly performed, there must be a spiritual correspondence between the root of the Kabbalist's soul and that of the deceased zaddik with whom he seeks to maintain spiritual contact.

In addition, every detail of the process must be performed meticulously and accurately: "These are the *yiḥudim* that were orally transmitted to me by my teacher— from mouth to mouth [i.e., in privacy], word by word, and letter by letter."[23] The ARI himself was qualified to perform them because he received revelations from heaven. R. Joseph ibn Tabul further says: "This is the wording of my teacher and master, R. Isaac Luria Ashkenazi ZLHH, who communicated this to me from mouth to mouth, and in great secrecy and this is proven and tested and of great benefit to the individual who knows it." Interestingly. R. Joseph ibn Tabul adds the following: "Thus far the statements of the perfect rabbi, the Luminary of the Diaspora, as he transmitted them to me, Joseph, by the grave of Abba Saul, from mouth to mouth. I had forgotten them, but after his death I recalled them in a dream. And he gave me some proof, which I checked on the graves of the zaddikim. And it turned out that he was truthful and his words were true." A wealth of material on this point is to be found in *Sha'ar Ru'aḥ ha-Kodesh* and in *Sha'ar ha-Yiḥudim,* both of which are by R. Ḥayyim Vital.

In a letter dated 1621 that was addressed to his sons, R. Isaiah [ha-Levi] Horowitz makes the following point: "And there is a special prayer for each and every zaddik. By the grave of R. Simeon bar Yoḥai, of blessed memory, one studies the *Zohar* in fear and awe and great *devekut* [enthusiasm]." Afterwards one's heart experiences total bliss, unspoiled by any trace of mourning and sadness, for this is what Rabbi Simeon bar Yoḥai wants and it is proven and tested."[24] Thus, there was special interest in studying the *Zohar* beside the grave of R. Simeon bar Yoḥai, where the profound meaning of the secrets hidden inside it was supposed to be revealed. There are many biographical stories that attest to this phenomenon.

Significantly, the custom of prostrating oneself by the graves of the zaddikim is also mentioned in halakhic books. For example, R. Ovadiah Yoseph points out in his responsa that "the wondrous Luminary, the ARI of blessed memory, has already confirmed that when one prostrates oneself by the graves of the zaddikim, and especially if he knows how to perform a *yiḥud* that is associated with that particular zaddik, the soul of that zaddik will be of great help and assistance to him."[25] In fact, the Halakhah books deal with various aspects of this issue.

Another technique that is partly connected with graves is known as *gerushin* (wanderings in exile). This practice branches out into several intertwined offshoots. One is that the Kabbalist detaches himself from his family for a certain period of time and goes out to nature. The narrative episodes in the *Zohar* therefore often take place in nonpopulated areas. R. Elijah de-Vidas,[26] the disciples of Sabbatai Ṣevi,[27] and many others attest to the practice among their contemporaries. There is withdrawal from the world in order to ascend to the Root, and participation in the suffering of the Shekhinah, who, like the people of Israel, is in exile. The close identification with the Shekhinah helps one to attain secrets, for the Shekhinah is "the gate of heaven."

Another offshoot is walking in the desert or visiting the graves of the zaddikim in order to establish spiritual contacts with them and achieve union with their souls. Many descriptions of this practice appear in *Gerushin* by R. Moses Cordovero and in *Sh'ar Ru'aḥ ha-Kodesh* by R. Ḥayyim Vital. It should be noted that Cordovero explicitly states in several places that the Kabbalists used to stand barefoot beside the tomb of the zaddik, as an indication of mourning for the exile of the Shekhinah and sharing her sorrows.

Still another offshoot of this practice of *gerushin* is related to the Rabbi Moses Cordovero and his circle. Cordovero describes

> what I and others have experienced in connection with gerushin, when we wandered in the fields . . . discussing verses from the Bible suddenly, without previous reflection. On these occasions, new ideas would come to us in a manner that cannot be believed unless one has seen or experienced it many times.[28]

Though the Kabbalist is willing to drop some hints about what has occurred, he insists that only the person who has either experienced it himself, or at least witnessed it "many times," is capable of truly and thoroughly understanding it. The Kabbalist runs out to the field, where a biblical verse or a talmudic saying comes out of his mouth spontaneously, without any deliberate preparation on his part. And all of a sudden he finds himself producing a discourse that revolves around this intuitive utterance "and the words of Torah were shining in us and the words were spoken of themselves."[29]

Here are some detailed descriptions of this striking experience:

> We were still in the study of R. Simeon bar Yoḥai when I concluded my exposition on the subject. Then we fell down [in prayer] in the sepulchre of Rabbi Simeon and Rabbi Eleazar, and with my lips still moving I said a short prayer from the depths of my heart. Then my master arose and expounded [several verses from Deuteronomy} in a manner different from his previous explanations, and so did some other participants. I stood up and looked. I was facing south—to my right was the tombstone of R. Eleazar; to my left, that of Rabbi Simeon, of blessed memory. And I opened my discourse by explaining the verse . . . and I said. . . .[30]

After mentioning the discourse of Rabbi Solomon ha-Levi Alkabez, which was held by the tomb of Rabbi Yehudah bar Illay, Cordovero adds: "And all of this was said by my teacher, for it was the gift of R. Yehudah bar Illay, with whose assistance we expounded . . . and we also elaborated on this."[31] In other words, the spirit of the deceased assists the Kabbalists in penetrating mysteries. This is implicit in the following description: "And we, some of the companions, entered into the cave [of the tannaitic rabbis in 'Akhbara] and recited a short prayer and then we went into the field to the rock, where we expounded a scriptural verse. . . ."[32] By entering into the cave and praying there, they were endowed with a special power that enabled them to spontaneously produce an insightful discourse.

R. Immanuel Ricchi, an Italian Kabbalist of the eighteenth century, reports a similar experience of intuitive knowledge. In the introduction to his book *Yosher Levav,* he recounts that sometimes, as soon as he wakes up, a scriptural verse "comes to my mouth." An almost identical story appears in the *Zohar* (II, fol. 61b). Now, although the Talmud recognizes and applauds this kind of occurrence,[33] it makes no mention of the mystical practice of *gerushin*—the sudden departure for the countryside as described above. On the other hand, similar spiritual exercises are customary in Christian and Muslim sects. In Judaism there seem to be no testimonies about this practice prior to the time of Cordovero and his circle.[34]

A special technique is employed in a magic ritual of the adjuration of the "Princes of the Torah," those in charge of the secrets of the Torah. Written testimonies on these ceremonies, which were held precisely on the eve of the Day of Atonement, originated in Babylonia and France around the year 1200, and perhaps even earlier.[35]

A similar technique is that of pronouncing the names of God so as to reach a state of ecstasy. This technique also involves adjuration and performing of certain acts, such as holding the fingers in a special way or breathing in a certain regular rhythm. Music played an important part in the array of means leading to the peak of mystical experience. Even combining the letters according to well- defined rules was likely to draw man nearer to his destination.[36]

By virtue of a special technique, man's soul ascends upward and sublime secrets are revealed to it. For example, the Besht relates that on the day of Rosh ha-Shanah (the New Year), when every man purges and purifies his soul, "I performed an incantation for the ascent of the soul. . . . And in that vision I saw wondrous things, which I had never seen until then from the day that I became spiritually aware. And it is impossible to relate and to tell what I saw and learned in that ascent hither even in private."[37]

7 • Evaluation of the Kabbalah

Predictably, the Kabbalists extolled the science of the Kabbalah on various occasions, designating it by all sorts of appreciative appellations. Some of these capture the character and distinction of the Kabbalah; others applaud its merits. I will begin by introducing these appellations, following which I will cite a selection of sayings in praise of the Kabbalah. Finally, I will demonstrate how the laudatory terms led to important conclusions and at the same time stirred up problems.

There is a well-known verse from the Book of Ben Sira (3:22) that is cited in the Talmud (*Ḥagigah* 13a) as follows: "Do not explore that which is concealed from you; do not expound that which is hidden from you. Think about that which is permitted to you, but do not occupy yourself with mysteries." These statements, in their given formulation, are recurrent in the literature, and especially the word *nistarot* (mysteries). The Talmud also uses the phrase *sitrey Torah* (mysteries of the Torah), as do the Jewish philosophers, following their own orientation. Furthermore, apparently on the basis of the ending of the Book of Ben Sira, the mysterious vision of Ezekiel in chapter 1 is named *ma'aseh merkavah* (the account of the chariot) (Mishnah, *Ḥagigah* II,1). The mystics belonging to the period of the *Heikhalot* literature are designated *yordey merkavah* (descenders into the chariot). This appellation is somewhat obscure and lends itself to several interpretations. One of them is that *yordey merkavah* are those who go deep down into the innermost recesses of their soul to the point of envisaging themselves riding the divine chariot. A similar appellation is *ṣofey merkavah* (the observers of the chariot), which refers to those who wish to fulfill the verse "Thy eyes shall see the King in his beauty" (Isa. 33:17). *Sefer ha-Bahir* speaks of the mystic as one "who beholds the chariot" (par. 68), but it also designates the mystics as *maskilim* (par. 139): "and when there is among Israel those who are *maskilim* and know the secret of the glorified Name." This appellation, which originates in the Book of Daniel 12:3 ("And they who are *maskilim* shall shine like the brightness of the firmament") is interpreted in the *Zohar* as follows: "It is the wise man who, of himself, looks upon things that cannot be expressed orally."[1] The mystic has reached such a high level of contemplation that he is capable of understanding even those things that cannot be verbalized. Interestingly, the term *maskil,* which overlaps with the "natural" designation of the philosopher, is recurrent in kabbalistic literature, probably under the inspiration of Ps. 14:2 (as well as 53:3): "a *maskil* that did seek God." Thus, Rabbi Asher ben David writes in *Sefer ha-Yiḥud* that the Kabbalists are "the *maskilim* among Israel, those who seek God, the pious followers of the Most High." Similarly, the Geronese Kabbalists speak of the "*maskilim* of France," and Rabbi 'Azriel speaks of "the *maskilim* among Israel." Naḥmanides, in his commentary on Lev. 20:12, designates them as *ha-yode'im* (the knowledgeable), which is a sort of translation of "gnostics," or perhaps it alludes to another appellation that was widespread among his colleagues in Gerona: *yode'ey ḥen* (those who know grace). This appellation probably derives from Eccles. 9:11 and perhaps was interpreted as the acronym of *ḥokhmah nistarah* (hidden wisdom).

A definition cited in the book of Yehudah the Barcelonian[2] may address the secrets of the Kabbalah: "The supreme science is called *madd'a ha-Elohi* [the science of the Divine] and this is the finest wisdom to understand the Unification of the Blessed One and the wisdom of his Torah and Commandments, which is the highest and most excellent of all sciences." Whether this definition concerns the Kabbalah is difficult to establish conclusively, all the more so since the book was composed circa 1130, and the given definition is cited in the name of an earlier sage, David of Babylonia, who according to another passage in the same book[3] is David Al-Mukammis of the tenth century. It is also possible that this definition refers to theology ("the science of the divine"), and not necessarily to esoteric matters. Therefore I propose it as a mere conjecture.

What is said in the same book about things that the sages "transmit to their disciples and to the sages in whispering and in privacy *be-kabbalah*"[4] qualifies the nature of transmission (by word of mouth, as received tradition) and the term *kabbalah* in this context has nothing to do with the Kabbalah proper as Jewish mysticism. This also holds true of the statement of R. Eleazar of Worms in reference to "the *kabbalah* that we have received from the ancients" and a similar statement by the Kabbalist R. Moses de Leon.[5]

According to the Mishnah (*Avot* VI), he who learns Torah for its own sake merits many things, and "to him are revealed the secrets of the Law." What precisely these secrets are is not quite clear. In *Merkavah Rabbah* (and in the *Heikhalot* literature) it is said: "And you revealed to me the power of the enquiry into the mysteries of above and below and the secrets of hidden things above and below, the secrets of understanding and the mysteries of wisdom." Later on, the word *raz*—whose numerical value, namely 207, is equivalent to *or* (light), hence the great value attached to it—became one of the basic appellations. Thus R. Kook spoke of *ḥokhmat ha-razim* (the science of the secrets.)

The use of the term "Kabbalah" in the sense of esoteric teaching is found in the writings of Rabbi Asher ben David: "bi-leshon [in the language of] ha-Kabbalah"; "ba'aley [masters of] ha-Kabbalah"; "al-pi derekh [by the method of] ha-Kabbalah"; and so forth. Apparently, it originates with his uncle, Rabbi Isaac the Blind, whose other disciples in Gerona, such as Rabbi 'Ezra and R. Jabob ben Sheshet, also employed this term. But in his letter to Naḥmanides, the same Rabbi Isaac refers to "my ancestors who were well-versed in the *ḥokhmah,* in the wisdom." This suggests that it was enough to use the word *ḥokhmah,* without qualifying it, for the recipient to know that it signified the Kabbalah. Indeed, even his disciples used this appellation (perhaps under the influence of the appellation *maskilim* in *Sefer ha-Bahir,* as cited above). Accordingly, the Kabbalists are named *ba'aley nefesh ḥakhamah* (those with a wise soul).[6]

A well-known appellation is that used by Naḥmanides in his commentary on the Torah (as well as in the beginning of *Ha-Nefesh ha-Ḥakhamah*): *'al derekh ha-Emet.* Even R. Joseph Gikatilla sometimes uses the term *derekh ha-Emet* (introduction; fol. 55a). Identical to it is the Aramaic phrase in the *Zohar* (II, fol. 95a) *be-oraḥ keshot* (according to the way of Truth). But Naḥmanides also uses another appellation. In his commentary on Job he writes: "Ba'aley [the masters of] ha-Kabbalah said." Close to this is the term *Kabbalah penimit,* which is mentioned in *Iggeret ha-Kodesh* and is recurrent in *Ta'amey ha-Miṣvot* by R. Joseph of Ḥamadan. R. Joseph Gikatilla speaks of *ḥakhmey ha-penimiyyut* (the sages of the interior).[7] Three hundred years later, Elijah de Vidas would write similarly about the *ḥokhmah penimit* (inner wisdom),[8] a term that in our days was frequently used by Rabbi Kook. In connection with this, let me mention *ḥakhmey ha-Kabbalah ha-kedoshah ha-kadmonim* (the ancient sages of the sacred Kabbalah), an appellation that apparently was first used by Rabbi Moses of Burgos.[9] This Kabbalist also designates his contemporaries as *geoney ha-midrash ha-ne'elam.*[10] The Geronese Kabbalists use other appellations, such as *ba'aley emunah* (masters of faith);[11] *ba'aley Kabbalah; yode'ey ḥen* (those who know grace); *mevinim* (those who understand); *mekubbalim* (Kabbalists); *mekabbeley ḥokhmat ha-Emet* (receivers of the wisdom of Truth); *maskilim; maskiley Emet;* and so forth.[12]

Another designation of the early period of the Kabbalah is *doreshey reshumot* (those who expound verses metaphorically). The Talmud (*Babba Kama* 82a) uses this term in reference to the sages, the exponents of the Torah who expound every verse by the method of *derash* (homiletic interpretation). The Kabbalists, too, use it in the sense of expounding verses—though in their own way. For example, R. Jacob ha-Kohen, circa 1270, comments that *Sefer ha-Bahir* found its way to "the rabbis of Provence, who pursue all sorts of *ḥokhmot ha-reshumot,* being versed in the knowledge of the Most High." Also widespread is the appellation *ba'aley reshumot.*

The *Zohar* uses several designations, such as *emet ve-emunah* (truth and faith) and *mehemanuta* (faith). The Kabbalists are *ḥavrayah* (group of companions); *ḥakimin* (wise); *yad'ey ḥokhmata* (those who are versed in wisdom); *beney mehemanuta* (men of faith) (III, fol. 12b); *beney heikhala* (the sons of the palace);[13] and *meḥaṣdey ḥakla* (reapers of the field). The latter appellation, which originates in the *Idra,* appears together with *beney heikhala* in the well-known hymns of the ARI for the Sabbath meals. R. Moses Ḥayyim Luzzatto (the RaMḤaL) provides an interesting explanation for *meḥaṣdey ḥakla:* "For *sadeh* [field] is the mate of Shaddai [the Almighty]";[14] "And this concerns those who attended the talmudic academy of R. Simeon bar Yoḥai of blessed memory, who used to take long walks in the countryside, where they explored the secrets."[15]

Another well-known term is that used by the author of *Ma'arekhet ha-Elohut: ba'aley ha-'avodah* (masters of the worship). It seems that he used this term exclusively and others Kabbalists followed suit, among them Rabbi Menaḥem Ṣioni in his commentary on the Torah, Rabbi Meir ibn Gabbay, Rabbi David ben Zimra (the RaDBaZ), and even the philosopher Rabbi Abraham ibn Migash.[16] Significantly, some Kabbalists used this term only in reference to the *Ma'arekhet ha-Elohut.*[17]

Other typical appellations are: *ba'aley emet* (possessors of the truth),[18] *ba'aley ha-'einayyim ha-me'ayyenim be-tapuḥey ha-zahav asher be-maskiyyot ha-kesef* (those with [sharp] eyes who contemplate the apples of gold in ornaments of silver),[19] *yode'ey madd'a* (those who know science),[20] *meviney madda'* (those who understand science),[21] and *moṣe'ey da'at* (those who find knowledge).[22] Finally, let me mention an appellation used in a debate that was held in Candia in the fifteenth century and revolved around the issue of transmigration. The given appellation connotes mockery: *kabblanim* (Kabbalah makers).[23]

It turns out that there is a wide range of appellations. In the beginning, this multiplicity of terms resulted from the fact that things were not yet crystallized. In the course of time, the Kabbalists tended to simply vary the terms they used.

In *Tikkuney Zohar* (fol. 147a) it is stated aphoristically: "Halakhah le-Moshe mi-Sinai—Kabbalah le-Moshe mi-Sinai." As explained by R. Moses Isserles, this means that "the words of the *Zohar* were given in Sinai."[24] At about the same time, the Kabbalist Rabbi Meir ibn Gabbay, who was exiled from Spain, wrote the following: "Kabbalah is the soul of Torah; hence, there is no perfection to Torah without it, just as there is no perfection to the body without the soul."[25] In the second half of the sixteenth century, R. Elijah de Vidas writes that the Kabbalah "is that which is called *ḥokhmah ba-amitut* [real wisdom]."[26] Others call it "pure philosophy"[27] and say "[T]he wisdom of the Kabbalah is the wisdom of philosophy, only they speak in two different languages."[28] The Kabbalah is so exalted that "no one is truly God-fearing if he fails to learn this wisdom."[29] Or, in a similar wording: "The wisdom of the Kabbalah . . . is the source and essence of the Torah, and all of it is nothing but the fear of heaven."[30] Therefore, "he who has not seen this wisdom, has seen no lights in his life and the fool walks in darkness."[31]

The gnostic Kabbalists of the mid-thirteenth century used to call themselves by terms of praise, such as *ha-ma'amikim* (the penetrators)[32] and "the remnants whom the Lord calls."[33] They also believed that they were, so to speak, *beney 'aliyah mu'atim* (the sons of high [namely, the spiritually exalted], who are few), as R. Simeon bar Yoḥai called himself and his son, according to what is told in the Talmud (*Sukkah* 45b).

According to Tishby's analysis, the same arguments that were raised in the *Zohar* in favor of the Kabbalah are precisely those that led both to its dissemination and to the trend of concealing it from the public.[34] Thus, the *Zohar* (II, fol. 247b) praises the one who contemplates the glory of God by contemplating the hidden wisdom, and, conversely, warns about the grave consequences entailed in desisting from doing so. In *Tikkuney Zohar*[35] it is said that he who avoids studying Kabbalah repels the fountain of wisdom. And already in the ancient *Shi'ur Komah* "he who knows this secret" of *shi'ur komah* (the measure of the Creator) was promised all sorts of spiritual rewards.[36]

Beginning with the sixteenth century, many voiced approval for studying the Kabbalah on a large scale. The belief was widespread that by virtue of reading the book of the *Zohar,* the Jews "will emerge from exile."[37] It is as if the duty of concealment was limited up to their period, and from 1540 onwards "it is one of the best religious precepts for all to occupy themselves in public [with it] . . . for by virtue of this, and not for any other thing, the messianic king was destined to come."[38] This conviction is reminiscent in the contemporary trend to study the Kabbalah. For instance, in the collection of *hanhagot* written by the members of R. Moses Cordovero's circle, it is recommended that one "occupy oneself every day with Scripture, the Mishnah, the Talmud, the Kabbalah, and halakhic rulings."[39] In practice, part of the public in the Safed synagogues studied the *Zohar* regularly, as attested to by Rabbi Solomon of Dresnitz in his letter to his family, dated 1603. There are many other testimonies, which cannot be dealt with at length in this context.[40] Nonetheless, it is worth mentioning that the ARI and his disciples insisted on the duty to be engaged in the Kabbalah every day and decided upon a specific sequence of studies: "It is incumbent upon every person to study every day the Bible, Mishnah, Talmud, Kabbalah."[41] As mentioned, they even discussed special times that were deemed the most appropriate for this lofty study. For example: "The engagement in the wisdom of the Kabbalah and its sources is successful on Friday after midday, and inside the *sukkah* on the festival of Sukkot. Also the night of the festival of Shavu'ot is a good time for studying the Kabbalah."[42]

Indeed, in various works from the sixteenth century onward, one is likely to find reading material for the regular study of the Kabbalah, especially the *Zohar*. Among the people there spread out the belief, cited by R. Moses Ḥayyim Luzzatto in his introduction to his book *Kalaḥ Pitḥey Ḥokhmah,* that "even if one does not understand, the language is precious for the soul."[43] This view is sometimes attributed to R. Moses Cordovero. Thus, the editors of *Arb'a Meot Shekel Kesef*[44] write as follows: "But the Holy SheLaH [acronym of Sheney Luḥot ha-Berit] stated in the name of the Pardes [*Pardes Rimmonim* by R. Moses Cordovero] that even he who does not understand the language, but reads in depth on matters of the Torah in order to uncover its inner meaning, 'is rewarded for his efforts' [after Isa. 40:10]." This view finds a clear and positive expression in the works of R. Ḥayyim Joseph David Azulay: "The study of the *Zohar* is superior to any study, even if one does not know what it says, and even if he misreads it. And this is a great *tikkun* for the soul for . . . [in the *Zohar*] the secrets themselves are visible, and the reader knows that they are secrets and mysteries of the Torah, but the text is not intelligible because of his intellectual deficiency and the depth of the matter."[45] In Smyrna, it was Rabbi Elijah ha-Kohen (d. 1729) who summed up this point: "The conclusion from this is that a person should occupy himself in every sort of wisdom: the Scripture, Mishnah, Halakhah, Talmud, Kabbalah, the Account of Creation and the Account of the Chariot, and any other thing of Torah, even if he does not understand it, so that for him it is nothing but a commandment of men learned by rote."[46]

However, with regard to this issue, other opinions were voiced as well. For example, according to R. Shneur Zalman of Lyady, one should not read the *Zohar* "without knowing the meaning of the words," "for otherwise one does not do his duty concerning the study of the *Zohar*." It is noteworthy that precisely among the Hasidic circles there were dissenting voices.[47] As R. Simḥah Bunim of Przysucha ironically observed: "An intellect that is not divested of corporeality does not understand even a single point of the holy *Zohar;* and yet, it seems to them that they do know."[48]

Apparently, it was the post-Sabbataian crisis that gave rise to agitation and retrogression among the East European Jews with respect to the position of Kabbalah in Judaism.[49] Various conditions that were laid down by the contemporary sages in order to restrict the study of the Kabbalah resulted in a diminished interest in it, which was accompanied by fears of its potential dangers.

But if we go back several hundreds of years, we find ourselves facing the very requirement to study Kabbalah. The ancient texts of the *Heikhalot* literature display a tendency to disseminate its teaching. For instance: "Rabbi Yishmael said to me in the presence of his pupils: 'I and Rabbi Akiva vouch for this, that whoever knows this measure of our Creator and the praise of the Holy One, blessed be He, he will surely be a son of the world to come, provided he learns it regularly every day.'"[50] Similarly, "He who does not know this measure, does not know his Creator, blessed be His name and blessed be His memory forever and ever. And he who does know it, knows his Creator and his faith." This statement concludes the *Sefer ha-Navon,* which is authored by one of the Ashkenazi Hasidim.[51] Yet there is also the view that even though one should know, he ought to conceal his accomplishments: "One should not disclose these things to any one but to he who is wise and *maskil* and understands of his own knowledge and whose heart is constantly anxious, and who is a God-fearing person. Happy is he who knows, and all the more so—he who conceals."[52]

Jewish history moves in devious ways. It so happened that in spite of the awareness of one's duty to maintain secrecy, an external historical factor—the need to commit things to writing—prompted the promulgation of the Kabbalah. The decrees issued against the Jews in 1096 and the pogroms initiated by the Crusaders intensified the sense of uncertainty and the concern for tradition and "urged the teachers of Hasidism [in Ashkenaz] to disseminate their teaching and transmit it to the public. . . . Some of their teaching, addressed to the public at large, was disseminated by the Ashkenazi Hasidim in popular literature out of spiritual motivation, while another part, which in their opinion was best kept in secret, lest it falls into the hands of those who are unworthy of it, was equally written in books and disseminated, out of concern that a teaching entrusted to a few families faced the danger of being utterly destroyed."[53]

A similar reasoning, though from a spiritual point of view, namely the spiritual-religious decline of the generations, emerges from the writings of Jewish leaders at the beginning of the twentieth century. In his pamphlet *Eṣ Ḥayyim,* the fifth Hasidic rabbi of the Ḥabad movement, Rabbi Shalom Dobber, urged his disciples to study the inner meaning of the Torah: "The first generations did not need this because they were perfect zaddikim and learned Torah for its own sake. . . . But in the last generations . . . the hearts diminished. . . . It is a *miṣvah* to disclose, and generation after generation, the matter of unveiling the inner nature of Torah becomes more and more urgent."[54] And Rabbi Kook stated: "To purify the hearts and to engage the mind in lofty thoughts that originate in the secrets of the Torah became an absolute necessity in the last generation for the survival of Judaism. . . ."[55]

Kabbalists that approved of disseminating the Kabbalah sometimes posed an intriguing question, namely, how to treat the individual who does not occupy himself with the Kabbalah. It is interesting to consider what R. Moses Cordovero says about this issue. In discussing the well-known controversy between Maimonides and R. Abraham ben David of Posquières (the RABaD) in *Hilkhot Teshuvah* (III,7) concerning the extent of attributing corporeality of the Creator, he tries to reconcile the two stands by stating that a deep-thinking person "to whom the chapters of the fundamentals have been revealed" and yet he believes in the corporeality of the Creator is nothing but an atheist and a heretic. Conversely, the person who is not adept in speculative study, and has a simplistic religious faith, is not an atheist. Cordovero goes on to express his own opinion that even as far as the understanding of the higher Sefirot is concerned, the sages concealed these things, and therefore a person who has not studied them is not to be considered a heretic. "However, we are right in saying of him that he has never seen the light in his life and has never tasted of the sweetness of the Torah and the honeydew of its pleasant sayings, and he shall die without having acquired any knowledge or experiencing any good."[56] It follows that the person who has not been exposed to the Kabbalah is not blamed for this failure, but is considered to have a marked flaw.

A stricter approach was expressed fifty years later by R. Isaiah Horowitz:

> After he has filled himself with Scripture, the Mishnah and the Talmud, he will preoccupy himself, with fright and fear, holiness and purity, in the wisdom of the Kabbalah, in the *Zohar* and the *Tikkunim* and their commentators and the rest of the sacred books that draw on the waters of the Zoharic well. . . . It is a well-established rule that man is obligated to know His blessed name. And whoever has not seen this wisdom, has seen no lights in his lifetime. Now, I have found written that just as among the tradesmen, some earn only four or five *levanim* per day, because they make coarse garments, while others earn twenty or thirty *levanim* per day, because they

> make refined clothes—so it is concerning the rewards of the *miṣvot:* He who knows the secret of the *miṣvot* may earn in a single day what he who is ignorant of their secret may earn in a whole week. . . . This is analogous to the superiority of light to darkness. . . . Indeed, just as the reward of he who knows the secrets of a *miṣvah* is greater than the reward of one who does not know them, so is one's punishment for making a transgression or failing to observe a *miṣvah* greater than the punishment of one who does not know.[57]

In the above excerpt, the extravagant praise lavished on the person who fulfills the commandments in the spirit of the Kabbalah goes hand in hand with the insistence on punishing the adept who fails to observe a *miṣvah* or transgresses the Law. A similar approach emerges from another book, *Pele Yo'eṣ,* composed by Eleazar Pappo, who served as a rabbi in Bosnia and whose books were widespread outside his native country. According to R. Pappo, "[A]fter he has filled himself with all the studies and knowledge according to the plain meaning *[peshat],* he should try to occupy himself with the wisdom of the Kabbalah. . . . And he is bound to suffer the consequences if he could learn but did not do so. . . . And certainly the Holy One, blessed be He, does not criticize his creatures severely, and everything is according to what is incumbent upon man to attain, according to his own ability."[58] This suggests that there is no complaint against the person who is incapable of studying the Kabbalah, since this is not ingrained in the root of his soul.

Let me conclude this discussion by proposing the stand taken by the *Zohar,* as summed up by Tishby: "In its evaluation of worship without *kavvanah,* the *Zohar* is not at all consistent." On the one hand, there is a sympathetic attitude "toward those whose mental or spiritual deficiencies prevent them from praying with proper sincerity and concentration." On the other hand, "several passages denigrate and criticize very sharply those who pray without *kavvanah.*"[59] Indeed, the conflicts that emerge from the *Zohar* itself have not been resolved by later Kabbalists, so that the two approaches coexist side by side.

THE OBJECTIONS TO THE KABBALAH

So far we have discussed the appreciation of the Kabbalah as expressed in its own writings. The question is how it was treated outside its ranks. Well, the unfolding of the Kabbalah was not a peaceful and uneventful process. *Shi'ur Komah,* with its excessive anthropomorphism, was subjected to strong criticism from the Karaites as well as from those who were faithful to traditional Judaism. Even Maimonides, who at a certain stage must have been unfamiliar with the nature of the book, later recanted and utterly rejected it. Nonetheless, this criticism was directed at the book, or the trend it represented, many years after it had been composed, and thus had no practical significance.

When the Kabbalists entered the historical arena and the first book, *Sefer ha-Bahir,* fell into the hands of the masters of the Halakhah, it was categorically denounced. In his book *Milḥemet Miṣvah,* Rabbi Meir ben Simeon, president of the rabbinical court of Narbonne, expressed strong criticism that threatened the "young" movement. Undoubtedly, this echoed the struggle between the traditional conservative worldview and its mystical counterpart. The former rests on historical continuity while the latter assigns an important place to personal experience and even favors substantial innovations. In the mid-thirteenth century, the Kabbalists were active in the polemics against studying the apocryphal sciences, and this placed them on a par with those faithful to tradition. Furthermore, historically speaking, the Kabbalah has never disappeared from the map of Jewish society. This is because, first of all, from the Middle Ages up to our own days, the outstanding Kabbalists were also distinguished men of Halakhah, who legitimized the preoccupation with the Kabbalah by their very personality and authority.[60] Secondly, the Kabbalists did not object to tradition, but rather were nourished by it. While the philosophers tended to underrate the value of the practical Commandments to the point of dismissing them altogether, thus infuriating the religious leadership, this was not the case with the Kabbalists. On the contrary, they strengthened the restraints of the Halakhah and even broadened its scope. The Kabbalists' loyalty to halakhic tradition allowed them to form an integral part of "all Israel."

Even though there was no formal warfare between the Halakhists and the Kabbalists, some of the sages expressed their disapproval by ridiculing the doctrine of the Kabbalah, the reliance on extraordinary religious experiences, the hallowing of the *Zohar,* and so forth. These sages occasionally declared war on the Kabbalah. In particular, a polemical dispute emerged when the attempt was made in the mid-sixteenth century to print some kabbalistic books, and especially the *Zohar.* The words of the opponents, scattered here and there in various works, some published and others still in manuscript, have been the subject of recent research,[61] and I will mention some of the arguments that were raised. Incidentally, it should be noted that even among the Kabbalists themselves there were some who forbade the printing of the *Zohar,* such as Rabbi Jacob Israel Finzi.[62] To counteract his arguments, the publishers of the *Zohar*[63] introduced the ruling of R. Isaac de Lattes, who permitted the printing. Another halakhic ruling, that of R. Moses Bassola, who also addressed other objections, was printed at the top of *Tikkuney Zohar.*

What, then, were the grounds for the opponents' objections? Briefly, they were as follows:

1. Objection to the Kabbalah in general, as a false doctrine, and to the *Zohar* in particular as a late work of forgery.

2. The Kabbalah is bound to lead to heresy. Indeed, the Christians availed themselves of its writing in order to provide proofs in support of their beliefs. The corrector's apologetic preface to the Mantua edition of the Zohar attests to this practice.

3. The "mysteries of the Torah" should not be disclosed in public, since "the glory of God is to conceal a thing" (Prov. 25:2). Rabbi Yehudah Aryeh of Modena wrote that in addition, the mysteries of the Torah should not be expounded in public.[64]

4. This wisdom is not within reach because of the shortcomings of the student and the profundity of the subject.

5. There is a talmudic prohibition against committing the oral Torah to writing.

6. A pragmatic objection anchored in the historical circumstances: fear that printing will result in further decrees to burn the Talmud, as happened several years before that, in 1553.

7. A halakhic-formalistic objection: contrary to the Kabbalists' insistence, spiritualistic intentions should not be placed at the center of religious life.

Against the arguments of the opponents, those who were in favor of printing raised various counterarguments, of which I will indicate just a few. Concerning the dangers inherent in divulging secrets, a tactical argument was raised: whoever does not understand, will not understand anyway, and if someone deliberately distorts, "thorns will vanish from the vineyard."[65] But even more important than these is one of the major motivations for printing that is still in force: stressing the importance of the spiritualistic conception for the fulfilling of the Commandments, which necessarily requires the study of the Kabbalah and its dissemination in public.[66]

It is worth noting that less than a hundred years later, the echoes of the debate once again reverberated. Rabbi Naftali Bakharakh (Frankfurt, the first half of the seventeenth century) continued to refute the claims raised by those who opposed the printing of kabbalistic writings and harshly criticized them.[67]

Outside the context of the debate about publishing kabbalistic works, many other arguments were voiced. Let me mention some of those that are a matter of principle.

In their prayers, the Kabbalists concentrate their mind on some particular Sefirot, shifting their attention from one Sefirah to another. This is a matter of idolatry. "They desired many gods," states a rabbinic saying referring to those who committed the sin of the golden calf, and this wording was borrowed by the above-mentioned Rabbi Meir ben Simeon of Narbonne to qualify the Kabbalists. Well known is the telling remark, "The Christians who believe in the trinity and the Kabbalists who believe in the tens,"[68] which is meant to express abhorrence toward the Kabbalists. In other words, the Kabbalists are even worse than the Christians, even though in principle, once the monotheistic notion is dismissed, there is no significant difference between three and ten. An argument was voiced in the period of the Renaissance that the Kabbalists are even worse than the Christians, because "they attribute to Him plurality, materiality, and passion."[69]

The very fact that the Kabbalists concentrate on an intermediate being, rather than on God himself, shocked many sages. For example, "It is inconceivable that by means of the Sefirot we shall draw down the *pleroma* as do the exponents of forms and images, for if we consider the words of Torah, we will find them contrary to this, and these are of the practices of idolatry."[70]

Another argument was addressed against the numerous references to the male and female entities that form part of the divine world. These references were embedded with erotic images, some of which were extremely bold.

There were also objections to the Kabbalah on the grounds that it was a late phenomenon in the Jewish world and criticism was especially directed against the *Zohar*. The claim was made that it was not composed by R. Simeon bar Yoḥai, but rather by someone of a much later period, who dared deceive the public by attributing the book to an ancient tannaitic sage. I will not go into the details of the arguments and proofs that the *Zohar* is a late work, many of which have been incorporated into contemporary research literature.[71] In this context it is sufficient to call attention to the total denunciation of a book that was particularly hallowed by the Kabbalists.

History teaches us that the Kabbalah spread into various countries despite the objections raised against it, while in others it was accepted either with some reservations or just by few sectors of the public. At any rate, even during the Renaissance and the Enlightenment, whose ethos was in sharp contrast to the essential teaching of the Kabbalah— the Enlightenment movement and its contemporary historians depicted the Kabbalah as a dark reaction of the *mordey or,* those who defied the light of rationalism[72]—the Kabbalah proved to be indestructible. It increasingly penetrated the public, especially after the expulsion from Spain, exerting strong influence on the world of Halakhah (mainly as far as prayers and daily practices are concerned) to the extent that its imprint is well discerned in Judaism.

This raises a different sort of question. What limits must be set on the popularization of the Kabbalah and what is the price of this popularity? Is it possible for everyone to meditate upon its secrets? Various texts, amongst them those written by the men of Kabbalah themselves, express strong objection to the prevailing state of affairs. As ironically observed by Rabbi Moses Isserles, in a large number of Jewish communities many congregants would rush to study the *Zohar* without even having sufficient knowledge to read the weekly portion of the Torah.[73] Or, to quote R. Ḥayyim Joseph David Azulay (eighteenth century): "And in this orphaned generation, whoever slightly opens a book considers himself an instructor in halakhic matters, and whoever engages in a cursory reading of the *Zohar,* considers himself a Kabbalist."[74] About the same time, an Italian rabbi and Kabbalist complains:

> This is what I have grieved about all my life, that some of our contemporaries rush to study the matters of Kabbalah and whoever has seen a little of it, takes pride in it, and one stone in a pitcher cries

> out, "rattle, rattle." And they argue and settle issues and make up controversies and issues and a number of times they depart from the true method. And this results in their being incomplete in this wisdom. For not everyone has the opportunity to be exposed to most of the books that deal with this wisdom, especially the ones that were composed by those who have delved into its depth, for they are all in manuscript form. . . . Therefore my counsel is that anyone who is well versed in it should keep silent and not attempt to innovate anything, whether big or small, until he knows himself to be an adept who can innovate and argue in matters of wisdom according to its traditional introductions.[75]

Nonetheless, one should not forget that the Sabbataian crisis and its challenge to the binding authority of the Halakhah—"Blessed be He who releases the prohibitions," as defiantly stated by the followers of this movement (replacing *mattir asurim* [releases the bound] with *mattir issurim*)—produced distrust and tremendous confusion. The outburst of the Frankist movement in East Europe was nothing but another testimony to the depth of the crisis and bewilderment. This is what motivated the debates in Lemberg and Kamenitz circa 1756 and the ban that was issued afterwards, which among other things imposed stringent restrictions on those wishing to study Kabbalah. The result of this state of affairs is described by a Lithuanian rabbi, author of *Darkhey No'am,* which was written sometime before 1760: "Because of the slander that is practiced in these generations, due to the increase of the infamous heretics, Sabbatai Ṣevi and his sect—may they breathe their last!—whoever occupies himself with this wisdom, even if he is righteous and pious, is said to be of their company, heaven forbid. And for this reason, many refrain from getting into this matter, *as is known*."[76]

In conclusion, attention should be drawn to the interesting ruling of a distinguished man of Halakhah who was also familiar with the world of Kabbalah. Responding to the words of a doctor from Amsterdam who slighted the Kabbalah, this scholar wrote as follows: "His mouth is full of scorn directed at our sages of blessed memory and their Aggadot. The wisdom of the Kabbalah, too, is the target of his tongue. He derides this wisdom, the wisdom of the Truth, and slanders it and says he holds nothing in esteem save philosophy, which addresses every man. . . . Undoubtedly, this man deserves to be cursed, excommunicated, and condemned to death. All the more so he who mocks the words of the sages and defames the wisdom of the Kabbalah, which is the source and essence of the Torah and all of it is the fear of heaven. And since he casts away the wisdom of the Kabbalah and the words of the Kabbalist sages, he should be treated with utmost severity and should forcefully and unequivocally be excommunicated."[77] These words were written by one of the most important codifiers in the context of a halakhic responsum and they have a binding halakhic validity.

8 • The Origins of the Revelations

SEEING AND HEARING

A close contact between man and God is impossible because of the absolute gulf that separates them, not to mention the fact that God, the supreme being, is not corporeal. Occasionally, man attempts to bridge this enormous gap by some sort of visual or auditory communication. Adam, the first man, did not see God, but he heard his voice while "walking in the garden" (Gen. 3:8). And Moses our master hid his face "for he was afraid to look upon God" (Exod. 3:6), "for no man shall see Me, and live" (33:20). In the classic story of the theophany, the Sinaitic revelation, "all the people perceived the thunderings, and the lightnings" (20:15). Under certain circumstance, man is allowed to catch a glimpse of the divine glory, but not of God himself: "And thou shalt see my back; but my face shall not be seen" (33:23), says God to the greatest of all prophets, Moses our master, adding, "Thou shalt see but the utmost part of them, and shalt not see them all" (Num. 23:13). This is the secret of the tension and attraction in the relationship between man and God.

Nonetheless, the Torah also attests about Moses: "With him I speak mouth to mouth, manifestly, and not in riddles, and the similitude of the Lord does he behold" (Num. 12:8). So did the prophet Isaiah, who discloses: "For my eyes have seen the king, the Lord of hosts" (Isa. 6:5). Ezekiel is struck by a similar vision: "[T]he heavens were opened and I saw visions of God" (Ezek. 1:1). Isaiah sees God "sitting upon a throne, high and lifted up" (Isa. 6:1) and even hears the singing of the angels. But for Ezekiel, the impact of this experience is overwhelming: "I fell upon my face and I heard the voice of one that spoke" (Ezek. 1:28). And again, "then a spirit took me up and I heard after me a voice of a great rushing" (3:12). Afterwards, all he can discern is but "a likeness as the appearance of fire" (8:2), or "the shape of a throne" (10:1). Nothing beyond that is accessible to him.

It is interesting to juxtapose those prophets with Daniel, who attests to having seen the divine spectacle, though in a "vision" (Dan. 8:2). He says he "heard a holy being speaking" (8:13), but not the Lord himself. Yet, whether he has seen Gabriel (8:16), or "a certain man clothed in linen" (10:5), his description deserves attention, as it highlights the phenomena that haunt the mystics. "I was afraid, and fell upon my face . . . I fell into a deep sleep on my face towards the ground . . . and was sick certain days . . . I was astonished at the vision but none understood it" (chap. 8). "And I, Daniel, alone saw the vision; but a great trembling fell upon them so that they fled to hid themselves. So I was left alone, and saw this great vision, and there remained no strength in me for my comely appearance was horribly changed and I retained no strength in me, yet I heard the sound of his words and when I heard the voice of his words I was in a deep sleep on my face and my face toward the ground . . . there remains now no strength in me, nor is there any breath left in me" (10:7–9, 10:19). Daniel is ordered to stand up in order to hear the message. Daniel says he "stood trembling" (10:11), and only thanks to the touch of "one in the likeness of a man" was he "strengthened" (10:18–19). Afterwards, he was told: "Shut up the words and seal the book, until the time of the end," for these things cannot be public property, "and none of the wicked shall understand but the *maskilim* [the wise] shall understand" (12:4, 12:10). Here lies the key to the mystical explorations. Things are sealed, but not completely. The *maskilim* are able to contemplate and reach beyond. During the revelation, or while preparing themselves for it, the mystics are surrounded by special psychological, physical, and mental phenomena. Nevertheless, they do not and cannot withdraw, as if this experience is imposed upon them. This bipolar tension is captured in various expressions, such as the following: "at times they are silent at times they speak" (*Ḥagigah* 13b); "and if your heart runs, let it return to its place" (*Sefer Yezirah* I,8); "and the living creatures ran and returned" (a verse from Ezek. 1:14 in widespread use by Kabbalists and Hasidic Jews); "an everlasting pleasure is no pleasure," and "descent for the purpose of ascent" (spoken by the Hasidim); and the like.

Significantly, the *ophanim* (wheels) seen by Ezekiel are described as having "their rims full of eyes" (1:18), and similarly, the angels in the *Heikhalot* literature are "full of eyes." The meeting occurs, so to speak, by means of the eyes. Even when a man dies, what he sees in the final moment is the Shekhinah,[1] as if he returns to his natural state. At any event, the man who seeks eye contact with the supernal faces a dynamic situation. "Whenever the prophet or the 'unifier' contemplated these holy lights, he knew that sometimes they would spark forth and immediately vanish, as in a constantly changing vision, and then, once again, they would appear and disappear, and so on."[2] Apparently, there is a reason for the stated behavior of the "holy lights": it indicates the alternation between acceptance of man (revelation) and remoteness from him (concealment). When man cannot see with the eyes of the flesh, he may see with the eyes of the intellect,[3] which allow for a sublime kind of visualization.[4] Or, perhaps, it is the other way round, so that the mind transcends the eye: because of the limitations of normal sight, one channels his vision in the direction of thought as the only way of communication open to man. Hence the common practice of contemplation: "Many have expounded the [account of the] Chariot without ever beholding it" (Tosefta, *Megillah* 3).

Sometimes man gets a glimpse of a partial and somewhat dim sight, and then it seems to him as if he saw the "back" of the Shekhinah.[5]

Yet the mystics in the first half of the first millennium—the "period of the *Heikhalot*" as we name it—had the aspiration of "observing," "beholding," "peering," "gazing," "looking at," and "seeing" the king on his throne (or something close to it). These synonyms are found in the sources and perhaps they point at subtle differences in vision. However, they all signify a face-to-face and eye-to eye encounter with the Divine. No wonder, then, that many mystics stumble and fall in the course of the intermediate stages, or find themselves shaking and trembling.[6] "When I heard the loud voice, I recoiled and became silent and fell backwards until Hadarniel the Prince came over and gave me strength and spirit and put me on my feet and said to me: 'Friend, what has happened to you?'"[7] Yet, the attraction is so strong that the mystic does not pay attention to the dangers inherent in it. Sometimes he gets assistance from heaven, as in the passage just quoted and in this one: "He grasped me and placed me in his lap and said to me: 'What do you see . . . ?' He said to me: 'My son, conceal [the sight from] your eyes so that you would not be shaking." At other times, the mystic utters a special personal prayer for assistance.[8] At any rate, the urge to ascend as high as possible and reveal the mysteries above is very strong. During this early period, the mystic was supposed to attain this by "seeing" or "hearing" the King, or any of his celestial retinue. Things were different in the later period, the second millennium, which as a rule is designated "the period of the Kabbalah."

INTELLECTUAL ATTAINMENT

Generally speaking, the spiritual disciplines use the human intellect to follow their pursuits. Philosophy deals with rational thinking, on the basis of which it makes inferences and draws conclusions; the Halakhah develops along the lines of halakhic and juridical thinking; and so on. In contrast, the Kabbalah borrows from various sources.

As already mentioned, an important condition for the preoccupation with the Kabbalah is knowledge of rabbinic literature, namely, familiarity with discursive speculation. But these are just the early stages of the process. One of the Kabbalists stated in reference to the philosophers: "As to the philosophers whose wisdom you praise, you should know that where their head is placed is the very point where our feet stand."[9] It is as if the uppermost boundary of intellectual attainment is only the point of departure for spiritual attainment. It is not enough to use human intellect, for it is limited by its very nature. True "enlightenment" is a matter of the striving of the soul, which is directly connected to its divine source. The human soul serves as an instrument of attainment. This is because, according to the Kabbalah, it is a particle of God, a spark of the Godhead. Before it descended into this world the soul resided in the supernal world. Its descent is intended to realize the knowledge it has acquired in the supernal world. Therefore the soul aspires to return to its Source. Relying upon talmudic sources according to which the soul ascends night by night to heaven, the Kabbalists explain the purpose of its ascent: to gain further knowledge, to complete itself. Thus, the connection of the soul to its Source is invisible and eternal, and thanks to this bond, the soul is constantly charged with supernal powers. Having this fundamental conviction, the Kabbalist is certain that the sources of his knowledge are competent. Consider, for example, the following passage about the ARI:

> He also merited that every night, when his soul ascended to the heavens, the ministering angels came to accompany it to the celestial academy. They asked him: "To what academy do you wish to go?" Sometimes he said that he wished to visit the academy of R. Simeon bar Yoḥai, or the academy of R. 'Akiva . . . or that of the prophets. And to whichever of those academies he wished to go, the angels would take him. The next day, he would disclose to the sages what he had received in that academy.[10]

Another interesting story puts the ARI, the outstanding Kabbalist, on a par with R. Joseph Karo, the great codifier of the Halakhah. Each of them, in his own way, reached the same truth. But the ARI did so earlier, probably because of the direct attachment of his soul to the higher worlds, as described above. Thus, it is told that R. Joseph Karo

> used to pray in the synagogue every day together with the ARI of blessed memory. Now, the rabbi [the ARI] of blessed memory would pray the *shmone 'esreh* prayer (The Eighteen Benedictions) with *kavvanot,* frequently pausing [to linger on the text], while the master [R. Karo] of blessed memory used to pray by paying attention only to the literal meaning [so that his prayer was shorter]. Once, the rabbi of blessed memory prayed as was customary for him and completed the prayer, while the master, of blessed memory, did not complete his. The rabbis who were with him in the synagogue were wondering about this. Then the rabbi of blessed memory summoned the beadle and said to him: "Go to this master and whisper to him that this is implicit in tractate *Kil'ayim.*" The master, may his memory be blessed, heard him and said: "Indeed, this is so, and I have not produced anything new in my prayer . . . but when I was praying, it occurred to me . . . and I forgot that it was implied, and therefore I was pondering about its halakhic ruling and was not praying."[11]

PERSONAL TRANSMISSION

Another factor that enhances the authority of the Kabbalah is the whispered transmission of tradition from the rabbi directly to his disciple.

Because the Kabbalah is shrouded with mystery, it is not entrusted to the public at large; consequently there is no fear that it has become corrupted in the process of transmission. Its reliability is unquestionable. Thus, for instance, one of the kabbalistic epistles lists names of several respectable persons who "all received by way of transmission *[kabbalah],* [namely], without getting any definitive proofs [about what they were told], just as he who tells a secret to his friend does not need to prove it."[12] The reliability of the Kabbalah also springs from the fact that this tradition is very ancient, going back to Moses, or even Adam—hence its authority. Naḥmanides says: "I do hereby firmly make known to him [the reader] that my words will not be comprehended nor known at all by any reasoning or contemplation, excepting [if received] from the mouth of a *mekubbal ḥakham* [the wise Kabbalist who, having already received the Kabbalah is thoroughly steeped in it] into the ear of a *mekabbel mevin* [the recipient who grasps it by his own intelligence]."[13] The teacher too has received this as a long-standing tradition that originated in ancient source: "These things and the like of them cannot be grasped by one's own knowledge, but through the *kabbalah* [received tradition] . . . and this is the chain of tradition that stretches back, receiver by receiver, up to Moses [who has received it] from the mouth of the Almighty."[14]

Such transmission of received tradition is much preferred to other methods of inquiry: "And the sage cannot know them through his own wisdom, and he who understands cannot understand them with his understanding, and he who inquires cannot do so by his inquiry, except for the *mekubbal,* the receiver, as he received them by an oral tradition that goes back to the chain of the greatest of all generations, who, in turn, received from their masters and their ancestors up to Moses."[15]

REVELATION FROM ELIJAH

In some cases, Kabbalists receive revelations not from an ordinary human being, a creature of flesh and blood, but rather from Elijah the prophet. In the beginning of the Kabbalah, the apparition of Elijah was a rare phenomenon. Only few Kabbalists are mentioned as having merited it, and the revelation itself concerned only the secrets of prayers. R. Isaac ben Jacob ha-Kohen tells about a wondrous sage of Narbonne who possessed secret knowledge, which he received by word of mouth from an old man and a rabbi. And his master, too, the Holy Old Man, was known to have been visited by Elijah of blessed memory every year on the Day of Atonement.[16] Attention should also be drawn to the recurrent statements used by the Kabbalists in support of the contents of their works. For example, in his introduction to *Sefer ha-Kanah,* the author announces: "I have not made up these things, but state them just as they were revealed to me from the celestial academy." In other words, this was a direct revelation from above.

The Kabbalists also use the phrase *ka'asher horuni* (or: *her'uni*) *min ha-shamayim* (as I was taught [or: shown] from heaven).[17] At first sight, this statement suggests a higher, celestial power that informs man of certain truths. Yet opinions differ on its interpretation, because this phrase also appears in the writings of the Geonim, where it signifies some sort of inner certitude about the ideas presented in the text. In view of their assumptions concerning the transmission of the Kabbalah, the Kabbalists probably feel that their revelations are indeed the gift of God and whoever is gifted with them serves as a vehicle or channel through which the secret is passed on. Thus this wording suggests the humility of the Kabbalist, who presents himself as a mere vessel, and at the same time it qualifies his knowledge as intuitive and hence beyond rational explanations. As an example, consider the following words of Moses Cordovero: "There are many explanations and different formulations of the statements made by R. Simeon bar Yoḥai and we are going to interpret his words as they were taught to us from heaven."[18] He means he doesn't need to justify and account for his explanation, for this is the tradition he has received.

SPIRITUAL ILLUMINATION

Another source of revelation is the *he'arah* (illumination) or *barak* (a flash), as Maimonides defines it in his introduction to the *Guide of the Perplexed.* In contrast to the vision of the Descenders into the Chariot, which emerges on their own initiative, illumination is perceived as truth that is revealed from above to the person who is found worthy of it. In this connection, it is appropriate to mention *Sefer ha-Orah* by R. Jacob ben Jacob ha-Kohen.[19] Similarly, Rabbi Abraham Abulafia records: "And when I was thirty-one years old, in the province of Barcelona, the Lord woke me up from my sleep . . . and the hand of the Lord was upon me . . . and my spirit was revived and the spirit of God came unto my mouth and the spirit of holiness sparkled inside me, and I saw many awesome and wondrous visions by way of signs and wonders."[20]

DREAMS

While illumination is likely to occur in one's waking state, revelation may also assume the form of a dream. In the Middle Ages, dreams were supposed to have a prophetic nature, though of a lower level.[21] Like other mystical experiences, dreams vary in character from dreamer to dreamer. While asleep, a person may see or hear Elijah, the angels, or the supernal souls. It must be kept in mind that in the Middle Ages, the apparition of Elijah was sometimes associated with the teaching of the Halakhah, as suggested by the well-known book *She'elot u-Teshuvot min ha-Shamayim,* which was written by one of the Tosafists, Rabbi Jacob of Marvège.[22] Dreams had a special value in the doctrine of the Ashkenazi Hasidim,[23] though some of them strongly denounced the use of them. Thus, *Sefer Ḥasidim,* par. 211, reads as follows: "Whoever occupies himself with the adjuration of angels will not come to a good ending. . . . This man should refrain from doing all of these, including dream questions. . . . And there is nothing better for man than praying to God." Nonetheless, the Kabbalah too is concerned with dreams and generally displays a favorable attitude toward them. "The dream is a mirror in which the pure soul sees the light that illuminates its life. . . . And the seer who has a pure soul constantly sees everything without mixture and without doubt. This sight is fixed in his mind and inscribed in his intellect and burns inside him like fire."[24] Many dreams emerge on the initiative of the Kabbalists. Such a dream is called *she'elat ḥalom* (a dream question); there is also the phenomenon of *she'elah be-hakiṣ* (a waking question). The technique of *she'elat ḥalom* was very widespread among the generation of those who were expelled from Spain. Important material on this is found in a work that is still in manuscript form, namely, *Sefer ha-Meshiv*.[25] Another book, written about a hundred years later, is *Gle Razaya,* which was "composed by visions and dreams and according to what was revealed to him from heaven."[26]

THE APPARITION OF THE *MAGGID*

The appearance of the *maggid* (heavenly messenger) is documented primarily from the sixteenth century onwards and was explained by Gershom Scholem as "elements of the mystic's unconscious, crystallizing and coming to life and behaving in an autonomous fashion as if they were agents with an identity of their own."[27] In other words, this is the unconscious, or the superego, which is revealed to the individual. It guides him and divulges to him future events.

Probably this phenomenon originated in the circle of Rabbi Joseph Taitazak in Turkey and Salonika and spread out among his disciples, such as Rabbi Joseph Karo, who left behind a book (later entitled *Maggid Meisharim*), in which he committed to writing the revelations of the *maggid* that appeared to him. Though some people doubted the correctness of the tradition according to which R. Joseph Karo was involved in such metaphysical communication, there is some solid evidence to this effect.[28] The phenomenon of the *maggid* is mentioned time and again by the Safed Kabbalists and is also explained in the writings of the ARI. Even the Sabbataians made use of it. In addition, this type of revelation is attributed to Rabbi Moses Zacuto, Rabbi Moses Ḥayyim Luzzatto,[29] the Gaon of Vilna,[30] and so forth.

Karo's *maggid* said to him, "[I]t must be evident to you that for several generations no one has attained this high level but the few privileged men."[31] The *maggid* continued: "[R]ight now you see that I am speaking to you as one speaks to his friend"—though the speech was somewhat mechanical, "a voice pounding inside [Karo's] mouth, sounding of its own."[32] An interesting description was left by Karo's friend, Rabbi Solomon Alkabez, who writes: "Our Maker bestowed upon us this privilege that we heard the voice speaking through the mouth of the pious man, a powerful and articulate voice. And the voice became louder and louder. We prostrated ourselves and none of us had the spirit to lift his eyes and face, out of fright."[33] Now, just as the *maggid* in this case encouraged Rabbi Joseph Karo to settle down in the Land of Israel, so another *maggid* warned Rabbi Samson of Ostropol about the impending slaughter of the Jews during 1648–49: "Among them [those who were to be killed in Polonnoye] was a wise and intelligent man, a godly Kabbalist named our master, R. Samson of Ostropol, who was daily visited by an angel with whom he studied the mysteries of the Torah. . . . And this *maggid* had told him before the decree was issued that they should do repentance in order to undo the decree. So the rabbi preached in the synagogue several times, insisting on the need for profound repentance for their misdeeds in order to prevent the occurrence of the calamity."[34]

All the Kabbalists mentioned so far in connection with the *maggid* were pleased with his appearance, even though they did not initiate it. But we also have the testimony of a man who adamantly refused to receive such revelation. Rabbi Ḥayyim of Volozhin tells about his teacher Rabbi Elijah, the Gaon of Vilna: "I have heard from his holy mouth that *maggidim* from heaven had come to him a number of times in order to reveal to him the secrets of the Torah without any toil on his part. But he refused to accept their intervention. And one of these *maggidim* exceedingly urged him to do so, yet he refrained from beholding his majestic vision."[35]

It is interesting to add that the maggid of R. Joseph Karo appeared to him while he was studying the Mishnah, whereas the *maggid* of Nathan of Gaza used to make contact with him while he was studying the *Zohar*.

Another phenomenon, which emerges as an "initiative" from above is involved in the process of *gerushin*.[36] In connection with this, Cordovero mentions "the gifts which I received and which fell to my part during these *gerushin* by God's mercy upon me."[37] "For there the words were shining forth of themselves."[38] In this case, one does not speculate on his own initiative, but rather absorbs the influx that flows into his mouth: "So far the proceedings of that day. Thanks be to God that we were vouchsafed all this, for these things are all supernal, infused without reflection whatsoever; they are sweeter than honey, the gift of the queen to them that wander with her in exile."[39]

JOY AND WEEPING

The Kabbalist's gift of a revelation from above makes him happy, as suggested by his beaming face. For example, in the *Zohar* we find: "Meanwhile Rabbi Isaac awoke and smiled, and his face shone. Rabbi Simeon noticed, and looked at his face. 'Have you heard something new?' He said. 'Yes,' he replied. . . ."[40] But according to the description of Rabbi

'Azriel of Gerona, which was elaborated by R. Menaḥem Recanati, it emerges that joy is an integral part of the process of revelation. Drawing on an exchange between R. 'Akiva and ben 'Azai in TY *Ḥagigah,* which concludes with the statement: "while I am studying, the words come down and rejoice before me," Recanati adds another rabbinic saying (*Shabbat* 30b), according to which "the Divine Presence rests [upon man] neither through gloom, nor through sloth . . . [nor through frivolity, nor through levity, nor through talk, nor through idle chatter] but only through a matter of joy [in connection with a precept]." It follows that when the Kabbalist "binds his soul to the supernal soul," then "these things increase and expand and out of his joy they reveal themselves to him."[41] What follows in this description is very interesting: "And perchance he will be so overcome by this joy that he will burst out into a mighty weeping, and his soul will desire to separate itself from his body. And this is death by kiss, which signifies the connection between the kisser his beloved. For then his soul will attach itself to the Shekhinah." Thus joy leads to weeping,[42] to the point of the expiration of a man's soul and his passing away from this world. And Recanati adds as follows: "And therefore you will find in the *Zohar,* in the context of the unveiling of mysteries, that Rabbi so-and-so arose and wept.[43] And perhaps he would be so overpowered by his weeping that his soul will be collected."

In connection with this point, mention should be made of the Zoharic description of the ecstatic death of three companions who attended the *idra rabba,* the great assembly of R. Simeon bar Yoḥai. These men were savoring the wondrous secrets revealed in the discourse of Rabbi Simeon bar Yoḥai when they received the divine kiss that took away their souls.

Yet weeping does not always end in death. Sometimes joy and weeping are mixed up, as in the following episode from the *Zohar:* "Rabbi Simeon wept, and Rabbi Eleazar wept. Rabbi Eleazar said: Weeping has penetrated my heart on the one side, and joy is in my heart on the other, for I have heard things that I had not heard before. How happy is my portion!"[44] At times, the Kabbalist finds out that weeping is not in his control, but nevertheless it is connected with the revelation of the secret. Once again let me illustrate by a text from the *Zohar:* "He [the Old Man] wept again and said: Friends, the tears which I shed fall not on your account, but for fear of the Lord of the universe, that perchance I have revealed mysteries without permission. It is, however, known to the Holy One, blessed be He, that all I do, I am doing not for my own honor nor for the honor of my father, but because my sole desire is to serve Him. I discern the glory and honor of one of you in the other world; and as to the other one, I know that he is likewise worthy; at first this was not revealed to me, but now I see it clearly."[45]

Another motif, that the Kabbalist who has revealed the secret passes it on and weeps in relief, and so does the recipient of the secret, occurs in the *Zohar* a number of times. For instance, it says: "The companions rejoiced and wept and said nothing. And he also wept, as he had at the beginning."[46] Or: "But when Rabbi Simeon communicated the secret of this verse, the eyes of all the companions streamed with tears, and all the things that he said were revealed in their sight. . . ."[47]

Sometimes weeping bursts out when a person is waiting for inspiration from above. For example, Rabbi Abraham Halevi testifies that the ARI advised him concerning the matter of attainment "that he should arrive at midnight and weep over his deficient knowledge."[48] Occasionally, it is difficult to figure out the meaning of the weeping. For instance, in the *Zohar* (II, fol. 97b) it is said: "The old man prostrated himself, and prayed, and wept, as he had at the beginning." The context does not make it clear whether the weeping resulted from the prayer, or whether this was an ecstatic outburst. Perhaps, too, prostrating oneself[49] is part of praying and together with the weeping they served as means of receiving inspiration, for immediately afterwards the old man began to deliver a new discourse. At any event, it is obvious that weeping occupies an important place in the process of the mystical life. Similarly, the motif of weeping appears in the *Heikhalot* literature, where it is sometimes related to excitement and at other times to the content of the revelation.

THE DISCLOSURE OF SECRETS

One of the difficult problems facing the mystic concerns the disclosing of secrets to others. On the one hand, the mystic labors strenuously to merit the illumination from above. On the other hand, the mystic who has received a revelation feels a strong urge to communicate it to someone else. The resulting tension is difficult to bear. How can the Kabbalist let someone else instantly enjoy what he himself has labored so hard to achieve? And—who knows?—perhaps that individual is unworthy of the revelation, so that he will be led to interpret things incorrectly. Indeed, these fears were openly discussed by the Kabbalists. For instance, we find in the *Zohar:* "The old man wept as he had at the beginning, and said to himself: 'Old man, old man, how greatly you have toiled to master these holy matters, and yet you have narrated them in a single moment!' Yet, upon reflection, he says: 'If you maintain that you should have more respect for these things and not disclose them, it is written (Prov. 3:27): "Do not withhold good from those who possess it, when it is in the power of your hand to do so."'"[50] Another passage in the *Zohar* relates to the same issue: "R. Simeon, having heard them, wept and said: 'This is one of those sayings whose significance was revealed to me in a whisper from the school of knowledge in Paradise itself, and which should not be repeated openly. Yet in spite of all this, I will now reveal it unto you, O my beloved children, my children whom my soul loves! What else can I do? It was told to me in a whisper, but I will tell it to you openly. . . ."[51] These conflicts arise not only with respect to the way in which the secret is attained, but also with respect to its transmission to others. "Rabbi Simeon wept and said: "'Woe is me if I speak! Woe is me if I do not speak!' If I speak, the wicked will know how to serve their master; if I do not speak, the companions will be deprived of this thing."[52] Conflicts of this sort are displayed by R. Joseph Gikatilla, who befriended the author of the *Zohar*. As he puts it, "I want to write it down and I am not allowed to do it, I do not want to write it down and cannot entirely desist."[53]

The hesitations concern both oral and written transmission and the Kabbalists convey these hesitations even in later periods. For instance: "Many times I asked myself: How can I reveal that which the ancients, whose little finger is thicker than my loins, were reluctant to reveal? And I was hesitating like this for a day or two, not wanting to write down the secret that was lingering in my heart. But it was stirring in my heart and making me discontent, until I wrote it down in that book of mine."[54] And also: "And I stood trembling, wavering whether or not to elaborate on these things and write them down in a book. For on the one hand, I was afraid lest, heaven forbid, I break the barriers by disclosing things that were veiled by the Ancient of Days, things that are the mysteries of the world. . . . On the other hand . . . 'For it is time to act for the Lord' (Ps. 119:126) after the preceding generations have filled themselves with the doctrines of the Greeks and corrupted the words of the living God into vain and empty things."[55] Because of these hesitations, Naḥmanides announces that his commentary on the Torah "will not be comprehended nor known at all by any reasoning or contemplation, excepting from the mouth of a *mekubbal ḥakham*" (wise Kabbalist). Naḥmanides wants the readers to regard his commentary only as "novel interpretations of the plain meanings of Scripture and Midrashim," and says, "'Let them not break through unto the Eternal to gaze, For the Eternal our God is a devouring fire' (Deut. 4:24)."[56]

These conflicts caused many Kabbalists to prefer a face-to-face talk rather than to commit things to writing, which makes them widely accessible. "And do not expect more than I do to publish and write and disclose in writing because this is like putting a finger in one's eyes, except *from mouth to mouth* so that it won't be like a target for arrows. For it is inappropriate to write down in a manuscript what the pious men of the world toiled [to achieve] all their lives."[57] Therefore, many times we find "promises" on the part of the Kabbalists to the effect that they will explain the things at length in conversation and not by a letter: "It is impossible to explain this well in a letter, for this requires much toil, which is by no means possible. Only, if you please, send one of them, a distinguished member of the community, so that, God willing, I shall speak to him face to face about this."[58]

The *niggun* (melody) plays an important role in Hasidic mysticism, since the mystical experience is better captured by music than by words. Yet, even as far as the *niggun* is concerned, we learn that all persons do not absorb a given melody with the same ears. For music is a special language, which appeals to the ear as well as to the mind.[59] R. Shneur Zalman of Lyady, who composed some well-known melodies of *devekut,* discusses the various types of melodies, which correspond to different levels of perception, or of cleaving to God.

Before concluding this section, let me cite what is said in the *Zohar* about R. Simeon bar Yoḥai: "'Happy are you, O land, for your king is a free man' (Eccles. 10:17). What does 'a free man' mean? A man who lifts his head to reveal and interpret things, and does not fear—this is a free man. He says what he pleases and does not fear. What does 'your king' mean? This is Rabbi Simeon ben Yoḥai, the master of the Torah, the master of wisdom, for when Rabbi Abba and the companions saw Rabbi Simeon they ran after him, saying, 'They shall walk after the Lord, who shall roar like a lion' (Hos. 11:10)."[60] This excerpt conveys a hidden wish that the disciples would be able to enjoy and drink of their rabbi's teaching, whose fountains flowed fearlessly wide and far. In contrast, the ARI said to his followers: "My companions, know that flames of fire surround us and standing together with us are R. Simeon bar Yoḥai and his friends and the souls of other zaddikim and tannaim and the ministering angels, who all came to hear from me *torat emet* [the real Torah]. . . . For though the words are said as they were given in Sinai, permission for the eye to see [them] was given to me alone."[61]

MYSTICAL RAPTURES

Occasionally it so happens that the Kabbalist is given with such an abundant illumination that technically it is impossible for him to say, and all the more so to write, all that he has heard. Thus it is reported that the ARI said: "I summon heaven and earth as my witness, that had I expounded for eighty successive years, I could not have exhausted what I have learnt this time." Also, once the sages of Spain said to the ARI: "Our rabbi, the Candle of Israel, the Blessed One bestowed upon you so much wisdom. Why don't you write a fine discourse so that the Torah shall not be forgotten among Israel?" He replied: "If all the seas were ink and all the reeds were quills, and all the firmaments were parchments, still they would not suffice to write down all my wisdom. And when I begin to reveal to you a single secret of the Torah, it cascades like a river and I seek strategies with which to open up for you a small and thin pipe through which to transmit to you a single secret of the Torah that is not too much to bear. For otherwise you will lose everything just like the baby who would choke upon sucking too much milk."[62]

In this case, the ARI himself refrained from disclosing secrets. In another case, it is told that the souls in heaven gathered to protest against the book that was written by R. Isaac Yeḥiel of Komarno, on the grounds that it disclosed many more secrets than was advisable.[63]

In contrast to this approach, there were some Kabbalists who believed that it was a duty to write "for the sake of heaven and for the *tikkun* of my soul."[64] It was considered important to share with others the benefits of one's personal progress and to reveal the secret itself.

Significantly, some revelations were communicated by the mystics just before they died. It is written in the *Zohar* that during the last thirty days before one's death, the soul is in the process of parting from the body and then all sorts of secrets are revealed to it.[65] In reference to this notion, an Ashkenazi Kabbalist of the fourteenth century writes as follows: "Now, we cannot deny . . . and we have already seen and heard of an instance of this, that the sick who are about to die see and recognize the dead who come toward them, while others do not see them. And the thing is that once their physical power is eliminated, they no longer see or hear by means of the vessels, such as the eye and the ear, but rather through the eye of the soul alone, and this is the true and correct way of seeing and hearing."[66] Similarly, the Tosafists attest that when R. Kalonymus of Lucca was dying, he "uttered three things as if by prophecy."[67]

At times the revelation of a secret by the dying person expresses the peak of the mystic's ecstatic ascent, following which there can be nothing but death. Thus, according to the description of "The Child's Prophecy," Naḥman Katofah (or Ḥatofah) passed on to his parents lofty things and immediately thereafter departed from the world.[68] This may account for the following words as written by R. Emmanuel Ḥay Ricci: "What the rabbi [Moses our master] attained in his life is impossible for the student to attain in its entirety, save when he dies, and provided that the rabbi transmits this to him at that particular moment."[69]

Death may also be perceived as a sign that man has reached the peak of his achievements. Menaḥem Recanati expressed this notion by a beautiful image:

> Know that just as the ripe fruit falls from the tree, it no longer needing its connection [to the tree], so is the link between the soul and the body. For when the soul has attained whatever it is able to attain and cleaved to the supernal soul, it removes its raiment of dust, severs [itself] from its place, and cleaves to the Shekhinah; and this is [the meaning of] death by the kiss.[70]

The Hasidic world abounds with stories of wondrous zaddikim who died while they were still young, such as Rabbi Abraham the Angel, son of R. Dov Baer of Mezhirech, who passed away when he was only thirty-six years old. The friends of these righteous men explained that they had fulfilled their "task" in the world and had reached the uppermost heights, from where they were bound to descend. To prevent this fall, their soul departed from their body and ascended to the high heavens. "And this is death by the kiss!"[71]

Part II

The Basic Concepts of the Kabbalah

9 • The Doctrine of the Sefirot

Understanding the nature of the Divine—this is one of the central problems that has concerned thinkers of many nations throughout the ages. Not surprisingly, many definitions of that entity have been proposed. The Kabbalists' reflections on this question are especially interesting.

The fundamental problem that troubled the Kabbalists seems to have been how to resolve the contradiction between the philosophical-Neoplatonic concept that God is infinite, transcendent, inconceivable, and ineffable—a *Deus absconditus*—and the religious viewpoint portraying a desirable and immediate relationship between man and his Maker, a personal and familiar God, "near to all who call upon Him,"[1] who reveals himself to the individual and to the Jewish nation; He ordains, communicates his will through human prophets, and man for his part appeals to him in prayer. Prayer then is a continual and intimate connection, an "I and thou" relationship.

This dialectic becomes more tangible when we recall the deceptively simple expression frequently used in the liturgy: "Our Father, Our King." Though it addresses only one side of the problem, i.e., man's relationship to God, it is a paradoxical expression, and sheds some light on our discussion. On one hand, the word "father" signifies kinship and profound closeness. Yet "king," on the other, implies distance. Hence the midrash: "Love combined with awe and awe combined with love—this attribute is used exclusively concerning the Omnipresent *[ha-makom]*."[2]

More extensive, lyrical expression of this duality, this time from God's perspective, may be found in a poem attributed to R. Solomon ibn Gabirol. "Adon 'Olam" is found, in varied contexts, in the prayer books of all Jewish communities. The first part of the poem describes a "Lord" *(adon)* above and beyond the world, existing before and after it, beyond human comprehension; no other can be compared to him, and though he is sovereign of the universe, He dwells solitary. In the second part, though, he is portrayed as a personal deity: ("my God"; "my Saviour," etc.), very near to man, who casts his soul's burden upon him. How, then, can the incongruity between these two identities, which coexist in the consciousness of the Jew as he prays, be resolved theoretically?

Kabbalistic theology[3] seeks to authorize these two aspects by tilting the balance in favor of philosophy. In other words, in a purely theoretical sense God truly is transcendent,[4] inconceivable by the human intellect because no equivalent to him exists in human language or experience. His absolute hiddenness makes verbal description of him impossible. His being is ineffable, for any statement about him imposes limitation or multiplicity. All definition is reductive by its very nature, and neither man's intellectual language nor human speech have the words to describe such tremendous unity. He is 'Eiyn Sof (endlessness), so called by R. Isaac the Blind and his students after him, the name eventually becoming a constant in the Kabbalists' vocabulary. This 'Eiyn Sof has no human characteristics[5] and cannot be described; in essence, none of the divine names appearing in the Bible are appropriate in relation to him. In a work dating from the second half of the thirteenth century, we read: "Of the Holy One blessed be He, who is called the Cause of Causes blessed be He, one can speak neither of being nor of non-being, neither of measure nor stature nor length nor breadth, not of limit or border or schism, neither of movement nor rest, for nothing is external to Him and nothing divides Him."[6] Or in the words of a Kabbalist (probably R. Abraham ben Eliezer ha-Levi) who lived in the early sixteenth century, in his work *Ohel Mo'ed* (Cambridge MS 673, fol. 20b): "No object can contain Him and no idea can grasp Him, for it is forbidden to ponder over Him. That is the poet's meaning when he said: Examine His works, but do not lay your hand upon Him." Even the negative formulation of the expression "'Eiyn Sof" emphasizes his total concealment from us. And nevertheless, for reasons unknown to us, God wished to reveal himself to humankind.[7] This revelation, of course, is only partial. In the

Hasidic parable appearing in the opening of *Maggid Devarav le-Ya'akov*, it is "like the father who contracts his intellect to chatter with his little son." That is, the father seems to lower himself by speaking in childish language so that his son will understand him, yet he preserves his own integrity nonetheless. Only a single aspect of God's "personality," his attributes, or his acts is apparent to us and accessible to our understanding. In effect, even the Bible says nothing about God in and of himself; its very first verse already speaks of the Divine as revealed in his acts and their effect on something outside of himself. In the famous statement in the work *Ma'arekhet ha-Elohut*: "Know that the 'Eiyn Sof we have mentioned is not referred to in the Torah, the Prophets, or the Hagiographa, or in the words of the rabbis, but the worshippers [i.e., the Kabbalists] have received a little indication of it."[8] The Bible speaks only of the relationship between him and the cosmos, humanity, the Jewish people, the individual, etc.

The distinction between "the thing itself" *(das Ding an sich)* and "the thing as it appears to us" (phenomenon, *Anschauung*) is particularly appropriate in this context. At issue are not two separate entities, but rather two sides of a single coin. Expressions such as "from his perspective," "from his point of view," "as for the receivers," and "as for created beings"[9] are thus prominent and highly significant in kabbalistic writings. This emphasizes that when we speak of God, we should be well aware that we are relating not to some totality but rather to its revelation limited to a single aspect. It is the use of symbols,[10] moreover, that empowers us to *speak* freely and allows us, or perhaps even obliges us, to employ symbols frequently; the special quality contained in a certain symbol serves certain ends, and at times we make use of a series of symbols to express an entire idea.[11] Clearly, then, the Kabbalists read the Bible, all other religious sources, and even the world itself in their symbolic language. This is particularly true in the case of man, for "through my flesh I would see God" (Job 19:26), man being created in the image of the Divine, and in the case of the Torah, which is a revelation of divine will. The Kabbalists' contention that the Torah offers multiple possible readings comes as no surprise,[12] for other aspects unarguably exist in addition to the simple reading revealed to us. All is thus a transparent reflection of the Divine. In the words of *Ma'arekhet ha-Elohut:* "Indeed, of the many names of the ten Sefirot used by the Kabbalists, some they understood through their own intuition from the events occurring in the lower world; others they drew from the mysteries hidden in the books of the Bible, and still others from the secret meanings of aggadot and midrashim."[13] At times, God takes on the "image" of a certain Sefirah, appearing in a form appropriate to that Sefirah, yet that appearance does not prevent him from employing all the other Sefirot as well. The problem is ours, for it is we who are unable to grasp his endless fullness and variegation.

However, though the Sefirotic order represents the Divine as he reveals himself, in a personalistic form—as opposed to the sublime source of emanation, transcendent, 'Eiyn Sof immersed in the depths of himself—it is nonetheless not completely identical to the biblical concept of a personal God. The Sefirotic order still represents only one aspect of divine being, that part which is immanent in the world, dwelling as it were outside of himself (though in truth there is nothing "outside" of the Divine), which determines the form of the cosmos and its natural and moral values, as well as the measure of effluence needed to sustain the world and man. Thus, on one hand the Kabbalist can comfortably see the Sefirotic system as what actualizes divine providence without engendering any change in 'Eiyn Sof itself.[14] On the other hand, no harm would be done to the Divine itself if we were to say that man, through prayer or cleaving to God, activates the divine order inherent in nature, arouses the Sefirot, and even causes miracles to occur. It must be remembered, though, that miracles are not irregularities or changes in the world order, but rather part of the wholeness of nature. For that reason the Kabbalists took care to emphasize that the recompense of a *miṣvah* is not a "promise" or reward (for if it were, that would imply that something is unplanned or unwilled by God), but rather a natural result necessarily dependent on the act itself.[15]

To make their theoretical perception of God more tangible, the Kabbalists often adopt philosophical language in speaking of God: 'Eiyn Sof,[16] the Root of all Roots,[17] the First Cause, the Cause of Causes.[18] Yet, as we have said, the mystic draws his life force from his religious environment, and even the Kabbalists, who sought a living religious relationship, were forced to describe God in vital language, familiar to human speech and understanding. Thus the concept of the "Sefirot" was devised in order to create a situation in which the Divine may be described as both transcendent and immanent. That is to say, the revealed aspect cannot appear to us in its true essence, but rather in a form our intellect is able to receive; thus the Divine reveals himself through the ten Sefirot. Each Sefirah expresses a different aspect of this revelation, for our boundedness allows us to perceive things only partially. An illustration of this might be the sun,[19] with its many and contrasting effects (light, heat, melting of certain substances, turning certain liquids to solids, such as the cooking of an egg, etc.)—although they share a single source, that truth is difficult to grasp.

THE TERM "SEFIROT"

In the thirteenth century, various difficulties remained concerning the doctrine of the Sefirot. What, for example, is the connection between the Sefirot and the thirteen attributes of God, both in respect to their number and the way they are designated? Scholars of the thirteenth century offered varied solutions, most of them concerning the disparity between thirteen, ten and three. For instance: there are three forces which are the root of all ten (a famous response attributed to R. Hai Gaon). At times, the thirteen were seen as an aspect contained within the first Sefirah,[20] and sometimes within Tiferet;[21] perhaps they split off from Malkhut, or, alternatively, the three may be effects in the manner of Ḥesed, Din, and Raḥamim. In any case, the words *middot* (attributes) and Sefirot are used without inhibition as synonyms.

In the fourteenth century, a certain crystallization took place. A number of Kabbalists considered the names of the Sefirot and their symbolic significance more extensively, and in the process the question of the relationship between the ten and the thirteen was almost forgotten. Yet in the sixteenth century, R. Moses Cordovero proposed a new solution to the contradiction, based on the ethical view that was becoming more and more widespread. He contended the thirteen truly are God's moral attributes embodied in the first Sefirah, and it is man's responsibility to emulate them.

As we have said, God reveals himself primarily through the ten main attributes. In early Kabbalah, the Kabbalists used many different appellations. In the terminology of the *Sefer ha-Bahir*, for example, we find names such as: treasures, forces, pleasant vessels, crowns, utterances, attributes, kings, voices, etc. In the *Zohar*, more names are added, such as: lights, places *('atarin)*, colors, words, levels, powers, days, forces, diadems, garments, fountains, visions, brightness, plants, springs, sides, supports, ornaments, worlds, pillars, heavens, names, gates, and more.[22] In thirteenth-century literature, others appear as well: mirrors, essences, finite entities,[23] etc. In the "'Iyyun" circle of thirteenth-century Castile, the names of the bodily parts of the Adam Kadmon (primordial man) were used. The description of the process of emanation and the world of divine powers offered by that circle was, in fact, unique. Yet their influence paled before that of the school of R. Isaac the Blind and the Geronese circle, and was nearly forgotten.[24] Thus, numerous names were invented throughout the thirteenth century, the formative period of the Kabbalah; the most widely used among them, though, was "Sefirot." In effect, the system of the ten Sefirot as a whole was given various epithets, such as the world of holiness (particularly as opposed to the world of evil), chariot, the world of emanation, essences (R. Isaac the Blind), glory (*Perush ha-Aggadot* by R. 'Azriel), supreme glory (Naḥmanides' commentary on *Sefer Yeṣirah*), supernal glory (*Zohar* II, 155a), etc.

The term "Sefirot" ספירות (not to be confused with the Greek word for "sphere") makes its first appearance in *Sefer Yeṣirah*. That book begins with the words: "In thirty-two mystical paths of Wisdom. . . . He created the world . . . ten Sefirot of nothingness and twenty-two letters of foundation." The context indicates that the word "Sefirot" is paired with "letters," and refers to the ten primary numbers that are the foundation of existence according to the Pythagorean school. Indeed, because *Sefer Yeṣirah* was a basic book for the first Kabbalists, even a thousand years after its composition the Kabbalists readopted the term, though charging it with new meanings.

In addition to the numerical connotation of the word, which indicates the sum of ten,[25] it is read by some as *sfar* (boundary). This is meant to suggest the theoretical aspect. That is to say, the hidden side of God truly is infinite, yet another, apprehensible aspect is within the reach of our intellect due to its very limitation or, more precisely, it appears to us in limit and measure. It acts to a restricted extent within the confines of a limited reality.

The word *sappir*, another alternate reading of the term Sefirot, bears an additional meaning. *Sappir* is a precious jewel glimmering with many beams of light, each of them reflected in the other, yet all of them emerging from a single stone. Audible here, too, are echoes of the theoretical view in the background. That is, although we may speak of various Sefirot, that implies no polytheistic concept of the Divine, but rather a single unity revealed in its multiplicity.

Another meaning is suggested in the *Bahir* in the following laconic explanation: "Why are they called Sefirot? Because it is written: 'The heavens tell of God's glory.'"[26] The simplest interpretation of the statement would be that it is the Sefirot that disclose *(meSaPRot)* the nature of the Divine; without their action, as suggested above, we would be unable to discover that true nature. The Kabbalists, in their commentaries on the *Bahir*, did not hesitate to charge the original sentence with other meanings; however, these postdate the text itself.[27]

In sum, the term "Sefirot" encompasses all the multiple senses we have considered, thus serving the Kabbalists well in expressing their view of God as he reveals himself.

At issue are the "ten Sefirot" of revelation. The sum of ten stems both from the original expression in *Sefer Yeṣirah* and from other phrases such as the "Ten Commandments" (or the "ten Words," as in Deut. 4:13) in which God is revealed as legislator; or the "ten utterances"[28] in which he revealed himself as Creator of the world, etc.[29] There really was no other possibility,[30] for as soon as we permit ourselves to speak of "manifold" aspects of the Divine, an explanation can be found for any number, as well as better alternatives to that explanation. The number "ten," on the grounds suggested above, was thus well justified.

The Kabbalists themselves, of course, treated the question as well, generating, among others, the following explanations. There is the geometrical interpretation of R. 'Azriel;[31] a simpler formulation of the same idea was made by the author of *Sefer ha-Shem* in its opening pages: "There is no point without length and thickness and width—three. Each of these has a beginning, end, and middle—nine in all. Counting the boundary of its space makes ten. In truth, the Sefirot are nine, and the space containing them is the tenth." R. Yehudah Ḥayyat, who lived during the time of the Expulsion from Spain, explains the decimal structure of the numbers. In *Ma'arekhet ha-Elohut* we read: "The ten Sefirot are the basis of all that is defined numerically; thus you see that the total quantity of numerals is no more than ten, as mathematicians well know."[32] R. Moses Cordovero, similarly, dedicates the second section of his seminal and extensive work, *Pardes Rimmonim,* to the same question. Yet even after a long discussion and review of his predecessors' views, he offers no "logical" reason. Rather he contends that it is a given, an axiom, and thus beyond question. (The same was also suggested by R. Shem Tov ibn Shem Tov in *Sefer ha-Emunot*, IV, chap. 6).

THE NAMES OF THE SEFIROT

What, then, are these ten Sefirot? In effect, because the Kabbalists, as mystics, make use of symbols, they may choose among an almost infinite number of symbols to name those same ten Sefirot which define the ways in which divine influence is manifest. For practical reasons, though, the Kabbalists more or less agreed upon the following names:

Keter
Ḥokhmah Binah
Ḥesed Gevurah
Tiferet
Neṣaḥ Hod
Yesod
Malkhut

Before we elucidate these ten names, though, we must point out that in wake of the influence of Neoplatonism, which speaks of the emanation of abundance from the One to the elements inferior to him, down to the nethermost kernel, the Sefirot are also described as evolving downward. This evolution is portrayed as an ongoing emanation *(aṣilut)* or effulgence *(shef'a)*. Two fundamental images widespread in Neoplatonism are used—*light* and *water*. The choice of these symbols was not accidental. Light represents vitality, purity and lucidity, nobility and spirituality in general; it is an expansive entity that travels quickly. Water is pure and clear as well, represents the fundament of physical existence, and has the basic quality of fluidity. To make the similarity between these two images more perceptible, let us consider the symbol of a river *(nahar)*. Light *(or)* is implicit in the word itself (see Job 3:4), particularly in the Aramaic of the *Zohar (nehora – nahir)*, while it also suggests the streaming *(nehirah)* of water. The river thus offers itself as a symbol of luminosity flowing and branching into rivulets. Indeed, in the *Zohar* we find a long series of terms describing emanation, all of them expressing the same idea. Among them: extension, prolongation, expansion, flow, illumination, sparkling.[33] We must add, though, that while in Neoplatonic thought the process of emanation takes place outside of the "Oneness," in the Kabbalah the processes of emanation of the Sefirot occur within the Divine. Even in that realm, moreover, there is no permanent hierarchy as in Neoplatonism. Rather, there are internal relationships, mystical unions, and a vital dynamic that bear witness to a realm fermenting with life, as it were (hence the reference of modern scholars to kabbalistic "theosophy"). Certain theoretical problems arise from such assumptions, and we will consider them in the course of our discussion.

The process of downward evolution is described in three ways: (1) as the continual path of a descending line, in the order of the names mentioned above; (2) in the form of three lines: right, left, and center; (3) in groups of three.

Having sketched the arrangement of the Sefirot,[34] let us now consider their names in greater detail. We must point out that the representative names of the Sefirot we have used are the most commonly accepted, their format having been conceived and consolidated in the school of the Kabbalists of Gerona (the *Bahir*, in contrast, still lacks consistent terminology).

1. Keter or *Keter 'eliyon* (supernal crown],[35] was apparently chosen because it is the highest point associated with the image of royalty; one of the most indubitable names used to designate God is "King," particularly in the esoteric tradition of the *Heikhalot* literature at hand for the earliest Kabbalists. Other popular terms synonymous with Keter are as follows.

Raṣon (will). In some instances the Kabbalists indicate the numerical equivalence or *gematria* (= 346) between *raṣon* and "His Name" *(shmo);* the word "Name" was widely used among the Kabbalists as an expression of divine revelation.[36] The element of will, in fact, played an important role in Neoplatonic philosophy and in the Jewish trend influenced by it.

Maḥashavah tehorah (pure thought) is a potential spiritual element, a divine idea, primordial and all-inclusive.[37]

Afisat ha-maḥashavah (the nought) is a point at which human thought ceases because it can no longer grasp anything.[38] For that reason, we frequently find the injunction, "Do not inquire into what is too wonderful for you."

Similar to this name is *ayin* (nothingness). In the words of R. Moses Cordovero: "All agree this name belongs to Keter, and is called thus because that realm is beyond conception."[39] Or as R. Joseph Gikatilla explained more fully: "Because of the hiddenness of the Sefirah Keter, utterly remote from all creatures, it cannot be gazed upon but only heard."[40]

Hefsed (annihilation) or *he'eder* (absence) is used in the sense of the incapacity of human thought to grasp it, or that it itself is absent in the sense of an unattainable objective; alternatively, the terms may signify such an overabundance of being that all laws of existence and absence are irrelevant regarding it, making it incommensurable with any other word designating being and mandating the euphemism of absence, nothingness. In the expression of a Kabbalist writing near the year 1300: "There is more of Him than all the being the world contains, but because He is utterly simple, uncomplicated, and the most simple creatures appear complex in comparison, He is called "nothingness" in contrast to them."[41]

Ḥoshekh (darkness) was a name widely discussed in early Kabbalah,[42] and follows the same logic as the names mentioned above;

Similarly, the appellation "He," in the third person, designates the most hidden and inconceivable Sefirah. Another interesting designation is *'olam ha-mitbodded* (the lonely world),[43] signifying a unique, self-contained realm.

It may sometimes be said, as well, that by the very will to create an Other that will receive his nature, Keter crowns itself, so to speak. R. Moses Ḥayyim Luzzatto also considers the term Keter as a positive relationship to the world. "And it is called Keter because all are crowned [i.e., surrounded] and protected by Him. This source has also been called *ayin*, to tell of His great hiddenness, like the root of a tree concealed in the earth."[44]

Another important point in the description of Keter is that it is a primeval root of all reality. Opposites and contradictions coexist harmoniously within it; only when they are revealed in our world does the conflict between them find expression. Keter then means "indifferent unity"[45] or "the symmetry of unity," as in Neoplatonic philosophy. Interestingly, in the early seventeenth century the German mystic Jacob Boehme stated that all truth is a *complexio oppositorum*, that is, a compound (and perhaps a complexity) of opposites.[46]

Finally, note that in the work *Tikkuney Zohar* and the writings of

Kabbalists following it, other names are used as well, such as Adam Kadmon (primordial man) and Adam Kadma'ah 'Ela'ah Dekhulhu (primordial man, supreme over all).[47]

2. Ḥokhmah (wisdom) signifies the upper and exalted part of the body of the king. In addition, the attribute of Ḥokhmah is associated with God by philosophers such as R. Sa'adyah Gaon, and even according to Maimonides it is one of the attributes of essence inseparable from his very being. The downward evolution from Keter begins to be revealed in this Sefirah, though it is yet extremely limited. Thus the name: *reshit* (beginning), or *yesh* (being), in contrast to *ayin* mentioned above. A verse from Job (28:12) is illustrative: "From whence *[me-ayin]* shall wisdom be found?" In its biblical context, the verse serves as a question, yet the Kabbalists transform it to an affirmative statement—"Wisdom emerges from nothingness *[ayin]*." (Such sleight of hand is common on the part of the Kabbalists, and deserves notice.) The transition from "nothingness" to "being" is the first step made by infinite Will toward the Other. We must emphasize that the Kabbalists perceive the evolution of being from nothingness, and Creation itself as an event occurring within the Divine (as opposed to the philosophical concept of creation ex nihilo); it is a stage in the emanation of Ḥokhmah from Keter. Ḥokhmah is "the first expansion of thought, the beginning of emanation," in the words of *Sha'arey Orah* (fol. 94a).

Ḥokhmah is also called *nekudah* (point) as a symbol of minuteness. Yet the point is the basis of all geometric constructs as well. In other words, all of creation begins from this point, as it is written: "God founded the earth upon wisdom" (Prov. 3:19). In this context, the word *ḥokhmah* is read with its letters inverted as *ko'ah ma* (the force *[ko'ah]* of the most basic essence [*ma*])—i.e., that foundation is the potential and the power of all entities in cosmic existence.

3. Binah (understanding) is a development emerging from Ḥokhmah, in the sense of intuitive knowledge. That is, the scant abundance present in Ḥokhmah is further revealed in Binah. The point expands to a circle. The comparison is often made to the relationship between father and mother. The tiny quantity of seed present in the father's body is not outwardly visible, yet it grows prominent after conception in the mother's womb. These two Sefirot are thus intimately related and are called by the *Zohar* (III, fol. 4a): "Two lovers who do not separate." Despite the oppositions between them, they are empowered to continue the process of

creation. By this principle, in effect, the dualism of opposing male and female valences in our own world, which exist in human, animal, and plant life, combine to create "one flesh" (after Gen. 2:24).[48]

Ḥokhmah, as the first sparkling, could continue to glitter, perhaps endlessly, if not for the limitation inherent in the receptacle of Binah. Yet Binah does not merely halt emanation and keep it from continuing, but shapes what it has taken into itself, just as a mother does. Hence the image of "matter and form"[49] in reference to these two Sefirot, in the sense of a mutual relationship that is creative and viable. There are two aspects to this role of shaping: one positive and creative, suggested above, and the other negative and limiting. They are two sides of the same coin, because if not for limitation, formation would be impossible. Thus one quality of the Sefirah of Binah is limitation and contraction; in the language of the Kabbalists, "Judgment *[dinnim]* is aroused through it." For this reason, Binah is perceived as the root of the left side of the Sefirotic system,[50] while Ḥokhmah serves as the root of the right side—the benefactor.

The feminine symbol of mother reappears in various guises, especially in the context of the second female image—the lowest Sefirah. And as that female image is the mother of her offspring, so Binah was conceived as a mother of children—in the more narrow sense of mother of the seven Sefirot beneath her, and in the wider sense of the world's mother. From then on, as it were, the world grows and develops. The verse "In the beginning *[bereshit]* the Lord created the world" (Gen. 1:1) is sometimes interpreted as saying: the Lord *(elohim),* which is an appellation of Binah, created six *(bara shit),* i.e., the six days of Creation.

The relationship among the three upper Sefirot may be clarified by aid of the following analogy.[51] A person wishes to study a certain object. Will is completely general at this stage; he does not consider details, nor even the distinctiveness of the object. He sees, for example, a house (= Keter). At the next stage (= Ḥokhmah) he considers the singularity of the house more closely, noting its construction, height, materials, color, location, attractiveness, and so on. At the third stage (= Binah) he looks at more details: the number of floors and rooms, their shape and functionality, the internal relationships among the house's components, and so forth. At that stage a full picture of the house is reached—in other words, the world's creation, its realization in the material being of our world.

From an eschatological perspective, the path from the divine womb to the nadir of being in its first moments of becoming is the same as the path of ascent back to the source, like the ladder to the End of Days. "All are of dust and all return to dust" (Eccles. 3:20). Or, like the familiar Neoplatonic precept: all comes from the One and all returns to the One.

We have used the verb "return" as it is used in the Bible and, indeed, Binah is called *teshuvah* (returning), not only in the moral sense but, in this context, in a cosmological and eschatological sense. Another quality characterizing Binah must be mentioned—redemption. This element is bound up with various symbols: the biblical book of Exodus (which concerns the redemption from Egypt), the jubilee year (the year when slaves are freed and property is returned to its original owners), the shofar (a means of heralding either repentance or redemption), the world to come ("What great goodness You have hidden away for those who fear You" [Ps. 31:20]), and so forth.

The three upper Sefirot form an autonomous group,[52] and there is a commonly accepted division between those upper three (called "the first three") and the seven after them (called "the seven days of building" or "the lower seven"). The group of seven that emerges from Binah reflects the story of the seven days of Creation told in Genesis; in it, divine emanation becomes revealed, the divine attributes begin to affect the world, and their influence is manifest. This, apparently, is one of the reasons R. Joseph ben Shalom Ashkenazi, in the fourteenth century, described the seven lower Sefirot as "renewed."[53] His comment aids us in understanding this second group. Indeed, it is characteristic of the Kabbalist to contemplate the lowest Sefirah and then lift his gaze upward.

The seven lower Sefirot are dependent on the upper three; this is simply expressed by Gikatilla (*Sha'arey Orah*, beginning of chap. 9) in his observation that the Tetragrammaton, which unites all the Sefirot, is formed in such a way that the first half of it (the letters *yod*, *he*, signifying Keter, Ḥokhmah, and Binah) can appear independently as a divine name, while the second half (the letters *vav*, *heh*) cannot stand alone.

The group of seven, once again, stems from Binah and is collectively called "sons" *(banim)* or "son" *(ben)* (designating six Sefirot) and "daughter" *(bat)* (the lowest Sefirah). The names of most of the components of this group are taken from the verse in 1 Chron. 29:11: "Yours, O Lord, is the greatness *[gedulah],* and the power *[gevurah],* and the beauty *[tiferet],* and the victory *[nezah],* and the majesty *[hod],* for all that is in heaven and on earth." Let us examine this notion more closely.

4. The first Sefirah of this second group (i.e., the fourth Sefirah) is called Gedulah, after the formulation in the biblical verse. Others among the first Kabbalists, though, used a different name: Ḥesed. This appellation came to replace the former because it more aptly expresses the nature of this Sefirah, which is an endless giving of abundance and light. This is compared to the light created on the first day, which all creatures freely enjoy.

5. In contrast, the fundamental role of the next Sefirah, Gevurah, is to test and try the recipient of that efflux of Ḥesed to determine its worthiness. Thus, it has the character of a court of law, a trial, and even of punishment in the form of a restriction of effulgence. This is why it is also called "the attribute of strict judgment" and why the account of the second day of Creation, telling of the act of separation and distinction, does not evoke the words "And it was good" as on the other days. This separation (as opposed to the light of Ḥesed, which flows indiscriminately) is what engenders objects in their individuality and their distinctiveness from one another; it is also responsible for regulating the flow of abundance in quantities appropriate to the worthiness of the recipient. The parallel, in effect, to the relationship between Ḥokhmah and Binah is striking: an expansion from Ḥokhmah and concentration in Binah; primacy and primordiality versus formation and definition.

Ours is a world of contradictions. That situation is rooted in the world of the Sefirot, especially in Ḥesed and Gevurah. No negative connotation is implied in such a statement, but merely a simple recognition that such is the nature of the world. Neither of the two opposing sides thus has the power to act autonomously. The male needs the female; the ideas of Ḥokhmah likewise need the formulating power of Binah, and the endless abundance of Ḥesed must have the circumscription of Din.

6. These two extreme qualities of Ḥesed and Gevurah threaten this world's existence, as the Midrash says,[54] and thus the next Sefirah, Tiferet, comes to temper them, to mediate between them and balance the oppositions. Its role is to "make peace on high" (Job 25:2), and thus is also called *shalom* (peace).[55] It contains characteristics of both, and is sometimes called *midat ha-raḥamim* (the attribute of compassion). The world's existence is possible by grace of its quality of compromise. Harmony is created by a tempering of the two poles: freedom and limitation, oneness and differentiation, mercy and judgment. This Sefirah is thus of central importance. Indeed, on the third day of Creation—the parallel to this is

the third Sefirah in the group of the seven lower Sefirot—the phrase "And it was good" appears twice, for only on that day could reality become viable and begin to function.

Its importance is expressed in the placement of Tiferet at the central axis of the diagram of the ten Sefirot. For this reason it is symbolized in the letter *vav*, whose form is a straight line, like "a middle bar in the midst of the boards reaching from end to end" (Exod. 26:28, concerning the construction of the Tabernacle in the desert). Moreover, there are many parallels between Keter and Tiferet. For example, Keter is called *arikh anpin* (long countenance] and Tiferet z*'eir anpin* (short countenance].[56] Additional characteristics and, in their wake, additional symbols were invented on the basis of this centrality. The "Ineffable Name" (YHVH) is identified with the Sefirah of Tiferet. Tiferet represents the world of maleness as opposed to Malkhut, femaleness, and it is the center of the six Sefirot (extremities) surrounding it, which are called "the branches of the tree." It is a symbol of the written Torah, which embodies the religious-national essence of the Jewish people, and it is the object of that people's prayers (although the intent of those prayers is toward the unification of all the Sefirot).

7–8. Divine efflux descends to the next two Sefirot, a pair like the Sefirot of Ḥesed and Gevurah in miniature. Among other things, these two lower Sefirot serve as a source of inspiration for the prophets. Their names are Neṣaḥ and Hod.

Neṣaḥ signifies both eternity and victory. "Neṣaḥ graces Israel with its mercy . . . issues decrees in Israel's favor . . . and never goes back on itself." Hod "clothes itself in the attribute of Gevurah, gaining the power to overcome enemies, be victorious in battle, and rescue those who love God. And in the place where wars were won and miracles and wonders performed [!]—that is the site where words of thanksgiving *[hoda'ot]* are said."[57]

These two Sefirot often appear as a pair, represented by *yakhin* and *boaz* (the two central pillars of King Solomon's Temple), the two willow branches used at Sukkot, the two kidneys, and so forth. The quotations cited above also clearly demonstrate the internal connection between them. Indeed, the classic work describing kabbalistic symbolism, *Sha'arey Orah* (along with its counterpart, *Sha'arey Ṣedek*, by the same author, R. Joseph Gikatilla) devotes a single chapter to both these Sefirot, while each of the other Sefirah is treated in a separate chapter.

9. The Sefirah called Yesod[58] not only intermediates between Neṣaḥ and Hod but draws into itself all the abundance flowing from the Sefirot above it and passes that abundance on to that after it. Thus it is called *kol* (all) in the list of designations in 1 Chronicles cited above. It is also called *ṣedek*, for the world stands on a single pillar named *ṣaddik* (righteousness).[59] In other words, this attribute actualizes in the world the divine attributes above it through the prism of morality.

This brings us to one of the central points in Kabbalah, a point that may well have aroused sharp opposition because of its sexual connotations, and that may indeed have engendered the prohibition against an unmarried man's learning Kabbalah in general. That is, the Sefirah of Yesod serves as a connection between the Sefirot above it, which represent *'alma di-dekhorah* (the world of maleness), and the Sefirah below it, *'alma de-nukbah* (the world of femaleness). It thus represents the male sexual organ, signified by the word *berit* (the sign of circumcision).

This means that the Kabbalists interpreted literally the verse in Gen. 1:27: "For He created him in the divine image, male and female He created them." Man is not only a world in miniature *('olam katan),* a microcosm, but reflects the Divine as well. Here the Kabbalists adopted yet another verse almost as a motto: "Through my flesh I would see God" (Job 19:26). In other words, one of the fundamental characteristics of the human species—and, in effect, of other parts of nature as well—is its bisexuality; the two opposing sexual valences striving for unity are the root of existence itself and its perpetuation. The same two elements likewise exist, so to speak, in the Divine, though they are not perceived, as in polytheistic religions, as completely separate but rather as a unity, a principle within divine action as a whole. Kabbalistic teaching was certainly daring in including the feminine aspect in its doctrine of the Divine. Thus, in the world of the Sefirot, the aspects of male and female are present as separate Sefirot, like all the others, yet their aspiration is toward union, toward becoming one. If the Sefirot as a whole must necessarily be brought to a state of oneness, demonstrating strict monotheism despite multiplicity and variegation, then this responsibility is particularly relevant vis-à-vis the images of male and female. But while the unity of all the Sefirot is desirable "for God's own good," so to speak, and directed to him as the One God, the union of male and female is demanded more for the sake of the lower world. For that oneness and harmony draw a great efflux down to the worlds beneath the world of *aṣilut*, an efflux that is essential to their existence. In the words of the *Bahir* (s. 173, according to Munich MS 209): "Neither the upper nor the lower would could exist without the female."

A large part of man's religious action is therefore dedicated to removing obstacles and maximizing the nearness and the union between these two Sefirot. The male figure, which actually characterizes all nine of the Sefirot, as abundance flows from all of them, has its focal point in the figure of Tiferet. Not accidentally does that Sefirah descend as a straight line directly from Keter, with nothing else on that line but the Sefirah of Yesod,[60] which connects to the figure below it—that of the female.

10. Myriad images are used in kabbalistic literature to portray the lowest Sefirah, and prominent among them is the element of reception. This appears as early as the *Bahir*.[61] Some of the other names, with no apparent connection among them aside from that element of reception, include: earth, land, cabinet, Ark of the Covenant (remember that "covenant" = Yesod), palace, sea, vessel, lower Mother, woman, daughter, lady *(matronita),* queen, etc.

The term "Malkhut" was already routinely used in the early Kabbalah.[62] Some Kabbalists, though, such as the author of *Ma'arekhet ha-Elohut,* replace it with a similar term: *'atarah* (crown). Other terms frequently used include Shekhinah,[63] an appellation that is meant to speak of divine immanence in our world; and Knesset Israel (the Assembly of Israel), which suggests the historical aspect. Attached to these two names are descriptions of the destiny of the Jewish people and the struggle against evil, the exile of the Shekhinah and her redemption.

Many of the designations for Malkhut stem from their connection to the corresponding Sefirah of Tiferet, since Tiferet is the source of efflux and the Malkhut is its receiver. The designations include *heaven and earth, day and night, sun and moon, east and west, son and daughter,* and *body and soul.* Important as well is the symbolism of Malkhut as the totality of all that is above it. One symbol is *sea* (and sometimes more specifically, the sea of Ḥokhmah), after the verse "All rivers flow to the sea" (Eccles. 1:7); another is *ma'arav* (west), in the phrase of the *Bahir* (s. 156): "Because there all seed is combined *[mit'arev]*"—"seed" meaning the abundance from all the other Sefirot. Note, as well, that according to the Talmud (*Baba Batra* 25a): "The Shekhinah is in the west." Malkhut is called *kallah* (bride), for it contains all *(kollelet kol).* It is also called *diokanah* (likeness), *mar'ah* (image), and *temunah* (portrait), for it contains all images. The color blue *(tekhelet)* is associated with it because blue is also interpreted as containing all *(khol)*. Malkhut is thus a sort of all-inclusive amalgam. With that, the divine schema comes full circle. On one hand, Malkhut acts as a gateway leading to the upper world; it is an opening for orientation and devotion. On the other hand, effulgence descends from it toward the lower world.

We must remember, though, that effulgence does not flow freely downwards. A certain valve, as it were, impedes that stream, so that it not reach someone unworthy of it. Divine providence is thus double: of the world in general, and of each individual in particular. Malkhut is an emissary of judgment, a messenger of Gevurah; for that reason it is called the attribute of gentle judgment *(middat ha-din ha-rafah)*, *elohim*, the Lower Court, and so forth.

In some cases it corresponds with a particular Sefirah, as in the instances of the "lower Shekhinah," the "lower letter *heh*" as opposed to the "*upper* Shekhinah," the "upper letter *heh*." The latter represent the Sefirah of Binah. Most important is the notion of continuity, in which each stage represents a successive level of revelation. For example: the primordial Torah *(Torah kedumah),* the Written Torah, the Oral Torah (= Ḥokhmah, Tiferet, Malkhut); thought, voice (without enunciation of words as such), speech (Keter or Ḥokhmah, Tiferet, Malkhut); thought, speech and action (same as above); He, Thou, I (Keter, Tiferet, Malkhut).

Because Malkhut receives the effulgence of other Sefirot yet none flows from it, it is described as "having nothing of its own." The light emanated from it is reflected light, like that of the moon. For that reason it is portrayed in images of poverty *(dalut)* (including the letter *dalet*), privation and darkness. Following that sense, it is even compared to David, for according to aggadic tradition King David received all seventy years of his life from Adam. The situation of Malkhut clearly reflects that of a woman—there are times when she is not permitted to her husband, and thus cannot receive his abundance; as a result, no abundance can come from her either. This, then, is the status of the Shekhinah when she is alienated from Tiferet.

Another aspect of the portrayal of Malkhut concerns its position: it is at the lowest point in the Sefirotic order, adjacent to the world of evil, the first of all the worlds beneath the Sefirot. She is the World-mother (as well as a miniature of Binah, the mother of children, i.e., the seven lower Sefirot), a gateway and opening that serves both as a channel conducting efflux downwards and as a step on the ladder of ascent used in meditations on divine mystery or in directing mystical intent toward the unification of the Sefirot, as we mentioned above.

Particular importance is given to the Shekhinah as representing the higher Knesset Israel.[64] That is, the people of Israel is summoned to represent, in the lower world, the Shekhinah—who is an embodiment of the higher world. The Shekhinah, which in midrashic literature designates the presence of the divine in the world, and Knesset Israel, which is a personification of the people of Israel, both serve in kabbalistic literature as symbols of a force containing all the divine powers, the entire Sefirotic system, and the historical destiny of the Jewish people. Divine essence and human essence are thus eminently united. This metahistorical perspective is a cornerstone of the kabbalistic worldview.

The reader has doubtless noticed the unusual length of the list of symbols representing the Sefirah of Malkhut. This is no accident. One of the most prominent of Kabbalists remarked on the wealth of symbols corresponding to that Sefirah:

> I would like to consider the names for the Shekhinah, which are more numerous than those of the other attributes . . . the name of almost everything in existence recalls her . . . each of her names reflects not the material nature, heaven forbid, of the entity bearing that name but the special quality that entity receives from her.[65]

The hierarchy and the internal connections among them is, in the words of the Kabbalists, the Tree of Emanation *(ilan ha-aṣilut)*. Thus, as the *Bahir* says: "All the powers of the Holy One blessed be He are ordered one above the other, and resemble a tree" (s. 119).

DIVISION OF THE SEFIROT INTO GROUPS

The Sefirotic system as a whole can be divided into various subgroups. Above, we considered the division of three and seven, and of male and female (9 + 1). Another division, less common, originates in *Sefer Yeṣirah* 1:3, and suggests five upper and five lower Sefirot. The same idea appears in a text that deals exclusively with the nature of the

Sefirot, namely, *Sha'ar ha-Shoel* by R. 'Azriel of Gerona. To cite a passage from *Ma'arekhet ha-Elohut*:

> The Kabbalists have said the ten essences are five parallel to five—the first five are more spiritual than the second five. They did not imply, heaven forfend, any change occurring within the Sefirot, but rather that the lower ones were called thus because they have greater propensity to act in the nether world than the first ones, which are concealed.[66]

An alternative division constructs a parallel to the Neoplatonic hierarchy of the world of the intellect, the world of the soul, and the world of nature,[67] making the triad of the intellectualized world, the perceived world, and the innate world.

There is the division of right, left, and center, as mentioned above. Nonetheless, the most popular of all is of three and seven. Perhaps this is because these two numbers—and not only in Jewish culture—have the aura of completeness, holiness, and so forth. And, as it says in the midrash *Pirkei de Rabbi Eliezer* (chap. 3): "The world was created with ten utterances and concentrated in three."[68] It may also be that seven reflects the days of Creation, the phenomenon of revealing, thereby making room for the higher level of the hidden aspect of the Divine. All three reasons may well play some part.

We have already spoken of various qualities associated with three and seven; I would like to point out a later characterization, found for the most part in Habad Hasidic teaching, of intellect and attributes or intellect and emotion. That is, the first three Sefirot designate the intellectual level, and that level influences and arouses the emotional level of the lower seven. The importance of this view lies in the inclusion of the two elements as a unity within the Sefirotic system—i.e., mind and heart are intimately joined.

A division of three triads is also possible. In that case, the first three designate the intellectual aspect; the second the ethical aspect; and the third, authority in the world. The lowest Sefirah contains all of them, and acts as their representative in the world beneath the divine realm.

In some instances, the seven is divided into six and one—six sons and one daughter. Yet the sons may also gather around the central Sefirah, Tiferet, as the antithesis of the female. In any case, the six are designated "six extremities" *(shishah keṣavot),* an expression originating in *Sefer Yeṣirah*; there, it is used in the sense of spacial dimensions. They are like the branches of a tree growing from the trunk, from Tiferet. In this context, let us recall that the image of the Sefirotic system as a tree appears as early as the *Bahir* and is very common. The tree, of course, stands upside-down, with its roots above, in 'Eiyn Sof.

THE HUMAN FIGURE

An anthropomorphic likeness of the Divine may be found at the very dawn of Jewish tradition. Numerous biblical verses explicitly compare God to man; he is described as a "warrior," as one who saves "with His right hand," whose "eyes rove to and fro through the whole earth" (Zech. 4:11). Yet, deep in the subconscious, the words of the prophet Isaiah were always inscribed: "To whom then will you liken me, that I should be his equal? says the Holy One" (Isa. 40:25). The world of the Sages, as well, particularly in the realm of Aggadah, partook of this material representation of a personal God. The mystics of the *Heikhalot* literature, who lived in the first half of the first millennium, were audacious enough to reach the state of "Your eyes shall see the king in his beauty" (Isa. 33:17); they described the *shi'ur komah*—the physical stature and dimensions, as it were, of the Divine.

Many saw them as going too far, and the fury of more traditional and mainstream Jews was aroused; even the Karaites did not remain silent.[69] The fact that the Kabbalists frequently felt compelled to defend the institution of *shi'ur komah*[70] indicates that they had not abandoned the possibility of anthropomorphization. Thus, without believing in it, the Kabbalists present extensive descriptions and fantastic images of the Divine based upon the parts of the human body.[71] One motive here is clearly man's need to describe the unknown in terms more comprehensible to himself. Another motive is the need for identification; it is certainly easier to identify with something familiar than with something wholly abstract. In any case, the Sefirotic system was described in human form,[72] and its general structure is as follows.

The first three Sefirot symbolize the head. Ḥesed and Gevurah symbolize the arms; Nezah and Hod, the legs; Tiferet, the navel; Yesod, the male sexual organ; Malkhut, femaleness. Various erotic descriptions were founded on this basic schema; in the *Zohar* such images are particularly frequent and elaborate, and this is another reason the study of Kabbalah was restricted to married and mature men.

Other anatomical parts are considered as well, such as the sections of the brain, which are meticulously described in *Idra Rabba*, a part of the *Zohar*. In the *Zohar*, brain, heart, and liver usually symbolize Ḥokhmah, Tiferet, and Malkhut, respectively. Yet in other kabbalistic writings, "heart" represents additional Sefirot as well.[73] The kidneys symbolize Nezah and Hod. Two appellations previously mentioned are particularly striking: "long countenance" *(arikh anpin)* and "short countenance" *(z'eir anpin)*. The Kabbalists employ these names in varied ways. In the *Idra* of the *Zohar*, for example, the former signifies Keter and the latter the other nine. At other times, *z'eir anpin* designates Tiferet,[74] while in Lurianic teaching *z'eir anpin* relates to the six Sefirot from Ḥesed to Yesod.

In concluding our brief discussion, let us note the warning voiced by R. Joseph Gikatilla:

> Know and believe that, although all these matters demonstrate and testify to His greatness and His truth, there is no creature who can know or understand the nature of the thing called "hand" or "foot" or "ear" and the like. And even though we are made in the image and likeness [of God], do not think for a moment that "eye" is in the form of a real eye, or that "hand" is in the form of a real hand. Rather, these are innermost and most recondite matters in the real existence of God, may He be blessed. From them, the source and the flow go out to all existing things, through the decree of God, may He be blessed. But the nature of "hand" is not like the nature of a hand, and their shape is not the same, as it is said (Isa. 40:25): "To whom then will you liken Me, that I should be his equal?" Know and understand that between Him and us there is no likeness as to substance and shape, but the forms of the limbs that we have denote that they are made in the likeness of signs that indicate secret, celestial matters, which the mind cannot know. . . .

He presents this simple proof: when we write the name of a person, the name and the person are two separate things, yet the name clearly points to that specific person and everyone knows who is meant. The same is true in kabbalistic usage; the mention of limbs merely implies an allusion to the secret hidden beyond the subject.[75] Blessed is he who knows![76]

THE DIVINE NAMES

The Bible contains a diversity of names signifying the Divine. One of the Kabbalists' basic assumptions is that in this plethora of names, all are not synonymous, but rather that each suggests a particular nuance. In their eyes, each of them indicates a specific Sefirah. The Divine as a whole, for example, is designated by the "Ineffable Name," the Tetragrammaton,[77] which is utterly concealed; even its correct pronunciation is unknown to us. That knowledge was entrusted to the High Priest alone, who would pronounce it at the climax of the holy service on the Day of Atonement while the Temple stood; today, that secret tradition is lost to us. This name was thus chosen to indicate the entire Sefirotic system. And just as that system is composed of ten Sefirot, the Tetragrammaton can be broken down into various elements.

Keter is the tittle of the first letter, *yod*; Ḥokhmah is the *yod* itself; Binah is the second letter, *heh* (i.e., the higher *heh*); the six Sefirot of Ḥesed, Gevurah, Tiferet, Nezah, Hod, and Yesod are the third letter, *vav*;[78] and Malkhut is the fourth letter, the second (i.e., the lower) *heh*. Sometimes, though, the Sefirah of Tiferet is designated by the Tetragrammaton as well, for as we have said, it is the axis of the Sefirotic system[79] (although all the Sefirot are the multiplicity contained in unity). He is called, in the Aramaic of the *Zohar,* "Kudsha Berikh Hu" (The Holy One Blessed Be), a name adopted by many Kabbalists afterwards.

In some instances, a name is associated with a particular Sefirah. This is the basic table:

	Ehyeh	
YHVH (with the vocalization of *Elohim*)		Yah
Elohim		El
	YHVH	
Elohim Ṣeva'ot		YHVH Ṣeva'ot
	Shaddai	
	Adonai	

Another point of singularity shared by these names is that, according to the Kabbalists, they are the ten names mentioned in the talmudic tractate *Sanhedrin* that are never to be erased; all other names are considered "appellations" *(kinnuyim)*, and the Halakhah permits their erasure.[80] Let us add a few words explaining the relationships between the names and the Sefirot.[81]

The name Ehyeh appears in the Bible only once,[82] and in a manner that conceals more than it reveals, for the implications of that name are never made explicit. Many, many interpretations have thus been offered, and it is the name designating Keter.

The name Yah is presented here as a symbol for Ḥokhmah; the Kabbalists sometimes associate it with Binah.[83]

The name YHVH, when vocalized as the name Elohim (as in Deut. 3:24) is given the quality of the left side, reflecting the attribute of judgment *(din),* as we shall see below.

The name El is related to the Sefirah of Ḥesed already in the verse "The love *[ḥesed]* of God endures for all time" (Ps. 52:3).

The name Elohim is related to the attribute of Gevurah, because the root of that name has the connotation of potency and strength. In addition, the intrinsically plural form of it in Hebrew indicates strength as well.[84] Thus Naḥmanides interpreted the name Elohim as "the Master of all forces."[85] In the Bible, moreover, the name is often associated with justice, whether that imposed by heaven or by human beings.[86] The attribute of judgment, we may add, concerns not only the act of judgment itself but also its realization, as in the punishment of the wicked. Thus, according to most of the Kabbalists, evil is enrooted in the Sefirah of *din*.

The name YHVH and its identification with Tiferet has been discussed above.

The name Ṣeva'ot never appears on its own in the Bible. At the same time, it is binary in form, and we spoke earlier of the binary nature of the Sefirot Nezah and Hod. The two names accompanying Ṣeva'ot—namely, YHVH and Elohim—were aptly chosen in order to distinguish between them, as in the Bible as well those two names appear in juxtaposition. Here, too, attention is focused on their significance. In rabbinic literature they were interpreted as symbols of the attribute of *raḥamim* and the attribute of *din*, and in kabbalistic thought their symmetry becomes complete—Nezah on the right and Hod on the left.

The name Shaddai, which is explained by the Sages through the pseudo-quotation "It is I who said to my world, Enough! *[dai]*"[87] marks, so to speak, the conclusion of the act of Creation and the stream of divine efflux. The nature of the Sefirah Yesod is conceived in the same way in kabbalistic teaching. The Sefirah after Yesod, Malkhut, merely reflects light, and is itself not a source of light, as we said above. Let us add that the name El Ḥai is also connected to the Sefirah of Yesod because it serves as the source of life. This is the reason for the Kabbalists' emphasis in their prayers on the expression *ḥei ha-'olamim* (who grants life to the world), and not *ḥai 'olamim* (who lives forever), as was accepted in some versions.

The name Adonai, which suggests authority and control in the world, was chosen, not surprisingly, as a symbol of the lowest Sefirah, in keeping with what we have explained above.

ELEMENTS OF NATURE

The natural elements find expression in the order of the Sefirot as well. Ḥesed, again, corresponds with water, the basis of existence and flow, vitality and goodness.

Gevurah is fire. It, too, is a vital element, yet can also be destructive and incendiary. For a full picture of this duality, compare our explanation above of the name Elohim.

Tiferet is *wind*. It evaporates water and extinguishes fire—in other words, it balances the opposition between Ḥesed and Gevurah.

Malkhut is earth, soil. As the lowest of the Sefirot, its symbol is terrestrial existence. Akin to these is the symbolism of the metals: silver, which is white, thus represents Ḥesed; gold, which has a reddish tint, is Gevurah; brass, tin, lead, mercury and iron. Other divisions also exist.

COLORS

The colors of the spectrum serve as kabbalistic symbols as well,[88] although not everyone agrees on what each one represents. Keter is usually portrayed as supernal whiteness or snow as the epitome of purity, just as Keter's place is the highest point of the tree. Ḥokhmah is Lebanon (Song of Songs 3:9), the azure of the sky. Binah is green.[89] Ḥesed is white because it indicates water and light. The High Priest, when clothed in the "white vestments" for his divine service, represents that Sefirah as well. Gevurah is red, like fire, but at times also black, in the role of the forces of judgment that punish and darken the destiny of those subject to that Sefirah.

The colors of certain pairs mentioned in the Bible, such as milk and wine, and silver and gold, may recall those of Ḥesed and Gevurah.

Tiferet is purple, a combination of colors, as it is central in the Sefirotic system. Malkhut is azure (in Hebrew, *tekhelet*, from the root *kol*), suggesting its all-containing nature, as we said above. Yet it may also be black, signifying the absence of color or of its own light; in addition, it is a miniature form of Gevurah in its attribute of *din*.

Another color division may be found in the writings of R. 'Azriel in his interpretation of the ten Sefirot. In it Keter is disappearing light (i.e., a color invisible to human eyes); Ḥokhmah is azure *(tekhelet),* containing all the colors. Binah is green; Ḥesed is white; Gevurah is red; Tiferet is a combination of white and red; Nezah is whitish red; Hod is reddish white. Yesod is a mixture of the four colors above it, and Malkhut is an "amalgam of all colors."

THE POINTS OF THE COMPASS

These, too, symbolize Sefirot. The concepts are based on the geography of the Land of Israel. When a person faces east he looks toward Tiferet, the sun. His back is turned toward "the uttermost sea" (Deut. 11:24) in the west, or toward Malkhut.

When he stretches his arms to the sides, his right hand faces south. In Hebrew, this direction may be called *teiman*, *negev*, or *darom*; the word *yamin* means "right" (compare Ps. 89:13: "The north and the south *[yamin],* You have created them"). Indeed, the right hand signifies help and aid, and is therefore a symbol of Ḥesed. His left hand points toward the north, which in the Bible is sometimes called "left" *(smol),* as in Gen. 14:15. Jeremiah prophesies that "Out of the north, evil shall break forth" (Jer. 1:14), and "the northern one" mentioned in Joel 2:20 is a harbinger of evil as well. North is thus an appropriate symbol of Gevurah.

Just as east and west relate, as a pair, to Tiferet and Malkhut so north and south, along with their symbols, often function as a pair. According to the Talmud, for example (*Yoma* 33b), in the Tabernacle the menorah was placed on the southern side and the table on the northern. The lamp symbolizes light, Ḥesed, and is thus in the south. The table, on the other hand, symbolizes wealth, gold, the color of Gevurah. Consistent with this is another talmudic source (*Babba Batra* 25b): "He who wishes to become wise should face south; he who wishes to become wealthy should face north." We might add that Ḥesed is below Ḥokhmah (wisdom) on the tree of the Sefirot, and hence the connection implied between gaining wisdom and facing south. Moreover, the south is often used as a symbol of the place where sages live. Thus, for instance, we find the expression in the *Zohar* III, fol. 10a, "Our colleagues who dwell in the south." Perhaps it is also relevant that kabbalistic teaching developed in a number of southern locations, such as France, Morocco, and Yemen.

Religio-ethical symbols are also related to Ḥesed and Gevurah, such as love and awe.

BIBLICAL FIGURES

Another important symbolic system, this one in the realm of moral attributes, concerns famous personalities. It is also related to the tradition in the *Zohar* of the seven guests *(ushpizin),* who visit, each on a successive day of the festival of Sukkot, an individual worthy of such an honor. In order, Abraham symbolizes Ḥesed (Micah 7:20), for it was he who succeeded in most fully realizing that attribute in his lifestyle. In the words of R. Isaac of Acre: "The body of Abraham our forefather was pure, for he was prepared to receive the brilliant radiance of God's Ḥesed, and he became clad in it, as if *he were it and it were he*."[90]

Isaac symbolizes Gevurah, after the phrase (Gen. 31:42): "The Fear of Isaac." It is important to remember that in early Kabbalah, fear *(paḥad)* was one of the most common appellations of Gevurah.

Jacob symbolizes Tiferet. The figure of Jacob was understood as mediating between the first two Patriarchs. The name Yisrael sometimes also serves as a designation for Tiferet.

Moses is Nezah; Aaron is Hod. It should come as no surprise that the younger precedes the elder, as temporal and spacial dimensions have no significance on the spiritual-symbolic level; they are a function of our world alone.

Joseph is Yesod. Historically, Joseph lived before Moses and Aaron, yet this, too, is inconsequential. Joseph won the distinction of maintaining sexual purity against assault (Genesis 39), and in the Midrash (*Genesis Rabbah, Vayigash*), the rabbis gave him the name of Joseph the Righteous *(Yosef ha-Ṣaddik). Ṣaddik,* we recall, corresponds with the Sefirah of Yesod, as does the male sexual member, the sign of the Covenant.

The last of the figures is David, the symbol of royalty for the Jewish nation. He is associated with royalty both in the well-known phrase used in the prayer sanctifying the New Moon, in which the moon is compared to kingship ("David, King of Israel, lives on") and in the aggadic tradition[91] that Adam gave David all seventy years of his life as a gift. David, then, is portrayed as an impoverished figure in need of help from others, and he is like Malkhut, which has no autonomous source of light.

At times, the three Sefirot of Ḥesed, Gevurah, and Tiferet are indicated through the triad Kohen (the priest, symbolized by whiteness, as we said above), Levi (see Exod. 32:26–28), and Israel. We should take this opportunity to point out that the three *maṣot* mentioned in the Passover seder as corresponding to Kohen, Levi, and Israel actually refer to the three Sefirot in question.

The three Patriarchs, with the addition of David, are sometimes spoken of as "the four legs of the throne" in the prophet Ezekiel's vision of the Divine Chariot. Indeed, the "higher chariot" sometimes serves to designate the world of *aṣilut,* while the various Sefirot are "parts of the Chariot" *(pirkei ha-merkavah).* A particularly relevant prooftext of this idea for the Kabbalists was the midrashic statement: "The Patriarchs themselves are the Chariot" (*Genesis Rabbah*, 47).

We must remember, though, that all this is no simple symbolic approach, but is rather bound up with practical conclusions putting great emphasis on the value of actions. For example, a poor person symbolizes the Shekhinah, for both of them are dependent on what others give them. Thus, "He who holds the hand of a poor man and deals charitably with him, it is as if he makes peace *along with the Holy One blessed be He*" (*Zohar Ḥadash*, Midrash Ruth, fol. 26d).[92] In other words, he engenders harmony and union in the upper worlds, as well as causing abundance to flow down to our lower world.

Thus, a radical change took place once it became possible to speak of God through the doctrine of the Sefirot, which claimed wide horizons for itself using the principle of symbolism. Many restrictions suddenly seemed lifted, and freedom was granted to compare creatures to their Creator, to make use of such a wide variety of examples that the fundamental tenet of the Jewish faith risked being driven into obscurity. Without any doubt, this is a danger that darkens the doorstep of people who have glimpsed the esoteric world but have not fully contemplated or comprehended its hidden wealth; suspicions of personalizing the Divine are palpable. For these reasons, we find numerous warnings voiced by the Kabbalists not to take their words literally. I will offer only two examples. R. Menaḥem Recanati, in his commentary on the pericope *Vayeḥi*, writes:

> And you, son of Man, when you see statements . . . teaching of personalization, beware and be not led to iniquity, guard your soul well, that you not falter and destroy the world by saying God has material attributes that can be described and defined. This, heaven forfend, is absolutely untrue. "To whom would you liken God, or what likeness would you compare to Him?' (Isa. 40:18)

During approximately the same period, R. Isaac of Acre, in his book *Meirat 'Eynaim,* wrote: "God forbid that you should think any of these matters or forms are actually present in heaven. For not a single aspect of all the forms inherent in human beings exists there—all is intellectual light, devouring fire—but the Torah spoke in the language of the people."[93]

Some Kabbalists with a philosophical bent sought a conceptual interpretation of various symbols. Their attempt, though, ended more or less in failure, because symbols are laden with much more content and significance than can be expressed in conceptual terms. To shrug off the bounds of conceptual language—that, in effect, was the Kabbalists' original desire. Thus we find Kabbalists, particularly the author of the *Zohar* and R. Isaac Luria, unreservedly and "innocently" describing matters entangled in symbols and mythic figures of the most radical nature. As Isaiah Tishby has shown, tension between these two approaches, "personalization" and "abstraction," has existed throughout the history of Kabbalah, one or the other temporarily gaining the upper hand.[94]

In our survey of basic motifs, we mentioned a long list of symbols, yet have explored only a few of them. Common to all those we mentioned is their nature as definitively affirmative, even material names. This, again, is in complete contrast to the expression "'Eiyn Sof." That multiplicity of names demonstrates, on one hand, how far we are from an adequate portrayal of the divine realm; on the other hand, it evinces the aspiration to come to know, to grasp, and to express that understanding as fully as we can.

Indeed, the Kabbalists themselves wrote tracts such as the "Commentary on the Ten Sefirot;"[95] their primary intent was to interpret the various names of each Sefirah in order and to present the particular meaning of each Sefirah. Some Kabbalists truly outdid themselves in this endeavor, noting a multitude of names and even indicating the various internal relationships among the Sefirot, as well as many other motifs.

There were Kabbalists who even compiled quasi-dictionaries of kabbalistic terms. Some of them were arranged according to content, such as *Toledot Adam* by R. Joseph of Ḥamadan, published in *Sefer ha-Malkhut*; *Shekel ha-Kodesh* by R. Moses de Leon; *Ma'arekhet ha-Elohut* by an anonymous author, chapters 3–7; *Sod Ilan ha-Aṣilut* by R. Isaac; *Sefer ha-Shorashim* by R. Joseph ibn Waqqar (unpublished).

Others of these works were arranged after the order of the Sefirot, as, for example, those texts mentioned above that were devoted to an explication of the Sefirot. Of particular importance are *Sha'arey Orah* and *Sha'arey Ṣedek* by R. Joseph Gikatilla;[96] *Sefer ha-Shem*, attributed to Moses de Leon and published in the book *Heikhal ha-Shem*; and *Ma'arekhet ha-Elohut*, especially chapter 4. The Yemenite composition *Leḥem Shelomo* (ed. M. Ḥalamish), Gate II, followed *Ma'arekhet ha-Elohut*, as did the sixth section of *Netivot ha-Emunah* by R. Yaḥya Ḥarazi (Benayahu MS T29).

There is an alphabetical cataloged list in *Mafteḥot 'Arakhey ha-Kinnuyim* by R. Solomon ha-Kohen (Jerusalem, 1890). A work by Elijah Peretz, *Ma'alot ha-Zohar*, has recently been published; it treats different works individually. Mention should also be made of the indexes at the end of *Perush ha-Aggadot* by R. 'Azriel (ed. I. Tishby) and at the end of *Perush Parashat Bereshit Rabbah* (ed. M. Ḥalamish).

The book *Mafteḥot ha-Zohar* (Venice, 1744) by Israel Berakhiah Fontanila has its first section organized by subject in alphabetical order. Also in alphabetical order is *Sha'ar 'Arakhey ha-Kinnuyim*, which is Gate XXIII of R. Moses Cordovero's seminal work, *Pardes Rimmonim*. After this work came alphabetical dictionaries based on Lurianic teaching. These include: *Me'orot Natan* by R. Meir Poppers; *Ya'ir Nativ,* which contains important notes on *Me'orot Natan* compiled by R. Nathan Net'a Mannheim; *Sefat Emet* by R. Menaḥem 'Azariah de Fano; *'Arakhey ha-Kinnuyim* by R. Yeḥiel Halperin; *Kehilat Ya'akov* by R. Jacob Ṣevi Yoelish; *'Eden mi-Kedem* (Fez, 1940) by R. Raphael Moses Elbaz; and *Regel Yesharah* by R. Ṣevi Elimelekh Shapira, a Hasidic leader. Another Hasidic work is *Or 'Eynayim* by R. Eleazar Ṣevi Safrin; and finally, there is *Yad Eliyahu* by Aaron David Slotki. Other important works are *Mevo Petaḥim* at the end of *Shomer Emunim* by R. Joseph Ergas, which also deals mainly with Lurianic names, and *Yashresh Ya'akov* by R. Jacob Ṣevi Yoelish. The work *Ohel Mo'ed*, written in the first years of the sixteenth century, should also be mentioned, as it is a lucid introduction to kabbalistic teaching; it is, however, still hidden away in Cambridge MS 673, fol. 13–55 (written in Cairo in Nissan 1559).

A list of symbols and names, as well as commandments related to each Sefirah, can be found at the end of *Midrash Talpiyyot*, 'Anaf "kinnui."[97] The works *Yalkut Re'uveni* and *Yalkut Ḥadash* are also somewhat helpful.

In recent years, indexes to the *Zohar* have been compiled according to concept or subject, such as: *Aderet Eliyahu* by R. Aaron David Slotki; *Oṣar ha-Zohar ha-Shalem* by R. Daniel Frisch; and *Mafteḥot ha-Zohar ve-Ra'ayonotav* by R. Ḥayyim David ha-Levi. An important aid is *The Wisdom of the Zohar* by I. Tishby, arranged by subject. The work of Reuben Margaliot, *Sha'arey Zohar* can also be used—at the end is an index by subject. *Perakim be-Millon Sefer ha-Zohar*, by Y. Liebes, is an extremely detailed work yet contains only selected subjects, and may well be helpful.

A concordance of the *Heikhalot* literature has recently been compiled by Peter Schaefer, entitled *Konkordanz zur Hekhalot-literatur* (Tübingen, 1986).

Other indexes have been arranged by biblical verse. The earliest of these is *Mafteḥot ha-Zohar*, mentioned above. Another very useful source is *Beit Aharon ve-Hosafot* by Abraham David Lavat, which presents numerous rabbinic and kabbalistic sources indexed by verse.

Some descriptions include diagrams as well, a number of them corresponding to specific kabbalistic theories. I will list only a few of them. In manuscript form: *Ilan ha-Ḥokhmah ve-'Igul ha-Sefirot*, composed in Rome in 1284, still extant only in Paris MS 763. The "tree of the Sefirot"[98] is drawn on a very large page, and surrounding it are explications of various kabbalistic terms. The work was copied in another manuscript in Venice in 1533. Other diagrams are inserted in the catalog *Ohel Ḥayyim*,[99] in *Sod ha-Ilan* by R. Meir Poppers, and at the end of *Sefer Naftali*.

'EIYN SOF AND REVELATION

As we have said, the ten Sefirot are revealed in the emanative process. Understandably, the Kabbalists were compelled to ask some vital theoretical questions concerning the catalyst of that process.

First of all, the act of emanation, which radiates effulgence to levels beneath it, would seem to cause a state of lack or deficit in the source. One response to the problem could be found in the midrashic analogy: "When one candle is lit from another, the first candle is not diminished." Emanation engenders no change in the emanating source itself.

Various explanations of the primary transition from 'Eiyn Sof to the following phase were offered in the earliest stages of kabbalistic teaching. The first Kabbalists, such as the author of the *Bahir*, speak of "Thought" as a primordial act in the process of Creation, although implicit even in thought is the element of infinity, as R. Isaac the Blind stressed. Yet at a later stage, particularly in the teaching of his student, R. 'Azriel, the status of thought was diminished; it was now identified with the second Sefirah, Ḥokhmah, which plans the process of Creation. The place formerly occupied by thought as the initiator of the process was taken over by "will" *(raṣon)*. Under the influence, apparently, of Solomon ibn Gabirol, will came to be perceived as the source of all, and as the active element in the process of Creation. Will represents a directed and intentional action on the part of the Emanator, which by force brings him "closer" to the world, watching over it and responding to man's appeals to him.

The Kabbalists were intensely engaged in the task of defining the status of will with precision. Some saw it as a primary element, as we have said, engendered along with the very process of emanation. Others considered it to be as primordial as 'Eiyn Sof, thereby concluding that the emanative process began with the second Sefirah, which they thus called *reshit* (beginning), as discussed above. In any case, the relationship between 'Eiyn Sof and the Sefirot is treated from the perspective of the relationship between 'Eiyn Sof and the first Sefirah.

The problem of this relationship may also be formulated in another way: What factor causes emanation. Does 'Eiyn Sof participate actively in the process of emanation? In effect, 'Eiyn Sof could remain concealed and still be a personal God connected to entities outside of himself. Hence the role of the Sefirotic system, which serves as a bridge between 'Eiyn Sof and the world. The only way to understand the relationship between 'Eiyn Sof and the world is through figurative language. One of the most famous analogies, to which we will return later, is that of body and soul. The soul is unknowable, utterly spiritual. It acts in a variety of ways by means of the body, which is its instrument, and we have no conception of how it acts. Similarly, 'Eiyn Sof remains passive and unchanging; its instruments alone are active. Each "instrument" *(keli)* is responsible for a different sphere of divine activity. This means that although they are not 'Eiyn Sof, they nonetheless embody within themselves the infinite essence of the Divine. But if we wish to keep any such action separate from 'Eiyn Sof,[100] "crediting" it to the first Sefirah—what will be the status of that Sefirah among the other Sefirot? That question—whose concerns are essentially philosophical and theoretical, such as the desire to prevent the transition in 'Eiyn Sof from non-emanator to emanator—received no unanimous answer. For example, in various places R. Joseph ben Shalom Ashkenazi clearly grants Keter supremacy over the ten Sefirot. Yet "nothing differentiates between it and its cause but that one is cause and the other caused."[101] At times they are considered to be identical. For instance, "The most outstanding and profound thinkers have agreed that the supernal Keter should truly not be numbered among the ten, for it is like 'Eiyn Sof."[102] The first Sefirah is here conceived of as the emanator, while the nine below it are emanated. In any case, 'Eiyn Sof is directly bound up in the process of Creation. According to another opinion, 'Eiyn Sof is the emanator, and Keter the first emanated entity. In the responsa attributed to R. Joseph Gikatilla, a clear distinction was made between them. R. Meir ibn Gabbai also speaks of "those who misunderstand the teaching they have received, and say that Keter is 'Eiyn Sof."[103] The contention that the two are distinct became increasingly accepted from the sixteenth century onward.[104]

In the thirteenth century a compromise was suggested in which 'Eiyn

Sof is perceived as the emanator and Ḥokhmah the first emanated entity; Keter, which is not identical with 'Eiyn Sof, "acts as a kind of transitional stage, which has both the characteristic of the Emanator and the marks of emanation impressed upon it."[105] In this view, adopted by a few of the Kabbalists of Gerona, Ḥokhmah is thus held to be the first Sefirah, and in order to complete the sum of ten, Ḥokhmah is divided into two, and Haskel or Da'at are added. In Lurianic teaching, it is also usually said[106] that Keter is intermediate between the Emanator and the emanated entities, and Da'at is added. The contention is particularly widespread in the thought of R. Shneur Zalman of Lyady, the founder of Ḥabad Hasidism in the eighteenth century (the very name ḤaBaD is an acronym of the three Sefirot Ḥokhmah, Binah, and Da'at, and testifies to the centrality of that teaching in the Ḥabad worldview). In the works of R. Moses Cordovero, Keter is given the status of an intermediary between 'Eiyn Sof and the nine Sefirot, yet it is always presented as the first emanated entity.[107]

The conceptions outlined above serve more or less as a framework, for within each of them are additional differentiations and views. For instance, R. Joseph Gikatilla states in a few places that 'Eiyn Sof is identical with Keter, yet at the same time holds that Keter separates into various aspects, manifesting itself in the nine Sefirot it emanates.[108] The same is true in the *Zohar*. On one hand, 'Eiyn Sof and Keter are apparently not identical, yet Keter—conceived of as a sort of primordial essence, though different from 'Eiyn Sof—is not the first emanated entity. That distinction belongs to Ḥokhmah, which emerges from it. Nonetheless, Keter is numbered among the ten Sefirot. These things are not presented unequivocally in the text of the *Zohar* and, indeed, some Kabbalists interpreted them in the opposite way. R. Yehudah Ḥayyat, for instance, learns from the *Zohar* that even Keter is emanated.[109] R. Simeon ibn Lavi, in contrast, understands the *Zohar* differently; in his opinion, Keter is not emanated but emanates, and acts as an intermediary between the Emanator and the emanated entities.[110] Yet we should add that in R. Moses de Leon's Hebrew writings, the appellation Cause of Causes (*'illat ha-'illot; sibbat ha-sibbot)* alludes to Keter,[111] while in another work he writes: "The Cause of all Causes is the cause of Nothingness *[ayin],* which has no equal anywhere."[112] This implies that the Cause of Causes is 'Eiyn Sof. It could be, then, that de Leon himself is uncertain whether or not a distinction should be made between 'Eiyn Sof and Keter.

Because 'Eiyn Sof is hidden, it may be assumed that it does not participate directly in the process of emanation. Thus, as we have said, various intermediary stages exist: the Sefirot, and another stage even before the Sefirot themselves.

At times, the Kabbalists speak of the presence of three roots concealed in the depths of 'Eiyn Sof; these are called *ṣaḥṣaḥot*. They are conceived as three lights: primordial internal light *(or kadmon),* polished light *(or ṣaḥ),* and clear light *(or meṣuḥṣaḥ)*. These are so hidden as to be unattainable. Though originally linked, they represent an intermediary stage prior to the emanation of the Sefirot. This conception originates in a famous responsum attributed to R. Hai Gaon, but actually composed in the 'Iyyun circle.

Another position speaks of ten *ṣiḥṣuḥim* preceding Keter, which are none other than ten roots of the ten Sefirot. This idea, first expressed by R. David ben Yehudah he-Ḥasid, made its way into many kabbalistic works and influenced Lurianic teaching as well.[113] It also made its mark on the Kabbalists of North Africa, who flourished there after the expulsion from Spain. In any case, the purpose of this theory is to emphasize, on one hand, the gap between 'Eiyn Sof and the Sefirot; on the other hand, it stresses that the Sefirot originate in the depths of 'Eiyn Sof and its light.

ONENESS AND MULTIPLICITY

The presence of the Sefirot is the origin for all that exists in the lower worlds; it is the source of variety, difference, hierarchy, and the various processes unfolding in the cosmos. Indeed, though the Sefirot themselves are rooted in infinite oneness, they are empowered to function as a source of multiplicity: in that capacity, they exert a certain limited effect in Creation, and created entities are able to receive their action. The notion of divine providence, claims R. Moses Cordovero, can be explained through their changeability, and not through the Cause of Causes;[114] in his wake, it seems, R. Moses Ḥayyim Luzzatto stated:

> The Sefirot are His attributes . . . which He invented for the sake of His creatures . . . attributes engendered by His will and desire according to the needs of the creatures He wished to create, and they

> include all the aspects related to Him through His acts. . . . It must be understood, though, that while man's attributes are actually engraved in his soul, the same cannot be said of the Lord; we cannot say they are His qualities, for "qualities" apply only to created entities and not to the Creator. Rather, the attributes of the Creator can solely be forms of Providence and the light He casts on His creation.[115]

An active dynamic thus takes place within the Sefirot themselves. It is portrayed through various terms, such as *yiḥuda 'ila'a* (mystical unions). Even here we find gradations: the union of Ḥokhmah and Binah as father and mother is eternal, but the union of Tiferet and Malkhut as son and daughter is not eternal. Even the relationships among the Sefirot are variously described. In principle, there are ten Sefirot, yet each one contains something of all the others within it, like beams of light reflecting one another and creating the impression of tremendous multiplicity. The idea behind this image is that the division into Sefirot does not give way to true multiplicity; rather, each Sefirah embodies something of the nature of the others while maintaining its own unique identity.[116] In the phrase of R. Solomon Alkabez, of the sixteenth century:

> You must know, when the Kabbalists said that each of the Sefirot is composed of ten, do not suppose that every aspect found in one attribute, yet originating in another, belongs only to the attribute where it is found, separate and cut off from all the other Sefirot, heaven forbid. Rather, each and every aspect is embodied in all of them. (*Berit ha-Levi*, 41a)

In any case, there are highly complex internal divisions. These became even more complicated in descriptions in the *Idra* literature of *'attika kaddisha*, *'arikh anpin,* and z*'eir anpin*, particularly in commentaries on the *Idra Rabba* and *Idra Zuta* by R. Isaac Luria in his doctrine of the *parṣufim* (divine configurations). Another such division is that found in *Tefillat ha-Yiḥud* [Prayer of unification] of R. Neḥuniya ben ha-Kaneh, according to which there are 620 pillars of light in Keter (corresponding to the numerical sum of the letters of the word Keter), 32 paths of Ḥokhmah, 50 gates of Binah, 72 bridges of Ḥesed, etc.

That division, which reappears in partial or complete form in other works as well, is artificial to some extent, essentially based as it is on separate concepts drawn from earlier traditions. What is important, though, is the principle behind the division: the vital internal dynamic of the Sefirot, which is responsible for the complex dynamic of our own world.

The main point is that the Sefirot are interconnected, and joined to their source of emanation "as a flame is attached to a burning coal."[117] The flame appears in varicolored beams of light, yet all of them are inherent in the coal and sustained by it.

To the question of how multiplicity was generated from unity, and, most essentially, how the oppositions between them came to be, the Kabbalist would respond that, at their source, all are equal. R. 'Azriel asserts that Keter is "equal to all permutations of an entity." In the same manner, the seed of a tree is tiny, and contains no perceptible sign of internal oppositions; only when it grows and becomes a tree can one distinguish its multifaceted nature, comprising trunk, branches, fruit, leaves, flowers, etc. In an image in the first pages of *Sefer ha-Shem*:

> Regard the vine, from its roots to its branches and leaves and tendrils and clusters and grapes and seeds—clearly, each has its separate being. Yet in truth all are a unity, emerging from the root of the vine; all of them are intertwined with it, and when one grasps the vine all of them move together in his hand.

Similarly, R. Simeon ibn Lavi writes, "For a single heart may think one thing and its opposite,"[118] and only when that thought is realized do its contradictions become apparent. The images we have mentioned, and others like them, demonstrate that multiplicity and contrast are related phenomena that actively influence our world, though the root of all being is undifferentiated unity.

On the idea of internal unity despite the multiplicity inherent in unity, R. 'Azriel commented: "The essence of the Sefirah is equal in every entity and every opposite to that entity . . . their essence can be compared to the soul's will, which is manifest equally in all objects and all thoughts extending from it."[119] An appropriate image might be a candle. From its center, rays of light seem to scatter in all directions, yet that is only an optical illusion; the candle truly does not separate, though to our eyes it appears to. Similarly, says R. Moses Cordovero, when a man strikes flint, sparks of fire are emitted. The multiplicity of sparks and their differentiation from the stone hint at some hidden reality. The stone, in any case, is one despite the myriad forces emerging from it. We recall the image of the sun, a unity despite its diverse characteristics.[120] In a popular phrase drawn from *Sefer Yeṣirah*, "their end is fastened into their beginning, and their beginning into their end."

To stress the unity of the ten Sefirot, the Kabbalists adopted other images as well. It was said, "All the powers of the Holy One blessed be He are one upon the other, resembling a tree."[121] Hence the widespread term "the Sefirotic tree" (although the tree image is also used in early Gnostic thought). An even more common image is that of the human form (the internal divisions of which we have described above), which in essence includes both female and male, for "in the Lord's image He created them"; some also call it *shi'ur komah* (the divine man).[122]

The image of the candle serves an additional purpose. Although the Sefirot are emanated one from another, each is "as a candle lit from another; the first candle [the initial emanator] lacks nothing." In other words, no change occurs in the Emanator and his strength is not diminished, as suggested above. In this context, we recall Naḥmanides' interpretation of the verb *AṢL* which appears in Num. 11:17—"and I will take of the spirit *[aṣalti]* which is upon you [Moses] and put it upon [the seventy elders]." He relates the verb to the preposition "with" *(EṢL),* thereby implying that the Sefirot are not separate from the Emanator but rather that they act under his influence and are empowered by him.[123] The process of disintegration and differentiation from the divine realm thus begins only after the ten Sefirot, and the Kabbalists call this lower realm "the world of separated entities" *('olam ha-niPhRaDim)*, based on the verse in Gen. 2:10, "And a river went out from Eden to water the garden, and from thence it was parted *[yiPaReD]* and branched into four streams."

The disciples of R. Isaac the Blind, perhaps under his influence, used the expression "the essences preexisted, but the emanation was new."[124] This was meant to imply that the Sefirot were always potential in the Emanator, and at a certain point became actualized as they were emanated and thereby revealed. In that way their connection to the Divine is maintained. To express this idea, some Kabbalists also used the image of the flame and the coal mentioned above. This enabled them to avoid the problem with which other Kabbalists grappled—namely, just when the Sefirot were emanated. R. Moses Cordovero, for example, contended they were emanated "in a timeless time," i.e., in a dimension of time unknown to human experience.

The analogy of the Sefirot as a flame demands additional consideration. Examining the second part of the analogy, we realize that, in essence, the process of emanation (the flame's bursting forth) causes the emanator to become visible (for the coal, in and of itself, serves as no more than a base for the flame). But let us take an even more popular analogy, that of the garments. First of all, we have the midrash that speaks of *ten* garments worn by God.[125] Secondly, we have the widespread kabbalistic image of the relationship between the Emanator and the Sefirot as "like the locust whose garment is part of its body."[126] On one hand, the locust's "garment" is not separate from his substance, because it originates as part of his nature. On the other hand, there is nonetheless a difference between the locust and its "garment." The importance of this duality is its expression of the idea that although the Sefirot are part of God's essence, there is a differentiation between the emanated Sefirot and the Emanator clothed within them. In any case, the purpose of being clothed is to conceal the Emanator, and such a notion contradicts the above image of the flame. Two explanations may be offered to solve the conflict: First, in principle, every implication arising from an image may not necessarily be relevant.[127] Secondly, the contradiction is, in fact, relevant. For concealment makes revelation possible.

This brings us to another widespread analogy, that of the soul and the body. The soul is concealed within the body and functions through it; without the soul the body would be lifeless.[128] (As we saw above, this analogy also serves to elucidate the possibility of multiplicity acting out of unity.) We have now reached a vital question that, as R. Moses Cordovero testifies, has confused many: the issue of *'aṣmut* and *kelim*, or "essence and vessels."

ESSENCE AND VESSELS

What is the relationship of the Sefirot to the Emanator; is there some identity between them, or are they differentiated from the Emanator, serving only as his instruments? Are the Sefirot hypostases with real existence, or is their reality no more than nominal and intellectual? This latter possibility, of course, is akin to the philosophical view.[129] In any case, the problem is known in Kabbalah and in scholarly research as that of "essence and vessels" (*'aṣmut ve-kelim*).

Remember, in early Kabbalah, the Kabbalists' discussions of the nature of the divine were not philosophical ones. For that reason, theoretical questions that trouble us—or the Kabbalists themselves in later generations as they became more aware of the world of philosophical inquiry—are not exhaustively treated in those earlier tracts. At times we can only outline the issues based on what is extant in the sources, the full picture remaining incomplete; at other times, we find the Kabbalists, whose hearts throbbed with the whisperings of myth, expressing themselves freely, unencumbered by philosophical formulations.[130]

In the thirteenth century the Kabbalists had not yet used the terms "essence" and "vessels." Only at the end of the thirteenth century are the terms used by R. Menaḥem Recanati[131] as part of a wider discussion and presentation of his view of the Sefirot as vessels. A philosophical inquiry into the concept of essence is found in the early sixteenth century in the writings of R. David ben Yehudah Messer Leon.[132]

The extent to which the Kabbalists were unaware of the problem becomes apparent in an ambivalent formulation found in a commentary on the ten Sefirot originating in the 'Iyyun circle. The work, extant in manuscript form, was copied by Gershom Scholem; it speaks of the Sefirot being, on one hand, "the essence of the Holy One blessed be He, as it were," yet it also states that the Sefirot were created. Thus:

> The Sefirot are the essence of the Holy One blessed be He, as it were, like the fundamental elements of man inherent in man . . . for all of the Sefirot are *differentiated powers*, utterly simple, and they are all *divine glory, unseparated and undifferentiated*, though *in the aspect of their effects* which reach us [they seem to be differentiated]. And all these Sefirot were *created* by the Lord, blessed be His Name in His honor. All of them come together in a single unity. And all were called "soul" *[neshamah]*, while He is the soul of that soul.[133]

The first Kabbalist to use the term *kelim* (instruments, vessels, tools) was R. Asher ben David, in the thirteenth century, in speaking of "the craftsman and his tools."[134] R. Asher sought to respond to the accusation that the Kabbalists' writing style created the impression that the Sefirot were an autonomous unity, thereby implying they believed in a duality inherent in the divine. To that end, he offered two analogies in the attempt to prove the unity between 'Eiyn Sof and the Sefirot. The first is the image of the cluster of grapes. Intrinsic to the cluster itself are grapes, leaves, etc.—that is, a multiplicity and diversity of elements—yet a single source waters all the divisions of the vine. This watering, the fundamental lifeline of the cluster, is what finally transforms all the parts into a unity. The distinction, of course, between the "spring watering all" and the vine itself is clear. The same is true of the second analogy, that of the candlestick that stood in the Tabernacle in the desert and later in the Temple. The Bible describes the various parts of the menorah (Exod. 37), yet mandates it be fashioned of a single block of gold. The oil flows from the central shaft, spreading through all the other branches to their wicks. Though the oil is not an integral part of the candlestick, it sustains it and grants it meaning. The olive oil, like the spring, originates in an external entity and offers vitality. Clearly, then, a unity exists between the efflux emerging from the source and its reception in the vessels. We see that the Sefirot are receptacles for divine abundance, and though their light shines forth in diverse colors, the fundamental light uniting them is one.[135]

R. Menaḥem Recanati chose a different perspective. He reacted to the view expressed in the rabbinic composition, *Sefer ha-Ḥinukh*, which explicates the biblical commandments. In that work, the author argues that there is no connection between sin and recompense. Punishment, rather, is a sign of God's concealment as a result of sin, thus abandoning the sinner to the caprices of nature. Recanati disagrees and presents an analogy to illustrate his point. A king commands his two servants to observe his subjects and to recompense each individual for his behavior. The servants act autonomously, yet in accordance with a preestablished order. In the same way, "The Creator blessed be He empowers His attributes to act, yet His own action remains unaltered; it is the attributes that act."[136] At the same time, multiplicity is an inherent aspect of the Sefirot due to the diversity of their effect. Hence "the Creator's essence is indivisible." Clearly, then, the ten Sefirot are not his essence, but only instruments. They did radiate or "spark" from the light of 'Eiyn Sof, yet they serve as servants or as a craftsman's tools, a means through which the higher will of 'Eiyn Sof is actualized. 'Eiyn Sof is the source of their substance, and his essence flows forth through them. Thus the *kelim* serve both as instruments and as vessels receiving infinite divine light. In that way they differ fundamentally from the tools of the human craftsman, which exist independently from him.

Recanati was aware that Kabbalists of his time disagreed with him, and this led him, apparently, to try to buttress his view. Although the text of the *Zohar* proper could not substantiate his argument, the later sections of *Ra'aya Meheimna* and *Tikkuney Zohar* did support his view (though he may not have been familiar with them) that the Sefirot are vessels that the artisan may even break without harming the water they contain. These vessels were created as *tikkunim* (regulators) of the world's order.[137]

The various analogies presented thus far point to the indisputable and real precedence of 'Eiyn Sof vis-à-vis the Sefirot, which are ontologically different from his essence. The utter simplicity of a transcendent God may thus be preserved without attributing diverse actions to him. No difficulty arises from seeing the Sefirot/vessels as "attributes of action."

This basic view of *kelim*[138] was shared by Kabbalists such as R. 'Ezra of Gerona,[139] R. Yehudah Ḥayyat, and R. Yoḥanan Alemanno. R. Abraham ben Eliezer ha-Levi, who arrived in the Land of Israel in the second decade of the sixteenth century, deserves particular mention for his affirmation, "They are not He and He is not them." Audible in his words is a polemic against the formulation in the *Zohar* itself.[140]

Interestingly enough, it was Recanati who first mentioned the term '*aṣmut* (essence),[141] although the concept itself was already present in the thirteenth century in most of the Kabbalists' writings. The term serves to affirm that the Sefirot have no ontological status but are rather the extension of what was hidden in 'Eiyn Sof, "a revelation of that sealed and concealed power, emerging from potentiality to actuality."[142] In a later formulation, it is said that their being can be probed only "from the perspective of the receivers." By such a statement, the charge that the Kabbalists addressed their prayers to various Sefirot, separate from 'Eiyn Sof, was proven to be unfounded.

As we have said, the Kabbalists did not initially conduct philosophical discussions defining the Sefirot as essence. Thus we hear various formulations, such as the definitive statement of the *Zohar:* "He is they and they are He" (III, fol. 70a), or the affirmation voiced by the author of *Ma'arekhet ha-Elohut:* "The 'laborers' [Kabbalists], in their study, have received the knowledge that the Godhead is the emanation of the ten Sefirot, which are manifest as attributes and order in the lower world."[143] This, then, was the majority view,[144] adopted by prominent Kabbalists, and it gained popularity among Kabbalists throughout the second half of the fifteenth and the early sixteenth centuries. For example, R. Isaac Mor Ḥayyim, a Spanish Kabbalist who resided in Italy in 1491 and apparently settled later in the Land of Israel, stated unequivocally: "The Holy One blessed be He created the world through no medium aside from Himself and His truth." All of being, in other words, is the Creator's essence, and even the Sefirot have no separate existence.[145]

Conflicts between thinkers holding such disparate views began to arise. To present the conflicts as occurring exclusively between two diametrically opposed factions would be unfair. Certain differences existed even between Kabbalists belonging to the *kelim* school, and likewise between those belonging to the *'aṣmut* school.

The concept of essence *('aṣmut)* raises various questions. For instance, if the *Zohar* stresses that the Sefirot are essence, virtually united with the Emanator, while the lower realms are completely separate *('alma de-peruda)*, how can one speak of divine immanence in our world? Indeed, it is not a matter of the dispersion of divine essence but rather of the Shekhinah's presence in the lower worlds.[146] Another question relates to the significance of the Sefirot themselves—if they have no reality, what are they? It seems that even the proponents of essence did not contend that the Sefirot are devoid of real content or existence. In their eyes, the Sefirot should be regarded as real entities. This view does indeed lead to the question of the Emanator's unity, for the Sefirot are his essence. That problem, though, did not trouble the Kabbalists, at least not overtly; they remained willing to accept the Sefirot in all their paradoxicality. Let us compare Maimonides' position, as presented by Ephraim Gottlieb:

> It appears that in philosophical thought as in Kabbalah, the problem of multiplicity within the Divine cannot be resolved through a denial of positive substance. Rather, it must be assumed that the entirety of the various positive qualities are paradoxically united in God, and form a unity with His essence. It is a unity of subject and object, and a unity among the myriad objects. If we indicate any particular quality of God, it is only to make our point more intelligible; in truth, all qualities are identical.[147]

An alternative solution to the problem of change occurring within God, a problem that burdened the proponents of essence, was proposed by R. Joseph Karo in the sixteenth century. In his view, the Sefirot are essence and thus wholly unchanging. Indeed, the Kabbalists' statements regarding change relate to the lowest level of the tenth Sefirah, Malkhut, which he calls the Shekhinah. Thus R. Joseph Karo makes a vital distinction between two domains while adopting existing kabbalistic terms. Essentially, we can speak of change only regarding the Shekhinah, in the "feminine world," and not regarding any of the Sefirot, even Malkhut.

Other discussions of the subject may be found in the works of R. David Messer Leon and R. Meir ibn Gabbay.[148]

A multifaceted debate was aroused in the sixteenth century by R. Moses Cordovero, who directed a number of important arguments against both positions. In brief, he opposes Recanati with a theological contention that the latter robs God of action and estranges knowledge of God from himself, placing it entirely in the domain of the Sefirot. "God forsakes the world to the hand of His attributes," as he says. He also opposes the assumption likely to arise from the concept of essence that the Sefirot are a substantial extension of the Emanator's essence. This despite the fact that a nominalistic outlook mitigates, in effect, the theosophical significance of the Sefirot, rendering meaningless the notions of mystical unions, intention in prayer, and spiritual cleaving. In that manner, R. Moses Cordovero sought to strike a compromise between the two positions.

In his view, the Sefirot may be considered essence only in the sense of 'Eiyn Sof spreading through them and animating them, and for that reason they are not separate from him. "He and they—all form a complete unity." However, no interaction or differentiation of cause and effect exists between them until they are considered as *kelim*. The essence of 'Eiyn Sof exists equally in all and extends outward without engendering change. Yet it expands into a certain framework, and that framework is the *keli* (vessel). The *keli*, in the sense of a receptacle, is what limits essence and gives it a particular nature. Each Sefirah has its own uniqueness. R. Moses Cordovero offers five analogies with varied nuances to illustrate his point. The first is of water poured into glass vessels of different colors. In each, the water appears to have a different color, though in truth it remains unaltered. The second is of light and lanterns. Rays of light pass through lanterns with tinted glass and appear to change color. The third concerns body and soul. Though the soul is present in all the limbs, it manifests itself differently in each one. Each has its own function, despite the unity of the soul's essence. The same is true of the Sefirot, each with its separate nature. What is special in this analogy is the spiritual quality of the soul, making it particularly apt to illustrate the role of the Sefirot.

R. Moses Cordovero sensed the affinity between this view and pantheism, and this led him to add the rejoinder: "God is omnipresent, yet everything in existence is not God." Essence is indeed instilled in every entity, but that does not imply its identicalness with every one of its vessels. The lower one descends within the Sefirotic system, the more distant the connection between essence and the vessel becomes. This graduation exists in the vessel alone; essence remains unaltered. "He is in all and all is in Him, and nothing is void of His presence." What varies is only the mode of revelation.

The question of essence and vessels, which concerns not only the Sefirot but the very formation of the worlds, was a seminal issue for medieval thinkers. R. Moses Cordovero's solution that the Emanator acts, as it were, in the manner of a living organism, by means of both essence and vessels, apparently relieved some of their distress. Even R. Isaac Luria largely assimilated that view, while making some changes to adapt it to his own system.

Another approach, developed by a few Kabbalists of North Africa, should also be mentioned. R. Simeon ibn Lavi, a commentator on the *Zohar*, contends that the Sefirot are essence. For example, "All the attributes of God are called by the appellation 'the Holy One blessed be He' because they are part of His holy essence."[149] Yet he does not refrain from introducing analogies that present the Sefirot as vessels. It may be that R. Simeon Lavi, like R. Jacob Iffargan (author of an extensive commentary on the Torah entitled *Minḥah Ḥadashah*, Liverpool MS 12044, written in 1619) perceived the Sefirot as series. It is the higher series—also called *ṣiḥṣuḥim* (as in the teaching of R. David ben Yehudah he-Ḥasid, an Ashkenazic Kabbalist who lived in Spain and North Africa) or *sefirot de-'aṣilut* (the Sefirot of emanation)—that is seen as essence. The lower Sefirot, in contrast, serve as their vessels, apparently in the sense suggested by R. Moses Cordovero.

As we conclude, I would like to remark that this debate among the Kabbalists whether the Sefirot are essence or vessels was ridiculed in a work by one of the most prominent thinkers of the Haskalah (Enlightenment), Samuel David Luzzatto.[150]

Thus far, we have described the doctrine of the Sefirot in its classic form, as a direct development originating in the Emanator (whether by means of other forces such as *ṣaḥṣaḥot* or without them). Indeed, some Kabbalists[151] use as a prooftext a famous statement in the midrash *Genesis Rabbah* concerning the worlds created before our world and destroyed by their Creator. They combine that text with the biblical narrative of "the kings that reigned in the land of Edom" who died "before there reigned any king over the children of Israel" (Gen. 36:31ff.); the *Zohar* honored them with the title "ancient kings" *(malkhin kadma'in)*. Those Kabbalists were part of the circle centered around the brothers Isaac and Jacob ha-Kohen in Castile in the thirteenth century. They give a radical description of the harsh powers of judgment that were initially emanated; because of their redness (implied in the word *edom* [red]), symbolizing their sternness as judges, the world could not survive. Thus, "It was decreed that such emanation would no longer come into the world." A "sweetening" or mitigation *(hamtakah)* of that harsh judgment was needed, and came about when harmony was achieved between male and female—i.e., when a complete and properly formed Adam Kadmon was created. We must point out that in this description the gentle nature of the feminine is restored to the female image, while in many other kabbalistic descriptions, woman is portrayed as *din* (judgment) and a constriction of abundance.

The above portrayal of Ur-worlds destroyed in prehistoric time serves, on one hand, to explain the existence of evil, presented once again by Isaac and Jacob ha-Kohen in gnostic and mythic terms and pungent with the odor of dualism. On the other hand, it is a gesture of subordination to the world of holiness. The concept of evil in kabbalistic thought will be our central concern in the next chapter.

10 • Good and Evil

A description of the divine realm would be incomplete without some consideration of its reversal or negation, the realm of evil. The presence of evil and of suffering is an existential concern that has stimulated people throughout the ages to formulate diverse and sometimes bizarre conceptions; it is also, however, a philosophical and theological question of the first order that has interested Jewish and non-Jewish thinkers alike. Indeed, it is not difficult to find fundamentally pessimistic views assigning a separate source for good and for evil; in these views, the two opposing forces are engaged in a continual cruel struggle for survival. This battle, which seems to transpire on the divine plane, has parallels on the cosmological and human levels. Entire myths were invented describing heroic battles between the gods of good and evil and their allied forces. Some worldviews are patently dualistic, while others gesture only obliquely toward dualism. There are other, fundamentally optimistic views, however, which emphasize the positive reality of the good as divinely created and confront the question of evil in various ways. In any case, the nature of evil is a central dilemma treated with great seriousness in the world of kabbalistic thought. That, in fact, constitutes one noticeable difference between the Kabbalah and philosophy—the latter has treated the question of evil and its source much less extensively.

The problem of evil is of major concern in every monotheistic worldview. How can the existence of evil be explained if the Creator is a benevolent God and the source of goodness? Does this internal opposition not compromise his unity and completeness in some way? If evil is, in essence, a matter of defect and deficit, how could God's completeness be lacking? What is the place of evil in the world?

The question is usually approached in kabbalistic thought from two perspectives:

1. Using the Divine as a starting point—what is the relationship between evil and the divine realm of intrinsic goodness? How does evil correspond with God in its origin, status, role, and effect?

2. Using man as a starting point—how does humankind deal with evil? What influence does evil exert upon man? How should he react to it? Is evil not a reflection of injustice? Does evil appear only in a human framework, or does it have a place in some realm beyond man?

These two perspectives often intermingle in the attempt to describe the problem and propose a solution. Before we explore the world of Kabbalah on this subject, let us review some of the views that preceded it.

In the Bible, God is portrayed as "Former of light and creator of darkness, maker of peace and creator of evil" (Isa. 45:7). The world is thus seen as the handiwork of a benevolent God, and he, in his thought and plan, assigned a role and a place for evil. Evil is nothing but a medium through which God attains his benevolent ends. In that way, the problem of evil becomes a moot point, although the question of divine recompense does remain—why do the wicked flourish while the righteous suffer?[1]

The Neoplatonic worldview, which exerted a tremendous influence on Christian mysticism, held that the world originated in supreme goodness. The light descends from that source and through emanation forms the lower worlds, but in the process it gradually darkens and becomes more dense. In its final nullification, it becomes matter, which is evil in its essence; in other words, what was formerly light is no longer an entity, for it has no existence—rather, it is the *absence* of light and goodness. Our world is the world of matter, and a place devoid of light is naturally filled with darkness. This, therefore, does not contradict the perception of the Divine as a sublime and complete entity. The Neoplatonic view is fundamentally monistic, brimming with the optimism that in truth, our world is good and its source is goodness.

Gnosticism, in contrast, influenced by Persian religious views, is dualistic. It contends the existence of two autonomous realms. Evil is a real and destructive force; our world is the kingdom of the lord of evil, the Demiurge. In opposition is the lord of good, represented by the human soul. Man's role is to free the soul, a spark of goodness, from its enslavement to the lord of evil. Gnosticism did offer a solution to the philosophical and theological problem, but it placed man in the throes of a continual and terrible struggle.

Postbiblical Judaism opposes both these theories. It recognizes the existence of the power of evil, yet sees it as an instrument through which the world is controlled and a means to attaining ultimate goodness. "Light can be perceived only within darkness"—this declaration was voiced by many in a variety of forms.[2] Evil acts as a divine messenger and is subject to God's will. As for man, before him are good and evil, and the free choice between them is his.[3]

This is the general attitude. Maimonides, however, a giant of Jewish thought, took the path of the Neoplatonists. Evil, for him, has no autonomous existence, but is rather the absence of good, just as darkness is an absence of light.[4] Evil action cannot be attributed to God, for his role is solely to bring realities into existence. "And all that He did—it was very good" (Gen. 1:31). Human experience, however, does not seem to correspond with such a view. Emptiness and absence have no power, and yet most people intuitively feel and believe that evil does have some real existence. For that reason, most Jewish philosophers did not adopt the position of the *Guide to the Perplexed* on that subject.

The Kabbalists, for the most part, did not accept the Neoplatonic view. One work that did express some sympathy for it is *Ma'arekhet ha-Elohut*, which says:

> He who chooses a twisted path and allows himself to become alienated from the goodness ordained by the Lord receives the opposite, which was *also* decreed by Him. Yet from the *perspective of God*, nothing evil or impure comes from heaven.[5]

Later in the same work, however, in a discussion of the lowest Sefirah, a kabbalistic view similar to that of the Geronese Kabbalists is presented; we will examine it more closely in the following pages. It contends that the source of evil is in Gevurah, and from that Sefirah onward there is a *mixture* of good and evil.[6]

The Kabbalists usually held that evil does have some actual existence in the world, and that its spiritual roots are planted in a higher realm. They spoke incisively of the two forces and unhesitatingly portrayed evil in somber colors as a power battling with good and with those aspiring to goodness. Their treatment of evil, though, is not homogeneous; various problems are approached in diverse ways.

In the *Bahir*, for instance, the problem is not approached systematically, as the work itself is homiletical rather than systematic in nature. Yet the figurative language and the images it uses suggest that both good and evil are attributes of the Creator—right and left hands, as it were; both are emissaries of God, although the role of evil is not clearly defined. Even the "Satan" mentioned in the *Bahir*[7] is conceived as a seductive and accusing force while remaining within his role as emissary. He is called "evil," "left" *(smoll)*, and "north" *(ṣafon)*—names with clearly negative connotations. Evil is thus not absence, devoid of reality, yet it is not an autonomous entity either. Its power is equal to that of the good; it does not stand in opposition to the Divine, and does not exist outside of it.[8] A similar view was expressed by Ashkenazic Hasidim as well.

The question of how evil was engendered is a particularly serious one in the framework of kabbalistic thought, for the basic view is that all evolved from divine essence. The process of Creation out of nothingness *(yesh me-ayin)* was interpreted by the Kabbalists not as *creatio ex nihilo*, an evolution initiated in utter nothingness, but rather as emerging from Keter, the fullest Sefirah in the divine world. It is for this reason that the question of evil and its origin in absolute goodness arouses such serious and fundamental thought.

In the beginning of the thirteenth century, more profound and extensive discussions on the issue of evil were conducted. R. Isaac the Blind of Provence, in southern France, and his circle of disciples in Gerona, northern Spain, take another step in relating to the realm of evil. A verse from Ecclesiastes, "God has made one as well as the other" is commonly used as a prooftext for the conviction that evil, darkness and death have a positive origin within the divine world. The source of good and of evil is in the Sefirot of Ḥesed and Gevurah. This is the most widespread view.[9] Evil has real existence, yet is not an essential and substantial part of the divine world. The analogy is made to a vessel full to the brim, all the excess liquid spilling out of it. The divine unity in which good and evil are *enrooted* allows the attribute of judgment *(gevurah)* to exist for purposes such as punishing evildoers. As the evil deeds of mankind increase, so the power of judgment, emanated from the higher attribute of *din,* gains force in the world. Thus, here as well, evil is not an organic part of the Sefirotic world, although it originally emanated from the left aspect of the Sefirot, and a connection to its source does endure.

This stance, which was widely accepted and reinforced through various presentations, indeed solved the problem of dualism but did not answer the theological question of how evil emerged from a benevolent God. One thinker who did consider this question was R. Asher ben David (nephew of R. Isaac the Blind), who argued that the very assumption that the Emanator is complete and omnipotent mandates his being the source of evil as well. If he were not, some element could originate outside the Divine—and the assumption of his completeness and omnipotence would be undermined.[10] A second response, taking diverse forms throughout the generations, was to the effect that no distinction between good and evil is evident at their root, and only in their revelation in the world outside the Divine do they receive separate ontological status as opposing forces. This view, expressed by many Kabbalists, is founded on a simple esoteric assumption. Just as all of reality originates in the Divine and its existence outside the Divine is unlike its state within the Divine (in terms of multiplicity, complexity, change, etc.), so evil was not originally evil but became so after emerging from the Divine. In this approach, it is man who draws evil (or good) to himself, thereby empowering the force he has chosen. In essence, it is the law of free choice that is at work here. Evil exists for man's sake, so that he may negate it and by that act realize divine intention—to promote goodness in the world. We recall, in this context, R. Moses Ḥayyim Luzzatto's contention that evil was created so that the uniqueness of the Divine could be revealed in the overcoming of its opposite.[11] This takes place through man's own actions—the task is his to triumph over evil. Evil, in that case, has but imaginary existence.

A second association made by the Kabbalists of Gerona, and in the *Zohar* in their wake, is related to the esoteric view of the "Tree of Knowledge." In the Garden of Eden, the Tree of Life and the Tree of Knowledge were originally joined as a single entity; it was Adam who created the schism between them. His eating engendered a composite evil drawn from the Tree of Knowledge of Good and Evil and actualized in the "evil inclination" *(yeṣer ha-r'a)* now implanted in his heart. Thus it was the primordial Adam himself who gave form to the evil hidden in the Tree of

Knowledge by distinguishing it from the Tree of Life and by separating the fruit of the Tree of Knowledge from its source. This event is symbolically designated as "the cutting of the shoots" *(kiṣuṣ ba-neti 'ot),* the archetype of all sin. Every evil act is essentially perceived as bringing schism into the world of holiness. Primeval man's sin was in engendering "disunion above and below" in what was meant to be united. From then on, all sin is a reenactment of that first act of separation.

Another important position appears in the thirteenth-century esoteric thought of the Kabbalists of Castile, among them the brothers R. Isaac ha-Kohen and R. Jacob ha-Kohen, R. Moses of Burgos, and R. Todros Abulafia. The subject was extensively discussed in a famous response by R. Isaac on "the left emanation" *(ha-aṣilut ha-smalit).*[12] It is based on the biblical story in Genesis 36. Its sole importance seems to be historical, yet because the Bible is not a history book, the description must bear some symbolic meaning. The account begins, "These are the kings that reigned in the land of Edom, before there reigned any king over the children of Israel." The Kabbalists came to conclude that the kings of Edom reflect the redness *(odem)* of harsh judgment, a terrible concentration of evil that the world cannot bear. Moreover, R. Isaac ha-Kohen, citing the verse (Job 22:16) about wicked men "who were cut down out of time"[13] and the statement by R. Abahu[14] that before the creation of the present universe the Holy One blessed be He "formed and destroyed many worlds" points to three "cruel forces that began to accuse and confound emanation." At that moment, a divine voice proclaimed, "It is not the will of the King of Kings, the Holy One blessed be He, that they should exist in the worlds"; immediately, they "returned to their previous state and melted away—the spring of their emanation became the cause of their extinction. The sages of contemplation have compared it to . . . the wick that draws the oil—when we wish to extinguish it, we submerge it in the same oil whence it drew its light and flame, and there it dies out and becomes extinct."[15] Without explicitly naming the original source of evil and its nature, R. Isaac contents himself with a highly figurative and detailed description of the event. An important description, presented later in the text, states that from Binah,[16] ten princely accusers were emanated, parallel to the ten Sefirot in the world of holiness. Leading this formation is the "primeval snake" or "the evil Samael," although it is emphasized that "he himself is not evil[;] rather, he seeks to draw close and cleave to an emanation that is not his own."[17]

Similar to this Castilian view that the source of evil is in a "left emanation" is a statement in the commentary entitled *P"Z* by R. Reuben Ṣarfati, cited by R. Yehudah Ḥayyat: "*Din* is revealed in the world through these husks *[kelippot],* for no evil ever emerged from God, but only absolute good."[18] Thus R. Moses Cordovero contends that "the husks have absolutely no part in holiness."[19]

This fundamental conception found its way to the *Zohar* as well. There, though, we find descriptions[20] in which parallel structures are proposed for the Sefirot and for *sitra aḥra* ("other side," a euphemism for the powers of evil),[21] as well as scenes of fierce battles between the two forces, creating the impression of a radically dualistic outlook. That, apparently, is the way two series of opposing symbolic terms should be understood as well. One side includes God, king, living waters, pure waters, holy waters, land of the living; the other includes other gods, an alien god, an old and foolish king (Eccles. 4:13), stagnant water, turbid water, impure water, stolen water,[22] wasteland, and so forth. The symbols of evil may also be understood as indicating inferiority. To recognize evil as inferior renders it less frightening, severe, or dangerous than otherwise.

The *Zohar* hints at that possibility by indicating, through diverse images, the subordination of evil to good. Evil was created for the sole purpose of testing or seducing mankind. If man falls into the net spread at his feet, it is the force of evil that punishes him. The *Zohar*'s famous "Parable of the Whore"[23] addresses the subject directly: A king wished to put his son to the test, and so he had a woman stand in the doorway of a whorehouse to seduce him. If you argued she was no better than a wicked whore herself, you would be wrong, for she was merely fulfilling the king's wishes. In other words, evil is in the service of good and no more. The doctrine of recompense mandates that man have the opportunity to choose freely between good and evil,[24] and hence the seductive attraction of evil. If, then, evil is subservient to the good, why is it called "evil"? The answer is that, in practice, evil goes beyond the task assigned to it, and seeks to extend its reign and its power in the world,[25] so that it may seize a larger portion of emanated abundance.

The conception emerges, as in Neoplatonism, that as divine effulgence descends, the emanated light gradually fades, and more and more room is made for darkness. Even the husks, in certain contexts, are presented as belonging to the realm close to that of darkness.

In many instances, the power of evil and its source are ridiculed. Evil is "like the ape that imitates human beings, but cannot really pull it off."[26] Evil is no more than "gold residuum" *(hitukha de-dahava),* "wine dregs," menstrual blood, turbid water in the natural world, a bitter branch in the plant world. The image of the bark *(kelippah)*[27] from the "Tree of Emanation" is particularly common; it spread throughout kabbalistic literature, permeating Jewish folklore as well.

This notion of the *kelippah* demands more attention. Despite its negative connotation, the husk or peel does precede the fruit. That is, "evil" comes into existence even before the good. This, though, does not indicate any real advantage, for the peel serves to preserve and protect the fruit. In other words, it is evil that makes the existence of good a possibility. In the words of the *Zohar:* "*[S]itra aḥra* always appears first, growing and maturing and protecting the fruit. Once it has matured, it is thrown aside."[28] Yet another aspect of the image of the *kelippah* is that in order to reach the fruit one must cut away the peel. This would imply that evil is but a temporary state, which man must combat for good to triumph.

The image of the husk, like that of the nutshell, teaches that there is no absolute good or evil in the world, but rather that the two are necessarily interconnected. Indeed, evil is but a challenge, put in man's path to give him the opportunity to prove himself and to earn his reward. The challenge is part of the game. The Hasidim made frequent use of the expression "Evil is a chair [i.e., a means] to the good."

The concept of the *kelippah* appears in another context as well. As we mentioned above, the Kabbalists of the thirteenth century held that the internal structure of evil is parallel to that of the world of holiness, though inferior in status. Some Kabbalists sought to emphasize the inferiority of evil even more, and did so by proposing a structure not of ten but of four *kelippot*. The four are derived from the verse in Ezek. 1:4, "And I looked, and behold a *storm wind* came out of the north, a *great cloud* and a *fire* flaring up, and a *brightness* was about it." Thus, the four *kelippot* surround, as it were, the world of holiness or, to put it more precisely, are beneath that realm. This idea was developed in interesting directions.

The Kabbalists distinguished between three *kelippot* directly associated with the realm of evil and impurity, constituting evil in its essence, and a fourth, known as *kelippat nogah* (brightness), which was the fourth element in the prophet Ezekiel's vision. It surrounds the world of holiness, serving as an intermediary linking that world with the realm of impurity. This is explained by the fact that a mediating agent must stand between two opposing forces, and that such an agent must contain some of the qualities of each; inherent in *kelippat nogah* are both good and evil. The biblical term "The Tree of Knowledge of Good and Evil" suggests a similar bivalence. As a result, *kelippat nogah* may be drawn toward evil but, alternatively, it may be sanctified. Another explanation is that the connection must also be mutual, for evil is not an autonomous force but rather a part of holiness. The abysmal opposition between them necessitates the existence of *kelippat nogah*—akin to both sides, it bridges between them.

Another aspect of the image of *kelippat nogah* is manifest in life itself. Man vacillates between good and evil, yet reality should not be seen in such polar terms, but rather as a middle road that man is commanded to restitute; the choice is his to tend toward the right or to the left. In other words, the existence of *kelippat nogah* has great practical, as well as theoretical, importance.

In any case, the subordination of evil[29] to holiness is expressed in a crucial point. Like all of being, which draws its vitality from the supreme and holy Emanator, evil, too, is nourished by the effulgence flowing down through the Sefirot. This takes away its independence, yet the path toward its rebellion is also thereby broken. Thus, the fact that *sitra aḥra* is part of Divine Creation mandates its sustenance, and even man is summoned to contribute to the cause. We might compare the belief that parts of the ritual sacrifices were designated for feeding *sitra aḥra*. Indeed, *sitra aḥra* is sometimes allotted some portion connected to the performance of a *miṣvah;* this, though, is perceived as a way of bribing or pacifying it. The hope is that *sitra aḥra* would, then, mind its own business and not interfere during man's performance of holy acts and, perhaps more importantly, that it would not need to corrupt mankind in the attempt to receive its food. We recall, for example, the commandment concerning the scapegoat sent off to the wilderness for 'Azazel (Lev. 16:10), which was perceived as a bribe offered the devil to persuade him not to disrupt the process of purification and repentance in which the Jewish people was engaged on the annual Day of Judgment. Similar is the custom of washing with finger-bowl water before reciting the Grace after Meals, a practice that was also meant to preoccupy or entertain *sitra aḥra* with something material while man, through his blessing, seeks spiritual transcendence.

Clearly, though, evil grows ever stronger and is never satisfied with the abundance given it, but forever stalks a larger portion; this very fact expresses its negative nature. For evil, in a sense, oversteps its role as messenger and servant, and becomes an independent agent. Evil sucks greedily, demanding an increasingly larger share of divine efflux. Yet how can its will be realized? Here a third factor enters the picture, constituting one of the Kabbalah's greatest innovations. When man, and a Jew in particular, transgresses a negative precept, he cuts off the Sefirah of Malkhut from the influence flowing down to it, rechanneling that stream to the realm of "the other side." *Sitra aḥra*, then, receives its spiritual sustenance from mankind's evil deeds, his meditations on sin, and his impure thoughts. This counterbalances the belief that fulfillment of positive precepts engenders union between the Sefirot of Tiferet and Malkhut and a greater flow of divine influence into the lower world. The force of evil, then, seeks to seduce and accuse mankind in the attempt to draw as much effulgence as possible to itself. Its prime aim is to gain strength.

When Malkhut is thus denied that effulgence originally flowing down to it, evil gains strength and Malkhut weakens; this is reflected in the talmudic dictum that "Tyre was filled only by the destruction of Jerusalem."[30] What we have is a situation in which the world of holiness nourishes *sitra aḥra*, thereby upsetting the internal unity of that realm, harming the union of male and female, breeding disharmony, and causing a constriction of the flow of abundance to the lower worlds. As a result, the efflux to be produced is generated by sinister powers, and war and wickedness in the world inevitably follow.

This condition may be put in yet more extreme terms. As *sitra aḥra* gains strength, Malkhut—a female image with no autonomous power—necessarily deteriorates; she becomes a victim of *sitra aḥra*'s desire to enslave her to his own ends, "to assault the queen *[malkah]* in [the king's] own presence," in the biblical phrase (Esther 7:8). This danger continually menaces that hypostasis of the feminine which is Malkhut, threatening to diminish her sanctity and defile her; it is man's holy responsibility to prevent such a disaster.

This situation of "assaulting" the Shekhinah, i.e., severing her from the configuration of Sefirot above her, is generally called "the exile of the Shekhinah," "the Shekhinah in the dust," and so on. The experience of estrangement has a potent effect on the state of Knesset Yisrael, as the Jewish nation is in exile as well, and its situation is unnatural. Even the nations of the world are indirectly affected by that condition.

According to I. Tishby's analysis, the *Zohar* offers four explanations of the exile of the Shekhinah, and they are central to the Kabbalists' worldview. The first explanation links the exile to the basic condition described above, in which the sins of the Jewish people created a schism between the Shekhinah and Tiferet, thereby strengthening *sitra aḥra*; the latter then "assaulted" the Shekhinah. The trauma of being driven from her natural and ideal place is what caused the assault upon Knesset Yisrael by the nations in the lower world as well, and the exile of the Jewish people from their land.

The second explanation is that the Shekhinah, as a mother guiding and raising her offspring, is punished for "educational failure," for the Children of Israel had not understood how to live as they had been commanded, according to the laws of the Torah. This is the prophet Jeremiah's intent in his description of "Rachel weeping for her children" and the basis of the accusation the prophet Isaiah directs to the people: "For your transgressions was your mother sent away" (Isa. 50:1).

These two justifications link the suffering of the Shekhinah with her "punishment" and exile against her will. The following two explanations, in contrast, transform the suffering to a voluntary exile. The third explanation stresses the profound connection between the Shekhinah-mother and her children. She willfully takes their anguish and estrangement upon herself as a sign of identification with them. The description of Rachel in Jeremiah 31 and the midrashim in which the rabbis developed those biblical motifs provided an appropriate background against which the Kabbalists could frame their own ideas. In their eyes, this voluntary exile was a rend in the upper world, causing all of being to sink into an unnatural state.

The fourth explanation concerns a voluntary exile decreed by God, through the agency of Tiferet, upon the Shekhinah. He drives her away as a gesture of sympathy with and participation in the Jewish nation's exile. Yet another factor is at work here as well. The talmudic statement: "The Holy One blessed be He has declared, 'I will not come to the heavenly Jerusalem until I have visited the earthly Jerusalem'"[31] is amended by the author of the *Zohar*, who comments that the temporary dissociation serves as a kind of pledge to the lower Knesset Yisrael that she, too, will be restored to her place, her land, and her former status.

Descriptions such as these found various forms of concrete expression in Kabbalists' lives. For example, in response to the estrangement of the Shekhinah—who, as we have said, symbolizes the Jewish nation—individual Jews imposed certain practices upon themselves so that they could share her suffering. These included leaving their homes and families during the week, or even longer. Such people were said to have taken "exile" upon themselves (prominent among them were the brothers R. Elimelekh of Lyzhansk and R. Zusha of Hanipoli, important Hasidic leaders). Other practices included going barefoot as mourners must, thereby expressing the anguish they felt at the Shekhinah's sorrow.[32] In the sixteenth century, when the Kabbalah flourished in Safed, the custom spread not to eat meat or drink wine during the week; one was to indulge only during religious ceremonies (weddings, circumcisions, and so on), the Sabbath and festivals. It was also decided to recite the mournful Psalm 137, "By the Waters of Babylon," on weekdays before the recitation of Grace after Meals.[33] R. Isaac Luria, and many in his wake, would daily stand and joyfully give alms, as a symbol of encouragement and support for the Shekhinah, who is also poor and downcast ("she has nothing of her own"—and if the Shekhinah is always in need of strengthening, how much the more so in the present period of exile). The act of standing was also meant as a gesture of raising the Shekhinah from the ashes in which she sits dejected and setting her back on her metaphorical feet. Thus, certain *miṣvot* and customs were emphasized because of the unifying element inherent in them. For example, before entering the synagogue each morning, every individual was commanded to say: "I hereby take upon myself the precept, 'Thou shalt love thy neighbor as thyself.'" Likewise, in the evening before retiring (at the beginning of the Recitation of Shem'a before Bed) one must say: "I hereby forgive all who have angered me. . . ."[34]

The intent of such declarations is to deepen the sense of mutual responsibility and national unity as a precondition for the Shekhinah's gaining strength and courage.

The most important practice concerning our subject that the Kabbalists instituted was doubtless *tikkun ḥaṣot*. The custom, now well known, is to rise at midnight (many Kabbalists stressed the necessity of rising at the halfway point of the night), sit on the floor near the threshold, place ashes on one's head as mourners do, and lament the destruction of the Temple and the anguish of the Shekhinah. The mourner begins by reciting a confession *(vidduy),* meant to indicate the human factor in the Shekhinah's current predicament. The confession serves to deepen consciousness of the necessity of repentance and of doing good deeds, so that one's personal state may be improved, as well as the state of the Shekhinah.

Essentially, the *tikkun ḥaṣot* consists of two parts, one relating to the figure of Rachel and the other to Leah. The first is *tikkun Raḥel*, in which the motif of lamentation and mourning is most prominent. In the second part, hopes for redemption join in; even the symbols used echo that change in key. *Tikkun ḥaṣot* is to be recited nightly, but on the Sabbath and festivals only the second part, *tikkun Leah*, is said, as Jewish law forbids ritual mourning on those occasions.

THE DESTINY OF EVIL

Another seminal question concerns evil's ultimate destiny. We recall that the problem of the origin of evil and its present nature was raised within the fundamental Jewish conception of monotheism; the question of its end is addressed within the same framework. A variety of possible answers have been suggested.

The definition of evil as a peel or husk that serves a certain preliminary function leads to the natural conclusion that when its task is completed, evil will disappear—the husk will be stripped off and cast upon the ground, so that the fruit may be eaten. There is another opinion, however, that since evil originates from a sublime Sefirah, its present negative state is but a mask, a disguise. In time to come, evil will be revealed in its primordial form, and will return to its source within the good. After fulfilling its mission, so to speak, it will be restored to its original state of being. Naḥmanides[35] expresses such an idea, saying that the evil inclination *(yeṣer ha-r'a)* will eventually be no more, and man will fulfill all that he is commanded to do in a purely natural manner. The notion of free choice will be rendered meaningless, for man will choose the good with no particular effort or intention. The talmudic idea that "in time to come the *miṣvot* will become void"[36] is understood according to the same logic, for in that utopic future, no heteronomous commanding will be necessary; people will fulfill the commandments autonomously.

This idea is connected to another—with parallels in Neoplatonic thought and in the conception of many Kabbalists from the Geronese period onward—that all being is ultimately destined to return to the source; as Ecclesiastes says, "All are of dust and all will return to dust" (3:20). The world will return to its origin by the same path on which it set out, and only that primordial good will remain.

R. Joseph Gikatilla holds the somewhat similar view that the forces of evil will return to the place first designated for them before Adam's primordial sin.[37]

Others go further, claiming that of its own volition evil will become a driving force of holiness, one of its internal powers. In a work entitled *Kaf ha-Ketoret*, from the early sixteenth century, Samael himself is portrayed as regretting his wicked ways and reforming; he turns into a good angel and draws with him the entire camp of wreakers of judgment. One hundred years later, R. Menaḥem 'Azariah of Fano, Italy, presented a similar scenario.

The teaching of R. Shneur Zalman of Lyady incorporates an idea along the same lines. He says the zaddik is an individual who has succeeded in converting his animal soul, and the entirety of evil forces within himself, to the level of a divine soul; in other words, evil itself has become a component of the good and the holy.

There is a view that because the presence of evil is so potent, and because its very existence is devoted to driving mankind to its downfall, evil's power can be silenced only through an active battle against it. There are varied means to that end: physical mortification, forcing the submission of destructive inclinations, annihilating one's desires, deliberate avoidance of committing negative precepts, seeking to perform positive injunctions—perhaps even to the point of causing others to uphold the commandments out of a sense of national unity and common destiny: "To unify the Holy One blessed be He and his Shekhinah in the name of all of Israel." All these are weapons against the world of evil.

Another view calls for the avoidance of "contact wrestling with the enemy." The verse from Psalms (34:15), "Depart from evil and do good," is interpreted in Hasidism in the simplest way possible: Don't sink into the mud. Even if you have failed and are aware of it, don't dig around in the filth surrounding you. Filth is always anathema; concentrate your energies on doing good, as much good as possible, and evil will fade away. In the words of R. Kook:

> The pure and righteous do not lament about wickedness, but rather increase righteousness; they do not lament about apostasy, but rather increase faith; they do not lament about ignorance, but rather increase wisdom.[38]

In essence, such a view boasts important lineage. Lurianic kabbalistic teaching, which presents evil as existing by grace of the divine sparks imprisoned within it, also teaches that every good act one performs engenders some kind of restitution *(tikkun)*—both in the Divine itself and in the soul. For, in addition to performing the *miṣvah*, and thereby fulfilling one's individual obligation, one enables the holy spark encaged in matter (representing the *kelippah*) to ascend by the very performance of a *miṣvah* entailing simple physical action. In this manner, the divine spark is redeemed and returns to its source; in the same moment, the *kelippah*, in the form of matter, is left bereft of its animating and vital force. This, of course, marks its demise. The process described is the future messianic redemption: goodness will multiply, and the world will shrug off the chains of evil, which will disappear utterly. Hence the vision of a wholly good world, revealing "eye to eye" the Kingdom of God on earth.[39]

There is another view quite similar to this one, but with the difference that in it, evil will return to good. R. Moses Ḥayyim Luzzato explains:

> The achievement of this last stage depends on man's actions, which will empower the force of holiness; evil will then lose all relevance, for everything will exist solely in honor of the Creator . . . and all will reach its full *tikkun*. If these vessels and garments provide a basis for evil—that is no failure but, on the contrary, is the fulfillment of the intent in the completeness of Creation to reveal supreme unity. . . . True evil must return to the good through human acts of restitution until evil itself exists in the King's own honor, accomplished by human beings. . . . And when the restitution is completed and it has returned to the good, all is restored to its original state; the actual presence of evil is no longer necessary, for it was present and then restituted.[40]

In the teaching of R. Isaac Luria, every individual is a participant in the active process of the world's *tikkun* by the very act of doing good. This process is called "clarifying the sparks" *(berur ha-niṣoṣot)* or "raising the sparks" *(ha'ala'at ha-niṣoṣot)*. The completion of the process takes place with the arrival of redemption itself. This brings us to the question, asked not only by the Kabbalists, whether redemption is a process or an event that will be revealed but a single time. R. Isaac Luria chose the first possibility. Less than one hundred years later, though, Sabbatai Ṣevi claimed to be the Messiah himself, come to restore the world. But since the mission of the Messiah is to restore the world, he contended, the resolution of evil must take place within the world of evil itself. Evil, then, must be combated and destroyed within Islam. He thus offered entrance into the world of evil through the gate of religious conversion to Islam.[41] Jacob Frank made a similar argument—enter the Christian world, and combat evil from within it. This program, presented here in greatly abbreviated form, was aptly described by G. Scholem as "redemption through sin" and its historical result was, of course, catastrophic.

The problem of the existence of *sitra aḥra* and its powers, and all the attention to that domain, had an unavoidable result. For the realm of evil is, of course, not strictly metaphysical, but relates to myriad aspects of human life—religious, ethical, existential. Thus the Kabbalah came up against one of the most troubling situations any individual could pose; it is only natural that man should seek protection and a resolution of his problems. As an outgrowth of the kabbalistic myth, practical Kabbalah developed. It was a world of magic and adjurations, a folklore that drew its vitality from the images and symbols of that kabbalistic mythology. Such was the price paid by the Kabbalah to be received in popular circles. This does not mean that, were it not for the Kabbalah, no one would have thought about the evil eye, adjurations, etc. The Talmud does speak of such subjects,[42] and medieval Ashkenazic Jews were preoccupied with thoughts and acts concerning the world of evil.[43] Various concepts in kabbalistic thought,[44] such as the *kelippot* and their powers, *sitra aḥra*, the transmigration of souls, etc., penetrated the consciousness of the people and found diverse expression in folklore, folk beliefs, and practical Kabbalah.

11 • The Doctrine of Creation

SOME POSITIONS

The monotheistic idea presented in the Bible concerning God's reign in the world, his omnipotence, and his continual omnipresence in all aspects of Creation is expressed there in various ways. Among them are the second of the Ten Commandments ("Thou shalt not make for thyself any carved idol or any likeness"); Isaiah's vision with the angels' hymn ("The whole earth is full of His glory"); and the poetic phrases of Psalm 139. The monotheistic idea was handed from generation to generation; the appellation "the Omnipresent" *(ha-makom* [the Place]), for example, used in the talmudic period to speak of God, was explained by the paradoxical contention that "the Holy One blessed be He is the Place of His world, but the world is not His [exclusive] place." In other words, he is immanent in the world, yet there is no hint of pantheism. Another similar expression, originating in the midrash *Exodus Rabbah*, that "no place is devoid of His presence," became even better known in its Aramaic form used in *Tikkuney Zohar*;[1] these, like the statement in the midrash *Tanḥuma* that "The Holy One blessed be He wanted an abode in the lower realms," were given a literal interpretation in many later works, particularly in the *Tanya* by R. Shneur Zalman of Lyady (although there, different methodological conclusions were attached). Other forms in which the idea was expressed include the song *Adon 'Olam*, part of the liturgy of every Jewish community; the Hymns of Unity *(shirey yiḥud)* of Ashkenazic Hasidim, with their hyperbolically poetic descriptions of that immanence;[2] the poem by R. Yehudah ha-Levi, "Lord, where shall I find You? Your place is lofty and secret. And where shall I not find You? The whole earth is full of Your glory!";[3] a variety of formulations akin to Neoplatonism in the writings of R. Abraham ibn 'Ezra, such as "He is all and all is from Him,"[4] or, "the Name is one, Creator of all and He is all—I cannot explain further";[5] the comment by R. Eleazar of Worms that God is closer to all being than the soul is to the body;[6] the proverb that "the numerical value of Elohim [the Lord] equals that of *tev'a* [nature],"[7] a suspiciously pantheistic remark discussed in various contexts (such as by Ḥakham Ṣevi in his famous responsum 18); or another saying like it, "Nature is the Shekhinah."[8] This entire system of images and expressions amassed from diverse literary genres, and others too numerous to mention here, indicates a certain aspect of God: his dwelling in a world he himself brought into being, guarding it and reigning over it. Clearly, for the Kabbalists, the question of immanence, of God's presence permeating the world, is a matter of central importance.

Influenced by Jewish tradition, as well as the Neoplatonic view that the world emanated from the very existence of his "oneness,"[9] which was accepted with some reservation, the Kabbalists, in their teaching, concentrated on the idea of 'Eiyn Sof as the source of the world's emanation. Everything was revealed at a certain stage within the innermost essence of the Emanator, yet no change occurred within him. The idea of ceaseless, all-pervading immanence is a basic principle, for the process of Creation is conceived as a process of the Creator's revelation. In the saying often invoked by the Kabbalists (associated with R. Isaac the Blind) in the thirteenth century, "The essences existed but the emanation was new." That is, only the external process of emanation is continually enacted, while the beings (the Sefirot and all that evolves from them) were preexistent; they were not first created at that moment.

The present chapter is devoted to a more extensive presentation of the process of Creation and the problems it involves.

Much thought has been devoted to the task of describing the way in which the world was created, yet no single system has yet been proposed—whether scientific, philosophical, religious, mystical, mythological, or folkloristic—which fully answers all aspects of the problem. Even in the Kabbalah, certain elements were left as inscrutable by the human intellect and inaccessible even to man's heart or soul. In any case, we have juxtaposed the subject of Creation to the subject of the Sefirot because the Kabbalists also draw an intimate link between them. The very evolution of the Sefirot is perceived as a stage leading to the future creation of the material world. First, though, let us review some other positions.

The first chapter of Genesis describes the world's Creation as planned and organized over a six-day period. Creation proceeds in stages, and there is no remnant of any kind of battle. The process culminates with the appearance of Man and he, from then on, is the protagonist of the biblical story and the commandments. According to a literal reading of the narrative, the world was created by divine utterances: "And God said, Let there be . . . and there was. . . ." This, most likely is the contention echoed in Ps. 33:6, "By the word of the Lord were the heavens made, and all the host of them by the breath of His mouth."

This principle continued to evolve throughout the generations. The notion of "utterance" evokes the well-known conclusion voiced in the Mishnah, "The world was created through ten *ma'amarot* [utterances]" (*Avot* 5:1). There, a certain framework has already been introduced; while in and of itself it seems to point only to an account of how many times the verb "said" appears in the Creation story,[10] it in fact transfers the issue to a higher level of other important values related to the number ten, as the Mishnah goes on to enumerate. This becomes even clearer in the addition of the number ten to the word *davar* [thing, word] used in the verse from Psalms mentioned above. Hence we learn in the name of Rav that "By ten things was the world created—by wisdom, by understanding, by knowledge, by strength, by rebuke, by might, by righteousness, by judgment, by lovingkindness, and by compassion" (*Ḥagigah* 12a). At first glance, Rav appears to have strung together the various expressions connected to the biblical account of Creation. The truth is, though, that his approach is predetermined.[11] That is, his list is somewhat artificial, for the verses he uses do not speak directly of Creation. Rav's intent was clearly to indicate certain properties (and the word *davar* here does not mean "sayings" but rather "things," values) upon which the world is founded from its inception. It should be pointed out that Rav was one of the greatest Amora'im in Babylon, and among the most prominent of Rishonim (early third century); his was close to the esoteric teaching adopted by the authors of the *Heikhalot* literature.

Rav's conception recalls, in part, the famous comment at the beginning of the midrash *Genesis Rabbah*: "The Holy One blessed be He gazed[12] into the Torah and created the world." The Torah is presented here as a sort of architectural plan used in the construction of the universe. Once again we find an emphasis on the world's values, without going into "techniques" and scientific or physical questions. Similar is the talmudic statement (*Ḥagigah* 12a) that the zaddik is the single pillar supporting the world. We may assume the intent is to indicate the ethical element, which is the true foundation on which the world stands.

Interestingly, these were not isolated comments; rather, they continued to arouse the rabbis' curiosity and imagination. The Talmud preserves Rav's statement: "Bezalel knew how to combine the letters by which heaven and earth were created."[13] At issue is not a mere utterance (though, indeed, a divine mandate) but an utterance composed of letters—Hebrew ones, to be sure[14]—conjoined to form complete and meaningful words. This description, then, pictures God as speaking in human language.

Rav's statement is not offhand. In the *Heikhalot* literature we read: "With letters, heaven and earth were created, the oceans and rivers were created . . . all the world's needs and all the orders of Creation. And each letter flashes over and over again like lightning."[15] Other sources in the *Heikhalot* literature also emphasize creation by means of letters, but mention another element as well. As we have said, Rav's expression was "to combine the letters"; a similar phrase is "the stamp *[ḥotam]* used to seal heaven and earth."[16] This formulation demands a brief explanation. "Seal" implies a certain divine name through which the various components of Creation are "harnessed," so that they may be complete and viable. (The synonymous term "affixing" *[keshirah]*, as in God's "affixing crowns to the letters" [*Menaḥot* 29b] usually bears magical significance and is frequently used in practical Kabbalah.) Thus even the divine names are an element in the world's creation. This innovation wore the mantle of esoteric truth, "the secret by which heaven and earth were created."[17]

Around the *Heikhalot* period, *Sefer Yeṣirah* was composed. Scholarly opinion conflicts concerning its date, but its first chapter, at least,[18] seems to have been written in the second to third century. In some manuscripts the work is attributed to the patriarch Abraham, and beginning in the thirteenth century it is attributed to R. 'Akiva as well. These two figures are archetypes in the Jewish imagination, and their association granted authority to the contents of the book. *Sefer Yeṣirah* opens with these words: "In thirty-two mystical paths of Wisdom He inscribed . . . creating His world with three books . . . ten *Sefirot belimah* and twenty-two letters of foundation."

Let us ignore, for a moment, some of the components mentioned in this statement, and concentrate on one in particular. First of all, certain elements used by God to create the world are enumerated. In effect, there are only two: letters and Sefirot, i.e., a complex rather than a simple utterance, as we said earlier. This utterance is composed not from letters alone, as we may have expected, but from Sefirot as well. These Sefirot, as Gershom Scholem has explained,[19] are ancient numbers that serve as the fundaments of Creation, a teaching voiced by the Pythagorean school as well. What we have, then, is a combination of letters and numbers through which the world was created. In any case, this text comes close to the basic view presented in Genesis, though with an important difference.[20]

It should be pointed out that from Tannaic times there was a tendency to avoid discussions concerning Creation. The point was brought home harshly in the Mishnah: "Whoever meditates upon four things, it were better for him if he had not come into the world" (*Ḥagigah* 2:1). R. 'Akiva's opinion is also presented that "the 'Secret of Creation' may not be expounded by two." In recent disputes, scholars have disagreed on how to understand R. 'Akiva's words. Is it preferable for a solitary person to study the question? Or does it mean the opposite: if not two, then certainly not one alone? In any case, the main thing for us is that the rabbis could not remain indifferent to the views of the non-Jewish world. The Talmud documents various instances in which the rabbis conduct philosophical disputes with non-Jewish figures. For the most part, though, the rabbis voiced radical opposition to Gnostic teachings about Creation. Their struggle is not recounted explicitly in the sources, but from the polemical tone of what is written, we can intuit the situation. Indeed, the Gnostic movement itself, wide-reaching in its prime, was not unanimous in all its views, even if the basic contentions were more or less officially accepted by all its various branches.

Many discussions about Creation took place in the Greek philosophical schools as well. According to Plato, the Demiurge created the material world out of hylic or formless matter by emulating eternal Ideas.

Aristotle taught that the world is primordial and was not created by any divinity. This assumption, though, did not impede him from recognizing God's existence. Even in Islam, theologians and philosophers debated various issues, such as whether the world was eternal or created at a certain stage, and, if created, was created with primeval matter or ex nihilo. Christian theology, of course, also considered the issue of Creation. An opinion akin to Plato's, that primeval matter was used to create the world, was expressed (by Clement of Alexandria, one of the church fathers), but in general the Church's loyalty was to the view that the world came into being ex nihilo; an edict to that effect was officially formulated by the Fourth Lateran Council in 1215.

Jewish thinkers were not unaware of these debates, and even reacted to them. In 2 Macc. 7:28 it had been said: "Look upon the heavens and the earth and all therein, and know that all you see was created by God out of nothingness." This is the first statement in Hebrew literature that speaks explicitly of Creation from naught. A trenchant discussion is found in R. Sa'adyah Gaon's philosophical work *Emunot we-De'ot* [The book of beliefs and opinions], and later Jewish philosophers continued to debate the subject (almost without exception, it seems), raising diverse claims. In any case, the assumptions that the world was created by God out of nothingness and that it was renewed attained the status of founding principles. Interestingly, though, study of Maimonides' work *Moreh Nevukhim* [Guide to the perplexed] uncovers a basic and innovative doctrine: the primeval nature of the world was not proven by the philosophers and cannot be demonstrated unequivocally even by the Creation story in Genesis. Nonetheless, we must accept the notion of the world's renewal as a necessary precondition for other fundamental and accepted assumptions.

In the course of time, more conceptions developed in general culture; they merit our attention as well.

One is the atheistic-naturalistic view, which holds that only phenomena worthy of being subjects of scientific investigation are ontologically real. The conclusion, then, would be that nature has no value or significance, even though it is the sole entity in existence. The pantheistic view, in contrast, contends that God himself is the sole ontological reality. But there was disagreement concerning the exact meaning of the equation God = nature. One popular view, claiming acosmism, denied the separate existence of the world on the grounds that it was but part of divine being. If so, one conclusion might be that human life and moral values are meaningless. All is perceived as a legitimate divine act. This, in fact, is the conclusion drawn in the Ash'ariya school of Islam.

Another approach is the theistic view. In it, both God and the world are thought to exist as separate entities. While God is infinite and thus eternal, noncomposite, and unchanging, the world is finite, created at a specific point in time, destined to end at any moment, composite, and subject to endless changes. The question whether there really is any connection between God and the world, and if so, of what the nature of that connection might be, is by no means a simple one. To a great extent, it depends on the perspective of the person asking. The philosopher would indicate changes that might occur in 'Eiyn Sof as a result of a certain relationship; a thinking individual might seek to evade or resolve such questions, his primary concern being a personal link with God. On the issue of Creation, however, there is a middle road between the latter two methods—and that is the theory of panentheism. According to it, the world is indeed part of all-encompassing divine oneness, yet it has autonomous existence as well, and is not identical with the Divine.

Most of the points outlined in our brief review were doubtless known to the Kabbalists. Let us mention one more important method: that of Neoplatonism, which influenced not only Jewish philosophers such as Isaac Israeli and R. Solomon ibn Gabirol but Kabbalists as well.

THE DOCTRINE OF EMANATION

One of the Kabbalists' central problems was the question of the world's origin in God, i.e., how finitude was generated from infiniteness. A secondary question also asked was: How did a flawed and incomplete world develop, where evil forces are so well represented, from a God whole and good in his very essence? In dealing with such questions, the Kabbalists' conception of Creation clearly bore the mark of Neoplatonic philosophy, and many fundamental beliefs were shared by both.

Earlier in our discussion we considered the path of divine emanation through the Sefirotic system and its internal dynamic. What concerns us now is how the nondivine world developed beneath the world of emanation. One opinion, interesting in its perspective although it never gained much currency, holds that the Sefirot and the lower worlds were emanated simultaneously. The Creation story in Genesis 1 recounts both the development of the Sefirot and how our own world came into existence. An allusion to this view may be found in Naḥmanides' famous phrase in his commentary on the first verse of the Bible: "Scripture speaks of the lower worlds and alludes to the higher worlds."

Another view is that the process of emanation is a natural one, issuing from its source in the Emanator and moving downward. Its light fades as it descends, allowing matter to come into being in the last stage. This view is predominant both in Neoplatonic philosophy and in Kabbalah.

The Neoplatonian view differs from Greek philosophical teachings[21] in its innovative concept of emanation. The primary principle is the "One"—infinite and utterly ineffable. He is a unified and unchanging entity, yet creative in his very essence by grace of the abundance ceaselessly flowing from him while in no way lessening his plenitude. Just as the sun radiates luminosity without end, so the law of God's nature as the all-encompassing "One" is that he emanates effluence from within himself, and that he creates and sustains the world. As we have said, all the various facets of the world continue to be created anew in the endless flow of influence from above while the emanating Source remains unchanged and undiminished. But as the entities generated become increasingly remote from their origin and as the spiritual element descends lower and lower, the spiritual element gradually constricts in the form of an inverted pyramid, and the spiritual is replaced with materiality. Just as light fades as it moves from its source, so the completeness of the emanated entities diminishes as distance from their source increases. Thus, something divine does remain in all of being, but for the most part it is coarse matter. The spiritual part that endures longs to return to its root.

The emanative process is continuous, although it does go through intermediate stages: the intellect, the collective soul, and nature. The intellect is the first to be emanated, and is, in a certain sense, identical with the One, but because it has been emanated, it differs from its source as well and becomes attainable even by man himself. The second element to be emanated is the soul or the general spirit. Incorporeal, it is allied with the higher world, thus enabling it to bond with the intellect and receive various forms of illumination; yet it is joined to the natural world emanated from it as well, which casts it under the influence of nature and immerses it in the realm of matter. The third element to be emanated is nature or the world of phenomena.

Although the Neoplatonic view was comprehensible in and of itself, simple metaphors were employed to clarify matters even further. Two images—light and water—were commonly used to describe the outflow, and they appear in kabbalistic thought as well.[22] Light, of course, cogently suggests a pure spiritual element inundating and sustaining reality. Water, likewise, is pure and clear, and vital for existence. Its fundamental property is to flow.

One important point should be added: in presenting this view, its originator, Plotinus, evaded the difficulties of how to explain the duality between the divine Creator and the created world and how to explain Creation as a temporal occurrence. As far as he was concerned, these problems had resolved themselves. Another difficulty: if some remnant of the Divine is indeed inherent in all parts of Creation, as it came into being from the efflux flowing from him, is this not tantamount to pantheism? Plotinus solved this difficulty as well by repeatedly stressing that God and Creation are not identical, and that he is not present to the same extent in all the world's details.

The Neoplatonians spoke of a continuous process of emanation. The question then arises whether, according to the central trend of kabbalistic thought, such an unbroken continuity from the world of emanation to the nondivine realms indeed exists, or whether, alternatively, some significant alteration occurs, perhaps even interrupting the order of descent.[23] Some Kabbalists used the expression "the chain of cause and effect" *(hishtalshelut 'ila ve-'alul),* i.e., a causal evolution, to speak of a continuous connection. This seems to be the position taken by the author of *Ma'arekhet ha-Elohut*: "For everything below has its counterpart above with the same name, and the latter is the fundament and the power of the lower entity, enabling it to exist. All [comes into being] through such a chain, whether animal, inanimate or plant life."[24] What is described, then, are stages that are parallel and yet joined without a break. The view is sometimes expressed that the "chain of cause and effect" creates some kind of inherent causal unity, while the assumption remains that the material world is, nevertheless, intrinsically different. Opponents to the notion of causal evolution, as we have said, argue there is an irreducible difference between spiritual and material entities. The Kabbalists were elaborate in their descriptions of the processes of emanation occurring within the Godhead and proposed, for the most part, a clear separation between the divine world and the world of matter. It was said the primordial light was hidden away,[25] causing darkness to invade, and from within that darkness the lower worlds were emanated. There was said to be a curtain or screen,[26] which cut off or impeded the sun's rays. And there was said to be a skipping over *(dillug, kefiṣah)* Creation rather than a direct emanation. The implication was that although the Emanator is the source of all being, the latter's existence is nonetheless separate from his. Others spoke of the world of the Chair, the Throne, the Chariot, the Shekhinah's hosts, and other expressions bearing a double connotation: the continuity of "the world of unity" *('alma de-yiḥuda),* in contrast to what is beneath Malkhut and called "the world of disunion" *('alma de-peruda)* or even "the world of separate intelligences" *('olam ha-sekhalim ha-nifradim).* Yet unlike the original philosophical term, used to speak of spiritual forms devoid of matter, in Kabbalah the term came to mean the opposite—forms devoid of spirituality. Some added another dimension, emphasizing the opposition to the world of unity. In other words, everything outside the realm of the Sefirot—down to this world and *sitra aḥra*—are realms of individuation, and each entity is as if autonomous. The Kabbalists even used the symbol of the "public domain" *(reshut ha-rabim)* in the sense of a place through which many people pass, each going his own way.

All this implies that the emanation present in our world is unlike that which fills the world of the Sefirot. One motive behind this conception may well be the desire to steer clear of any hint of pantheism. At a later stage, this view was expressed by R. Moses Cordovero in these succinct words: "The Divine is in all of being, yet all is not the Divine."[27] This is an indisputably panentheistic position.

The Kabbalah also differed from Neoplatonism on whether emanation was an immutable aspect of the very nature of the Emanator. The Kabbalists unanimously insisted on a clear distinction between 'Eiyn Sof and the act of emanation. Emanation depends solely on his absolute will.[28] In other words, a state of nonemanation preceded the world's coming into being. The possibility even exists that there can be no world. Destruction *(ḥurban)* implies a cessation in the descent of effulgence. Just as we know air, essential to our existence, is present though we cannot sense it, so divine efflux sustains the world despite its invisibility, and in its absence the world would cease to exist. Thus the Kabbalists interpreted the verse of the morning prayers, "He, in His goodness, daily renews the works of Creation," as speaking of a continual process of emanation, as if the world is created anew in every moment. R. Levi Isaac of Berdichev formulated the idea in this way:

> Thus the Creator, blessed be He, created all and He is all. His influence never ceases, for every moment He sends abundance to all his creatures and to all the worlds. . . . For that reason we say "He makes light and creates darkness" . . . in the present tense, for He creates continually, granting vitality to every living being, and He is the source of all.[29]

This matter bears great significance for the issue of pantheism. The central contention is that, were the effulgence to be interrupted momentarily, the world would cease to exist, yet the Emanator would endure. Clearly, an antipantheistic notion!

We must remember, though, that for the Kabbalists, emanation was a process that occurred, when it occurred, within the Divine, while the Sefirot are the stages through which that process is revealed. First to be emanated were the Sefirot and the attributes through which he is manifest, and as divine effluence descended, the worlds were formed one by one. The process of Creation is thus inseparable from the process of his revelation. It is an expression of his emanated and yet concealed essence. For this reason, the assumption of "creation out of nothingness" must not be accepted simplistically. The kabbalistic "from naught" signifies creation from within God himself; as we have said, *ayin* (nothingness) speaks of Keter, the supernal Sefirah. That nothingness is a positive entity, the true essence from which all is emanated. Thus the kabbalistic concept of "out of nothing" *(me-ayin)* differs radically from the philosophical notion, for at issue is not creation out of emptiness and naught, but rather the revelation of Ḥokhmah from its predecessor—Keter.

The Kabbalists, then, were compelled to refute the Neoplatonists' claim. Were they to concede that Creation had occurred at a certain moment in time, that would imply a transition had taken place from God's identity as "non-Creator" to "Creator." Their counterargument was that all had been concealed within 'Eiyn Sof, and the only change that occurred was its outward emanation; thus, no actual change took place in the Creator himself. The comparison may be made to saplings uprooted and replanted elsewhere. There they bear fruit, yet their produce existed in potential even where they were originally planted.

Another view, which contradicts the former to a certain extent, is formulated by Naḥmanides in his commentary on *Sefer Yeṣirah* and in the manuscript of another Kabbalist of the same generation. In their method, for "unlimitedness" to yield limitation, for infinity to bear finiteness, there must be some primary act arresting the flow of effulgence—"a contraction of His glory," in Naḥmanides' words.[30] In the kabbalistic manuscript we mentioned:[31]

> How did He invent and create His world? Like man, who takes in his breath, constricting himself so that his limitedness may contain plenitude—so He constricted His light in a handsbreadth, leaving the world in darkness; in that darkness He cut the cliffs and carved out rocks to draw forth the paths called "wondrous knowledge."

The first stage, then, is an ingathering of breath, engendering darkness, the absence of emanation. Note that this act does not occur within the confines of 'Eiyn Sof himself: the purpose of this contraction *(ṣimṣum)* is not to engender the first Sefirah, for that entity is "more filled with His glory than the heart can imagine." The first Sefirah, like 'Eiyn Sof, is eternal. Emanation, therefore, began after the transition from Keter to Ḥokhmah. The importance of this explanation lies in the fact that, in contrast to the usual description of emanation as a ceaseless outflow from the source, here we have some sort of interruption in the form of contraction. G. Scholem suggests that Naḥmanides may have been trying to adapt the kabbalistic view to the philosophical notion of creation ex nihilo.[32]

Yet a different conception should be mentioned as well. As early as *Tikkuney Zohar*, we find discussion of four stages: *aṣilut* (emanation), *beriyah* (creation), *yeṣirah* (formation), *'asiyah* (making). The source of this nomenclature is Isa. 43:7: "I have created him *[berativ]* for my glory; I have formed him *[yeṣartiv]*; yea, I have made him *['asitiv]*. In a slightly later text, *Massekhet Aṣilut*, dating from the early fourteenth century and penned by an anonymous Kabbalist, we read of four worlds called *aṣilut*, *beriyah*, *yeṣirah,* and *'asiyah*. In the same period, R. Isaac of Acre used, for the first time, the acronym ABY'A to speak of those four realms, which became prevalent from the sixteenth century onward. In the fourteenth century, though, there were other Kabbalists who made no mention of those four worlds, like the author of the seminal work *Ma'arekhet ha-Elohut*.

The four worlds represent the realm of the Sefirot, the realm of Creation beneath it *(yeṣirah),* the angelic realm (sometimes called the World of the Seat), and our world *('asiyah).* The nature of that lowest world is evaluated in a variety of ways; central to most is an account of the relationship between it and the world of matter, the realm of evil. The contention is sometimes made that the central image of a primeval man [Adam Kadmon] is found in each of these four worlds—in the first, an Adam of *aṣilut*, then an Adam of *beriyah*, etc. Even the realm of evil is spoken of as a satanic creature, "Adam of *beliyya'al.*"

Other subdivisions of reality are proposed as well. The above-mentioned *Ma'arekhet ha-Elohut* distinguishes between the supernal world of the Sefirot *('olam 'elion),* "the world of the separated ones" *('olam ha-nifradim),* "the world of the wheels" *('olam ha-galgalim),* and the lower world *('olam ha-shefel),* i.e., our own. Others went in a more Aristotelian direction, naming the lower stages "active intellect" *(sekhel po'el),* soul *(nefesh),* form, and matter.

The description outlined above of the process of 'Eiyn Sof's revelation through the Sefirot is not the only one that was offered. Prominent Kabbalists spoke of various intricate processes. Some of these were presented in the context of commentaries on aggadic sources or biblical verses, and others without such pretexts. The general intent seems to have been to express the complexity inherent in the processes of revelation.

Another idea found in various forms is presented in relation to Genesis 36 as well as to R. Abahu's statement recorded in the midrash to the effect that before our present world finally came into being the Holy One blessed be He had created other worlds but, dissatisfied with them, had destroyed them. The difficulty of the midrash is evident; the enigma posed by the biblical text is why the historical period of the kings of Edom, "before there reigned any king over the children of Israel," a period seemingly irrelevant to the Jewish nation, is described in such detail. Some explained the matter as two instances in which the power of stern *din* threatening the world was at last contained. This teaches us of the necessity of preserving a balance between judgment and mercy in our world. The idea is sometimes expressed using the principle of masculine and feminine valences: the feminine is seen as softening and "sweetening" the quality of strict judgment intrinsic to the male figure. Until this dual figure—its counterpart in our world being man himself—was emanated, there was no balance *(matkela* is the term used by the *Zohar*) and the world was unviable. For that reason, the last verse in the passage on the kings of Edom gives the name of the eighth king's wife—a female figure comes on stage. Something similar may have occurred within each Sefirah, bringing them internal balance and stability. In sum, the primordial state finally secreted away is analogous to the "kings of Edom who died" or the "ancient kings" *(malkhin kadma'in)* as the *Zohar* called them; it represents a world destroyed and passed away, while the present world was emanated in measure and equilibrium from the very outset.

Another sort of process concerns the transition from 'Eiyn Sof to the Sefirot. Is there a direct connection between 'Eiyn Sof and Keter, or are there intermediate stages? Some speak of three prior stages, others of ten. Let us consider these two systems briefly. The first, attributed to R. Hai Gaon in the pseudoepigraphical literature, seems to be a product of the 'Iyyun circle active in the thirteenth century. It speaks of three lights: primordial internal light *(or kadmon),* polished light *(or ṣaḥ),* and clear light *(or meṣuḥṣaḥ)*, also called *ṣaḥṣaḥot*. All of them are hermetically sealed away, for they are the root of all roots. They are joined to the Emanator, and perhaps exist only in his essence. Nonetheless, they operate one step ahead of the Emanator. Thus, though this explanation is originally presented as a response to an "innocent" question, i.e., the relationship between the ten Sefirot and the traditional thirteen divine attributes (after Exodus 33), it actually teaches of the roots of the Sefirot themselves.[33]

In the fourteenth century we hear for the first time of ten *ṣaḥṣaḥot* or *ṣiḥṣuḥin* that preceded the ten Sefirot. Proponents of that theory include R. David ben Yehudah he-Ḥasid and other later Kabbalists, particularly those of Morocco. Their intent is to emphasize the distance between the Emanator and the Sefirot, as if to prevent any identification being made between them and 'Eiyn Sof. The same idea is expressed in calling the Sefirot "vessels" *(kelim)*, and the roots of the Sefirot "essence" *('aṣmut)*. Proponents of this view thus achieved two ends: (1) to indicate the complexity of the process of revelation, and (2) to settle the dispute over the nature of the Sefirot as essence or as vessels.

THE PURPOSE OF CREATION

Earlier, we stressed that the Kabbalah, in opposition to Neoplatonism, held emanation to be a willful act, and conceived of a "time" in which no outward emanation had taken place. This contention raises the question of what the ultimate goal of emanation then was. To what end did God reveal those forces? Various responses have been proposed. One is that the Emanator wished to reveal his goodness to benefit extradivine entities, and this necessitated the existence of objects to receive that goodness. R. Sa'adya Gaon, for instance, sees man as the focal point of Creation. "When we make our investigation with this [natural] criterion [as a guide], we find that the goal is man," and God's creation of him was an act of "goodness and mercy."[34] This is the response of a philosopher. Similarly, R. Moses Ḥayyim Luzzatto, a prominent Kabbalist, wrote: "The purpose of Creation was to bestow His goodness, blessed be He, upon others."[35] He added that it "permitted [mankind] to cleave to His divine attributes of true goodness and completeness."[36] The same response appears in the writings of many other Kabbalists, among them R. Moses Cordovero[37] and in *'Eṣ Ḥayyim*.[38]

A second response, perhaps more important than the first, takes the wind out of the question's sails. The entire subject is beyond our understanding, and we cannot know God's true purpose—"That was His will."

THE DOCTRINE OF ṢIMṢUM

The term "contraction" *(ṣimṣum)*, which we encountered earlier in Naḥmanides' thought, recalls the well-known Lurianic term. Yet the doctrine of *ṣimṣum* presented by R. Isaac Luria differs significantly from that of Naḥmanides. In Lurianic teaching, the relationship between 'Eiyn Sof and entities outside of it is scrutinized with great candor. A preliminary, "naive" question is backed up by ironclad logic: If, indeed, "The world is filled with His glory," how is there room for anything besides God? As G. Scholem put it, "How is it possible for the world to exist at all if there is nothing besides 'Eiyn Sof, the infinite Deity that is all and fills all? If 'Ein Sof or 'the light of 'Eiyn Sof' is all in all, how can there be anything that is not 'Eiyn Sof?"[39] For something else to exist, 'Eiyn Sof must recede. Hence, "the first act of the Creator was not His revelation of Himself to something outside . . . the first step was rather a withdrawal or retreat."[40] When God decided to begin the process of emanation, he contracted some part of his essence. "At a certain point within the light of 'Eiyn Sof . . . the light or essence drew away, receding to the depths of 'Eiyn Sof where it was enveloped, and leaving an empty void *(ḥalal panui)*. For 'Eiyn Sof, that void is but a minute point, yet for Creation there is space enough in it to contain all the worlds together. Only because 'Eiyn Sof hid itself away within its essence could the void be revealed. That empty space, in which all the complex processes of emanation and creation would later take place, was called in Lurianic nomenclature *tehiru*." The purpose of that act of contraction was to "create that hollow and void space, and then to emanate all the worlds into it."[41] Contraction, then, created an abyss between 'Eiyn Sof and Otherness. This is a rebuttal offered by Lurianic teaching to the contention that the doctrine of emanation gestures toward pantheism.

In the writings of R. Ḥayyim Vital, the point is stressed that the purpose of *ṣimṣum* was to enable the vessels to come into being. In other words, emanation has to occur, for without it nothing would begin to exist. But for something to be formed without returning to its original oneness with the divine, *ṣimṣum* must take place. If not for contraction, "the vast light of 'Eiyn Sof would annul the limited being of the vessels."[42] Thus contraction and emanation, withdrawal and expansion are two opposing movements, both of them essential to the world's functioning. A comparison may be made to the continual alternation of inhaling and exhaling on which man's very life depends.

We should point out that the understanding of the word *ṣimṣum* just formulated differs from that of the popular midrashic tradition that "The Holy One blessed be He contracted His Shekhinah into the Tabernacle"[43] or between the poles of the ark. For the rabbis, *ṣimṣum* means a concentration of divine being within a small space. In Lurianic teaching it implies the opposite: a withdrawal from a small space and creation of an empty place the size of a point, from which the Divine is, as it were, absent, from which he has contracted his essence.

Engendering the void space does not constitute the act of Creation; it is but a preparatory stage. Withdrawal occurs for the sake of expansion. Through the empty void, a line *(kav)* or thread *(ḥoot)* or the form of the letter *yod* emerges, a sort of beam of light that illuminates divine efflux and causes it to descend. Yet the line itself does not descend continuously; rather, recurring moments of contraction cause an alternation of hiddenness and revelation. "Every instance of new lights appearing is preceded by *ṣimṣum*."[44] It is the same process of breathing in and out suggested above.

One more point. The various descriptions offered teach us that even if contraction and involution did occur, some impression of the previous state of being nonetheless remains. "As it contracts, the receding light of 'Eiyn Sof leaves behind a trace *[roshem],* which fills the void and combines with the power of judgment revealed there along with the act of withdrawal. This composite trace provides, as it were, the material and basis from which the vessels come into being."[45] In the sources, it is called *reshimu.* R. Ḥayyim Vital, however, omitted the doctrine of the *reshimu,* perhaps because that concept implies some kind of relationship. Here an important difference is brought to light between R. Ḥayyim Vital and another prominent disciple of R. Isaac Luria, R. Joseph ibn Tabul. Regarding the primary act of withdrawal, there is no disagreement between them. They part company, though, on the question of how reality outside of 'Eiyn Sof came into being. According to Tabul, and R. Isaac Luria as well, it seems (in the commentary on the beginning of the *Zohar* attributed to the latter), all that was engendered from the *reshimu* is separate from God and external to him. Vital, in contrast, took a more radical stance. In his view, the *reshimu* itself contained something divine; that would necessarily lead to the same fundamental problematic possibility of an enduring connection with the Divine, and thus Vital chose to repress the doctrine of the *reshimu,* preferring to deepen the schism between the Godhead and the created entities.[46]

The doctrine of *ṣimṣum* as it is presented here makes one wonder how it could have been proposed at all, for if it truly had occurred, that would imply some change in 'Eiyn Sof, some constriction of his boundaries. The description of the event in certain works, such as those of R. Menaḥem 'Azariah de Fano, is doubtless meant to circumvent such a problem. In them, *ṣimṣum* is said to have taken place within the light or will of 'Eiyn Sof—not, that is, within 'Eiyn Sof himself, but at a stage emerging, as it were, from him. Two trends of thought, however, may be distinguished. Some understood *ṣimṣum* in a literal sense, while others saw it as an analogy. In either case, the field remained open to a wide variety of interpretations.

Leading the Kabbalists who favored a literal understanding of the notion of contraction was R. Emmanuel Ḥai Ricchi (1689–1743). He sought to adapt that doctrine to the concept of creation from naught. The act of *ṣimṣum*, understood as engendering a hollow point, represented, for him, the traditional "nothingness" *(ayin)*. An echo of this literal interpretation of contraction may be found in the detailed description offered by R. Sabbatai Horowitz: "He was compelled to contract Himself from Himself to Himself, and within and at the center of Himself."[47] The most vehement proponent was R. Jacob Emden. "In my humble opinion, the phenomenon of *ṣimṣum* is absolutely mandatory; *it is not opposed to the literal meaning [pshat] of Scripture*, and is one of the fundamental concepts for one of our holy faith . . . it is a simple matter, intrinsically mandate for any believer in the account of Creation, and why should it be any more difficult to believe it than to believe in the very notion of renewal[?] . . . The world's creation would be impossible without it . . . for it is not beyond His power to make a void and seemingly empty space, to gather His spirit and soul into Himself in order to vacate the place in which to create His creatures."[48]

This literal reading of *ṣimṣum* was vehemently opposed by R. Joseph Ergas (1685–1730). "Whoever chooses to understand the matter of contraction in its most simple sense stumbles into distortion and contradiction of most of the pillars of our faith."[49] Ergas's objections seem to have been focused on the Sabbatian Neḥemyah Ḥayun. In essence, Ergas claims a literal understanding leads to notions of anthropomorphism, changefulness, and complexity (in that one component disappears while the others do not, implying a combination of parts). Even R. Moses Ḥayyim Luzzatto argued that literalness was "food and water to cultivate an evil plant," i.e., Sabbatianism, which was accused of anthropomorphism. In any case, R. Moses Ḥayyim Luzzatto interpreted *ṣimṣum* not as an event that had indeed occurred, but as an analogy of 'Eiyn Sof wishing to leave what was "His infiniteness, and choose a limited mode of action,"[50] a mode already inherent in 'Eiyn Sof.

R. Ḥayyim of Volozhin holds that "all the esoteric teachings of the holy ARI [R. Isaac Luria] are meant figuratively *[mashal]*," and thus "it is forbidden to scrutinize and to meditate on the essence of *ṣimṣum*."[51]

He explains the term *ṣimṣum* in the sense used in the midrash *Genesis Rabbah* to describe Rebecca's act of covering and concealing her face—*ṣimṣema paneha*—implying that divine essence, which fills the universe, is wholly beyond our grasp. Yet he desired the "revelation of the vessels," so "that the existence of innumerable worlds and forces would become visible and attainable through their hierarchy and devolution, and that the light of His revelation might shine through them—a fine and tremendously fragile light—through infinite curtains." This minute light, which he calls a line *(kav)*, as in Lurianic teaching, symbolizes the devolution of his essence and its revelation, minimal as it is.[52]

The early Hasidic masters also rejected the literal understanding of *ṣimṣum* for two essential reasons. First, such an understanding involves anthropomorphism, as we have suggested. Secondly, while they strove to emphasize the presence of God in the universe, the notion of *ṣimṣum* stresses God's withdrawal. In the writings of R. Dov Baer, the Maggid of Mezherich, and his disciples, the analogy is often used of the father explaining something to his son (or the rabbi to his student) by simplifying and thereby contracting his own wisdom to suit his son's lesser understanding. It follows, then, that God's withdrawal is what ultimately makes expansion and revelation possible.

THE DOCTRINE OF THE *SHEMITTOT*

An important subject in the doctrine of Creation, which is, of course, bound up with other kabbalistic issues, is the topic of the *shemittot*.[53] The subject is not the Kabbalists' invention, although they do consider it "one of the Torah's great mysteries."[54] Similar and sophisticated theories were formulated in ancient times and in the Middle Ages. The philosopher R. Abraham bar Ḥiyya[55] presents an astrological conception of cosmic cycles lasting seven thousand years, each of them dominated by one of the seven planets. A few Kabbalists, such as the author of *Sefer ha-Temunah*,[56] related astrological teaching to the notion of *shemittot*, but this was not common. Some Kabbalists make no mention whatsoever of the doctrine of *shemittot*, among them R. Joseph Gikatilla and the author of the *Zohar*. Others rejected it out of hand, such as R. Moses de Leon, in his work *Ha-Nefesh ha-Ḥakhamah*,[57] R. Moses Cordovero,[58] and R. Isaac Luria.[59] We may assume it was due, at least in part, to the influence of the latter two

Kabbalists that the subject came to be ignored in subsequent kabbalistic works. The Sabbatians, however, did make use of the doctrine, particularly in its development in *Sefer ha-Temunah*, as we shall see below.[60] The doctrine is also a central issue in R. Jacob Koppel Lipschitz's work *Sha'arey Gan 'Eden*; he, too, had Sabbatian tendencies.[61]

The doctrine of *shemittot* is founded on the assumption that an intrinsic structure underlies the cyclical nature of the number seven. For example, the seven days of the week contain six days of Creation and the Sabbath; six years of working the land are followed by one year of *shemittah*, during which the land must lie fallow; and there are six Sefirot, each operating on those beneath it and the lowest, which "has nothing of its own." In the same manner there are seven cosmic cycles *(maḥzorim)* (or "orbits" *[hekef]*, as other Kabbalists call them),[62] each of them dominated by one of the seven lower Sefirot that determine the nature of the entire *maḥzor-shemittah* cycle. For instance, in the first *shemittah*, dominated by Ḥesed, a "wholly good world" may be anticipated. Interestingly, the author of *Sefer ha-Temunah* proposes the unusual idea that the Sefirah Yesod, also called "Sabbath," does not attain independent expression in its own *shemittah*, but rather shines forth in its own special way through the other *shemittot*, just as the Sabbath, in rabbinic tradition, casts its light upon the six weekdays.

On the basis of R. Katina's statement[63] that "The universe exists for six thousand years and lies in ruins for one," the entire cosmic cycle or *shemittah*, is described as lasting six thousand years, followed by a period of a thousand years during which the world remains destroyed. And like the laws of agricultural *shemittah* prescribed in the Bible,[64] seven *shemittot* combine to form a metacycle, called the "jubilee" *(yovel)*, and at its conclusion in the fiftieth millennium, all will return to its source in the world of the Sefirot.

In Naḥmanides' commentary on the verse "In the year of the jubilee the field shall return to him of whom it was bought, to him to whom the possession of the land did belong" (Lev. 27:24), the conclusion is drawn that the world is dependent on the will of the Emanator (*koneh*, in biblical Hebrew, carries the double meaning of "creator" and "buyer"), "who possessed the land." Should he choose, though, to annul that wish, "the field shall return" to its initial state. Thus, all returns to its source. Note that Naḥmanides' conception differs slightly from that of R. 'Ezra of Gerona. The latter contends that it is the natural aspiration of the Sefirot to mount once again to their source. "Their ultimate desire and intent is to cleave and ascend to the place whence they are nourished." However, to prevent all of reality from ceasing to exist, "Our sages established the blessing, the Kedushah and the Unification *[yiḥud]* in order to draw the source of life down to the other [i.e., lower] Sefirot." In other words, human religious acts exert a counterforce to the will of the Sefirot. In the jubilee year, in contrast, when man is no longer present, all obstacles will be removed and nothing will obstruct their desire; the world's viability will cease and all will return to the Source.

The first mention of the doctrine of *shemittot* is in the writings of the Gerona circle; from there it gained great popularity among the disciples of R. Solomon ben Abraham ibn Adret (RaSHBA). Their discussions revolved around the difference between the destruction of the universe in the seventh and in the fiftieth millennia. A brief but clear presentation of the two principal positions may be found in R. Menaḥem Recanati's commentary on the pericope *Behar*. According to one, the difference between the seventh and the fiftieth millennia lies in the extent of the destruction. In the seventh, the flow of effulgence is arrested, causing the death of all living creatures and plants, yet the cosmos itself endures. In the jubilee year, in contrast, the universe is totally annihilated. RaSHBA's students present, in their master's name,[65] the following theory drawn from a close reading of the biblical text: In the verse concerning the seventh year (Lev. 25:5), possessions are spoken of in the second person ("your harvest . . . your vine"), while in the verse concerning the jubilee year (Lev. 25:11), the third person suffix is used ("that which grows of itself . . . the vine"). This difference was held to support the claim that all returns to its source (third person) only after the jubilee year. A dissenting opinion, however, was voiced. According to R. Jacob ben Sheshet and R. Baḥya ben Asher,[66] the world will be renewed after its destruction in the jubilee year as well,[67] and R. Baḥya (in his commentary on Num. 10:35) even speaks of eighteen thousand jubilee years.

According to the second position, the world will be utterly destroyed both in the seventh and the fiftieth year, with the difference that while after every *shemittah* the world is renewed, this will not happen after the jubilee.

Once again, the unique view of the author of *Sefer ha-Temunah* deserves mention; as we have said, that work postdates Recanati (although the influence of his thought may be identified in subsequent generations).

In it, the contention is made that during the seventh millennium a change takes place in the paths of the stars and spheres; as a result, temporal dimensions there do not correspond to current ones. It may be, then, that in the next cycle, the world's "days" will be of much longer duration.

Interestingly, this process is seen as affecting the Sefirot as well. Recanati presents the view that in the jubilee year, the Sefirot return to their source, i.e., to Binah.[68] According to R. Joseph ben Samuel (who lived in Catalonia in the mid-thirteenth century), though, they will return to Ḥokhmah. In the view of R. David ben Yehudah he-Ḥasid,[69] they will return to Keter; in that of R. Baḥya, to 'Eiyn Sof.[70] In approximately the same period, R. Joseph of Ḥamadan, in his work *Ta'amey ha-Miṣvot*, accepts, in principle, the assumption of the Sefirot returning to their source, yet specifies that it will occur in the seventh millennium.[71]

The various opinions we have mentioned concerning the return of the Sefirot to the Source aroused the imagination of some later Kabbalists, leading them to suggest that the various opinions are based on differences between *shemittah* and the jubilee year, or that both are but stages in the process of return.[72]

Another question, rarely discussed in the thirteenth century but treated later, was whether each *shemittah* had some unique quality. R. Moses Cordovero wrote: "Beyond any doubt, the previous *yovel* differed from the one in which we live, and this one is unlike the *yovel* to come."[73] The question of which *shemittah* we are currently living in was likewise not raised in the early generations.[74] In *Sefer ha-Temunah*, however, penned by an anonymous Kabbalist in the mid-fourteenth century, great attention is devoted to the doctrine of *shemittot*.[75] There the idea that each *shemittah* is dominated by a particular Sefirah is further developed; the author even makes the startling suggestion that the Torah is read in varying ways depending on the presiding Sefirah. In that author's view, we are living in the second *shemittah*, that of Gevurah, in which the attribute of judgment reigns, and for that reason our Torah speaks of things forbidden, of negative and positive commandments, while in the coming *shemittah* under the dominion of Tiferet, the Sefirah of balance, the number of positive precepts will equal that of negative ones.[76] Moreover, the work *Kneh Ḥokhmah Kneh Binah*[77] states that in the *shemittah* of Tiferet, "The world will be filled with knowledge . . . all will come to know God . . . and filth and the evil inclination and sin will be no more." Many Kabbalists, in fact, held that we are currently in the *shemittah* of Gevurah.

In the view of R. Joseph Angelino,[78] though, we are living in the final *shemittah*. The possibility that ours is the first *shemittah* was raised by R. Moses Cordovero,[79] and in his wake Nathan of Gaza.[80] In contrast, R. Mordekhai Jaffe[81] contended that the twenty-six generations from Adam to the giving of the Torah at Mount Sinai were under the dominion of Ḥesed,[82] while from the time Israel received the Law, Gevurah has reigned.

The identity of our *shemittah* was thus a matter of contention; the author of *Ma'arekhet ha-Elohut* hesitates to take a definitive stand, although he is convinced we are not in the first *shemittah*, for then "the Holy One blessed be He was creating and destroying worlds."[83]

Many things are absent from this brief discussion; we have not mentioned biblical verses and rabbinic sayings interpreted by the Kabbalists as related to the subject, and have not explored the relationship between the doctrine of *shemittot* and questions of metempsychosis *(gilgul)* and the resurrection of the dead. Let us conclude with a citation from one of the Kabbalists of Gerona: "Blessed is he who knows what will be in the end of time; to meditate upon it is forbidden."[84] His words are echoed by R. Meir Aldabi at the end of *Shevilei Emunah:*

> It should not be revealed nor written; one should not ask what will be afterwards. Blessed is he who knows.[85]

12 • The Torah

DIVINE SPEECH

Sefer Yeṣirah offers some meditations on the nature of the Hebrew language, a language divine in its essence. Composed of twenty-two letters, its alphabet may be divided into three main groups: three "letters of foundation," namely, *aleph*, *mem*, and *shin* (alluding, among other things, to the three cosmic elements of air, water, and fire); seven "double letters," namely, *bet*, *gimmel*, *dalet*, *kaf*, *peh*, *resh*, *taf* (which may receive a *dagesh*[1]—they, too, symbolize elements, such as wisdom and foolishness); and the other twelve simple letters.

In the eyes of the Kabbalists, the Hebrew language is not a random collection of sounds, but rather the handiwork of the Creator. Every word is laden with meanings predetermined from the six days of Creation. Biblical accounts of figures being named after events affecting them are ripe with significance, for connections are drawn between the name and its bearer. The name reveals identity.

This linguistic theory is a cornerstone of the kabbalistic worldview, and is characteristic of the polemic initiated by Naḥmanides against the concept proposed by Maimonides. In opposition to Maimonides' explanation[2] that the term "the Holy Tongue" was associated with Hebrew because it has no specific words for the sexual organs, Naḥmanides contends that it is because

> the Torah and the prophecies and all holy utterances were spoken in that language, and it is the language in which the Holy One blessed be He, may His name be exalted, speaks with prophets and with His congregation . . . and created His world with it . . . that language is Holy of Holies.[3]

The Torah, written in the Holy Tongue, thus has special significance, and knowledge of the secret properties inherent in that language would allow one to discover new aspects of the text. The Torah may be read literally, in which case its narratives, for instance, are historical ones. The same texts, though, may be seen as vessels or garments containing sublime esoteric truths, and the conveyance of these truths is the reason for their presence in the Torah. If not, it would be difficult to understand why the Torah chose to recount certain historical events and omit many others. A particularly puzzling question is why the Torah devotes space to seemingly irrelevant information, such as the list of the kings of Edom at the end of Genesis 36. The Kabbalist, though, is not puzzled, for after breaking the code, the sublime significance of the text is revealed to him. Moreover, if the Torah is indeed eternal, why does it contain so many stories of merely local, temporary, and particularized interest? Clearly, if the narrative is perceived as but an external form concealing multiple and profound layers of wide-ranging spacial and temporal significance, the picture changes radically. Hence the vast wealth of interpretations of the Torah composed by Kabbalists throughout the ages.

Most commonly, in human experience, a person thinks about something and then expresses his ideas in words. Words, then, reveal human thought.[4] Similarly, it is said that the Sefirot reveal "the pure thought," the meditations of the Emanator. Already in the *Bahir* (s. 125), the meaning of the word "Sefirah" is related to Ps. 19:1—"The heavens tell [*meSaPRim*] of God's glory"—i.e., 'Sefirah' implies something about recounting the acts of the Creator. In other words, the Jew expresses himself in a rich language composed of twenty-two letters, and God expresses himself in the *language of the Sefirot*. That, apparently, is his spoken language, in which the whole world is engendered: "By His word were the heavens made"; "and the Lord said, 'Let there be' . . . and there was. . . ."

The Emanator's thoughts and will may be expressed through other means as well, such as the Torah. The midrash *Genesis Rabbah* opens with a homily on the Torah and Creation, in which it is said: "The Holy One blessed be He looked into the Torah and created the world." The Torah, then, serves as a sort of architectural plan guiding the world's construction. It provides its laws and governs its management. In a literal reading of the text, the direct relationship between its contents and the natural laws of the created world may not be clear. This indeed, is a central kabbalistic concern, and two responses are suggested:

First, just as man does not reveal the entirety of his thought at once, as thought is more active and moves much more swiftly than speech, so divine thought reveals itself only bit by bit. The further we ascend toward infinite being, the more the concealed dominates over the revealed. Stages of revelation thus exist within the Sefirotic system itself. Each subsequent Sefirah reveals more than its predecessor. The first three express the divine intellect in the process of its revelation. The process continues all the way to Malkhut. The same is true of the Torah: our Torah represents a certain stage in the revelation of that "primordial Torah" *(Torah kedumah)* by means of which the world was created. It may very well be, though, that additional elements are concealed in the same divine plan, elements invisible in the Torah we possess—just as a layman's reading of an architectural plan differs greatly from the reading of an engineer.

Second, in the same way that what we "see" in the world of the Sefirot does not express the full wealth of divine speech, so our simple reading of the Torah does not uncover all that is buried in it. New and more profound ways of reading must thus be found to unearth more meaningful, hidden layers. Man, for example, does not appear naked before the world, but rather clothed. An observer notices his clothes first of all, yet knows his body is beneath them; real insight knows more—even the body is but a container of his true essence, the soul hidden within. The *Zohar* gave bitingly ironic expression to this idea:

> How beloved are the words of Torah, because every single word contains supernal mysteries. . . . Consequently, when the Torah, which is the supernal *kelal*, produces a special story, the implications of that story are not limited to the story alone, but extend to celestial matters and supernal mysteries. . . . And if you think that the supernal King, the Holy One, blessed be He, does not have sacred words of His own, from which to make a Torah, but that He

> needs to collect the words of commoners, such as those of Esau, Hagar . . . and all the other stories written in Scripture, and makes a Torah of them, why is it called "the Torah of truth" [Mal. 2:6]? . . . But, in very truth, the Torah is holy . . . and every single word is there to demonstrate supernal matters. And a specific story is not limited in its significance to itself alone, but it extends to the whole [the *kelal*]. . . . When it [the Torah] came down into the world, the world could not have tolerated it if it had not clothed itself in the garments of this world. Consequently, the narratives of the Torah are the garments of the Torah. If a man thinks that the garment is the actual Torah itself, and not something quite other, may his spirit depart, and may he have no portion in the world to come. . . . Come and see. There is a garment that is seen by all. And when fools see a man in a garment that appears to them to be beautiful, they look no further. [But] the value of the garment resides in the body, and the value of the body resides in the soul. Similarly, the Torah has a body. The commandments of the Torah are the bodies of the Torah. . . . This body is clothed in garments, which are the narratives of this world. The fools in the world look only upon the clothes, which are the narratives of the Torah; they know no more, and do not see what is beneath the clothes. . . . The wise, the servants of the supreme King . . . look only upon the soul, which is the foundation of all, the real Torah.[5]

Thus divine language, which expresses divine and infinite thought, is a treasure-house as well. That language is expressed both in the Sefirot and in the Torah, but one must know its inner workings. It, too, has letters, vowel points, and intonations *(te'amim)* to vary its words. In any case, all aspects of Creation came into being through divine speech. This biblical notion underlies the *Sefer Yeṣirah* as well, which announces in its opening words that the Creator formed his world with thirty-two wondrous paths of wisdom, which include "ten *Sefirot belimah* and twenty-two letters of foundation." That the language is Hebrew is apparent from the mention of twenty-two letters, and it is honored with the name "the Holy Tongue,"[6] as God himself uses it. Clearly, though, even *Sefer Yeṣirah* does not fully reveal the mechanism of divine creation through speech; indeed, the text could hardly be more abstruse. But Jewish tradition does tell of various individuals who studied that mechanism, extracted its secret logic, and engendered entities of their own. One talmudic story concerns Rabba, who created a man, and other sages who created a calf and ate it in honor of the Sabbath (*Sanhedrin*, 65b); the medieval story of the golem is also famous.

We find, in a variety of contexts, the kabbalistic interpretation of the word *ot* (letter), as being derived from the Aramaic root *ata* (to come). In other words, everything issues from, or emerges with the letters. When they join forces, the letters form a language able to build worlds and reveal the thoughts of the Emanator. In a second linguistic analogy, the Kabbalists combine a number of sources treating Creation. Let us begin by recalling the midrashic statement in *Genesis Rabbah* 1:4 that six (in some versions, seven) things *(devarim)* preceded the world's Creation. The implicit etymological connection between *davar* (thing) and *dibbur* (speech) suggests that language existed before all of Creation. What is more, other texts state that it was by means of Ḥokhmah that the world was created: "In wisdom have You made them all!" (Ps. 104:23); "The Lord by wisdom founded the earth" (Prov. 3:19); or verse 8:22 from the renowned "Wisdom chapter" of Proverbs: "The Lord created me as the beginning of His way, the first of His works of old." In these, divine speech is divine wisdom, which, as it ramifies and evolves downward, creates worlds. On the basis of the "Wisdom chapter," the midrashic tradition was born that the Torah "was the tool for God's handiwork." In that context in *Genesis Rabbah,* the Ḥokhmah mentioned in Proverbs is explicitly linked with the Torah.

Thus, the speech that reveals divine thought (i.e., the Sefirah of Ḥokhmah) is the Torah. Once again, the analogy of body and soul illustrates the point: a Kabbalist would say that the Torah is the body in which divine wisdom, i.e., the soul, is concealed. Or alternatively, one could say the Torah was given to the human race at a certain point in history, at Mount Sinai, yet in essence it is the primordial Torah garbed in the words of the Torah we know. The latter represents a stage or additional step in the process of revelation to mankind with their inherent limitations. The common denominator between these two perspectives is, of course, that the Torah in our possession is the Emanator's means of communicating the wisdom forever concealed within him. Hence the longing to uncover the Torah's hidden messages. The Kabbalist reads the letters and the names in his own secret way and discovers treasures of understanding buried within the text. The Torah thus becomes the means through which man can transcend his own world and cleave to the realm of the Sefirot.

The connection between the Divine, the Torah, and Creation is also expressed in the idea presented in the *Zohar* (I, fol. 4b) that when a person formulates an innovative understanding of the biblical text, he creates a new dimension of heaven *(raki'a)*. This allowed the Hasidic master R. Ṣaddok ha-Kohen of Lublin to go one step further and declare that the act of Creation is renewed daily (after the verse in the liturgy: "Who in His goodness daily renews the act of Creation") only by grace of the innovations in understandings of the Torah formulated each day in the study houses of the Jewish people.[7]

The following conclusion was drawn by R. Ḥayyim of Volozhin, a student of the Gaon of Vilna:

> Since [the Torah's] descent from its concealed root, so to speak, down to this world . . . all the vitality and existence of all the worlds depends solely upon the breath of our mouths and our meditations upon it. And the truth, beyond all doubt, is that were the entire world, from one extremity to the other, to be voided, even for a single moment, from our study and consideration of the Torah, in that moment all the worlds, upper and lower, would be utterly destroyed, Heaven forfend. Thus the abundance of their light, or its paucity, God forbid, is wholly a function of our involvement in it.[8]

Hence the practice for which the Volozhin yeshivah was renowned; sounds of Torah study issued from it continually, day and night. (This seems to have been the background for Ḥayyim Naḥman Bialik's poem "Ha-Matmid.")

Let us consider, for a moment, some other practical conclusions related to the nature of the Torah study prescribed. Which particular aspect of the Torah and its branches one chooses to learn is unimportant. One's study should, preferably, be motivated by an aspiration to discover some truth planted in the text, i.e., the Torah's esoteric meanings or intentions. Yet even an amateur, someone who merely reads the text more than studying it—as they say in Eastern Europe, one who "says" Torah—can realize significant results. R. Shneur Zalman of Lyady expressed this conviction in straightforward terms: "The entire Torah, [when studied] in its simple sense, even merely read with no comprehension of its contents, wins life for all of Israel. And even doing one *miṣvah* in its simplest sense, with no understanding of it at all, wins life in the world to come for all who do it." It is true, he says, that "The life of Moses our Teacher, may he rest in peace, was unlike our lives, just as drinking water does not gladden men like the drinking of wine, and the life of one who knew a little or a lot is unlike that of one who knew nothing, one of the masses. For although all of them live, existing even on the lowest level of neither performing the *miṣvot* nor transgressing them, all are equal as living entities, and all have a portion in the world to come."[9] R. Shneur Zalman of Lyady reiterates his view in another context: "Thus the Bible is called *mikra*, for it summons *[kore]* and draws down [as he explains there] revelation of the light of 'Eiyn Sof through the *letters*, although the reader may grasp nothing of their meaning."[10] Interestingly, though, disputes did arise in kabbalistic literature over whether or not one was permitted to read the *Zohar* without understanding the text. According to R. Shneur Zalman of Lyady, one should not read "if he has no knowledge of what the words mean."[11] In opposition, R. Ḥayyim Palache wrote: "The *Zohar* has the *marvelous* power to purify and illuminate the soul" even of the reader who does not understand it.[12]

The words of the Torah were a gateway leading the Kabbalists to hidden worlds and extraordinary notions. The same fundamental text common to all, the order of its letters, the missing ones and the extra ones, provided the building blocks for complex new structures. The assumption that the Torah has body and soul, a revealed and a hidden aspect, the same basic structure shared by man himself, and the assumption that the Torah is composed of endless interconnected layers—for, indeed it is *Torat ha-Shem*, not in the sense of "God's teaching," but rather a teaching that expresses his great name, revealed in infinite aspects just as he himself may choose infinite avenues of revelation—these principles allowed the Kabbalists to interpret Scripture in myriad ways while preserving the immutable identity of the original text. R. Eleazar of Worms, a Hasidic master of Ashkenaz who lived in the early thirteenth century, contended that each verse of the Torah could be interpreted in more than seventy aspects. Four hundred years later, R. Nathan Shapira of Cracow, in his work *Megalleh 'Amukkot*, offered 252 (!) different interpretations of Moses' prayer in Deut. 3:23ff. And R. Elijah Ḥayyim of Ginazano wrote: "*Every single letter* of the Torah bears mounds and mounds of *halakhot* and profound secrets."[13] The biblical verse "The Lord's Torah is *temimah* [complete, untouched]" (Ps. 19:8) led the Hasidic master R. Menaḥem Mendel of Premyshlyany to comment that "No man has yet touched even the minutest part of it."[14] In other words, despite all the Kabbalists' efforts in seeking out the Torah's essence, the vast majority remains undiscovered. The Torah is compared to a well *[be'er],* a play on the verse "Moshe began explaining *[be'er]* this Torah" (Deut. 1:5). Were the verse grammatically correct, it would have used the infinitive form of the verb, *le-ba'er* (to explain); the fact that it did not implies that Moses transformed the Torah, so to speak, into a well endlessly flowing with water. The Kabbalist does the same, drawing from some hidden well of meaning. The water is different, yet the source is the same.

The Torah is the divine *logos*, addressing man without respite. Although the revelation at Mount Sinai was an unrepeatable historical event, it bears within it the seeds of eternity. At every moment, within every individual, a reenactment of the same experience may take place—if only he can sense it, if only he is able to incline his ear and open his heart. The Torah continues to flow forth and speak to man like a pure and eternally flowing spring, just as 'Eiyn Sof exists eternally despite all the world's vicissitudes; the question is only to what extent man is willing to sense the reverberations of the original Sinaic revelation. Hence the two main streams of thought: Torah study with the intent of penetrating its inherent mysteries, and the specific nature and spiritual connection each individual has to the Torah.

KABBALISTIC READING OF THE TORAH

The Kabbalist makes no claim to innovate; in his eyes, all is concealed in the Torah, and his role is but to make that hidden content visible. Many thinkers have pointed to the introduction often used in the *Zohar*, "R. So-and-so opened *[pataḥ],*" to state that the Kabbalist does no more than pull aside the curtain, revealing through that opening what was concealed. Such a contention, of course, empowers the Kabbalist to present audacious and even radical teachings. Indeed, many Kabbalists, or at least a portion of their commentaries, may seem very bizarre to us, perhaps even contradicting fundamental beliefs we hold. Nonetheless, the Kabbalists had a special sense of where to draw boundaries, and did declare, on occasion, that a certain statement must be rejected because it does not correspond with kabbalistic teaching.

Jewish thinkers have expressed the prismatic nature of the Torah in diverse ways. All of them—preachers, philosophers, Kabbalists—insist that a simple reading of the text is insufficient, and that additional layers of meaning must be excavated. This is true of the rabbis in their ramified talmudic expositions, of Philo of Alexandria in his allegorical explanations, of the philosophers' unearthing of "Torah mysteries."

Like them, the Kabbalists adopt the notion of multiplicity.[15] More precisely, the entire world of the Kabbalists, beginning with the fundamentally symbolistic approach intrinsic to mystical thought, is founded on the multiplicity revealed in the various levels of reality. If this is true in the created world, the Torah—considered to be God speaking to man—should surely contain even more layers upon layers. Thus the Kabbalists sometimes spoke in general terms of "hidden and revealed." As early as in Ashkenazic Hasidism, the analogy is used of the nut, composed of shell and fruit. The fruit is concealed within the shell, protected from the outside. Yet the nut in its entirety is not very nourishing; one must crack it open to extract its fruit, its raison d'être. R. Moses de Leon describes a person who fails to seek out concealed truths as "a beast who walks, head bowed to the ground,"[16] neglecting and even violating his God-given mission. In contrast, one who holds his head high, and walks with his eyes wide open, may well merit having a certain word flash before him, granting him a moment of inspiration.[17] Thus what is concealed is considered most important of all, a pure and divine spark. In the words of R. Moses Cordovero:

> As for the virtues of this wisdom in comparison to the other parts of our holy Torah . . . it is a divine occupation and surely offers tremendous potential for *devekut* [adherence]. Without any doubt, the extent to which a person's soul can cleave to the higher worlds depends on his occupation in the lower world . . . and he who devotes himself to Kabbalah *[elohiut]* will surely attain a higher level of adherence than one who deals with the other aspects of the Torah, even though the entire Torah is divine, composed of His holy names. . . . As it is said countless times in *Tikkuney Zohar*, the status of Kabbalists is far superior to that of scholars of Scripture or of the Mishnah.[18]

At times, two levels of interpretation are mentioned, namely, the hidden and the revealed; at others, as many as seven are suggested, though on a somewhat artificial basis.[19] For the most part, the Kabbalists speak of three or four hermeneutical paths including *ma'aseh*, *midrash*, *haggadah*, and *sod*.[20] R. Baḥya ben Asher enumerates "four paths": *peshat* (plain meaning), *derash* (homiletical meaning), *sekhel* (rational way), and "the path of truth," i.e., Kabbalah. The latter term appears frequently in the writings of Naḥmanides. The author of *Ra'ya Meheimna*[21] speaks of *peshat, re'iyah, derash,* and *sod.* This list, clearly, is akin to the famous PaRDeS, an acronym of *peshat, remez, derash,* and *sod.* Notably, the notion of PaRDe*S* does not appear in the *Zohar* itself. According to the findings of modern scholarship,[22] that notion does not seem to be an organically Jewish development at all, as traditional sources usually speak of three paths. Apparently, then, it is a product of influences from outside the Jewish world. That influence is already noticeable in a few of R. Moses de Leon's Hebrew writings, used more and more by Kabbalists after him until it became the "official" categorization. Another formula, less common yet also important, deserves mention as well. R. Moses Cordovero speaks of the following "divisions of the Torah": the "plain narrative" of the Bible, laws, Kabbalah, and combinations of letters.[23]

The most important statement related to our subject, and frequently cited in kabbalistic writings, originates in the *Zohar* (III, fol. 152a), part of which we quoted earlier in our discussion.[24] According to the author, there are three levels to the Torah: stories, commandments, and esoteric mysteries. Parallel to them are garment, body, and soul. Note that the Zohar's author does not mention the subdivisions of PaRDeS; his main concern seems to be with the simple meaning *(peshat)* and the esoteric message *(sod)*, although he does state that the future will bring the revelation of the Torah's greater secrets in an intimate "soul of the soul" fashion. In any case, whoever reads the Torah for its literal meaning alone yet insists he has grasped its essence is considered a sinner and apostate. For although, in this world, divine truths must inescapably be clothed in material, external garments, those garments must not be confused with the content they conceal. Certainly, the *Zohar* argues, a man's clothes are not his essence, and neither the taste of wine nor its purpose can be known from the appearance of its flask. Both the garment and the flask are means to an end, and should not be taken for more than that.

R. Moses de Leon goes even further, declaring that were we to hold the garment, i.e., the stories of the Torah, as the essence, we could compare masterworks of world literature and find stories of even greater artistic value! Clearly, though, the Torah did not intend merely to tell stories; the reader is obliged to consider each letter and every crownlet as an allusion to some higher meaning ensconced within it.

Another conclusion is that because the words contain such hints of sublime truths, nothing must be added or subtracted from the text, no detail of its appearance altered in the slightest. Any such change would put all its inherent allusions off target:

> Thus the Book is not vocalized, has no intonations, and lacks punctuation, for the Torah contains all wisdom, revealed as well as concealed. . . . And thus the Torah may be interpreted in many aspects as man inverts its verses one way or another.[25]

In effect, then, Halakhah itself serves as a tool, a legitimization even, for the Kabbalist's pursuit of radically innovative ideas.

This notion is expressed, inter alia, in the famous parable of the maiden in the *Zohar*:

> The old man said: It is not for this alone that I began to speak, for an old man like me does not rattle on or raise his voice for one thing only. How confused the inhabitants of the world are in their understanding! They do not see the path of truth in the Torah, but the Torah calls to them every day in love and they will not even turn their heads. It is true, as I have said, that the Torah takes a subject from its sheath, and it is revealed for a moment and then immediately hidden; but when it is revealed from within its sheath, and then at once concealed, it is revealed only to those who know it and recognize it. What can be compared to this? It is like a girl, beautiful and gracious, and much loved, and she is kept closely confined in her palace. She has a special lover, unrecognized by any one and concealed. This lover, because of the love that he feels for her, passes by the door of her house and looks on every side, and she knows that her lover is constantly walking to and fro by the door of her house. What does she do? She opens a tiny door in the secret palace where she lives and shows her face to her love. Then she withdraws at once and is gone. None of those in her lover's vicinity sees or understands, but her lover alone knows, and his heart and soul and inner being yearn for her, and he knows that it is because of the love that she bears him that she showed herself to him for a moment, in order to awaken love in him.
>
> So it is with the Torah. She reveals herself only to her lover. The Torah knows that the wise man walks to and fro every day by the door of her house. What does she do? She shows her face to

> him from the palace and signals to him, and she withdraws at once to her place and hides herself. None of those who are there knows or understands, but he alone knows, and his heart and soul and inner being yearn for her. And so the Torah is revealed, and then is hidden, and treats her lover lovingly, in order to awaken love in him. Come and see. This is the way of the Torah. At first, when she begins to reveal herself to a man, she gives him a sign. If he understands, good. If he does not understand, she sends to him. . . . She begins to speak with him through the curtain that she has spread before him, in the way that best suits him, so that he can understand little by little, and this is *derash* [homiletical interpretation]. Then she talks with him through a very fine veil and discusses enigmatic things, and this is *haggadah* [narration]. And then when he has become accustomed to her, she reveals herself to him face to face, and speaks to him about all her hidden mysteries, and all the hidden paths, that have laid concealed in her heart from ancient times. Then he becomes a complete man, a true master of Torah, the lord of the house, for she has revealed all her mysteries to him, and she has neither hidden nor withheld anything from him. She says to him: You saw the sign that I made to you at the beginning. These are the mysteries that were contained within it. This is what it really is. He sees at once that one should not add to these things or subtract from them. The real meaning of the text of Scripture is then revealed, [from which] one should not add or subtract even a single letter. Therefore men ought to take note of the Torah and pursue her, and become her lovers, as I have explained.[26]

This parable, used by many Kabbalists and developed in various ways, beginning in the sixteenth century,[27] touches on a gamut of issues, as the reader can easily see; what is important for us is the contention that the Torah contains, hidden behind a series of veils, layers of interpretation, all of which may potentially be revealed to one worthy of them. The end of the parable is important: a scholar who has been blessed with that wisdom understands why the text must be preserved unaltered. Due to the reigning state of limitation in the revealed aspects of Torah, many profound truths remain submerged, like the light that God hid away for the righteous in the first hours of Creation.

The same idea was expressed in another variation based, apparently, on the talmudic tradition preserved in the Land of Israel: "Ḥananya the nephew of Yehoshu'a said, Between each and every utterance, detail and letter of the Torah, as it is written "inlaid with emeralds" [Song of Songs 5:14] like the vast ocean. R. Simeon ben Lakish, upon reaching that verse, said, Hananya has taught me well . . . just as, in the ocean, between the big waves are small waves, so between each and every utterance, detail and letter of the Torah."[28] In Kabbalah, as we know, we find the image of the white expanse between the black words written on the parchment, a continuous and lengthy series of occult secrets, while the written words express that part accessible to human beings.

All this raises the question of how one should relate to the literal meaning of the biblical text. In some contexts, a negative view of the simple, revealed message is evident: it is referred to as "melancholy garments" that must be stripped away.[29] Others speak of three shells encasing the Torah; just as the Shekhinah is in exile and only a storming of the gates will lead to her redemption, so the shells around the Torah must be shattered to reach its true, i.e., esoteric, meaning.[30] A person who studies the Bible's literal sense exclusively, rejecting kabbalistic understandings, would be better off not studying anything at all.[31] In a harsh list of derogatory terms, the author of *Tikkuney Zohar* lambasts scholars of Halakhah and literal biblical interpretation; his is doubtless an extreme view. In most cases, despite the Kabbalists' esteem for study on the esoteric level, and their encouragement of such a practice, they did not deride those who favored literal interpretations, particularly those whose level prevented them from reaching higher and more profound planes. It is only fair to point out that Jewish rationalists also attacked proponents of literal interpretation. For example, it was said, "'This is not the way, neither is this the city' [2 Kings 6:19] . . . do not speak with anyone who has spent all his days exclusively in study of the Talmud."[32] Such an attitude is typical of elitist groups striving to claim their uniqueness.

The notion that the Torah entails more meanings beyond the literal sense extended, in the conception of various Kabbalists, to Oral tradition as well, particularly regarding aggadic literature. The first to speak of an esoteric understanding of Aggadah seems to have been R. 'Ezra of Gerona: "The same thing that happened with the Torah and kabbalistic teaching happened with rabbinic tradition as well—they relayed their wisdom in midrashim and *haggadot* through parables and riddles in order to conceal their true message. And they scattered them here and there to hide their real place. He who merely scans [the texts] will not sense their presence, taking them literally . . . and, bereft of knowledge or insight, it never occurs to him to ask how the Sages could write such things . . . indeed, a delightful treasure is hidden within them."[33] Among other Kabbalists who voiced similar ideas is R. Shneur Zalman of Lyady, who made the somewhat extreme statement that "*the majority of the Torah's wisdom is concealed in them.*"[34] Note that his comments regarding Halakhah were more moderate: "Each and every overt Halakhah contains hidden significance."[35]

THE TORAH AND ITS GIVER

An ancient midrashic text states: "The sections *[parashioteha]* of the Torah were not transmitted in order, for had they been, anyone who read them would have been able to raise the dead and perform miracles. Thus the true order of the Torah was hidden, and is revealed before the Holy One blessed be He alone."[36] This magical view of the Torah, later formulated as a reading "according to Names," enables the reader to achieve momentous and wonderful things by penetrating deep within the divine essence inherent in the words of the Torah. Not far distant was the conception that the entire Torah is in fact "the Name of the Holy One blessed be He," in the phrase of R. 'Ezra of Gerona.[37] Or, in the *Zohar*'s formulation (III, fol. 36a), "All the Torah is one single sublime and holy Name." Another approach avers that while "the entire Torah is a single holy Name" (*Zohar* II, fol. 124a), it is "a supreme name, containing all names."[38] Similarly, Naḥmanides writes (in the introduction to his commentary on the Pentateuch) that "the entire Torah is [composed] of the names of God." At issue is either a single name or a totality of names. In either case, Naḥmanides' is the most radical formulation. More moderate ones include the statement that "The Torah is the secret of His great name"[39] or that "In the secret of His blessed name are they contained."[40] For R. 'Ezra, though, the Torah and the Name are identical. A name discloses one's unique identity, and in that sense the Torah is God's name—in its form as a complete and continuous organic unit, without any subdivision even into words. No one, of course, is meant to, or even able to, pronounce that extended name; rather, the Torah is a sort of instrument through which God expressed his might and his essence. It may not even contain the whole of his essence, but rather only that portion he chose to reveal. Hence the ancient midrashic tradition, mentioned above, that God consulted the Torah in his creation of the world. If, indeed, the Torah expresses his essence, it speaks of the nature and quality of that essence as well. Thus the character of the world and all its laws, divinely chosen to be bestowed upon his handiwork, preexist in that Name, in that Torah.

Such a Torah, naturally, is not the Torah inscribed on parchment we currently possess and was not given at Sinai; rather, as the Talmud has it, the Torah predated the world by two thousand years.[41] Such a "temporal" scenario, truly irrelevant before the world came into being, is translated by the Kabbalists into symbolic terms. As early as the thirteenth century, this temporal scenario was identified with Ḥokhmah, the second Sefirah. The "primordial Torah" is thus parallel to the Sefirah also called the *reshit* (beginning) or *nekudah* (point) from which the world was created. These symbols do not contradict one another and may easily be seen as a single unit of meaning.

According to R. Joseph Gikatilla, the Torah itself is not the ineffable Name, but rather a commentary on that Name:

> Understand that the Torah is a manner of interpretation of the name YHVH, may He be blessed. And you shall understand the secret of "the teaching of God."[42]

In other words, the expression *Torat ha-Shem* speaks not of possession, i.e., "God's Torah," but rather indicates a more complex relationship, an identification of "God" and "Torah" in a sort of grammatical apposition. In another context, Gikatilla portrays the Torah as an interwoven fabric of the ineffable Name:

> All the Torah is woven from the appellations [such as "merciful" and "compassionate"], and the appellations from the names; all the holy names are dependent on the name YHVH, and all are united in it. Thus the entire Torah is woven of the ineffable Name.[43]

This concept may seem rather incomprehensible to an unassuming individual, and is, in fact, atypical of a work *(Sha'arey Orah)* generally formulated in more comprehensible style.[44] Nonetheless, the Kabbalists both accepted and made use of the principle that a process occurs in which the Name becomes an interweaving of warp and woof. Once the Kabbalist comprehends the message encoded in that process of transformation, he can reverse it and reach yet fuller understanding, even attaining a more real meeting with "the Name," and this enables him to realize other unique achievements.

Naḥmanides, a contemporary of R. Joseph Gikatilla, in the introduction to his commentary on the Pentateuch, states that the Torah is a sheet of names that Moses separated in a certain way, yielding the words that express the message of our Torah. Essentially, though, the Torah may be read in another manner through a redivision of the words and their vocalization. Approximately three generations later, the anonymous author of *Sefer ha-Temunah* concluded that in every *shemittah*, the Torah really is read in a different way. He went so far as to say that in our current *shemittah*, one letter of the Hebrew language remains unrevealed. This implies that in the future, when that letter is revealed and inserted in the text of the Torah, the Torah will be read differently than it is today. Such ideas harbored threats of antinomianism, which in fact surfaced in the Sabbatian period. At that time, those who professed them took license to stop observing the commandments, claiming the time of redemption had come, which mandated a new reading of the Torah.

A similar idea, emerging from another direction, is that the Torah, as an expression of 'Eiyn Sof, encompasses an infinity of meanings. This principle is drawn from the fact that the text of the Torah is unvocalized; the Halakhah actually forbids its vocalization. In the eyes of the Kabbalists, the reason is that as long as a word remains unvocalized, it may be read in a variety of ways (for example, the root *dvr* may be read as *davar* [thing], *dibber* [he spoke], *dever* [plague], *dabbar* [leader], etc.), thus taking on a plurality of meanings. The moment it becomes vocalized, though, this multiplicity ends; the word has but a single referent.

Undeniably, this, too, is a potentially explosive concept. R. Jacob ben Sheshet, a Geronese Kabbalist, was aware of its implicit danger, yet did not surrender, claiming it was possible to reject inappropriate readings. He said:

> A *Sefer Torah* is not vocalized, so that we can interpret every word as we wish, depending on the way we read it. . . . Do not think it absurd to interpret every word in any way that you think fit to read it, because, even if you find a word or so, the possible reading of which could *contradict true faith*, there is no harm in this, because

> the *answer to the problem is invariably at hand*, and no harm results. . . .[45]

The notion that the Torah is an organic unity is expressed in a variety of ways in the writings of the early Kabbalists. R. ʻAzriel of Gerona uses the image of the human body—though composed of separate limbs, it is a unified entity. One slight difference is that while the body functions as a unit, "there are some members upon which the soul depends and others upon which it does not";[46] in other words, an internal hierarchy does exist. Nevertheless, R. ʻAzriel stresses, "all of it forms a single structure."[47] Comparable is the conception of the Sefirot that developed in kabbalistic circles; the image of the human body is frequently employed to demonstrate that despite its internal divisions, the body is yet a unity. Another image of the unity of the Torah is the *merkavah* or Divine Chariot, which appears in the writings of R. Joseph Ḥamadan, for example. That thirteenth-century Kabbalist wrote: "The entire Torah is pure gems and pearls, and every single letter is a component of the supernal Chariot."[48] Here, as well, we find the image of the Sefirot as a chariot, and a central motif in that image is the intrinsic unity of composite entities.

In any case, the notions of unity and completeness explain "the need to count the letters and words, their plene or defective spelling, their written orthography as opposed to the way they are read, the final or open form of the letters, and their size, large or small."[49]

We may assume that the Kabbalists' view of the Torah, which embraced much more than the text's literal message, was not easily agreed upon by other circles. I would mention here, just as one example of the abyss separating them, the deprecating and polemical comments made by the philosopher Isaac Albalag: "Better that you should hold fast to the text's simple meaning and believe with absolute faith in its revealed aspect, without seeking the reason behind it, than to hold some alien belief originating neither in wisdom nor in prophecy. For if you belong to the occult sect in our land, you will be neither a sage nor a believer."[50]

THE TORAH AND THE JEWISH PEOPLE

Among the myriad developments and ramifications of the theme of the Torah in kabbalistic literature—too numerous to discuss in full in this context—I would like briefly to examine one of particular interest, and that is the connection between the Torah and the Jewish nation. In kabbalistic symbolism, the primordial Torah represents Ḥokhmah,[51] the Written Torah is Tiferet, and the Oral tradition is Malkhut. In that sense, the vital and continuous connection between the Written and the Oral Law has its counterpart in the connection between Tiferet and Malkhut; the two are interdependent like the two sides of a coin. The Oral Torah is not autonomous but rather draws its vitality and order from the Written Torah. Nonetheless, it expands, interprets, and reveals the Written Torah's true meaning. Such a relationship is mirrored in the link between the Sefirot of Tiferet and Malkhut, which symbolize the unity between masculine and feminine valences. In that framework, Malkhut often represents Knesset Yisrael as well. In the words of the *Zohar* (III, fol. 22a), for instance:

> The secret of the matter is that the Community of Israel [Malkhut] does not come into the King's presence save with the Torah. So long as Israel studied the Torah, the Community of Israel abode with them, but when they neglected the Torah she could not stay with them an instant. So when she presented herself to the King with the Torah, she was full of strength and confidence and the Holy King rejoiced to meet her.

It is the nation of Israel, then, which prepares the celestial Knesset Yisrael—the Sefirah of Malkhut—for her union with Tiferet. This belief gave rise to a variety of practices. One is studying the Oral tradition in the small hours of the night before dawn, followed by study of the Written Torah—thus joining the two "Torahs" at the nexus between night and day, i.e., between Malkhut and Tiferet. Another is the custom of learning Torah throughout the night on the eve of Shavuot.

The link between the Jewish people and the Torah, both Written and Oral, may thus be seen as a natural outgrowth. I would like to present one particular kabbalistic contention widespread in modern kabbalistic literature, though originating in the Safed school. It states that the Torah is composed of six hundred thousand letters. The most normal calculation, in fact, yields slightly more than half that number, but the Kabbalists claimed the sum of six hundred thousand for various reasons. Their primary impetus was doubtless the many midrashic sources in which the rabbis state that six hundred thousand souls were present at Mount Sinai for the Giving of the Law. The kabbalistic idea of the number of letters composing the Torah clearly expresses the conviction of a vital connection between the souls of the Jewish people and the Torah.

That conviction led to another notion. A link exists not only between Israel and the Torah, but between the Torah and every individual Jew. One may argue that the number of Jews far exceeds that six hundred thousand. The response is that the six hundred thousand souls are reincarnated throughout the generations until they seem to number many more. In fact, though, they remain but six hundred thousand.

Another principle follows: the enumeration of six hundred thousand is not merely a numerical matter. There are also six hundred thousand potential interpretations of the Torah, since the Torah addresses each individual according to his own unique identity. This idea was developed in a variety of psychological and educational ways in Hasidic thought. Most important for us is the notion that myriad interpretations of the Torah can all be authentic. Thus the idea we discussed above, which appeared for the first time in the thirteenth century, of the manifold meanings of the Torah as mirroring the relationship of the Torah to the Emanator, reappears in the sixteenth century in another form as well—in the context of the relationship of the Torah to the Jewish people.

These two motifs meet once again in the renowned saying that "the Holy One, the Torah, and Israel are one." The saying is often attributed to the *Zohar*, perhaps because it is in Aramaic. Yet although certain elements may be found in the *Zohar* indicating the connection between God and the Torah, the saying, with its trebled, proverbial form, was actually coined by R. Moses Ḥayyim Luzzatto in his commentary on the *Idra*,[52] composed in Padua in 1731, which became quite popular. In any case, the proverb adeptly joins three central axes and celebrates their inner and fundamental unity.

The letters that form the Torah are the same letters used in the world's creation,[53] and what occurred in the distant past is reenacted each day. Thus, one who understands the occult secrets of the Torah knows the mysteries of the created universe as well; his status becomes similar to that of the Creator himself, giver of the Torah. This concept does not contradict the assertion by one of the most prominent Kabbalists that "we believe the Torah, with all its themes and stories, from beginning to end, can be comprehended neither by the intellect nor by natural law."[54] That is, the Torah is necessarily connected neither to intellectual truth nor to the laws of Creation; these are not criteria for assessing the Torah's nature. The statement cited above that there is no direct connection between the Torah and Creation contradicts our earlier arguments. The contradiction is resolved, though, when we bear in mind the context in which the statement appears; there, the Kabbalist mentions various philosophical views of Creation:

> There are heretical sects who claim the world was preexisting *[kadmon]*... while others believe in its renewal yet deny any knowledge of its Renewer in the lower worlds. . . . Still others do recognize such knowledge but negate the Providence of God's supremacy over His humble creatures, claiming that man has no responsibility for his actions and censuring his behaving like the fish of the sea. In sum, in their eyes, God has abandoned the world to chance. Some believe in renewal and knowledge and Providence, yet conclude that such things are unacceptable by reason and nature, and that the world merely takes its course; thus, they deny the miracles inherent in natural changes. . . . And in addition to these sects there are many others . . . we need not describe them all.

In opposition to all these views, he argues that the Torah teaches neither philosophy nor physics, and no conclusions or proofs can be drawn from its simple message. What is most important is that "we have received it, handed down from one man to another to Moses our Teacher, may peace be upon Him, at Sinai, and the commandments practiced in the community of Israel are loyal witnesses to all our faith and our traditions; this is a great testimony to all the beliefs we have mentioned." In other words, the Torah's essence and significance is itself, the very fact of its being handed down from generation to generation throughout history; it needs no additional justification.

On the basis of this assumption, the Kabbalist seeks to perceive the Torah's contents as a complete unit, disallowing all possibility of fissures. Indeed, we find, for example, R. 'Azriel expressly combating those who believe the world was created and is controlled by God but who grant themselves the authority to decide what they will perform and what they will reject. This approach leads them to a total rejection of the Oral Law. Such people are called apostates *(apikorsim)*—"That is, he has exempted himself from the principle of the Creator's lordship and the wisdom of the Sages, as one who says, 'Who will be lord over us?'"[55]

THE CONCEPT OF THE COMMANDMENTS

A short comparison with philosophical views will aid us in understanding the kabbalistic view of the commandments, or *miṣvot*. Jewish philosophers assumed that the Torah is fundamentally rational in nature and saw the *miṣvot* as aids in achieving intellectual edification, ethical maturity, and physical fitness and in giving life some kind of moral and religious discipline. Man is the starting point, and the commandments are for his benefit. The philosophers speak of no extrahuman, and certainly no cosmic, influence stemming from performance of the *miṣvot*. At times emphasis is placed on man's perfection as a social and political being. Man is seen as recognizing the divine source of the commandments and God's greatness and relationship with man, the Jewish nation, and the world. An important question, then, would be whether the validity of the commandments is autonomous or heteronomous. A few philosophers concluded there is no specific need for the instruments that were prescribed, provided man can reach the desired goal by other paths. In other words, one may dispense with all the practical commandments whose aim could be realized, say, by intellectual or pedagogical means. Remember, as an intellectual trend, philosophy tends to put greater emphasis on spiritual aspects of life while the world of action and material concerns is given less weight. The conclusion many philosophers tried to draw from Maimonides' more relativistic explanations (regarding sacrifices, separations between milk and meat, etc.) was that commandments based on a certain historical reality may be done away with. According to Maimonides,

> The generalities of the commandments necessarily have a cause and have been given because of a certain utility; their details are that in regard to which it was said of the commandments that they were given merely for the sake of commanding something . . . (e.g., why one particular sacrifice consists in a lamb and another in a ram, etc.). . . . All those who occupy themselves with finding causes for something of these particulars are stricken with a prolonged

> madness in the course of which they do not put an end to an incongruity, but rather increase the number of incongruities.[56]

We need not bother seeking reasons underlying specific commandments, because we will uncover no explanations—the commandments were given to be performed. The only reasons we can find are general, relating to the commandments in their entirety.

Another point worthy of attention is the philosopher's relationship to the world of Halakhah. While he may have some personal connection to a halakhic way of life, Jewish law has no place in his philosophical *Weltanschauung*. Even Maimonides' attempt to integrate the basic principles of Jewish philosophical thought into Halakhah by presenting the *Sefer ha-Mad'a* [The book of knowledge] at the beginning of his *Mishneh Torah* failed to bring that world closer to the world of Halakhah.[57] Instead, the two remained disparate and mutually repelling realms. Much energy was given to the search for reasons underlying the commandments, but as we said, success led to a decrease in their observance.

Thus, despite the emphasis both philosophy and Kabbalah placed on the spiritual element of religious life, the two groups differ on many, many other points. In opposition to the philosophers, the Kabbalists viewed the commandments as an inseparable part of the Torah. The commandments are divine to the same extent as the Torah as a whole; each commandment is holy, its every detail significant. Moreover, not only the details explicitly mentioned in the Written Torah, but interpretations of those details, developed throughout the generations in the Oral tradition and instituted by halakhic authorities bear equal weight. R. Moses Cordovero says at the beginning of his work *Eilimah:* If a person "does not believe even in a single letter of the Torah, refuting it instead, he is an apostate *[min]*. And [this is the case] not only for the Written Torah but for the Oral Torah as well—if he denies even the smallest part of it or any of its elements, even the words of the Sages and their homilies," he is an apostate.

Shortly after Maimonides' death, the Kabbalists attacked some of his philosophical explanations on just those grounds. Naḥmanides, for example, assaults him on his stance regarding sacrifices (in his commentary on Lev. 1:9), as does R. Todros ha-Levi Abulafia. We have also mentioned Naḥmanides' opposition to Maimonides' interpretation of the expression *leshon ha-kodesh*.

In the opinion of the Kabbalists, once again, the Torah is preexisting, the world having been created according to it. It contains the world's order and the entirety of nature, to the extent that the commandments correspond with that order and are organically linked to it. They cannot, therefore, be altered. The commandments were meant not only to improve man on the individual level but to bring the whole of reality to a state of completeness. Thus, no discussion of the autonomous validity of the commandments took place. All the commandments, as a whole and individually, were given in correspondence with divine will. In a sort of play on words, the *miṣvot* were conceived as advice—*'eitin*, as the *Zohar* calls it (II, fol. 82b)—for the realization of divine will.

From approximately 1230 onwards, we find mystical interpretations of the commandments formulated by Geronese Kabbalists, particularly R. 'Ezra and R. Jacob ben Sheshet, both of whom quote their teacher, R. Isaac the Blind. In the course of the thirteenth century and the early fourteenth century, we find a growing trend toward interpreting the reasons for each commandment in its every detail, and explaining the processes taking place in various worlds and in the Godhead in each stage and detail of the commandments' performance. "No *miṣvah* contains even one element devoid of purpose and benefit in the soul's success and the unification of the great Name with His glory," declares a sixteenth-century Kabbalist.[58] We find extensive discussions in works such *Ta'amei ha-Miṣvot* by R. Joseph Ḥamadan or those of R. Menaḥem Recanati, as well as in the framework of commentaries on the Torah, such as those by Naḥmanides (to a certain extent), Recanati, R. Baḥya, and R. Isaac of Acre, or in *Ra'ya Meheimna* (a work slightly later than the *Zohar*, and penned by a different author). The general view was that expressed in the *Zohar* (II, fol. 218b): "Happy is he who gives heed to the precepts of his Master and knows their secret meaning, for there is no precept in the Torah upon which sublime mysteries and supernal radiance do not depend."

We have a collection of letters entitled *Minḥat Kena'ot* by Abba Mari, who is called "Don Astruck." This work clearly reflects the dire situation perceived by the sages of the time, and the imminent danger they saw in the allegorical homilies made by the rationalists of the miracles mentioned in the Torah and of the reasons for the commandments. Anxiety was particularly high in southern France, where translation of Spanish philosophical works from Arabic to Hebrew was currently being undertaken. One of the central figures in the affair around the year 1300 was

R. Solomon ben Abraham ibn Adret (RaShBA), a student of Naḥmanides in both the esoteric and exoteric realms. When we recall that RaShBA had students not only of Halakhah but of mystical teaching as well, we may understand why there was a tendency to delineate the significance of the commandments or to interpret Naḥmanides' mystical thought.

There was, therefore, a movement among a few philosophers and their followers to make light of the value and performance of practical commandments.[59] Various sources penned by halakhic figures in the thirteenth century clearly indicate this proclivity in Spain. For example, in 1235, R. Moses of Coucy lamented that myriad Jews do not perform the commandments of *tefillin, ṣiṣit,* and *mezuzah.*[60] R. Jacob ben Asher, too, writes: "It was the practice of the Rishonnim to be swift in fulfilling the commandments, and with affection. That is still the practice in Ashkenaz, but not in Sefarad, where the commandments are fled from."[61] Even the Kabbalists of the period declare that in their time, apostasy and an attitude of mockery had become widespread regarding the performance of commandments, for a variety of reasons. For instance,

> There are those among the people of Israel who act without restraint, inventing ideas to cast truth to the ground . . . saying there is nothing more to the *miṣvot* than that a few of them preserve physical health and a few preserve property . . . and a few ensure the world's habitation . . . yet their purpose is neither to punish nor to reward . . . They have erred after Greek wisdom and "have gone backward and not forward" [Jer. 7:24], forsaking the source of living waters, casting off the yoke of the Torah. . . . And each of them chooses according to his own judgment, and "they go from one nation to another, from one kingdom to another people" [Ps. 105:13] . . . mocking the pious and denigrating the Jews, etc.[62]

Or:

> Now there was a day when the sons of the Greek books came to present themselves before the Lord, and the adversary came also among them [after Job 1:6]. And they forsook the source of living waters and studied those books, and their minds were drawn to them, until they abandoned the Torah's words and its commandments, and cast them behind their backs [after Neh. 9:26]. . . . They scorn and ridicule and jest using the teachings of the Greeks and their

> cohorts. . . . And I even saw them during the festival of Succot, standing in their places in the synagogue, watching the servants of the Lord with their *lulavs* circling the Torah scroll in the ark, and they were laughing and mocking them. . . . And they said: "You think we need to bless God, or that He needs all this? It's all meaningless." More, when it was evident they had no tefillin and were asked why, they would say, "The only reason for tefillin is, as it is written, 'For a memory between thine eyes' . . . we prefer recalling the Creator verbally, even a few times a day, and that is a better and more reasonable sort of remembering."[63]

Faced with this religious laxity, we find, on one hand, emphasis on certain commandments, such as forbidden sexual relations, mixed marriage, the precept of tefillin, social precepts, higher status for the poor, etc.; and on the other, we find emphasis on the entire system of the commandments and inculcation of the various values we have mentioned. This undoubtedly raised religious tension even beyond the narrow sphere of kabbalistic thinkers. The works of R. Menaḥem Recanati and R. Baḥya ben Asher, which did contain kabbalistic commentaries on the Torah, were read by wider circles than those of the Kabbalists alone and, according to various evidence, were exceedingly popular among the general public. This certainly served as a counterweight to the tendencies toward disrespect, and helped to reinforce religious tradition.

A later period deserves mention as well, i.e., when Sabbatian theology caused a stir in the Jewish world and the contention was voiced that with the advent of the Messiah, the commandments would lose their validity.[64] It was Sabbatai Ṣevi himself who spoke the altered benediction "Blessed art Thou . . . who permits what had been forbidden" (substituting *isurim* for the word *asurim*—"who frees those in bondage" in the traditional benediction). In Salonica, the prayer book of the Doenmeh sect, the local Sabbatian converts, contained a radical emendation to the credo *Ani ma'amin.* To the traditional text "I believe with complete faith that this Torah will not be altered, nor another come in its place" was added "only the commandments will become void, but the Torah will exist for ever and ever."

Licentiousness and apostasy continued in the Frankist movement in Poland. Only after the ban in approximately 1756 did the movement die down. At the same time, the Jewish community of Poland and neighboring countries gained strength thanks to the spread of Hasidism, which also contained kabbalistic elements. The spirit of the movement finds expression in phrases such as "Torah and *miṣvot* are the essence of the divine,"[65] and order was restored.

THE COMMANDMENTS AND *DEVEKUT*

As early as R. 'Ezra of Gerona, the commandments were described as rooted in the world of *aṣilut*; thus, they are not merely symbols of divine forces but are a means of ascent to the upper realms, as well as the way the ten Sefirot are revealed in our world. "All the *miṣvot* are God's glory."[66] Performance of the commandments is a mystical act enabling contact with the divine realm and the experience of adherence, or cleaving *(devekut)*. The *miṣvot* themselves are a sort of drawing light, increasingly "indwelling" until "the soul is separated from the body like a drawwell to the soul."[67] Like a magnet, the commandments draw the soul up to its true and common root.

The commandments are sometimes seen as a means to the restoration of the upper worlds; in other words, they enable contact with divine forces that arouse the world or bless it with new effluence. Alternatively, they may cause the restitution of the divine realm itself, which is apparently in need of man's efforts.

As we will see in the next chapter, it is a fundamental kabbalistic principle that the soul has its source in the Divine. One conclusion drawn from this conviction is that the soul can also influence its source, destroy the nexus of connections among the various Sefirot, or increase the effulgence reaching the lower worlds and man himself. Man is perceived as a microcosm *('olam katan)*, and because he is composed of all and connected to all, he can also influence all. "Know that man may perform a *miṣvah* and thereby restitute all the channels from the highest wells of emanation to the last of the receivers; that is called 'a righteous one, pillar of the world' *[ṣaddik yesod 'olam]*."[68] Drawing from the basic assumption that man was created in the divine image,[69] an influence on the Adam Kadmon (primordial man) would, then, also be possible. Observance of the Torah and the commandments creates the direct link between man and the world of *aṣilut*. To perform positive precepts is to make internal links in that world, and to avoid performing negative precepts prevents complications and disturbances in the descent of divine effulgence. The law of the Torah became a symbol of the divine order, and even Jewish history came to be seen as bound up in that process. If we say that divine *aṣilut* fills all of existence, and that the Shekhinah represents the world of *aṣilut* down below, then man is obliged to realize that connection with the Shekhinah. This is particularly since the Shekhinah is connected to the historical Assembly of Israel, as we have seen. Thus, in his performance of the commandments, the Jew unites with the entirety of the Jewish nation and with the Shekhinah, which is but the innermost core of the People of Israel.

R. Isaac the Blind's commentary reads as follows: "Although Thy commandment seems finite at first, it expands ad infinitum, and while all perishable things are finite, man can never look upon the meaning of Thy commandment as finite."[70] That is, the practical performance of a commandment creates a doorway to infinity, though no man knows the whole length of the tunnel stretching from it. Thus, his student R. 'Azriel concluded that "All the *miṣvot* are glory *[kavod],*"[71] i.e., divine being. In his view, "Glory is the ten Sefirot." That idea penetrated to the *Zohar* and all kabbalistic works. Not only, as the *Zohar* (II, fol. 90a) says, do the ten commandments, which contain all the commandments, *correspond* with the ten Sefirot, but the performance of the commandments is an actualization of a mystical reality within the Sefirotic realm. Similarly, Recanati writes:

> The commandments form a single entity, and they depend upon the celestial Chariot, each one fulfilling its own particular function. Every commandment depends upon one specific part of the Chariot. This being so, the Holy One, blessed be He, is not one particular area divorced from the Torah, and the Torah is not outside Him, nor is He something outside the Torah. It is for this reason that the Kabbalists say that the Holy One, blessed be His name, *is the Torah.*[72]

Later, he adds that each commandment is linked to a certain part of the Chariot, and no commandment can take the place of another; although the two may seem similar to us, they are not. "Whosoever performs one commandment causes that power to descend upon the same commandment above, out of the 'annihilation of thought,' and he is considered as if he maintained one part of the Holy One, blessed be He, literally."[73] Recanati ends his introduction by saying:

> And if you are able to explain the reasons for the *miṣvot* and rejoin them with their primary source [in the Cause of Causes], that is good; but do not say [those reasons] were the intent with which the *miṣvot* were given, for we have never probed their depths; regarding my innovations concerning them, though, I would say if not for their hidden meaning, they may well have been given for the reason I will suggest.

In accordance with that conviction, he declares that the reason for some commandments is explicit in the Torah, while others are intellectually mandated. This conception of the commandments as a comprehensive system was extended by the Kabbalists, leading to the contention that the Torah is God's *name*, i.e., "in its exalted essence it is actually identical with God."[74]

In another view, mentioned above, the structure of the Torah is organic, like the human body and the world. Despite its complexity, it has a single form. "The *miṣvot* are a single knot, like the cloth of a garment, the threads of which are bound together."[75] The image of the human body, though, may be used to explain another idea as well, that of the distinction between "light" precepts and weighty ones as quantitative rather than qualitative. "All the *miṣvot* are glory; therefore, do not say that one is a light precept and another weighty, for one *miṣvah* may have many others connected to it, while another has few, just as the soul is much more closely linked to some of man's limbs than to others."[76]

COMMANDMENTS AND *TIKKUN*

The Torah is not a collection of commandments and narratives, but rather a treasure-house of divine forces and lights clothed in the guise of letters and revealed in a "material" Torah. Thus the relationship between the commandments and the Sefirot is not merely exemplary; rather, "He who subtracts even one commandment of the Torah diminishes, as it were, the image of faith [i.e., the Sefirotic system], for all [the commandments] are joints and limbs in the image of [supernal] Adam, and consequently, they all go to make up the mystery of unification."[77] By performing a commandment, one actualizes a supreme spiritual reality. One of man's principal roles, then, is theurgic, i.e., to enable the correct and harmonic functioning of divine powers.[78] Theurgic action is sometimes described as giving nourishment to the Shekhinah, as in the image of the candle, the wick, and the oil. The Shekhinah is the candle, the human body is the wick, and good deeds are the oil. It is man who must induce the flow. We recall the *Zohar*'s famous expression (II, fol. 135b): "arousal from below" *(it'aruta diletata)*. That is, arousal beginning in the lower realm serves as an impetus for a parallel arousal from above. Hence, the saying "For the sake of the unification of the Holy One blessed be He and His Shekhinah" found in many prayer books. Every human action must be devoted to the aim of engendering unity and harmony in the world of the Sefirot. This leads to the audacious belief that every human action, whether *miṣvah* or transgression, either restores or harms all realms of reality. Even man himself, in the performance of a commandment, cleaves to divine radiance and draws it from potentiality to actuality, opening a channel through which blessings can flow downward. Thus, through his material actions, man leaves the sensual world and rises to a sphere of divine holiness and light, reaching the apex of *tikkun* in cleaving to God. That is the mystical aspect of the *miṣvah*. It is, on one hand, a symbol of something wholly concealed from our conceptual system; yet on the other, it is more than a symbol, for man, through it, augments the light's intensity and cleaves to it. He is both the source and the receiver of influence.

It is worthwhile to note the formulation of this idea found in one of the most well known kabbalistic ethical works:

> To perform a *miṣvah* with intent is unlike performing it without intent, for intent *[kavvanah]* allows the *miṣvah* to ascend. . . . And with knowledge of the intent of a *miṣvah*, one must instill one's heart with awe and love, aware of the *tikkun* one enacts through that *miṣvah*. But if he does not know its intent, the tefillin upon his forehead and his arm are *as stones*, and cannot arouse awe and love in his heart. (*Reshit Ḥokhmah* IV, 10)

In *Gle Razaya*, fol. 24c, it says, in even more extreme terms,

> Anyone who attains knowledge of a commandment's essence and secret, and performs it—his recompense is ten times greater than

one who does not know its significance, for one who performs a *miṣvah* in ignorance of its secret merits is like an ape imitating men.

The *Zohar*, in contrast, is less concerned with the human aspect, and deals more with the mythic drama taking place on the divine plane as a result of performance of the commandments. Man's influence upon the upper realms is very important in that work. Indeed, the preeminent view among Geronese thinkers that reaching *devekut* was the climax of spiritual life reappears in the works of various Kabbalists and makes a vigorous comeback in the Hasidic teaching of *devekut*.

The conclusion to be drawn, then, is that external action is less essential than the mystical intent accompanying it.[79] Through that intent, the material-external aspect of the *miṣvah* expands and becomes an internal symbol which actualizes divine vitality in the world of the Sefirot. Man's every action oils the works of the Sefirotic machine. In such an atmosphere, in which every action is performed "for the sake of the unification of the Holy One blessed be He and His Shekhinah," every aspect of mundane life is filled with sacred emanation. Spiritual exaltation occurs in each and every domain of man's existence, for even in the most physical acts, holiness is concealed. As examples of works expressing this notion, I would mention two, both quite popular: *Shulḥan Shel Arb'a* by R. Baḥya ben Asher, which concerns the *halakhot* of meals; and *Iggeret ha-Kodesh* (whose authorship is not definitively known; it is customarily, but incorrectly, attributed to Naḥmanides), which concerns sexual relations. Each work teaches how physical deeds may become sacrament.

In such an approach, the most important aspect of human action is directed upward. As a secondary result, influence from above flows down to all the lower worlds, and to man among them. While performance of a *miṣvah* serves to augment the light and holiness emanating from above, committing a transgression causes that effulgence to flow to the world of *sitra aḥra*. R. Joseph Gikatilla aptly interpreted the word *ḥok* (statute) as "boundary," i.e., the performance of commandments is meant to set up an obstacle to the flow of influence to the world of "the other side."[80] In other words, there is a causal connection between performing a commandment and its recompense. Gikatilla expresses this idea very clearly, offering analogies from the natural world in order to demonstrate the connection between actions and their results. For instance, when man tills the soil as he should, "the earth will [certainly] bear its produce," or when a person dresses inadequately in inclement weather he catches cold.[81] Later, in the sixteenth century, R. David Messer Leon described God as a doctor, the commandments as medicine, and transgression as poison. Here, too, the intrinsic merit of the *miṣvot* is emphasized.

Man himself, though, must not perform the commandments with the a priori expectation of receiving a reward, not even in the world to come. The late Hasidic movement in particular emphasized serving God with no personal appeal and no request for recompense.

One can also find "philosophical" assumptions among kabbalistic thinkers. For example, the fourteenth-century Kabbalist R. David ben Yehudah he-Ḥasid said: "The Holy One blessed be He gave us the *miṣvot* for our benefit and pleasure, to grant us life this very day [after Deut. 6:24]."[82] Such assumptions are particularly prominent regarding a subject such as prayer, which may be seen as a religious act par excellence, but also as an expression of personal appeal and fulfilling of material needs. Indeed, in a classic kabbalistic work, composed in the fourteenth century by one of RaSHBA's students, we read: "Thus you must understand that the prayers and benedictions are only for our own benefit, for the upper realms lack nothing; all there is complete oneness."[83] One of the commentators on that work, R. Yehudah Ḥayyat, an exile from Spain, attacks him vehemently for his "philosophical speculation." The accepted view was that prayer was meant to bring the human world to perfection, yet its power reached far beyond, even to the divine realm. A detailed description of that process may be found, for instance, in certain passages in the *Zohar* and in commentaries on the liturgy inspired by it. Some Kabbalists, though, emphasized above all the metaphysical aim, the theurgic task of engendering harmony in the upper world "For the sake of unification of the Holy One blessed be He with His Shekhinah for the sake of all of Israel." The rectification *(tikkun)* of man and the world comes as a secondary result of the unity and wholeness achieved in the world of the Sefirot. The key phrase in this conception is *ha-'avodah ṣorekh gavohah* (worship serves a divine need). It appears frequently, particularly in R. Meir ibn Gabbay's *'Avodat ha-Kodesh*, R. Isaiah ha-Levi Horowitz's *Sheney Luḥot ha-Berit*, and R. Ḥayyim of Volozhin's *Nefesh ha-Ḥayyim*; a similar notion is expressed by R. Dov Baer of Mezherich, who writes in *Ṣava'at ha-Ribash*: "Do not pray for something you lack, for your prayer will not be accepted; rather, when you want to pray, pray for . . . what is lacking in the Shekhinah."[84]

Attention to the issue of the *miṣvot* was underlined in the Kabbalah by the famous phrase "worship serves a divine need." The term actually originates in the Talmud,[85] but it was Naḥmanides, I believe, who first infused it with kabbalistic significance,[86] in his commentary on Exod. 29:46. The idea was developed in the work by Ibn Gabbay mentioned above, who does not hesitate to point out the paradoxicality of the concept. In the introduction to his book, he writes:

> This is an extremely difficult matter, and no mind's net can capture it, for the human intellect could not conjecture that *tikkun* of the Most High should be in the hands of the lower worlds, and that divine service and prayer serve a divine need, had the Holy One blessed be He not revealed that marvelous mystery to the master among the prophets [Moses], evoking his astonishment.[87]

That, though, is not enough to negate the concept itself. Already in the *Bahir* we find something in the same direction: "Every person who learns Torah *deals mercifully with his Creator*, as it is written, 'He rides upon the heavens by your help *[be-'ezrekhah],'* that is, when you learn Torah for its own sake, you help Me, and I ride upon the heavens" (par. 185). This notion expanded to encompass the performance of all the commandments.

In accordance with the method of Ibn Gabbay, the talmudic expression, "The *miṣvot* were given for no other reason than to unite *[leṣaref]* mankind" was interpreted in the sense of welding together *[ṣeruf],* or engendering connection. In his words: "Connection and cleaving to the unique Name is through the *miṣvot*, for they are the thread binding those who perform them to the unique Name."[88] Similarly, in *Sheney Luḥot ha-Berit (SHeLaH),* the word *miṣvah* is interpreted as drawn from the Aramaic word *ṣavta* (together). Ibn Gabbay goes further and imparts another meaning to the word *leṣaref*—this time regarding negative precepts. As he says, the avoidance of transgression "also serves [His] glory, for defilement with them in the lower worlds reaches above as well, even to the Temple [i.e., Malkhut]."[89] To avoid impurity and the arousal of *sitra aḥra*, transgression must be avoided. This, then, is the significance of refining *(ṣerifah)* silver of all impurities: to separate out all dross, leaving pure silver.

Prayer *(tefillah)* was likewise seen as an act of joining by interpreting the term *tefillah* as drawn from the word *petil* (thread); prayer is the thread connecting man to God. God is conceived as the aim or goal, in utter rejection of the notion that man, in his prayer, presents himself as an object with needs to be answered. Consider Ibn Gabbay's understanding of the word *tefillah:*

> The hidden meaning of *tefillah* is in the phrase "Can that which is flavorless *[tafel]* be eaten without salt?" [Job 6:6], meaning that one should make his own needs unimportant *[tafel]* compared to higher needs. And he who requests and includes himself, it is as if he makes himself a partner of the Most High. Moreover, all requests and all needs are profane in nature, as all wise men know, and he who is preoccupied with them and asks for them in his prayer, which should be a moment of union, brings nonsacred offerings *[ḥullin]* into the Temple court and defiles the holy sanctuary.[90]

Ibn Gabbay, though, understands both prayer and the Torah and *miṣvot* as unifying elements. In the introduction to his work *Tola'at Ya'akov*, for instance, he writes: "The expression *tefillah* speaks of the bonding of the entreator's form to the Receiver of his plea for abundance and blessing from Him."[91] And in *'Avodat ha-Kodesh:*

> Just as a complete person, by preserving the relationship between the lower form and the higher in sanctity and purity through his involvement with Torah and the *miṣvot*—which is analogous to the thread that binds two pieces of cloth together—so the Torah and *miṣvot* are the intermediary joining the lower form with the higher. . . . In his cleaving to his Source through his deeds, his worship and his unification, he becomes beloved above and his will is done, and initiates marvelous actions in both the upper and lower realms.[92]

This interesting result is drawn as a "logical" conclusion from all that has been said thus far. That is, if man's actions are seen symbolically, and if the final destination is the higher world, then his actions do not merely "add strength to the might *[gevurah]* of the Most High," in the phrase of the talmudic Sages; he truly acts upon and integrates himself with the rhythm of theosophic life, with the order of the Sefirotic system. In this context, I would like to quote Gershom Scholem:

> Man appears here in his immediate connection with God, which was broken only after the primordial Sin. . . . Upholding the Torah and *miṣvot* returns man to that direct connectedness with God.

> Through Torah observance, man subordinates himself not to natural law but to the hidden law that determines the life of all the worlds, a law encompassed in the Torah. The life of the Israelite man is not enslaved to the laws of nature, but rather forms a single unbroken succession of "hidden miracles" through which God works, not as the Cause of Causes at the end of a long series of causes, but rather as the immediate cause of every situation and all events.[93]

The result, therefore, is that man has the power to change things in the world because the right key is in his hands. (The image of the key comes from Gikatilla, who uses it to speak of prayer.) R. Menaḥem Mendel of Vitebsk, one of the foremost Hasidic thinkers in the second half of the eighteenth century, used the concept of the changes and wonders the zaddik can initiate through his performance of the *miṣvot*.

This idea is linked to an important conception formulated in kabbalistic literature regarding miracles. In it, miracles are not God's direct intervention in and annulment of the world's order, but rather part of the existing system; according to its predetermined order, they will occur under certain conditions, as a natural outcome of a certain action. "And he who understands this will not find it difficult to accept natural change and new signs and wonders in the world; like a room in which all the world's species are contained—whoever merits possession of the key may draw all he needs from it, and what is the change of Will in that?"[94]

The Kabbalist's worldview thus combines two elements: the world's Creation is perceived, as we have seen, not only as born of the Emanator's will but as an expression of God's essence. Even the Torah and its commandments, as a "primordial Torah" *(Torah kedumah)*, were emanated from the Emanator. They flow from the essence of his being. Thus they are "the essence of purity and holiness."[95] Hence, by observing the commandments, one actualizes holiness in the world and thereby aids in the world's *tikkun*. The advantage is more than personal, in clear opposition to the position of the philosophers; pleasure is granted to the entire world.

This leads, of course, to a serious theological question. Is the Divine really lacking, that He should be in need of completion by man and his actions "serving a divine need"? The answer, from the Kabbalah's point of view, is simple. Man's actions are not directed to 'Eiyn Sof, to a transcendental God, but rather to the Divine revealed in the Sefirotic system and inherent in our world. Since that aspect of the Divine is wholly oriented to the world, and to man in particular, inconceivable power is granted to the human creature who is, as it were, the cause activating the Sefirotic mechanism; all, essentially, is in his hands due to the order determined by the Emanator. R. Ḥayyim of Volozhin trenchantly expressed the notion:

> In terms of His essence, His unconnectedness to the worlds, there is absolutely no need for the Torah and *miṣvot*, and thus it is said, "If you have sinned, what does it do to Him, and if you have been just, what does it give Him" [Job 35:7]. . . . For the essence of the Lord of all, blessed be He—no human action, whether good or bad, can affect His essence in the slightest, heaven forbid.[96]

VARIOUS PROBLEMS

The approach to the commandments described above circumvents a problem with which mystics of many religions have grappled: Is a mystic, at the height of his spiritual elevation, still in need of physical performance of the commandments? If he needs the material world in order to fulfill the practical commandments, doesn't that tie him to a degraded sphere?[97] The answer, according to the Kabbalists, is that the commandments are symbols of a more elevated state, and all of them form an organic unit; by the very performance of a commandment, the Jew abstracts it from its materiality. Thus the practical commandments are not an obstacle. Rather, they are perceived as steps on a ladder that are indispensable for the individual wishing to ascend.

In Hasidism, this notion acquired social significance. The zaddik, as leader of his community, cannot achieve spiritual elevation alone while ignoring the more common members of his congregation. Rather, he must bring about a situation in which he is able to raise those allied with him along with himself. He is forced to "descend" from his own level, although that would be considered "descent for the sake of ascent." The zaddik's condition is therefore a continual tension between "running and returning" *(raṣo va-shov).*

Another question emerging from this problematic was whether service for "a divine need" is reserved for a rare few, a religious elite, for Kabbalists alone, or whether an ordinary individual through his ordinary performance of the *miṣvot* also exerts some influence on higher realms.

This question was not answered definitively until the sixteenth century. Lurianic Kabbalah, in its teaching of a detailed and impressive system of *kavvanot*, nearly put an end to any presumption "the masses" might have had of participating in the noble effort. But while Lurianic teaching assigned complex rules for the performance of the commandments, Hasidism explicitly stated that not every individual should be burdened with knowledge of the entire complex system of the *kavvanot*. It emphasized the status of each and every individual in religious life, and tended to discourage overzealous attention to minor details.[98]

It claimed, "One should not multiply minute details *[dikdukim]* excessively in every act one does, for it is the will of the evil inclination to make a man fearful he has not fulfilled his obligation, driving him to sadness. And sadness is a great obstacle to worship of the Creator."[99]

In place of that, Hasidism made another, and by no means simple, demand: performance of the *miṣvot* in a state of connectedness, enthusiasm, desire, and *devekut*. Here is a somewhat ironic formulation of the idea:

> The essence of pleasure is when man decides and becomes inflamed with giving satisfaction to the Most High, that is, to fulfill His will. *For servitude in and of itself is not the main thing.* Indeed, sometimes a person learns because his natural desire is to learn, and a man also deals in trading if that is his inclination, and what is the difference between the two? . . . Yet the essence of God's pleasure in him derives from his desire to serve Him . . . *the fire of his enthusiasm.*[100]

A simple expression of this principle in everyday life would be a case in which a Jew, on his way to perform some commandment or to pray, met someone and stopped to converse with him. His delaying would imply he was not ardent enough in his desire to perform the commandment with the swiftness it demands, and that would be a serious flaw in his divine service.[101]

This position is fundamentally linked to a similar notion phrased in no uncertain terms in *Reshit Ḥokhmah* (II, 4):

> And his soul should cleave with ardent devotion in performance [of a *miṣvah*], so that even if he were given all the money in the world he would not cease from doing it, just as a man would not

> delay in making love with his wife, as all his desire is for her, even if he were given all the money in the world. Thus his ultimate desire should be in the *miṣvah*, for by fulfilling it he conjoins with the daughter of the King, the Shekhinah . . . and in that he cleaves to sublime life and his soul glows with the illumination of the supreme light shining from the performance of that *miṣvah*.

In Hasidism, then, adhesion was the highest ideal. As a result, performance of the commandments with intent extends into the realm of the profane. Thus, "in his every action, one should think that through it he gives satisfaction to his Creator, blessed be He, rather than fulfilling his own needs in even the smallest way."[102] That is, man is aware of a divine presence filling all of reality, and every step he takes is truly done in order to encounter God—*if only he seeks him out*, of course. Each renewed encounter is a realization of his adhesion. And that, in principle, *is possible for every person*.

The Kabbalah raised yet another point. Because the commandments are so powerful, people should do them joyfully. The importance of happiness had been emphasized by R. Yehudah ha-Levi,[103] and in Ashkenazic Hasidism great attention was indeed paid to that demand. For example, in the "Laws of Piety" at the beginning of the book *Ha-Rokeaḥ*, it says:

> It is a fundament of love that the soul be filled with love for God and bound with the cords of love with joyfulness and gladness of heart, and not as one serving his master against his will . . . for all who harbor God's wisdom in their hearts think with joyful desire of doing the will of their Creator, performing His commandments wholeheartedly.

In other sources we find similar formulations. But in the golden age of the Kabbalah in Safed of the sixteenth century, the demand was reiterated in a number of works. Many sources recall R. Isaac Luria's averment that all he attained was due to his fulfilling the commandments with joy (based on the verse in Deut. 28:47—"Because you would not serve the Lord your God with joyfulness and gladness of heart . . . "). That principle became widely accepted and revered, and was greatly stressed in the Hasidic world.

At this point I would like to cite some thinkers who attempted to "justify" the demand we have outlined. In the *Sefer Ḥaredim*, R. Eleazar

Azikri sees the commandments as a gift[104] from the King given to man—how could man not be gladdened by it? Similarly, his contemporary R. Elijah de Vidas wrote: "The commandments are the King's jewels with which He adorns Himself; one should be joyful."[105] R. Elijah ha-Kohen of eighteenth-century Izmir sees the commandments' greatest achievement as being that their holiness drives away the impurity of "the other side," and that, naturally, is a cause for happiness. In his words, "When a man performs a commandment, he should understand and know that with it, all his limbs are restored, that the sanctity of the *miṣvah* may enter within him, expelling all the impurity of the [evil] inclination, and thus he should perform it with great joy."[106] R. Moses Ḥayyim Luzzatto focuses on the very encounter with God, man "meriting the chance to serve the Lord, may He be praised, like unto no other."[107] R. Naḥman of Bratslav went in the opposite direction: "When a person performs a commandment in joy, that is a sign his heart is whole for his Lord."[108] That is, the feeling of happiness is an expression of his internal completeness.

These are only a very few examples, but the tendency is clear. We should add that the emphasis on the phenomenon of happiness is important in a psychological sense, for it serves as a counterbalance to the spiritual tension required in the actual performance of the commandments with profound mystical intent.

In examining kabbalistic works from the second half of the thirteenth century, the influence of historical reality is clearly visible. Although the Kabbalists' eyes are drawn aloft, they are by no means disconnected from their surroundings. Their concern is not only with metaphysical matters but also with the improvement of Jewish society, plagued by social ills and transgressions both in interpersonal relations and in man-God interactions. Thus R. Baḥya, for instance, in his commentary on Exod. 18:21, writes: "Come and see the power and greatness of fine virtues, for the zaddikim and the prophets were not extolled in the Torah for their wisdom, understanding, and knowledge but for their attributes . . . all this teaches that what is most important is not wisdom but the integrity of one's attributes, just as the tree is not of the essence but rather its fruit." Similar is his comment in *Kad ha-Kemaḥ:* "Wisdom is incomplete without correction of one's acts."[109] The comprehensive work of the time, the *Zohar*, dealt with phenomena of Jewish society in its day, and that reality is visible between the lines of other kabbalistic works as well. At times they treat halakhic issues such as the relationship between the community and the *misvot* or the pronunciation of the words of the liturgy as it is written in prayer books; at other times they deal with theological problems such as the Creation, eschatology, and so forth. Sometimes their concern is with economic issues, class differences, the plight of the poor, preaching charity, faith, trust in God, peace, honor, and protest against mixed marriage. In certain instances, they deal with security matters. Thus it is remarked, "There is no nation that denigrates them outright and spits in the faces of Israel like the sons of Edom" (*Zohar* II, fol. 185b). The implication is physical and spiritual aggression by Christians. In another passage, the author of the *Zohar* complains bitterly of injury inflicted by Muslims: "'A handmaid that is heir to her mistress' (Prov. 30:23)—that is Hagar, who gave birth to Ishma'el, and he did harm to Israel and ruled over them, and afflicted them with manifold afflictions and plotted their destruction numerous times. And to this day they rule over them, preventing them from practicing their religion. *No exile is as cruel to Israel as the exile inflicted by Ishma'el*" (*Zohar* II, fol. 17a).

The *Zohar*'s concern with this wide range of subjects demonstrates that its predominantly mystical interests were set against a background of *Sitz im Leben*. The Kabbalists' personal aspiration to spiritual exultation did not cut them off from reality. Perhaps that is a direct result of the nature of Judaism, with its concomitant system of *misvot* and strong emphasis on the social perspective. No one, including the Kabbalist, can ascend in disregard of those aspects of his religion. The Kabbalist's mystical life is an additional plane to that system.

The Kabbalist extends physical acts to mystical ones, thereby combining the two worlds; he neither disregards the material aspect nor presents it as an obstacle or negative element. This is reflected in R. Baḥya's interpretation of a socioeconomic commandment: "Thus the Torah warned that 'Her ways are ways of pleasantness, and all her paths are peace' (Prov. 3:17), that man should accustom himself to be compassionate, that he give some of his own blessing as charity to the poor. *And by doing that* he combines the attribute of *raḥamim* [the act of giving charity] with that of *din* [poverty, a constriction and limitation of abundance]—and by combining them enables the world to exist. For no existence is possible without both of them."[110]

Another example of the attempt to combine two planes comes in his discussion of a fundamental value, the preservation of the human species. He contends that sexual relations may be practiced for mere earthly ends, but in that case "man is no better than a beast." Thus, they must be practiced as "preparing for the reception of the intellectual soul, that man may be cognizant of his Creator and serve Him . . . unlike the intent of the wicked, [who think] they are to populate the world, to eat and drink as beasts; rather the intent should be for the sake of His Name alone."[111] The divine dimension is thus projected through the human, and that, in the eyes of the Kabbalist, is man's true essence.

13 • The Doctrine of the Soul

THE UNIQUENESS OF THE SOUL

No discussion of kabbalistic teaching, with its innovative explanation of the concept of the Divine and its highly tangible description of that entity, would be complete without treating the other side of the coin. We have already seen that the very description of the Divine is bound up with the lower world, so intimately linked to its source. That link is not one-sided. At the end of that lower world is man, and on the basis of the divine image within him, he is summoned to return everything to its origin, i.e., to raise, in a spiritual sense, all that has fallen. Such a task may, in a way, be even more difficult than that of the Emanator.

Philo of Alexandria exhorts:

> And why, treading as you do on earth, do you leap over the clouds? And why do you say that you are able to lay hold of what is in the upper air, when you are rooted to the ground? . . . Mark, my friend, not what is above and beyond your reach but what is close to yourself, or rather make yourself the object of your unimpaired scrutiny. . . . But before you have made a thorough investigation into your own tenement, is it not an excess of madness to examine that of the universe?[1]

The Kabbalist, though, thinks otherwise. For him, heaven and earth kiss one another. And he, for his part, is imbued with tremendous power enabling him to fulfill his mission. The *Zohar* says that in the verse "asher bara elohim la'asot" (Gen. 2:3), *bara* means God *(elohim)* and *la'asot* means man. That is, man accomplishes what God created. Likewise, we read in a Hasidic text:

> Man's excellence is in his power to join and link together all the worlds through his divine service, that is, to connect the lower world to the upper world and give pleasure to God, blessed be He . . . and to draw His Shekhinah down into the lower realms—that is the primary purpose for which all was created.

The Kabbalists base their view on certain rabbinic statements that are few in number,[2] but of vital importance. One is "Whenever Israel do the Holy One's will, they enhance the power of the Almighty, as shown by the verse 'And now, I pray thee, let the power of my Lord be great' (Num. 14:17); but when Israel angers Him, it is as if 'Of the Rock that begot thee thou art unmindful' (Deut. 32:18)."[3] Thus the *Zohar* comments on the verse from Psalms (68:35), "Ascribe strength to God," by saying, "How? In making good deeds" (II, fol. 32b). In other words, good deeds enable man to empower the Most High. R. Meir ibn Gabbay suggested a concrete understanding of the talmudic statement "The *miṣvot* were given for the purpose of refining society *[leṣaref bahen et ha-beriyot]*." Departing from the original meaning, Ibn Gabbay states that the commandments are not intended for man alone, but "joining and cleaving to the unique Name [occurs] through the *miṣvot*, for they are the thread connecting those who fulfill and perform them with the Unique God."[4] Thus *leṣaref* is understood in the sense of combination *(ṣeruf)* rather than of refining *(ṣerifa)*. In other words, the *miṣvot* join one end of the thread to the other—God, the source of the commandments, to man, their receiver. As mentioned, the word *tefillah* (prayer) was similarly explained as a connecting cord *(petil);* and the word *miṣvah* was drawn from *ṣevet* (group).

This is surely meant as encouragement that not only man's physical, creative power materializes before his eyes as he succeeds in conquering worlds, but that he is imbued with hidden spiritual power as well, and the results of the latter reach even to the heavens. Moreover, "If there is no arousal from below, there is no arousal above, and it is through arousal from below that there is arousal above" (*Zohar* I, fol. 235a). That merit, though, also gives him a tremendous obligation: the feeling that his actions touch the edge of the King's very cloak should surely instill him with fear of sin—and that is the religious aspect or achievement. If, though, he is daring and noble of spirit, that feeling would inspire him with awe of his majesty, and this is the beginning of the mystical aspect or achievement.

Thus, in the sixteenth century, R. Abraham writes: "I have copied this lengthy treatise that you may see the power man possesses to perfect or to destroy; do your utmost in joining the *middot* [the Sefirot] in your mouth, in your heart, and in the work of your hands."[5] And in the name of the Ba'al Shem Tov we have the statement: "One must believe with complete faith that even when man moves his little finger, he moves spiritual worlds."

A more radical statement is that "divine worship serves a divine need *[ṣorekh gavohah]*." It is as if the Emanator is lacking, and is in need of man to become complete. In fact, though, this was a sort of magic word for man regarding his own strength. It was not a weak God he would meet up on the mountain peaks, but his own self.

The Kabbalah presented man as possessing 613 organs (more precisely, 248 organs and 365 tendons), constructed parallel to the 613 commandments, and above them the 613 organs of the divine man. The Godhead exists, so to speak, with this same basic structure. R. Joseph of Ḥamadan, a thirteenth-century Kabbalist, coined the dictum often reiterated by other Kabbalists, "A limb supports a limb."[6] That is, a powerful connection exists between man's corporeal organs and their sublime spiritual counterparts. Thus, "Whosoever does harm through one of his limbs below, it is as if he has done harm above."[7] And, "When Israel do not do the will of God, that husk may cleave in the Pardes commensurate with the limb that lower man either sanctifies or pollutes, and all that is done below is done above."[8]

The declaration made in the first chapter of the Bible, "Let us make man in Our image, after Our likeness . . . in God's image He created him, male and female He created them," exerted a tremendous influence on the concept of man. Be our interpretation of the words *ṣelem* (image) and *demut* (likeness) what it may, the basic intent is clear. Man is placed above the entire framework of reality because he contains a divine element.

That element grants him the ability to judge and to choose, to create and to build, gives him understanding and attributes. He stands at the other pole, the nadir of the worlds, in this turbid world, but his basic qualities may give him strength and stability. Indeed, the two poles complement one another. On one side is God first of all, the source of all being, and on the other is tiny man, possessed of spiritual strength, summoned to draw forth all of creation and bring himself to perfection. Man is called to realize, in that material world, his original essence. The Neoplatonic principle, proof of which may be found in the Bible, that "All comes from the One and returns to the One" made man the turning point in the transition between descent and ascent.

The midrashic idea that man resembles animals in three things and angels in three others gave him equilibrium, and impressed him with responsibility for his actions and their results. The Kabbalists, for their part, added another layer in their view of man as responsible for what happens beyond his own self. Man is greater than the angels in that he was given inclinations, and obliged to contend with vital questions and his bodily needs, even with the seductions of the evil inclination, while the angels' existence is static.[9] He is also a microcosm *('olam katan).*[10] The Emanator, who projected all of being from within himself, concentrated the reflection of Creation within man, his direct link with it and influence upon it. Through man's actions and his omissions, man either causes effulgence to descend, enlivening and sustaining the world around him, or denies the world that abundance. When he succeeds in engendering "the union of the Holy One blessed be He and His Shekhinah," the world functions as it should and is immersed in an abundance of goodness. When he does not, the strength of *din* increases, effulgence in constricted, and all is visited with calamity. Indeed, the very phrase *horadat shef'a* (bringing abundance downward) implies that there is an influence upon the divine world, the world of *aṣilut;* and when the union of Tiferet and Malkhut takes place, the effulgence for the world is thereby increased. Thus, man's powers cover a vast area, beginning with the world of the Sefirot and extending down to the nethermost point of existence.

Here, then, is the secret of the Kabbalah's power: man ascends to God, and thereby gains strength. He gains strength—not in order to stand equal to God or in his place, as in polytheistic religions, but in realizing himself as a human being. That is the message of the *Zohar* in teaching that the soul refused to descend to this flawed world but was commanded to do so in order to realize the Divine in this world; if it is able to express the image of God implanted within it, that would be very good. R. Shneur Zalman of Lyady formulated the idea otherwise. Using the words of the midrash (*Tanḥuma*, *Beḥukkotay* 3), he reiterates the claim that the Holy One, blessed be He, desired a dwelling place down below. In other words, it is man's responsibility to cause the Shekhinah to reign in the lower realm. The direction, here, seems to be the opposite, but the intent is the same. In both cases, man voids himself and his material ego, and becomes an instrument enabling the Divine to dwell within him. R. Dov Baer, the Maggid of Mezherich, expressed it well in an interesting homiletical interpretation of the verse (Num. 10:2): "Make thee two trumpets." In his commentary, he weaves together various verses, combining them to express his message, and among other things we read that the word *adam* [man] is composed of the letter *alef*, the Alpha of the world, i.e., God, and the word *dam* (blood), i.e., flesh and blood in its simplest material sense. In other words, a complete person (ADaM) is none other than a combination of the Holy One blessed be He and of flesh and blood.[11]

Nonetheless, though the Kabbalists' soul flies high, they do not boast of it. On the contrary, their every action is done in a spirit of self-effacement and humility, with awe and reverence. Recall[12] that one quality required of the student of Kabbalah is modesty. Pride, in fact, distances the student by many thousand miles.

Hasidism saw the task in inner terms. Rather than accomplishing a theurgic task in which he acts in a higher world that "needs" him, so to speak, man acts within himself. A paraphrase of a statement from the Mishnaic tractate *Avot* is attributed to the Ba'al Shem Tov: "There is no man who does not have his hour" is read as saying: Man is not man if he does not have, for himself, an hour. In other words, a person must set aside some time for himself each day to examine his own character, to take stock of himself and ask whether or not he has realized his human potential. Hasidic masters indeed emphasized the unique individuality of every person. R. Simḥah Bunim declared: In the heavenly court I will not be asked why I was not Moses our Teacher, because Moses already lived his life, and God doesn't need a second Moses. Rather I will be asked why I was not Simḥah Bunim. Or, in the words of R. Naḥman of Bratslav: "God does not make the same thing twice" (*Siḥot Moharan*, par. 54). It was said, moreover, that every person was given a certain purpose to fulfill in his life—as if all of humankind were working together on a single cloth, each weaver given his own corner. This aids us in understanding the emphasis placed by the Hasidic masters and by Kabbalists on the unique importance of one certain commandment for a specific individual or even for a specific historical period.[13]

In addition, Hasidism stressed man's ceaseless striving for self-realization and perfection in his sacred worship. "Natural habit"[14] is man's worst enemy. He must surpass his own nature, go beyond what he imagines to be his natural capability. If you look for the middling way, the golden mean, so to speak, you are no better than a beast. Rather, you must summon your strength and advance beyond the norm. "A horse walks in the middle of the road," it is said in the name of R. Menaḥem Mendel of Kotsk. He also said: If you can't pass over the bridge, cross under it. In other words, nothing should prevent man from searching out a variety of paths leading him to the highest realization of his potential; there he will find God, benevolently awaiting him.

Philo of Alexandria appealed to man, stressing the goal of "Know thyself." Yet the Kabbalah and Hasidism went one step further: As long as he remains materialistic, he never fulfills his obligation. Only by transforming the ego אני to naught אין, only after emptying himself of worldly and material content may he be filled with divine brilliance. It is no accident that the wordplay between *ani* (I) and *ayin* (nothingness) also corresponds to the symbols of the Sefirotic world, Malkhut and Keter—the objective is to see them and bring them to a single unity. Man, as well, is to reach some kind of unification with the Divine.

These ideas about man's high status—in the phrase of Ibn Gabbay, "This man is modeled on a sublime paradigm and perfected in the likeness of the parts of the celestial Chariot,"[15] i.e., the Sefirot—are most true in the case of Adam. Man was meant, a priori, to act from within an intimate link with his Creator, but with Adam's sin, that connection was broken and the original harmony destroyed. Man, by sinning, caused a "breaking of the saplings," a severance among the Sefirot (although there are various explanations surrounding the precise nature of that disconnection), and the results of his deed accompany all of humanity. Echoes of the Christian teaching of Original Sin are surely audible here, yet one important difference must be emphasized: according to kabbalistic teaching, the primal sin does not taint man eternally. He is certainly able to free himself of it, improve his ways, and reach great heights. Every individual's personal redemption is attainable if only he wishes it. As R. Naḥman of Bratslav said: "If you believe it is possible to destroy—believe it is possible to rectify" (*Likkutey Moharan, Tinyana*, par. 112).

The notion of man's Fall is described through another image worthy of mention. At first, he was dressed in a "tunic of light (אור)," a wholly spiritual garment. After his sin, though, "The Lord God made for man and for his wife tunics of skins (עור)" (Gen. 3:21), material clothing. Now, it is the body that is material. Man does, indeed, weave his spiritual garment anew through every *miṣvah* he performs, but that garment *(ḥaluka de-rabbanan)* is useful only after his death. Yet even in his present state, man may transcend and make use of his highest powers. This is particularly true of the Jew, to whom the commandments and their fulfillment grants tremendous strength.

The Kabbalists attributed to man the power to influence the Sefirotic world. On what was it based? Was it really the Kabbalah's invention? There are a few midrashim that clearly suggest the possibility of influence upon higher realms. But though they may be rare, and even if we suppose they spoke metaphorically, they offered an important starting point from which the Kabbalists could create a complete conceptual universe. These sources combined with various verses also read literally—first and foremost, "And breathed into his nostrils the breath of life" (Gen. 2:7)—raised awareness of a significant internal connection, reciprocal in its very essence. The Kabbalists even formulated a saying to set that verse in relief: "Whoever breathes *[nofe'aḥ]*, breathes from within himself."[16] That is, man's origin granted him the privilege of influencing the various worlds. God planted in man, as it were, something from within himself, thus transforming man into a higher being, different from all other elements of Creation.

The Kabbalists made a clear distinction between man's body, similar in form and needs to that of animals, and his unique nature as man, i.e., his soul. Kabbalists often point out that the body is flesh, yet the flesh is not the man.[17] Thus, in every discussion of man's status, his soul alone is at issue.

> And when He gave him the *neshamah*, he rose to his feet, and was then like the lower and the upper worlds. His body was like the earth, and his soul was like the upper worlds in form, in honor and glory, in awe and fear. . . . What then constitutes man's similarity to

> Him? Rabbi Abbahu said: The *neshamah*, from His power and from His might. It is not like the body, which is taken from the ground and perishes, and becomes dust once more, as it used to be.[18]

In early Kabbalah, however, we may find views pointing out the unique nature and the exalted source of the soul without indication of the world of the Sefirot. These generally speak of the Throne of Glory *(kisse ha-kavod),* apparently under the influence of BT *Shabbat* 152b. Thus, for example, a thirteenth-century talmudic scholar at home in kabbalistic teaching, R. Asher ben Meshulam of Lunel, writes in his commentary on the tractate *Berakhot* that the soul "Is not composed of the four elements like man's body . . . rather it is a simple spiritual essence, emanated from the sphere of the intellect . . . which is the Throne of Glory."[19]

The contention that the soul has its source in the world of the Sefirot uses Job 31:2, "My portion from above," as a prooftext; it is a verse strongly emphasized by certain Kabbalists (such as R. Sheftel Horowitz and R. Shneur Zalman of Lyady) with the addition of the word "really" *(mamash).* The soul not only indicates its divine origin but also acts as a lighthouse. On the basis of the assumption, expressed in Greek philosophy,[20] that every part seeks to return to the wholeness it originally had, it follows that the soul also strives to ascend and cleave to its source. Hence the religio-mystical nature inherent to the soul. R. Shneur Zalman of Lyady interpreted the verse "God's candle is man's soul" to mean the soul is like a candle. Just as a candle flame is forever drawn upward toward the element of fire, so the essence and nature of the soul dictates that it return and cleave to its divine source.[21]

This notion of the return of the part to the whole, or to its root, makes adhesion *(devekut)* a natural aspiration, though here the initiative comes from the "part." Thus, when the part exhibits true initiative and progress, it is answered by the whole, as the poet, R. Yehudah ha-Levi, said: "When I went out toward you—I found you coming toward me." This principle of mutuality exists in the opposite direction as well: "When the Holy One blessed be He sees that man does not love him enough and forsakes Him—God, too is forsaken and separate from him." Moreover, that love contains an element of jealousy. That is, if

> One loves two women, their love from him is not complete, because they are rivals. For a woman's love to be well planted in her

> husband, she must see that he loves no other woman in the world but her alone. Then she will make a covenant of total love with him. Similarly, the Shekhinah will not bind her love to man as long as he is in love with worldly matters. Thus the essence of love is that man loves nothing else in the world more than his love for God, and his love for God must be greater than his love for his wife and his children and all other things of this world. For what causes man's estrangement from his love for God as he stands in prayer or occupies himself with Torah is the alien thoughts that come to him because he is not fixed in his love for the Holy One blessed be He with more love than for all earthly things—he loves both of them. (*Reshit Ḥokhmah* II, 4)

Man's soul gazes upward, intent on returning to the source. That is its nature. Thus, a person who goes astray from that path, although he realizes his freedom of will, also distorts his original essence. The aspiration to adhere to the Divine is not solely an instance of mercy extended from God to man, the mystic, but rather man's personal actualization, inspired with the divine spirit. Thus, the ego *(ani)* may become as naught *(ayin);* separate being is annulled as man merges with or ceases to exist within the divine nothingness *(ayin)*—the only true Being. For that reason R. Shneur Zalman of Lyady can draw the simple conclusion that an individual who sees himself as an independent entity, proud and self-confident, is like an apostate and idolator.[22]

In Kabbalah there is a difference between man's intellect and his soul. The intellect (שֵׂכֶל) is seen as a physical organ, and its ability and trustworthiness is therefore limited. The certainty of intellectual perception is incomplete. The soul draws from its source, and by grace of that continuous connection, like an umbilical cord, sublime truths reach the soul worthy of them. These truths, to be sure, are the fruit of man's own labors, yet their content is divine. Though intellectual attainments are the result of man's efforts as well, they are merely human in content and in nature. Hence the appellation the Kabbalists often used for themselves: the truly enlightened *(maskilim amiti'im),* sages of the truth *(ḥakhmey ha-emet),* etc. One expression of the soul's godliness is a dialogue between God and the soul as transmitted in the *Zohar:*

> When their time comes [i.e., for the souls to descend], the Holy One, blessed be He, summons each particular soul, and says, "Go

> to a certain place, and enter that man's body." She replies, "Master of the universe, I am content with the world I live in now. Let me not go to another world, where they will subjugate me, and I shall be defiled among them." "From the day you were created," says the Holy One, blessed be He, "you were created for this, to live in that world." When the soul realizes this, she descends unwillingly, and enters that place.[23]

The soul, then, is given an important mission: to realize its divine aspect in earthly life, to raise the human body into which it is planted to greater heights. Thus, particularly in the *Zohar*, the soul's descent into man's body is described in stages, meant to ease the process of its assimilation and adaptation to the material world. Although the soul is distressed to be bereft of a "world of pure goodness," it must experience the shackles of corporeality for there to be any ascent.

As I. Tishby has shown, the kabbalistic view that the soul may win completeness only if it dwells within a material body and uses its limbs to do good deeds was found among Jewish philosophers such as R. Sa'adya Gaon.[24] Moreover, in the *Zohar*[25] we find the notion, similar to that of Plotinus, that even when the soul descends to this world it does not do so completely; rather, some part of it remains in the higher world. The author of *Tikkuney Zohar*[26] says in regard to a verse in the Song of Songs, "Set me as a seal" (8:6), that the actual engraving of a seal *[gelufah]* is on high, while only its imprint descends, the stamp of the seal.[27] Here, too, the suggestion may be that the soul partakes of divine essence and thus cannot descend completely to this world, but even the part that did descend is not actually disconnected from its source; it is still vitally linked to the heavenly realm. (A few Kabbalists even teach that the soul has a double reality, for it exists contemporaneously within its divine root and in the human body.)[28] Hence the permanent connection and return to the origin are ensured. That also aids in explaining the view of the punishment of extirpation *(karet)* as the lower soul's being cut off from its root above.

In the *Zohar* and other kabbalistic works the soul's descent against its will finds expression in the Platonic image[29] of the soul's enchainment in the "prison of the body,"[30] as if it were buried alive. The contrast between the pure, divine world and the dim lower world, between the source in divine being and a reality under the reign of "the other side," is reflected in the relationship between the soul and the body.[31] They, too, are perceived as two different, and even opposing, entities. This view could lead to asceticism, but in fact only a few Kabbalists advocated practices intended to suppress physicality. Some Sabbatians were an exception; their asceticism and self-affliction reached fanatic proportions in the belief that through nihilism they would hasten the End and herald the advent of the Messiah. The general tendency, though, was to live a life of holiness within the framework of corporeal life, to raise the body as a participant through fulfilling the practical commandments. There were periods in which certain Kabbalists emphasized the necessity of being content with a minimum, of caring for the body's needs as much as basic existence required but no more. In kabbalistic ethical literature, the rejection even of fundamental satisfaction was encouraged, in order to accustom the soul to reigning over the world of matter. This demand was, in fact, common even outside of kabbalistic literature. R. Isaiah ha-Levi Horowitz used to say, for example, that MaHaRSHaL (R. Solomon Luria) did not eat fish on Rosh ha-Shanah because it was a favorite dish of his, and he sought to teach himself to overcome his bodily desires.[32]

The emphasis on the opposition between soul and body could have increased the lure of the forbidden, causing some to fall into a life of debauchery and licentiousness. Such things happened, for instance, in Gnosticism. The Kabbalah, though, proved resistant. The oft-repeated exhortation to uphold the Torah and the commandments, expressing the importance of its lore, the emphasis on the unique symbolic significance of man and of his soul as a creature whose feet tread upon the earth yet whose head is in the highest heavens, and whose power is inestimable—all these served to shield against extremist tendencies.

Juxtaposed with the dismal pictures of material existence, whose pleasures seduce the flesh, and reminders of their high price—torture and suffering at the hand of demons and baleful spirits or a life in a hell of snow and fire—the Kabbalists placed man's tremendous strength, with his ability to reach the peaks of Olympus and the mysteries of the Godhead. The burden of responsibility is placed upon his shoulders because he was given freedom of will, and the results depend on him. Thus he is able to enter the material world, to have a family; it obliges him to have a sexual life, to enjoy the beauty of nature—all on the condition that he not become absorbed in them but rather see them as a springboard to a higher state of being. This is not a sanctification of the profane for its own sake, but rather a process of becoming holy by means of the profane, perceived as a symbol and a mirror of a divine reality and, on a higher level of thought, as a symbol of parallel metaphysical processes.

Hasidim interpreted the following statement in the Mishnah *Avot* 3.7 in the name of the Ba'al Shem Tov: "He who walks along a road studying, and interrupts his studies and says: 'How beautiful is this tree!' or 'How beautiful is this field!'—the Torah considers it as though he transgressed against his own soul." The condemnation seems harsh. The Ba'al Shem Tov explains thus: If the landscape and nature appear to you to be a separate domain, different and segregated from the spiritual realm, that amounts to a dualistic view of two powers in the world, and hence the severity of the condemnation. Indeed, it is a small hand that covers the eyes, said R. Naḥman of Bratslav in the name of his great-grandfather, the Ba'al Shem Tov—yet that is what prevents them from properly seeing the Divine dwelling in all of reality (*Likkutey Moharan*, par. 133). It is as if man has only to pull away a veil for the light to shine forth.

This, then, is the central approach in kabbalistic literature: descriptions of extreme contrast on one hand, and the possibility of breaking a new path on the other. "Know yourself," man is told. The pearl planted deep within you can act as a magnet drawing upward to its eternal source.

Let us return to the subject of the soul's sublime origin. We cited Ibn Gabbay's statement that the soul is in the image of the Sefirot, from which it emerges. The Kabbalists, particularly R. Isaac Luria, compare the soul and the Sefirot at great length. The exemplary relationship enables man to understand the mystery of the Divine, as it is written: "And from my flesh shall I see God" (Job 19:26). Man gazes into his soul and looks, as through a mirror, upon the Divine. The comparison of the soul to a mirror originates in the writings of the philosopher Al-Ghazālī and was widely adopted in philosophical[33] and kabbalistic[34] literature. The mirror serves a double purpose. It reflects, on one hand, the divine world, just as the Shekhinah reflects the Sefirot above it ("the likeness *[diokan]* of all likenesses," etc.). As it is said, "We are really the Shekhinah, because the Shekhinah and the soul of a Jew are a single entity."[35] On the other hand, it reflects the souls of the entire Jewish nation. In other words, the mirror reflects both horizontally and vertically. The horizontal reflection speaks of mutual involvement among Jewish individuals. Thus, the reader should not be surprised at a statement such as the following, voiced in Hasidic sociology: "The zaddik is called a mirror *[aspaklariya]*, for whoever looks at him sees himself as if in a mirror."[36]

The relationship between the soul and its source, moreover, allows for the theurgic element intrinsic in human action. Man, by his deeds, aids the higher powers. It is he who engenders the conjoining and unification among the Sefirot, and he who is responsible for their disunion. This theurgic role is imposed as mandatory upon man.

At times it is said that the body originates in *sitra aḥra*, and because the soul's root is in the Divine, man reflects the wrestling of the mighty forces of impurity and holiness in this world. His decision in favor of holiness thus serves the divine realm. A similar view is that the body is but a battlefield on which the soul attempts to leave its stamp, while evil forces appear and prevent it from doing so. Even if we assume the soul itself is a "clean slate," man's decision in favor of his soul and its aspirations does strengthen, so to speak, the Divine.

The idea of the soul's having a divine source raises certain questions. One is the difficult theological problem of recompense: "If the soul *[neshamah]* is in the image of God and is derived from Him, how can He possibly judge himself, His own essential being, since it is actually His self"?[37] The problem is a serious one, and R. Moses de Leon's response is not particularly satisfying. In his view, because the soul is enchained in the body and defiled by its uncleanliness, the only way to purge it is to pass it through fire (due to its unique status, de Leon presents examples from nature). This solution is somewhat lacking, for in any case God "judges himself." The problem, then, like the enigma of Creation, is apparently one of God's mysteries. Just as we have no definitive and clear answer, beyond all question and doubt, about how finite existence came into being from infinity ('Eiyn Sof), so we have no answer concerning the soul's disconnection from its source. This, too, seems to be an axiom. Though the Kabbalists presented a variety of images and explanations appealing to the intellect, when all is said and done, we are forced to accept the assumption that, along with the outward emanation, alienation from the source occurred, for although that source continues to be an immanent part of the created world, some room is left for nondivine existence.

There is evidence, indeed, that the Kabbalists themselves struggled with this question. R. Joseph Gikatilla opposed the view of Naḥmanides that the source of the soul was within the Divine itself. Gikatilla wrote:

> Although our Rabbi Moses ben Naḥman said that the soul is from Him, blessed be He, and said that he who breathes into [something] breathes of his own breath . . . it was the opinion of our Sages of blessed memory, and of all who engage in divine secrets that the soul is from those close to Him, blessed be He.[38]

That is, the soul is "close" to God, but does not flow from within him.

The author of the *Zohar*, however, along with other Kabbalists as well, portrays the soul as growing from the tree of souls (an image reminiscent of the metaphor of the soul as a bird),[39] which is the Sefirah of Tiferet or Yesod, or as coming from the divine river that is Binah down into man's body. Some say the soul descends from Binah through Tiferet and Yesod;[40] others, from Binah through Tiferet and Malkhut.[41] According to a few Kabbalists of the Gerona school, the soul's source is in the Sefirah of Ḥokhmah.

The verse "Your fruit is from Me"[42] is often cited by the medieval Kabbalists in order to teach that the soul is a fruit growing on the tree of *aṣilut*. It is said that just as the conjoining of male and female in our world gives birth to the body, so the spiritual union between masculine and feminine—i.e., Tiferet and Malkhut—in the higher worlds gives birth to the soul. In both cases, the soul is a divine spark, a divine entity, and that makes it superior to all other entities in existence, for they originate from the lowest Sefirah; within the framework of the latter a coarsening takes place, a metamorphosis of divine light.

In the view presented in *Ma'arekhet ha-Elohut*,[43] the souls of the Jewish people have their root in Binah, and after death they return there. In the commentary on that work by Reuben Zarfati,[44] the soul's return to Binah is called "immortality." It should be noted that the author of *Ma'arekhet ha-Elohut* goes on to say that the soul of an ordinary non-Jew, whose soul comes from the world of angels, returns to that world after death, until it reaches the seventh millennium, at which point it will cease to exist. The soul of righteous gentiles, in contrast, will never cease to exist.

DIVISIONS OF THE SOUL

Thus far, we have spoken of the soul in a general sense as a defined unit, a homogeneous entity. Indeed, in early Kabbalah the soul was usually seen as an undivided unity. Later, however, this was not the case. It is no wonder R. Todros Abulafia wrote: "The matter of the souls and their mystery is a very, very great one, who can know it; it is so very deep, who can find it? (Eccles. 7:24)."[45]

In talmudic sources, we find the statement: "It was called by five names—*nefesh, neshamah, ḥayyah, ru'aḥ, yeḥidah*."[46] From the context, though, it is clear that the names are synonyms, just as they are in the Bible. That, though, was not the Kabbalists' thinking when considering the statement. In their view, the five are but appellations for various units or levels, while a single sublime and elect quality underlies them all: a divine soul. There is no special name, though, for the sum of those parts (such as the "body," which contains numerous separately named organs); as de Leon said: "Do not be confused when I sometimes use the word *nefesh*, and sometimes *ru'aḥ* and sometimes *neshamah*, without being precise in what I say."[47] Thus, kabbalistic texts must be read carefully with attention to details in order to distinguish when a particular part is intended and when the entity as a whole is meant.

In any case, the five parts are mentioned in ascending order, the *nefesh* on the lowest level and *ḥayyah* on the highest. Through the years, the order changed slightly, *ḥayyah* moving to the second level and *yehidah* placed at the top in its stead. In most cases, the Kabbalists speak only of the first three parts, often designated by the acronym *NaRaN*. The influence of Plato and Aristotle may be discernible here, as they, too, spoke of a tripartite division of the soul, although each suggested his own division, based on different elements. It should be recalled that the divisions they suggested permeated to medieval literature of Jewish philosophy; Jewish thinkers often link the Greek division to that of *nefesh-ru'aḥ-neshamah*. The use of the latter division is not entirely uniform, and various thinkers (such as Sa'adya Gaon, Ibn 'Ezra, Bar Ḥiyya, and Maimonides) ascribe variant qualities and purposes to them. Even in early Kabbalah, we see that the matter is not completely clear; in the Gerona school, we may find the terms *nefesh-ru'aḥ-neshamah* used synonymously, as they are in the Talmud. R. 'Ezra and R. 'Azriel, however, distinguished among them and even connected them to specific Sefirot.

We find a clear gradational division in the second half of the thirteenth century made by the Kabbalists of Castile, by Gikatilla,[48] and particularly by the author of the *Zohar*. From then on, the commonly accepted hierarchy became: *nefesh*, *ru'ah,* and *neshamah*, and their connection to the Sefirot was also generally standard and uniform.[49] In the *Zohar* itself, however, various views are still expressed, and the conception presented in *Midrash ha-Ne'elam* of the *Zohar* is certainly different.[50] Even later, we may find instances in which the places of *nefesh* and *neshamah* are reversed without attributing to them different powers or levels.[51]

In most cases, Binah is considered the origin of the *neshamah*, Tiferet the origin of *ru'aḥ*, and Malkhut that of *nefesh*. We may conclude, on one hand, that just as the Sefirot are a unity despite the multiplicity inherent in them, the same is true of *nefesh-ru'aḥ-neshamah*. On the other hand, each unit may be spoken of individually, as each is unique. Thus, when a person is born, only the *nefesh* enters him, and not every individual is fortunate enough to receive all the additional parts. When he sins, the *neshamah* quits him as he acts. Even after death, each part exists independently. Gikatilla explains that the *nefesh-ru'aḥ-neshamah* are interconnected like the links on a chain, and they function as a unit. If, though, the *nefesh* sins and is punishable by extirpation *(karet),* it is cut off from the *ru'aḥ* and *neshamah*, and wanders like a fugitive about the world. The Kabbalists compare it to being slung "out of the hollow of a sling" (see 1 Sam. 25:29).[52] R. Solomon Alkabez says the soul was given man "when he was pure in his ways"; for that reason, if the *nefesh* sins, it will die rather than the *neshamah*, because the sin is not dependent on the *neshamah*.[53]

What, then, is the role of the *nefesh-ru'ah-neshamah*? There is no clear, definitive, or unanimous answer to this question either. According to one passage in the *Zohar*, man has a *nefesh* and a *ru'ah*. The role of the *nefesh* is to arouse the body to perform the commandments. The role of the *ru'aḥ* is more spiritual; it motivates the body to occupy itself with Torah. Evil forces exist as well, pulling in the opposite direction, and their source is in impurity. Yet if man is able to summon his strength, holy arousal is awakened from above and ushers him into the world of mystery, allowing him thus to enter the presence of God. That power is called *neshamah*, and its source is apparently in Binah. But there is a yet higher force, emerging from Ḥokhmah and called *neshamah le-neshamah*.[54] The general assumption, though, is that *nefesh* is a part of every living creature, including animals. The *nefesh* is the vital, vegetative element that animates and motivates every body. The *ru'aḥ* enters man at a later stage,[55] as a result of appropriate religious behavior. The higher level, *neshamah*, enters an individual who fulfills the commandments and learns Torah with mystical intent. We find Kabbalists of the opinion that the *neshamah* enters man only from the age of forty onward (recall the statement in the Mishnah *Avot* "Forty years for understanding *[binah]*" and that the *neshamah*, according to the Kabbalah, originates in Binah). In any case, man needs maturity and readiness before he is worthy of assimilating his *neshamah*. For indeed, the *neshamah*, which is the most profoundly inward level, emanated from the highest Sefirot, is the means by which man becomes one with the Divine. When there is realization of religio-mystical values, the *neshamah* is realized as well, and actualizes itself.

At times it is said that the *nefesh*, *ru'aḥ*, and *neshamah* enter the body at birth, yet only function when a man becomes worthy of each of them.

In its descent into the world, the *neshamah* brings with it a treasury of secrets it learned while in the Sefirotic world, and in its descent it is commanded to actualize what it attained above. Knowledge of Torah in our world is but a process of "recollection."[56] Thus, the *neshamah* that does not occupy itself with mystical teaching in this world abuses its office.

The fact that man merits a *neshamah* has another dimension as well. Because the *neshamah* came about through the communion of Tiferet and Malkhut, man has the power to contribute to a renewed unification between them through his religious acts. He aids in equalizing the tension between Ḥesed and Gevurah, and creates harmony in the higher realms. Moreover, his every religious act influences a different Sefirah, and he thus contributes to the internal dynamic of the Sefirot. Imagine, then, what tremendous power man wields, and what power is inherent in the *miṣvot*. Even more, divine effulgence actually descends to the world because of him.[57]

As we have said, a few Kabbalists held that *ḥayyah* was the highest of all the soul's components, while according to others, especially in later periods, the ultimate stage was *yeḥidah*. The latter view may be found in the parallel between *yeḥidah* and the unique *(yaḥid)* element of Keter. In any case, the two are considered to be exceedingly high levels, and only a very elite few have been worthy of them.

R. Isaac of Acre considered the question of what happens when a person realizes himself and attains a high level. Does he depart for the world to come? In his eyes, that person does not remain at such a climax, but rather returns. This notion is particularly developed in Hasidism and is known in the context of the talmudic expression of "descent for the sake of ascent" *(yeridah le-ṣorekh 'aliyah).* The idea is that man, in this world, is in a continual process of confrontation, of searching for a path, aspiring to ascend. Thus, even descent, which may be connected to a weakening in the physical and spiritual effort demanded of the mystic, is not perceived as a true decline, for it will be followed by a gain of renewed momentum. This is particularly said of the zaddik, the leader of the Hasidic community; in the sociological teaching of Hasidism, the zaddik was required to consider not his own welfare alone, but to raise all of his community too. At times he rises higher and faster than his followers; then it is his responsibility to descend from his spiritual heights to join in the efforts made by those around him. That, too, is considered "for the sake of ascent."

THE PREEXISTENCE OF THE SOUL

Various prekabbalistic sources speak of the soul's existence before entering man's body. In the Apocrypha and in rabbinic literature, statements may be found assuming the independent preexistence of the soul, and the idea is also expressed in Greek philosophy. E. E. Urbach, however, indicates certain distinctions it the evolution of this conception, pointing out the difference between the elements in the view of the Rabbis and in the philosophical view, especially the Platonic.[58] In the *Heikhalot* literature, a "curtain of souls" *(pargod ha-neshamot)* in which the entirety of souls are woven hangs before the Throne of Glory. The souls of the righteous return there after their time in this world. The Aristotelian view which defines the soul as the body's form, cannot accept such a view, as form cannot exist without matter. But the Kabbalah presents the soul as a force external to the body, so it can exist before the birth of the body and remain after its death. The Kabbalists generally accepted the idea of the soul's preexistence, though there were some dissenting views. Let us mention a few of them. For instance, according to *Midrash ha-Ne'elam*, when the world was created, the souls were hewn from the Throne of Glory and placed in a storehouse until their entrance into bodies in this world. Processes such as those as in the *Zohar* are not mentioned here.[59] In most cases, it is said that the *neshamah* is hidden in thought, i.e., in the Sefirah of Ḥokhmah, yet afterwards undergoes various internal processes within the levels of the Sefirotic world, processes that serve to introduce the individualization of each separate *nefesh* and to suit it to the material world. These processes take place not only in the Sefirotic world itself, but also in chambers beneath the Sefirot and in the celestial Garden of Eden. At the conclusion of this process, the *nefesh* is taken down to the terrestrial Garden of Eden, and there it remains thirty days. During that period, it is shown the Garden of Eden and Gehinnom to suggest the future awaiting it in accordance with its deeds in this world.

Throughout its life, two angels accompany it, one its defender and the other its accuser. The idea behind such a picture is that man, as a thinking creature blessed with the ability to judge, is responsible for his actions. Thus, his deeds immediately create protectors or accusers in accord with their nature, and this result is expressed in the form of the angels.

The actions of the soul and its eventual reascent are important here, but the Shekhinah also plays a role in this scenario. Before the soul's descent, the Shekhinah has it swear it will occupy itself with mystical teaching, dedicate itself to a mystical life, and thus enable the Shekhinah to receive reinforcement from the lower realms and, eventually, make possible the union with Tiferet. That, in essence, is a mutual process binding the Shekhinah's destiny up with the destiny of the human soul, and ultimately with that of the entire world, which will benefit from the effluence that will descend as a result of that communion.

Thus, alongside the pessimistic view that the soul in this world is imprisoned in a place opposed to its essence, there is an optimistic view that sees the soul's descent as a part of a mission to raise the human body and the material world, and thus to aid the Shekhinah in the sense of "arousal from below" *(it'aruta diletata)*. Certain conclusions follow relating to the body and the world. The pessimistic view leads to a withdrawal from the world, perhaps even to bodily afflictions, while the optimistic view sees matter as a means to divine service—not a simple endeavor, but not impossible either.

The idea that a reascent is possible is reinforced by the tradition of the soul's nightly ascent. A famous midrashic idea, based on the Bible, describes the soul's ascent to heaven each night while the body sleeps, a sort of pledge man leaves in the hands of his Creator. Inspired by that idea, a well-known prayer was composed in the sixteenth century. The work *Seder ha-Yom* by R. Moses ben Makhir, head of the yeshivah 'Eiyn Zeitim, adjacent to Safed, renders it as follows: "I render thanks to You, everlasting King, who has mercifully restored my soul within me; Your faithfulness is great." Similarly, one of the Morning Benedictions—". . . Who gives strength to the weary"—was associated in halakhic literature with this idea as well.[60] Indeed, in the literature of Ashkenazic Hasidism, the suggestion is made that each evening one should render account of that day's actions. And in the list of *hanhagot* compiled by the Hasidim of sixteenth century Safed, we find this warning: "Take care to confess before eating and before sleeping."[61] This obligation to render an account or confession of one's deeds was meant to make one aware, and thus responsible for one's behavior. That would better enable him to fulfill the mission mentioned above. It is even said that if the soul, in waking hours, occupies itself with mystical teaching, then at night, in the upper worlds, it is able to draw down an abundance of sublime mysteries. And so the cycle continues.

BLEMISHED SOULS

Thus far, we have spoken of the soul as a general and sacred unit, but not of blemished souls and the souls of non-Jews.[62] At its origin, the soul is indeed pure, but during the stages of its descent into the body, as we have outlined above, and especially during its descent from the Shekhinah, its fate may be to come down at the very moment when "the other side" has gained force in the world due to man's evil deeds. This situation is described in the *Zohar*'s famous image of the *tikla* (scales).[63] The world's scales were tipped toward the side of guilt; "the other side" had gained the upper hand, blemishing even the holy souls that had descended at that moment from the Shekhinah to the world. Though the *Zohar* "sweetens the bitter pill" by not claiming there is an inherent blemish in the soul itself (but rather in its descent into the body of a non-Jew), the fact is that the soul does not enter the body as a "clean slate," in the sense of "The soul You have given me is pure."[64] Even if we seek additional explanations, such as the sin of Adam that blemished all human souls, or the sin of parents whose intercourse was halakhically illicit, there would be a challenge to the principle of the pure soul or the principle of the a priori equality of all people. It would even challenge the principle of free choice, for it would imply that certain individuals were born with an innate tendency to sin. On the other hand, though, the same assumption echoes the concept of mutual involvement, for better or for worse, and offers some sort of sanction that man should be aware of the long-term effects of his actions. (This, in essence, might also occur in the case of a flaw in man's physical condition, of various physical or biological flaws of his parents or those who bore him, or even flaws related to the concrete conditions of the intercourse or pregnancy.)[65]

We even find a radical view in the literature of Ashkenazic Hasidim indicating unarguable predestination:

> I declare that repentance is effective only for one who was born under a constellation for length of days, yet because of his sins was sentenced to death. For one not born under a sign for length of days, neither repentance nor prayer nor charity will help him live, even if he has not sinned.[66]

THE SOULS OF NON-JEWS

The Gerona school of kabbalistic teaching generally speaks of the soul *(nefesh)* as belonging to the human race as a whole. Essentially, we must assume, there would be no distinction between the soul of a Jew and that of a non-Jew. Yet near the end of the thirteenth century, a clear distinction was made between the two.

The Kabbalists' responses to the question of the religious status of gentiles sometimes express a continuation and development of views originating in statements made by the rabbis, while at other times they are a consistent evolution of a clearly kabbalistic ideological system. The main concerns of this system are conceptions regarding the Divine and the Torah, and sometimes the historical reality that dictated its positions and contentions as well.

Examination of the relationship between Jew and non-Jew must begin with a presentation of the relationship between the forces of holiness and of impurity, as these are represented respectively in a historical context by the Jewish people and the non-Jewish nations. Implicit in a presentation of the opposition holiness-impurity is a certain contradiction. On one hand, it suggests some kind of dualism, a fundamental, unbridgeable difference. On the other hand, the monotheistic outlook rejects a polar opposition, and mandates that evil be presented as part of good. Thus, when the model in the upper worlds is ignored, and attention is focused exclusively on the human realm, the dualistic stance is usually reiterated. As a result, the dominant view is a view of the essential opposition between holiness and impurity, of the world of the Sefirot and "the other side" as the source of Jewish souls and of the nations, respectively. (One problem that surfaces is the status of the convert.) Nonetheless, no attempt is made to set out on a crusade against the non-Jewish world in the attempt to subdue evil and cause good to reign, although that goal is considered a fundamental obligation in daily religious life. Perhaps the Kabbalists were realists, and knew how to distinguish between the ideal and the practical, between what was desired and what was; perhaps there was some other reason. Just as the existence of metaphysical evil is justified in kabbalistic literature by the existence of an accusatory force, tempting and punishing, so we sometimes find a justification for the existence of non-Jews, or for the presence of Jews in exile as a means of progressing, in the sense of "descent for the sake of ascent." Implicit in the notion of the chosenness of the Jewish people is not only merit but the imposition of certain obligations. Chosenness is thus conditional upon active behavior, and the punishment of Israel's dispersion among the nations may be perceived as a temporary nullification of having been chosen. R. Sheftel Horowitz, of the seventeenth century, writes:

> It is well known that the Israeli nation are divine in their essence *[ḥelek elohah mi-ma'al]* . . . the souls *[nefashot]* of the nations are from external forces, the forces of the husks . . . but the souls *[neshamot]* of the Israeli nation are emanated from Holiness . . . His true sons.[67]

The emphasis on "His true sons" bears a double connotation: both in the sense of source and lineage, and that of connection and continual obligation, as in the framework of a family. One outgrowth of this notion of connection to a divine source is the idea of the mutual involvement of the nation's members with one another, as if a single unit; no less important is the concept of the nation's eternity. "Just as the Holy One blessed be He is eternal, so Israel are eternal."[68] This, of course, is not said of the nations of the world.

Vital in this context is the comparison of the last Sefirah, Shekhinah, with the Assembly of Israel. The historical Knesset Israel is conceived as the body of the Shekhinah, through which the divine acts in the world. The Jewish people are called "the limbs of the Shekhinah" *(evrey ha-Shekhinah).* The connection here is profound; the same cannot be said of non-Jews. One characteristic element of this worldview is vehement opposition to mixed marriage. Moreover, because of this significant difference between Jew and non-Jew, even conversion is not viewed in a positive light—at least not by R. Isaac Luria. The mission of the Jewish people is to rectify the world, not the nations. It is the Jew's responsibility to free the holy sparks imprisoned among the nations; bereft of their source of vitality, their existence would thereby be destroyed.

A unique position is formulated by R. Isaac of Acre:

> All those people from the nations of the world who convert—their soul *[nefesh]* was a Jewish soul, and thus God brought them under the covert of His wings, that "none of us be banished" [2 Sam. 14:14]. This arouses me to say that the souls of apostates were wicked members of the nations, and God uproots the thorns from his vineyard and banishes them utterly, and they will return to the root whence they came, which is the left side.[69]

In other words, the convert is actually a Jew, one of whose ancestors abandoned Judaism for some reason and who returns to his true essence and root. Likewise, if you see a person become an apostate, it is because he was originally a non-Jew and is now returning to himself. Note the important principle that the source of an individual's soul, whether he is a Jew or non-Jew, whether emerging from holiness or from impurity, is a fundamental and unchangeable matter.

In contrast to Luria's rejection of conversion is a view based on the belief that the chosenness of the Jewish nation is an acquired quality, conditional upon observance of the Torah's precepts. Thus, among the Jewish nation itself there may be individuals to whom the fact of chosenness with its privileges does not apply; on the other hand, a convert attains the same status as an indigenous Jew. As Ibn Gabbay contends: "Just as there is a difference between a Jew and the other nations regarding souls, which do not share a single source, so within the Jewish nation itself there is a difference, for the soul of a righteous man is unlike that of a wicked man."[70] Following this train of thought, R. Menaḥem 'Azariah de Fano declared that "The righteous among the Noahides *beyond all doubt* have a portion in the world to come, for they were loyal to His utterance *in the seven commandments they were given*."[71] Some four hundred years earlier, the author of *Sefer Hasidim*[72] had already urged respect for non-Jews who observed the seven Noahide commandments, and did not even hesitate to state that such a non-Jew was preferable to an evil Jew.

There was an intermediate position as well. According to the author of *Ma'arekhet ha-Elohut*, "The righteous gentiles who observed the seven commandments given to the sons of Noah *will not be deprived of their reward*, for they have upheld what they took upon themselves, and they will dwell in the resting-place they deserve." R. Yehudah Ḥayyat, perhaps in the wake of his own experience of the horrors inflicted during the Expulsion from Spain, added: "But heaven forbid that they should be in the *Garden of Eden*, for 'the uncircumcised will not eat there' [Exod. 12:48]."[73]

In this context, Gershom Scholem's comments on our subject warrant attention: "Many Kabbalists in periods of persecution, and particularly after the Expulsion from Spain, voiced a Jewish version of the Christian doctrine *extra ecclesiam non est salus*—there is no salvation for those outside of the Assembly of Israel."[74]

This also aids in understanding the contention that "most of the Kabbalists agree the mystery of transmigration applies to Israel alone, and not to the nations."[75] Yet here, too, some reservation is present: "For some among them will return [in another transmigration to allow them to perfect themselves]."[76]

A glance at kabbalistic ethical literature reveals a positive view of non-Jews, and this may be seen as a continuation of the stance taken in rabbinical ethical literature. The latter, in general, called for respect and fairness toward gentiles, be it only for the sake of peace. Thus R. Ḥayyim Vital of Safed wrote: "And love all of mankind, even non-Jews."[77] Approximately two hundred years earlier, a Kabbalist from Byzantium wrote: "Welcome everyone with peace, even the non-Jew, that Israel may be beloved among the nations. And you are the cause, for by your peace are the ministers on high provided for."[78] Two aspects, then, are evident. On the social plane, the status of the Jewish people among the nations is important, at least in respect to profanation of God's name. On the metaphysical plane, the status of non-Jews is important in the cosmic system as a whole as representatives of "the other side"—it, too, is part of the divine plan and thus worthy of receiving effluence emanated from Malkhut. Hence the Jew's attitude is actively interwoven with this conception. Let these few examples suffice.[79]

MAN AT HIS DEATH

As we have said, the soul's origin is in the Sefirotic system, and man is thus obliged to raise it to its source. This duty is a continual undertaking, fulfilled day by day, and every *miṣvah* he does contributes to the cause. The more the soul realizes this purpose, the stronger its tie with the Sefirot becomes, and thus it wins eternal life. When its time comes to depart for the upper world, it merits a warm welcome and all celebrate its arrival. All this is in sharp contrast to what is happening in the earthly realm. The relatives of the deceased mourn his passing, and he himself watches with distress as his body deteriorates in the earth. For some time the *nefesh* (the lower part of the *neshamah*) wanders around the grave; the *ru'aḥ* enters the lower Garden of Eden according to its merit; and man's essence—the *neshamah*—begins a new life, so to speak. For it, death is not a final destination but rather a threshold between a material and a spiritual place. The word *histalkut* suggests this difference; it signifies parting, as in death, but in its original Aramaic connotation means "ascent."

For this reason, various accounts in folklore, in ethical literature, and in the literature of the *shevaḥim* (hagiography) describe the hour of death;[80] one outgrowth was also the notion of the *hillula*. It is a common practice—today mainly among Hasidim and Jews of North African origin, but formerly in other circles as well—that on the anniversary of a zaddik's death, a *hillula* ceremony is held in his honor. The great biblical and talmudic exegete, Rashi, states (in his commentary to *Yebamot* 122a) that on the anniversary of such a death, people gather about the grave of the deceased and study his teachings and his actions. The Kabbalists thereby demonstrate their sympathy for the deceased, who had merited rejoining his source, thus bringing an abundance of goodness to the world as a whole, and particularly to those allied with him in learning and in deed. Such moments also have the power to engender the soul's ascent.

In the ritual of *zi'arah* one prostrates oneself on the grave of a zaddik, and not necessarily on the anniversary of his death, for in truth he is still alive. At times admirers came from great distances to visit the graves of the righteous. As they prostrate themselves, some beseech the zaddik to be their advocate; others plead for spiritual transcendence; and still others ask for spiritual healing and material assistance. We recall the Prayer of the Righteous *(tefillat ha-ṣaddikim)*, said in the cemetery and included in booklets of *tikkunim*. Moroccan Jewry's admiration for holy personalities is particularly famous,[81] but in other countries as well certain graves serve as a focus for prostration and miracle stories. Among them are the grave of R. Shalom Shabbazi in Yemen, of R. Elimelekh of Lyzhansk in Poland, and of R. Naḥman of Bratslav in Russia. Unique in this connection is Lag ba-'Omer, which according to Lurianic tradition (and not earlier!) is the day R. Simeon bar Yohay, or RaSHBY, died. That sage is thought to be the author of the *Zohar*, a miracle worker, and knower of sublime secrets. Multitudes visit his grave, even lighting bonfires; during a certain period it was even the practice to throw clothes into the fires after the custom mentioned in the Talmud concerning kings. In the late nineteenth century, a vehement dispute broke out among the rabbis whether to permit or forbid such a practice.

It should be added that according to descriptions in the *Zohar* and other sources, thirty days before a person's death certain changes take place regarding him, and these are not only physical changes. For instance, the spiritual vision of some becomes clearer and they reveal mysteries of Torah, perhaps even foretelling the future. For some, their *ṣelem* begins to depart from their body as a sign it has completed its role in the world. And it is said of some that each night, as the soul ascends—especially the soul of the righteous—it is shown its place in the world to come. It sometimes happens that the soul refuses to return below. Sometimes, it is said, the announcement is made on high that a certain soul is soon to arrive.[82] Note the expression: "A person does not die until he sees the Shekhinah."[83]

Various ceremonies were created for the stages from the moment of the soul's departure until after the burial.[84] The *Zohar* graphically portrays how all the actions of the deceased stand before his soul as it is led to his grave.[85] It is also said that during the *shiv'ah*, the seven-day period of mourning, the soul itself takes part in mourning for the body because of the connection there had been between them. After that the process of judgment begins.

As we have said, for a while the soul *(nefesh)* hovers above the grave. Then, together with the *ru'aḥ* it passes through a river of fire that serves as a place of purification. From there it reaches the terrestrial Garden of Eden, and if it is worthy continues to the upper, celestial Garden of Eden.[86] At times the *nefesh* is described as being bound in the bond of life (after 1 Sam. 25:29), though that symbol is used in a variety of senses. Sometimes it indicates the celestial Garden of Eden and sometimes a certain Sefirah. Even in the latter case it may symbolize Binah, or Tiferet, or Malkhut. In contrast to the *nefesh* and the *ru'aḥ*, the *neshamah* returns directly to its origin in the Sefirot.

Entire works were dedicated to these subjects; among them let us mention only *Seder Gan 'Eden* and *Massekhet Ḥibbut ha-Kever,* which appear in *Bet ha-Midrasch,* compiled by Adolff Jellinek.

On the theme of the tortures of Hell, I would like to speak of a substitute for that punishment. In a fourteenth-century kabbalistic work, the story is told of a Hasid from Ashkenaz,

> Who was not wise but was simple and honest, and erased the pages of a book of prayers for the parchment [a common practice in former times was to reuse writing materials], though the name of God was written on them. After realizing he had sinned against God's name, he said: One who has decried His honour, blessed be He, should not defend his own honor either. What did he do? Each day, when the congregation came to pray in the synagogue and when they left, he lay down in the doorway on the ground, and great and small passed over him. And he would say: This is what should be done to one who took no care to defend the honor of his Creator. And if anyone trod on his body, inadvertently or under compulsion, he was joyful and thanked God. This he continued for an entire year, saying: The punishment of the wicked is twelve months in Gehinnom.[87]

Interestingly, a similar story of a man who lay in a sack at the entrance to the synagogue in order to inflict himself with punishment for various sins is told of R. Abraham Halevi, one of the Hasidim of Safed in the sixteenth century.[88] R. Abraham was a leader of a group of *ba'aley teshuvah*, many of whom were Marranos or their descendents, and they adopted harsh self-afflictions to repent for sins of the past.

So adamant was their belief in the idea of recompense that Kabbalists took issue with astrologers and their followers. "I wrote this treatise to crush the astrologers who read the constellations, for in our transgressions throughout our generations, many of the common people are drawn after their views and their suggestions; by their word they rest and rise, by their word they camp and move on [after 2 Kings 17:26], and are ignorant of the judgment of the Lord of the earth."[89]

THE DOCTRINE OF THE *ṢELEM*

Our first encounter with the term *ṣelem*, of course, is in the narrative of man's creation, "In His image *[be-ṣalmo]* and after His likeness. . . . In the image of God He created Him" (Gen. 1:26–27). The nature of this "image," though,[90] is not sufficiently clear. Much exegesis is devoted to these verses, and it is exceedingly difficult to pinpoint their exact meaning. The Kabbalists often introduce an additional verse, "For in the image man shall walk" (Ps. 39:7), to show that the *ṣelem* is an integral part of man on earth. What, then, is the *ṣelem* in their conception?

There is a basic assumption that two elements diametrically opposed by nature cannot exist together without some mediating entity. This also goes for the *nefesh* and the body. As R. Joseph Angelino said: "The *neshamah*, so great is its delicacy originating in the upper world, has nothing in common with the coarse body until it dons a fine garment from the upper world, although its fineness cannot compare with hers, which is more sublime."[91] Similarly, in Neoplatonic teaching and in ancient religions we find mention of an intermediary astral body; in the Kabbalah, the term *ṣelem* is borrowed to speak of the same idea. Thus we read in the *Zohar:*

> When a man begins to consecrate himself before intercourse with his wife with a sacred intention, a holy spirit is aroused above him, composed of both male and female. And the Holy One, blessed be He, directs an emissary who is in charge of human embryos, and assigns to him this particular spirit, and indicates to him the place to which it should be entrusted. . . . When the soul descends in

> order to enter this world, it comes down into the earthly Garden of Eden and sees the glory of the spirits of the righteous. . . . After this, it goes to Gehinnom and sees the wicked . . . and the holy image stands by it until it goes out into the world. When it goes out into the world the image is summoned for it and it accompanies it and grows with it. . . . A man's days exist through the image, and are dependent on it.[92]

Thus the "image" accompanies man all the days of his life and, according to R. Ḥayyim Vital, "Their ethereal body [that of the righteous] is the mystery of the image visible to those of pure sight."[93] In other words, certain individuals can see that "image" with spiritual eyes. The *ṣelem*, then, is sometimes identified with a shadow *(ṣel)* accompanying man. In that sense, the "image" constitutes the *principium individuationis*, the individual and unique element in each person. The *ṣelem*, which descends in the form of a human countenance, grows along with him.[94] In a few places in the *Zohar*, it is said that man has two "images." One is given him while still in his mother's womb, the other at his birth. At that point one surrounds the other. Thirty days before his death, both images disappear, as alluded to in the verse, "Until the day breathes, and the shadows flee away" (Song of Songs 2:17).[95] It is said that when the righteous "Depart from the world, their souls are bound in the bond of life whence they came . . . and they are given a whole, ethereal and exceedingly fine garment. The righteous attire themselves in it and it protects them at certain times, such as on especially blessed days when they can wear them and draw close to the Creator, and pray for their souls and their children."[96]

Involved with this concept of the shadow is a belief fundamentally related to the eve of Hosha'ana Rabba. A person goes at night to the bank of a river, and looks to see whether his shadow is reflected in its entirety. If so, he is assured of living out the ensuing year. If not, he will die in the course of the year. The destiny of his family members is revealed as well in the shadow of his various limbs. The subject[97] naturally engendered a variety of customs, which gave rise to disputes among scholars whether there was any truth in such "proof" or in its reading—for some doubt always remained whether dread had been needlessly sown in people's hearts or whether, on the contrary, one had not recognized warning signals because he had read them incorrectly.[98]

On the notion of the "image" above man like an aura, let us recall what is told of R. Isaac the Blind: "So great was the knowledge of R. Isaac son of the Rabbi, of blessed memory, that he could discern the feeling of the air though he was blind, and he would say what was living and what dead."[99] In other words, the penetrating vision of some individuals enables them to distinguish the nature of the veil surrounding those around them.

Similar is the notion of a person's smell. Every individual emits an odor unique to him. We speak, though, not only of a chemical fact but of its spiritual implications as well: a person's spiritual level finds expression in that odor. For this reason, not everyone is able to sense it. For example, the "feeling of the air" ascribed to R. Isaac the Blind in the account cited above may also be interpreted as the odor emitted by the person. In any case, it was considered a sign of R. Isaac's greatness. An indisputable instance of such a sense is attributed in the *Zohar (Balak)* to the "nursling" *(yanuka)*. Among his wondrous powers was his ability to discern by smell which of the sages had not recited the *Shem'a*.

Another external expression of internal spiritual essence is the *reshimu*. Man's every action is registered by some kind of mark on his forehead (see Ezek. 9:4); some people have the special gift of being able to read that secret language. Tradition has it that R. Isaac Luria, the Ba'al Shem Tov, and other zaddikim of Hasidism were particularly able to read the foreheads of those who stood before them. It is also said of R. Isaac Luria, or ARI, that "He could discern, in an ill person's pulse, which attribute of the ten Sefirot he had damaged, and would suggest how he could rectify it."[100]

All these subjects, discussed here with great brevity, express the notion of a connection between matter and spirit, between body and soul. All of them reflect a single entity. Spiritual elements combine with material objects, and are imperceptibly expressed through them, unseen by human eyes. The same is true, if you wish, of all the worlds, for they too are but a transparent reflection of divine essence.

Mention should be made of the garment called *ḥaluk*, and later also *ḥaluka de-rabbanan*. It first appeared in the *Ḥibbur Yafeh me-ha-Yeshu'ah* by R. Nissim Gaon, was adopted by the *Zohar*, and was developed further in subsequent generations. It even reached the oeuvre of S. J. Agnon in the form of the story "Ha-Malbush."[101] Found in many prayer books as well, it appears in the short prayer said before putting on the *tallit:*

"Just as I envelop myself in a *tallit* in this world, so may I merit the *ḥaluka de-rabbanan* and a pleasant *tallit* for the next world in the Garden of Eden."

The significance of the *ḥaluk* is that even in the Garden of Eden the soul is not naked but rather covered by some garment. That garment is woven from the individual's good deeds in this world. Each *miṣvah* fulfilled and each positive action adds, as it were, a thread in the cloth, until it becomes a finished piece. And in it, as we have said, man is clothed in the world to come.

THE DOCTRINE OF THE SOUL IN LURIANIC TEACHING

The midrash *Tanḥuma* (*Tissa* 12) relates that "When Adam was yet a golem [formless being], God showed each and every zaddik whose soul would come from his seed. Some are linked to his head, some linked to his hair, etc." Before his sin, Adam's soul was very great, containing all the souls of all future generations. As the midrash teaches us, though, all these souls are not equal. Whether the souls are linked to a certain limb or to another indicates a symbolic difference in value. It should be pointed out, though, that what we have here is not a claim for predestination. Freedom of will does exist, and man can climb much higher than his root, and to the same extent can fall as well. This is also true for astrological influence. The latter is not absolute or exclusive; it is in man's power to change it.

R. Isaac Luria divided souls in such a way that "[Adam's soul] consisted of six hundred and thirteen parts, precisely as—according to traditional rabbinic anatomy—the human body. Each part is a total configuration or gestalt *[komah shelemah],* that can again be subdivided into six hundred and thirteen parts or 'roots.' Each of these roots—one might almost call them 'soul-limbs'—constitutes a so-called major root or great soul, which subdivides into a number of minor roots or sparks. Each spark is an individual holy soul. . . . The human soul consists of different lights or aspects which together constitute the 'individual spark' of each man."[102] The soul of every individual is thus a spark from that root.

The idea of the root is important for a number of reasons: (1) It aids in explaining the existence of spiritual kinship between individuals, and the fact that a person often exerts a special influence on those of his own circle. As the rabbis said, for example, "When one member of a circle dies, all the circle is distressed" (*Shabbat* 106a). Reciprocal aid is given to the "family" members of that root. One person may benefit from the merits of another member of his family and they may benefit from him. This also relates to the notion of assistance given by a deceased zaddik in the form of his soul's *'ibbur*, as we shall see below. (2) The biological family does not necessarily indicate family in the sense of the soul's root. In other words, a biological family may have members from different roots. This thought, we may assume, was also influenced by the doctrine of the transmigration of souls. Thus, a soul may come "from outside" or from some generations earlier, according to God's will and ordering of the world. For this reason, parents whose soul is great may have a child whose soul is low, and the opposite. (3) "Man's task is the perfection of his individual spark on all levels; but all its levels or aspects are not necessarily joined simultaneously in one life. . . . The kabbalists took great pains to discover the root of their souls, as only such knowledge would enable a man to restore his soul to its supernal root or would tell him what precisely he was still lacking for the completion of his *tiqqun*."[103] Not everyone, however, is able to know his root and his past. It is told that R. Isaac Luria was skilled at revealing that system in detail to many important personalities. (Testimony of this is the book *Sha'ar ha-Gilgulim*.)

In a few Lurianic sources it is said that the *neshamah* itself does not enter the body; what enters is only a spark from it, bound in a secret and intimate bond with its source. In the teaching of R. Shneur Zalman of Lyady, in contrast, it is said that although the divine soul *(nefesh)* leaves a person's body if he is absolutely wicked, it does not ascend but rather hovers over him, as if waiting for the time it will be able to enter him once again. In R. Shneur Zalman's system, by the way, man has two souls *(nefashot)*—one divine and the other animal—and the two battle over control of the body.

> The soul of a human being pervades all the 248 organs of the body, from head to foot, yet its principal habitation and abode is in his brain, whence it is diffused throughout all the organs, each of which receives from it vitality and power appropriate to it, according to its composition and character: the eye for seeing, the ear for hearing, the mouth for speaking, and the feet for walking—as we clearly sense it that in the brain one is conscious of everything that is af-

> fected in the 248 organs and everything that is experienced by them. Now, the variation in the acquisition of powers and vitality by the organs of the body from the soul, is not due to the [soul's] essence and being, for this would make its quiddity and essence divisible into 248 diverse parts, vested in 248 loci according to the various forms and locations of the organs of the body. If this were so, it would follow that its essence and quiddity are fashioned in a material design, in a likeness and form resembling the shape of the body, Heaven forfend! But it is entirely a single and simple spiritual substance, which, by its intrinsic essence, is divested of any corporeal shape and of any category and dimension of space, size, or physical limitation. It is, therefore, impertinent to say, in relation to its quiddity and essence, that it is located in the brain of the head more than it is in the feet, since its quiddity and essence are not subject to the categories of physical limitation. But there are contained in it, in its intrinsic essence, 613 kinds of capacities and vitalities to be actualized and to emerge from concealment in order to animate the 248 organs and 365 veins of the body, through their embodiment in the vital soul, which also possesses the corresponding 248 and 365 capacities and vitalities. . . . But all the capacities flow from the brain, as is known, for therein is located the principal dwelling-place of the whole, so to speak, manifest soul, since the sum-total of the vitality that is diffused from it is revealed there. Only the [individual] capacities of the said general vitality shine forth and are radiated from there into all the organs of the body, much in the same manner as light radiates from the sun and penetrates rooms within rooms.[104]

We have included this long citation not only for what it teaches of R. Shneur Zalman's concept of the soul but also for its kabbalistic perception of the Divine.

14 • The Doctrine of Transmigration

Naḥmanides (in his commentary on Gen. 38:8)[1] called the belief in the transmigration of souls, or metempsychosis, "one of the great secrets of the Torah concerning human reproduction." Others saw the notion as "one of the essentials of kabbalistic wisdom" and "among the foundations of the Torah and its most basic elements."[2] Death is seen not as man's end but as the body's ruin alone,[3] while the soul reappears in the corporeal world clothed in another body. Logically speaking, "the mind is dismayed at the thought of such a supposition," but it is "a matter accepted by men of faith"[4]—that is to say, it is a long-standing kabbalistic tradition in need of no intellectual justification.

The underlying presumption, apparently, is the principle that the soul's nature is to return to its origin. That natural inclination, though, is necessarily contingent upon its actions: if found worthy, it may return and cleave to its source; if not, the soul is said to wander the earth disembodied—an exceedingly problematic condition. The concept of transmigration, it seems, offers a solution to that problem. We must hasten to add that transmigration is not the same as reincarnation. While reincarnation suggests a person becomes a stone or an animal, transmigration means that a person's soul "is clothed" *by* a new entity, yet maintains its original spiritual state.

This belief seems to have originated in India, where it was linked with the presumed existence of a moral world order: that is, every act yields results, yet these are linked to the wider complex of natural reality. These results may be undetectable to some extent, or they may occur over a period of time.

We find no allusions in talmudic literature to this belief, although Greek philosophers such as Pythagoras, Plato, and others spoke of it extensively. According to Aristotle's definition, the soul is the body's form and cannot transmigrate to another body, but in Plato, and the Neoplatonists such a possibility does exist. The view was accepted by some Gnostic and Manichaean sects as well.[5]

Official Christendom did not recognize the belief in metempsychosis, and in Islam we find it only in some sects, such as the Mu'tazilite. Karaites themselves disagree over whether 'Anan, founder of the sect, held it. During the same period, R. Sa'adya Gaon rejected it vehemently. He mentioned the Yudghanites who embraced such a belief, but expressed his radical opposition. Other Jewish philosophers reacted similarly, such as Ḥasdai Crescas in the fourteenth century, who contended that if transmigration really occurred, babies would have to be born as knowledgeable individuals. His student, R. Joseph Albo, rejected it as well. Others, such as Maimonides, saw no need to mention it at all, though they had surely heard of it. The only Jewish philosopher who accepted the doctrine of transmigration was Don Isaac Abravanel (1437–1508) in his commentary on the Torah *(Ki Teṣe)*. That, though, earned him the wrath of R. Yehudah Aryeh of Modena in the book *Ben David.*

Interestingly, the *Bahir*, the Kabbalah's earliest work, speaks of metempsychosis as a familiar and self-evident teaching, while in the course of the thirteenth century the doctrine is sheathed in veils as one of the world's greatest secrets, to be revealed only to those "worthy of them through received tradition *(kabbalah);* it is forbidden to decode them in writing, and to hint [at the true meaning] would be useless."[6] Anyone who mentioned the doctrine in the thirteenth century indicated its secrecy.[7] In the Geronese school, the doctrine is perceived as part of a broader and more abstruse teaching—"the mystery of *'ibbur*" [*sod ha-'ibbur*]. In the late thirteenth or early fourteenth century, however, the distinction was made between transmigration and *'ibbur.*

The doctrine of metempsychosis raised a variety of questions, and answers to them were not unanimous. Kabbalists differed among themselves on many points.[8] Perhaps for that reason R. Meir ibn Gabbay wrote: "The particulars of transmigration cannot be grasped, for their source is rooted in supernal wisdom."[9] In the fourteenth century, discussions of metempsychosis multiplied, and a range of commandments and biblical verses were interpreted in its context. By the sixteenth century the teaching had become quite extensive. An interesting theory was added, that only sparks belonging to the same family (in the nomenclature of R. Solomon Alkabez) or root (in that of R. Isaac Luria) are related by the internal connection of transmigration or *'ibbur*.

At the turn of the thirteenth century, R. Menaḥem Recanati writes: "One doubt remains in my mind, whether the mystery occurs for women as it does for men; on that matter, we must receive a tradition, *for logic would suggest either possibility* . . . blessed is he who knows the truth."[10] In *Sefer ha-Gilgulim* R. Ḥayyim Vital was more certain: "Know that men transmigrate until they are rectified. . . . The souls of females have no worship and transmigration, and are cleansed of their sins only in Gehinnom."[11] This, then, is an absolute denial of the possibility of transmigration for women. Later, however, we find some retreat from this extreme view.

It should be pointed out that a person whose soul transmigrates is completely unaware of the fact. He opens a new page in his life. The reason is simple—a person who in a previous life was wicked should not be discouraged; he may be terrified by the heavy burden imposed upon him, or fearful of another failure. We have already spoken of R. Isaac the Blind, who was able to distinguish "by feeling the air" whether a person standing before him had a new soul or an old one. Much is told about R. Isaac Luria as well, who knew all the details of a person's deeds in his previous lives *(gilgulim),* and intuited even the details of his *nefesh-ru'ah-neshamah* in their transmigrations. Such individuals, however, are out of the ordinary. An interesting and atypical stance is presented in a work close in spirit to Hasidism, *Darkhey No'am* by R. Samuel ben Eliezer of Kalvarija: "It seems to me, moreover, that if it is clear to a person that he has performed some *miṣvah* in the past [in a previous *gilgul*] and, were he to perform it again, he would lose what he had gained [as he might not perform it to the same degree of perfection as he had previously], that person has permission to avoid it completely."[12] At times, a person comes as an ignorant Jew, because "some rectification *[tikkun]* must be made. And blessed is he who knows what his *tikkun* is."[13] An interesting view found in the *Sefer Ḥaredim* (fol. 41b) is that an individual does not know about his past as a human being, but is only too well aware of his previous life incarnated in the body of an animal. It was commonly accepted, though, that no one knows anything about his own past. As it says in the *Zohar:*

> All souls must undergo transmigration, but men do not perceive the ways of the Holy One, how the revolving scale *[tikla]* is set up and men are judged every day at all times, and how they are brought before the tribunal, both before they enter into this world and after they leave it. They perceive not the many transmigrations and the many mysterious works which the Holy One accomplishes with many naked souls, and how many naked souls roam about in the other world without being able to enter within the veil of the King's Palace.[14]

REASONS FOR THE DOCTRINE OF TRANSMIGRATION

The concept of transmigration aids in understanding biblical verses, the problem of divine justice, the reasons for the commandments, and so forth. Let us address them in order.

1. *Biblical verses.* In addition to the many verses of the Bible interpreted by the Kabbalists as allusions[15] to metempsychosis, various biblical stories that seem superfluous or unjustifiably detailed are read as teaching of that doctrine.[16] Connections among figures, seemingly distant from one another in time and place, are explained in the context of transmigration. Statements about Cain and Abel and about Jethro and Moses reveal that those personages are linked through *gilgul*, and sins committed in a first stage had to be rectified in a second stage. From the days of R. Isaac Luria, talmudic sages were discussed this way as well as biblical figures. Over the years, books were written, dedicating tremendous thought to this approach and, truth to tell, tremendous artistry as well. Some of these are *Gle Razaya* by an anonymous Kabbalist, *Sha'ar ha-Gilgulim* by R. Ḥayyim Vital, *Gilguley Neshamot* by R. Menaḥem 'Azariah de Fano, and *Midrash Talpiyyot ('Anaf Gilgulim)* by R. Elijah ha-Kohen of Smirna. Even the entire book of Job was placed on the axis of belief in transmigration or its rejection.[17]

2. *The problem of divine justice.* The earliest kabbalistic work treating this issue[18] was composed as a theodicy—that is, a refutation of the

contention (or of the reality) that "the righteous suffer while the wicked flourish."[19] It is argued that although the body eventually perishes, the soul remains, and its "behavior report" accompanies it throughout its changes. Hence the possibility of transferring merits and guilt from one period to another. For that reason, a person who seems to be righteous may indeed be so, even from the point of view of divine justice, yet we are neither able nor permitted to stamp that individual with any label whatsoever as long as we lack information about previous periods of his life. A person who seems to be righteous may actually have a most negative past, and now is visited with his punishment in order to repent for that period. In the words of a fifteenth-century Kabbalist: "Know, when you find a zaddik who suffers, that he already was in the world, and 'remove the old because of the new' [Lev. 26:10]. And those transgressions he committed in his past—he receives punishment for them now, that he may merit, and that his portion be complete in the world of eternal life."[20] A prooftext is offered from Job's words (9:21): "'Though I were innocent, yet I would not know my soul' in its past—whether it was innocent or not," and, indeed, his suffering was meant to prove to him that in his past he really was not innocent. Thus, man has no right to judge certain events as God's injustice, since his judgment is based on appearances, while God sees all the events of a person's life in all its stages by means of the soul, which, essentially, is responsible for man's ultimate destiny. In terms of the soul, then, its life on earth is continuous, and its reward is thus calculated over the entirety of its time there. Clearly, then, nothing can be determined by considering the known present alone. The *Bahir* makes an analogy reminiscent of one by R. Yehuda ha-Levi in a different context: "A man planted a vineyard in his garden, hoping to produce grapes, yet produced noxious weeds; he saw that his planting had not succeeded, cut it down and destroyed it . . . and planted anew."[21]

Close at hand is an explanation of another, very distressing phenomenon: the death of infants. What, everyone wonders, could be the sin of nursling babes? The answer provided by the doctrine of transmigration[22] is the same as in the previous case: we are not permitted to decide according to what we see in the present alone. When you look at the entirety of periods that soul spent on earth, you can no longer consider it to be only an "infant." Such is the body's physical state, but not the soul's, and the latter is responsible for the body's happiness. The soul has just descended into the world in order to complete a certain task, and when it is done has nothing left to do in the world.[23] On the contrary, in his mercy, the Creator does not leave the infant any longer in this world of matter with its many seductions, where he could be caught in the snare laid by Satan or the evil inclination. Thus, from his point of view, it is actually better that God took him safely from this world.

The same approach serves to explain why people come into the world handicapped or with bodily impairments. This is no accident, nor is it "in the stars," i.e., an astrological fate determined by the constellation of stars and planets, for both those possibilities contradict the law of recompense.[24] In effect, such a condition itself serves as repentance for sins of the past.[25]

These two last points in particular, though, lead to a somewhat dismal conclusion regarding the body. It is generally agreed that a person is born as a "clean slate," innocent, pure and clean, in a fresh, new body. And yet it turns out that the body is but an object from which recompense is exacted, and even as it emerges into the world, it already bears the burden of years. This is because the body is really the soul's material instrument, without which it cannot function. Indeed, the freedom of choice granted it was intended to place full responsibility upon man with complete knowledge of what was to be expected.

An interesting view of transmigration was given by R. Isaac Abravanel in his commentary on the pericope *Ki Teṣe*. As he saw it, the soul is affected by bodily drives resulting from the level of balance between the various bodily fluids, the temperament, or the circulatory system. The soul therefore has no possibility of control or of acting from free choice, a fact that must be remembered in judging a soul that has transgressed. In Abravanel's view, transmigration is meant to test how the soul will act in a body of a different temperament, or to enable it greater freedom of action in a more balanced body.

3. *The reasons for the commandments*. The concept of metempsychosis also serves to explain certain *miṣvot*.[26] First and foremost among them is the precept of levirate marriage *(yibbum)*. Reading Naḥmanides' commentary on Genesis 38, the first narrative in the Bible concerning the issue of levirate marriage, one immediately becomes aware of the momentous importance and mysteries surrounding that subject. Even Naḥmanides' contemporaries in Gerona (especially R. 'Ezra, who was his senior) discussed it, and it served as a source for R. Menaḥem Recanati (in his commentary on the pericope *Vayeshev*), for R. Isaac of Acre, and

especially for the *Zohar* in its explication of the pericope *Mishpatim*, a text better known in kabbalistic and scholarly literature as *Sava de-Mishpatim* (which, in effect, is the only pericope in the *Zohar* where transmigration is discussed at length).

In short, as it says in Deut. 25, if a married man dies without having fathered any sons, his brother must marry his widow. The son born of that levirate marriage is himself the *gilgul* of the deceased, who returns to the world once again. The internal reasoning is that a person who did not occupy himself with the commandment to be fruitful and multiply, and certainly someone who did not want to bring children into the world,[27] will himself return once again to the world.[28]

Another precept, that of ritual sacrifice *(sheḥitah)* is also explained by metempsychosis. The rigorous precision in Jewish law requiring a clean cut and swift slaughter, meant to minimize the animal's suffering as much as possible, is essentially transferred to the man whose soul has transmigrated to the body of an animal. Kosher slaughter and eating according to religious guidelines enable the transmigrated soul of the animal slaughtered to ascend and become pure. This brings us to a new understanding of an interesting religious and social development. The Mishnah, at the beginning of the tractate *Ḥullin,* says: "All may perform ritual slaughter, and their slaughter is kosher, with the exception of the deaf, the mad, and the minor." This ruling, however, is not practiced today, not only because of the suspicion that the *shoḥet* (slaughterer) may not do his job properly due to unfamiliarity with all the laws concerning slaughter, but because of the deep-seated belief that the act of slaughter serves a higher end; for that end to be achieved, special intent is needed, and not everyone is capable of such responsibility.[29]

We even find a certain hierarchy of the powers various people have. For example, there are Torah scholars whose knowledge does not extend to Kabbalah; there are those who know the Wisdom of Truth (i.e., Kabbalah); and there are "those of supreme excellence in the Wisdom of Truth." Each is able to raise the soul only to a certain level, except for those expert in Kabbalah, whose power is very great.[30] Hence the status, both social and religious, of the *shoḥet*.[31]

A third commandment explained in this framework is the precept forbidding hybridism *(kilayim):* "There are some growing things, such as trees or seeds, into which souls transmigrate until the time decreed for them comes to an end. And if you mingle seeds with trees, you will cause greater evil and punishment for those souls that have transmigrated to them, for there are various aspects of *gilgul*, and not all of them are equal. Thus they should not be mingled together."[32]

Even the case of ritual sacrifices *(korbanot)* is perceived on a more profound level. When a person sacrifices an animal, he repents not only for himself, but for the sins of the soul transmigrated into the animal he offers as well.

A related matter is the prohibition against cruelty to animals. The Sages of the Talmud dealt extensively with the various aspects of that prohibition on the basis of certain biblical passages, while the Kabbalists offered their own explanation: concealed within the body of an animal is a human soul, and thus our treatment of that animal must be considered and cautious. It is told of R. Isaac Luria in particular that he would not strike any living creature, even a fly, and even if it annoyed him. Why? Because he was able to recognize the true nature of all the world's creatures, the human souls that dwell within them, and each one's past.

Another law associated with the doctrine of transmigration is that of burial. Deut. 21:23 forbids that a dead person be left unburied overnight; "You shall surely bury him that day." In the eyes of the Kabbalists, we have this obligation to bury the deceased the same day he dies because that alone enables its transmigration to another body for the sake of its atonement.

4. *Theoretical problems*. By means of the law of transmigration, the Kabbalists sought to resolve other religious difficulties. One central problem was how a person could fulfill his obligation to perform all 613 commandments. What is a person to do if he is not a *kohen* and is thus unable to realize the *mịṣvot* concerning priestly duties? Or suppose a person lives in the Diaspora and cannot therefore perform the commandments related to the Land of Israel? Some Kabbalists held that every individual must fulfill what he can within the framework given him, but others such as R. Isaac Luria were stringent and demanded that each person perform everything, including both the literal and the esoteric commandments. The doctrine of transmigration provides a solution. The soul would be able to live in a variety of situations, which would enable the fulfillment of the commandments in their entirety.

The teaching of metempsychosis answers another similar and essential question as well. In the view of R. Ḥayyim Vital, every individual must fulfill the entire Torah according to the four paths of the PaRDeS—

the literal, homiletical, allegorical, and esoteric levels. What, then, is a person to do if he has no knowledge of Kabbalah? Various solutions were suggested, and one of them was metempsychosis. In one phase of the body's existence, the soul will be given the chance to conduct itself in accordance with esoteric teaching. Another answer was given in the Lurianic teaching of the sparks. In this teaching, every soul *(nefesh)* is a spark from a more extensive "family" or "root," and a profound attachment and sympathy connects them. If a pleasant spark is in a family member, and his appropriate behavior radiates to another family member, he can save the latter from potential punishment. As a result, a person is exempt from a physical realization of all the paths of the PaRDeS if his kin support and assist him. There is the danger in this approach that a person might impose the burden upon others, expecting they will win him merit and come to his aid, and the windfall will be his, so to speak. We may assume, though, that justice would require a person to do what he is able. Moreover, we must remember that not everyone knows the sparks of his family members, and it would be a shame if one were relying on the merits of the family members—then both would end up the loser. R. Ḥayyim Vital expressed the point with great clarity:

> One might think that if all the sparks of the bodily parts together add up to the 613 commandments, even though each spark individually does not complete all of them, it would be enough. Know, however, that it is not so. For the limbs are also divisible into 613 or more sparks, and each spark is composed of all of them. . . . Thus every soul-spark must complete all of the 613 commandments, and if some *miṣvah* is missing, the soul must transmigrate once again. Not only that, every individual must perform all 613 commandments in deed, in speech, and in thought. And if some spark of the soul is missing, even one part of those three, it must continue to transmigrate until it fulfills all of them.[33]

5. *Various phenomena.* Affinities between rabbi and pupil were explained in the sixteenth century through the mystery of *'ibbur*. This "familial" kinship may exist between two people without any connection to their biological background; rather, it exists in the root of their souls. The kinship may evolve into a link in the spiritual realm of rabbi-pupil, or, alternatively, into an emotional-social relationship of love and friendship, such as that between David and Jonathan. What is more, the spiritual

affinity between rabbi and pupil does not arise only between two people sharing a single historical period; a person in our own times may be connected and guided by one of the Sages of the Talmud because, as we have said, the life of souls is not confined by temporal and spacial dimensions.

We haven't far to go, then, to reach the well-known idea of the *Tikkuney Zohar:* "The radiance [of Moses] is found in each and every generation."[34] That is, Moses transmigrates[35] to every righteous Jew and scholar who occupies himself with the Torah "to perfect all of them from their transgression." Thus all Torah scholars are Moses' spiritual sons and he is present, as it were, in each one of them as a spark transmigrated from him. (Note, by the way, that in the faith of Shi'ism, Mohammed is reborn in each generation in the soul of the Imam.)

Another phenomenon needing explanation is that of barrenness. If a woman is barren, it is because a male soul has entered her body, while a man is infertile because a female soul has transmigrated to him (this had already been taught by R. 'Ezra of Gerona). Clearly, this exchange of souls is in punishment for certain sins. The author of *Tikkuney Zohar*[36] adds that this is the reason the Jew praises his Creator each morning "For not making [him] a woman"—meaning he had been found worthy of not having his soul exchanged for that of a woman.

Another phenomenon is explained by means of the doctrine of transmigration and may be formulated as a proof of the verity of the notion of transmigration as a whole. Let us imagine a situation in which a man over seventy commits a transgression punishable by extirpation *(karet)*. According to the Talmud that punishment is enacted at the age of sixty. Thus, our septuagenarian would not be punished unless we assume the existence of transmigration.[37] The question appears in another form in other texts as well. For example, what happens when a person is punished with extirpation twice or more?

THE TERM *GILGUL*

One effect of the atmosphere of mystery surrounding the idea of metempsychosis in the thirteenth century is that we have no constant term for it. Indeed, the *Sefer Bahir* discusses the subject (par. 195) without using any term at all. This suggests that kabbalistic nomenclature had not yet crystallized. In the thirteenth century terms began to be coined, but we see that some Kabbalists still used the general expression of "the law" *(ha-middah)*.[38] The term we use, *gilgul*, is in fact the one most widely employed in talk of a person's return for an additional period of life. But its exact meaning is sometimes questionable. In his commentary on the Song of Songs, R. 'Ezra wrote, "And the souls return and transmigrate *[mitgalgelot]*."[39] Here it is questionable whether his meaning was really the same as our meaning. Gershom Scholem theorized that the term *gilgul* developed through a linguistic usage the Kabbalists found in the writings of authors before them, such as R. Abraham bar-Ḥiyya and R. David Kimḥi. Bar-Hiyya uses the word *hithgalgel* in his description of the wanderings of the disembodied souls of the wicked. R. David Kimḥi, as well, in his commentary on Ps. 104:29 writes: "For all living things will rise after their death, for the souls will transmigrate *[lehithgalgel]* and return to the world." Perhaps, then, the term *gilgul* was taken from these sources. It seems that R. Joseph of Ḥamadan, in the mid-thirteenth century, was the first Kabbalist to use the term. In any event, it was apparently in the wake of the *Zohar* that use of the term spread It should be noted that through the years, other terms were used, and these were not always completely clear, either.

The term "transference" *(ha'atakah)* is found in works by the Tibbonide family of translators, and its meaning is evident: the soul's movement from one body to another. For example: "Certain people, who call themselves Jews [Yudghanites, a Persian sect] . . . call it *ha'atakah*, meaning thereby that the spirit of Reuven is transferred to Simeon, and afterwards to Levi and after that to Yehudah. Many of them would even go so far as to assert that the spirit of a human being might enter into the body of a beast or that of a beast into the body of a human being, and other such nonsense and stupidities."[40]

The phrase "the mystery of *'ibbur*" also designates the transfer of a soul from one body to another. This term, of course, should not be linked to the astronomical-halakhic subject of the calendar (the calculation of which is also called *'ibbur*), nor with other kabbalistic uses of it. The term is found in early, i.e., thirteenth-century, Kabbalah. For example, Recanati writes in the name of Naḥmanides: "And the rabbi, of blessed memory, said that the mystery of *'ibbur* must not be written in his commentary, for fear that it would lead people to err."[41] No explanation is given why that mystery would lead to error. It should be mentioned that

Recanati himself did not heed that instruction, for he speaks of the subject in depth in *Ta'amey ha-Miṣvot* itself, and almost the entirety of his exegesis on the pericope *Vayeshev* is dedicated to the subject of transmigration.

At times, transmigration is conceived as part of a larger mystery, that of *'ibbur,* without the difference between them made explicit. For example: R. Todros ha-Levi Abulafia (1234–98, Castile) says in his book *Oṣar ha-Kavod* (in his commentary on *Ketubot* 111): "I am not permitted to tell you anything of the matter of *gilgul* and *meḥilot* [the underground rolling of the buried dead to resurrection in the Holy Land], which is an utterly concealed mystery, hidden in the mystery of *'ibbur.*" Yet the term *'ibbur* itself underwent a certain change. In *Ma'arekhet ha-Elohut* (fol. 127a–b), for instance, the two are explicitly identical: "The matter of the soul's *gilgul*, called the mystery of *'ibbur.*"[42] But the author of *Ra'ya Meheimna* and *Tikkuney Zohar*—who is not the same as the author of the *Zohar* itself—as well as R. Isaac Luria and others in his wake, do distinguish expressly between *gilgul* and *'ibbur*. In the simple language of R. Ḥayyim Vital:

> *Gilgul* is when, as the newborn emerges from its mother's womb, the soul enters that body, and it suffers all the sorrow and sufferings of that body from the moment it came into the world until its death, and it cannot leave until the day of death. But *'ibbur* is when the soul exists in this world after a person has been born and grown up; then, another soul enters him and that person is like a pregnant woman *['ubarrah]* who carries an infant in her womb, and thus it is called *'ibbur.*[43]

In other words, in the case of *gilgul*, an individual's soul returns for an entire lifetime. In the case of *'ibbur,* though, just as a pregnant woman carries within herself the soul of an infant for a limited period of time, so a living person carries, in the course of his life, an *additional* soul for certain period, similar to the "extra soul" *(neshamah yeteirah)* that enters a Jew on the Sabbath.[44] Clearly, then, "The pain of *gilgul* is much, much greater than the pain of *'ibbur,*"[45] for the period of *'ibbur* may be quite short. The reason is that *'ibbur* is meant to serve a particular purpose. For example, the *Zohar* says that the soul of Yehudah joined the soul of Bo'az during his marriage to Ruth the Moabite to strengthen him in his crucial act. The dictum of the Sages, "He who comes to purify himself is aided" (*Shabbat* 104a), is taken to mean he is provided with an additional soul. It is said that the soul of a zaddik descends to empower a person who fulfills a *miṣvah* with particular effort. For instance, the tale is told in *Shivḥey ha-ARI* that

> Once [the ARI] was sitting with the disciples before him, and our honored Master and Teacher, Rabbi Samuel Uceda entered to speak with the rabbi about a certain matter, and he was yet a young man. Yet when the rabbi saw him, he rose to his full height and said to him, "Welcome," and took his hand and seated him at his right, and spoke with him as long as he needed. After he left, R. Ḥayyim Vital said: "Master, I cannot contain myself from asking why you received that young scholar with such fear and trembling, which you have never done before—what, today, is different?" The rabbi said to him: "On your life, it was not before that lad that I trembled, but before R. Pinḥas ben Yair who entered with him, for today [the latter's] soul impregnated him because of a certain *miṣvah* he performed this same day, which R. Pinḥas ben Yair would do, and for that, his soul entered him to encourage him and help him with that *miṣvah*.[46]

The continuation of the tale is that on the morning of the same day, as R. Samuel Uceda was walking, he heard shouts coming from a house, and when he entered found a family whose home had been vandalized and emptied of their possessions, leaving them bereft of everything. Wasting no time, he went to his own home and brought them all the clothes they needed. That swift and important decision to provide a substantial amount of clothing to utter strangers won him the encouragement of R. Pinḥas ben Yair, who was famous for the efforts he had made in ransoming captives.

At times, the soul of a deceased person must complete its fulfillment of a minor commandment. When it sees that someone in its "family" is about to perform the *miṣvah* it lacks, it immediately enters that person, and thus the two souls act together and with combined strength. At times the soul of a zaddik returns to the world for the sake of everyone, causing good deeds to increase when the world is in need of such. There is an echo of the fundamental rabbinic concept of the unity of the Jewish people and their interinvolvement, and particularly the zaddik's activity for the good of the community. It is understood that there is no possibility of the soul's joining a person under the age of thirteen.[47]

Another passage from R. Ḥayyim Vital says: "When it is decreed that a certain soul must descend into the world and enter that drop [of seed], if, during its descent it encounters another soul in need of transmigration in order to perfect itself, it has the power to take [that soul] with it, and transmigrate with it, and both enter the body of that drop." Moreover, "It may be that one or two or three or four souls enter a single body. More than four souls, though, cannot be in one body."[48]

Another kind of *'ibbur* occurs while both parties are still alive. "When a person is intent upon his rabbi, and opens his heart to him, his soul is linked to his, and some of the influx upon him is transferred to him, and he receives an additional soul. This they call the mystery of *'ibbur* during both their lives."[49] See, then, how strong the link between two people may be, the smaller of the two radiating with light from the greater one.

The impression from all we have said thus far may be that the effects of *'ibbur* are exclusively positive. There are negative cases, however, and these, in the terminology of R. Moses Cordovero, are called "evil pregnancy" *('ibbur r'a)*.[50] The soul of a deceased wicked person may join the soul of a living one to augment the power of his wickedness. Even more serious is the tribulation inflicted upon the person impregnated with an evil *'ibbur,*[51] because the new soul does not want to leave him; throughout its wandering, it endured suffering and at last has found a certain measure of rest in his body. In contrast to that soul, the living person suffers because he carries two evil souls within himself. This phenomenon later became well known by the name of *dibbuk*. According to Gershom Scholem, that term does not originate in kabbalistic literature, but rather in spoken folk Yiddish, beginning in the seventeenth century.[52]

Another name for the phenomenon of evil *'ibbur* is *mikreh*. This term is commonly used by Jews of North African origin, and, barring the influence of the local language of Arabic, we may assume it originates from a statement by R. Ḥayyim Vital: "Sometimes, events *[mikrim]* and evil and difficult occurrences come upon a person suddenly."[53] Similarly, R. Abraham Azulay (born in Morocco, immigrated to the Land of Israel) writes: "At times, because of some sin, an evil event *[mikre r'a]* happens to a person, and he is impregnated with the wicked man's soul . . . and that is the story of that spirit."[54]

After this quick glance at some of the connotations of *'ibbur* and its metamorphoses, let us return to early Kabbalah. In the thirteenth century, we find the expression "to come in exchange for" *(behithalfut)*. It appears, for example, in the writings of R. Asher ben David.[55] The term appears, with minor changes, in other Kabbalists as well. Thus, there is reference to *ḥalifin*[56] and the statement: "Thus God prepares him another *ḥalifah* to purify him and make him meritorious."[57]

Another term is "exile" *(galut)*, found in the *Zohar* and the writings of Ibn Gabbay,[58] and especially in *Sefer ha-Temunah*.

R. Joseph ben Shalom Ashkenazi, who lived in fourteenth-century Spain, uses a number of terms, and it is difficult to distinguish the precise differences among them, or even whether the Kabbalists intended to distinguish among them. After the verse in Job 33:18, he speaks of "the mystery of the sending" *(sod ha-shelaḥ)*, and after Prov. 31:8 he speaks of "the cause of all such as are appointed to destruction" *(din beney ḥalof)*. It is as if he wishes to say that such a law applies to all being. Indeed, in his view,[59] all of existence is in continuous movement, including the Sefirot. Each transition or *hishtalḥut* from one situation to another, and from one state of being to another until completeness is reached, which is determined by Divine Providence, is called *din beney ḥalof*. The term became customary in subsequent generations of Kabbalists, such as in R. Meir ibn Gabbay.[60]

WHAT CAUSES A PERSON'S SOUL TO TRANSMIGRATE?

Concerning the development of the concept of *gilgul* in kabbalistic thought, another question of interest is: Why does a person transmigrate? In the *Bahir*, we find no particular statement on the subject. In the *Zohar* and in *Midrash ha-Ne'elam*, *gilgul* is limited to those who did not fulfill the *miṣvah* of procreation, especially if that failure was intentional.[61] It is no accident that Naḥmanides' extensive discussion of the subject, and Recanati's in particular, are placed in the pericope *Vayeshev* surrounding the issue of levirate marriage. We also find a position limiting *gilgul* to the realm of forbidden sexual relations, or even to other transgressions, such as singing songs with women or cutting one's hair in the manner of Christians.[62] The opinion was even expressed that transmigration does not occur if one fails to uphold the commandment of honoring one's parents. The reason given is that the parents may be zaddikim, and it would not be fair to trouble them by having them descend in another *gilgul* to permit their child to fulfill the commandment of honoring them. The limitations gradually disappear, and the incidence of *gilgul* extends to sins in a general sense.

R. Isaac Luria went further, as his student R. Ḥayyim Vital teaches us, in saying that a person must study and perform the entire Torah and its commandments, both in its literal and mystical sense—i.e., according to the PaRDeS. This approach arouses a certain sense of frustration, for what man can have the faith in himself that he will be able to realize such a mission? In the writings of R. Isaac Luria himself, the situation is eased somewhat by the doctrine of the sparks, in which a person benefits through the mutual involvement of the acts done by the other sparks connected to his soul's root.

We mentioned earlier that *gilgul* was linked, early on, to levirate marriage. This link has an important practical consequence. As it says in the Talmud (*Yebamot* 39b), the commandment of levirate marriage ceased to be practiced and was replaced with *ḥaliṣah*. The Kabbalah, though, which required levirate marriage, caused its resurrection. This becomes clear from the stormy debate that occurred in Candia in the fifteenth century. Luckily, the records of the debate were preserved in manuscript form.[63] One party sought to have a levirate marriage while the other party opposed it. The debate aroused an extensive and vociferous exchange of letters. The practice of levirate marriage existed in North Africa as well, and there the problem of bigamy did not exist; in Europe, if the brother of the deceased were married, his marriage to his brother's widow would be against state law.

Hence the innovative statement (which may have some justification, after the fact, because of the problem of bigamy) expressed in *Sefer ha-Kanah*: "Know that during the exile, there is no levirate marriage. . . . This *miṣvah* is permitted only in the Land of Israel, in the time the Temple stands."[64]

NUMBER OF TRANSMIGRATIONS

How many times does the soul transmigrate? On this question, the Kabbalists differed. The early Kabbalists usually[65] claim it may be no more than three times, and even introduce various verses as proof: among them, the "three transgressions of Israel" (Amos 2:6); "Lo, God does all these things twice or three times with a man" (Job 33:29); and "You shall reckon their fruit as uncircumcised: three years shall it be as uncircumcised unto you" (Lev. 19:23). Others speak of seven times.[66] The *Sefer Bahir* (par. 195) had said "until one thousand," based on the verse "Which he commanded to a thousand generations" (Ps. 105:8). Recanati, though, contends the latter verse cannot serve as a prooftext, for its meaning is that the doctrine of transmigration itself is in force as long as this world exists, and he cites a different verse as proof: "Showing mercy to a thousand generations" (Exod. 20:6). Is this, then, a "war of the sources" or does some sort of logic back it up?

If transmigration is conceived as an act of mercy on God's part, meant to give man the possibility of reaching completeness, that, in principle, has no bounds. As long as an individual needs to come down to this world, the opportunity will be given him, if only he strives to perfect himself. Thus it is said, "Even a thousand times." If, however, *gilgul* is fundamentally understood as punishment for a person's failure to perfect himself, he will be required to transmigrate only three times. And if, even then, he does not succeed, he will receive punishment in Gehinnom. That, for example, is the view of the author of *Ra'ya Meheimna* (III, fol. 216b), and many after him. (A few Kabbalists, though, contended that first a person receives his recompense, whether the Garden of Eden or Gehinnom, and only after that does the process of transmigration begin.)[67] Others say that three opportunities are given from the very beginning. But if he made an effort in the course of them yet did not manage, he may transmigrate a thousand times.[68] In some instances, the Kabbalists offer signs to indicate which *gilgul* a person is currently living.[69]

Some of the Kabbalists contend that the wicked and the middling transmigrate only three times, while the righteous do so without limit. The underlying assumption is that a zaddik transmigrates in order to receive the opportunity of fulfilling a commandment he did not succeed in fulfilling in his previous *gilgul*. Thus, for instance, R. Yehudah Ḥayyat writes: "For it extends to even a thousand times for zaddikim; for the wicked, though, it is only three [times]." The reason given there is that if, after the third time, they did not repent, chances are they will not.[70] In some cases, a zaddik transmigrates for the good of the world, which is in need of him; if so, it is also a perfect zaddik who transmigrates, once again without limitation. An indisputable example is that of Moses, whose soul, according to *Ra'ya Meheimna* (III, 216a), repeatedly transmigrates in order to support the Jewish people in their exile. This idea, of course, is related to the fact that social concerns and national responsibility have an important place in Kabbalah.

In contrast, some Kabbalists contend the soul of a zaddik should not be troubled more than three times, and it is the wicked alone who transmigrate up to a thousand times.[71] There is also one view that a perfect zaddik does not transmigrate at all, since a verse says: "I am always with you" (Ps. 73:23). There is no transmigration for an utterly wicked man either, for it says, "their worm shall not die" (Isa. 66:24).[72] From the fourteenth century onward, the view most commonly held was that the law of *gilgul* applies to the wicked. A zaddik has only a few transgressions he is obliged to rectify, so it is enough to have him undergo *'ibbur* alone. A similar view is expressed in the sixteenth century that *gilgul* is a punishment for the wicked, while "the soul of a perfect zaddik does not transmigrate, but only ascends and descends and sits in the hall of the King, 'to be enlightened in the light of the living' [Job 33:30]"; when he does descend into the world, it is just temporary, and he joins another soul "like one candle is lit by another."[73] Another view, voiced by R. Reuben Ṣarfati, is that the wicked do not transmigrate. "Do not think that the Holy One desires the utterly wicked; [He desires] only the righteous and the middling, not wishing to withhold their reward for what they have already done. Thus the Holy One prepares another 'suit' for him, to cleanse and purify him, that he may be worthy of returning and ascending to the place whence he was hewn."[74] In the fourteenth century, though, the author of the *Sefer ha-Temunah* writes simply: "He makes a covenant with the zaddik and the wicked, for He does not desire the death of the wicked but rather his return through transmigration."[75] An interesting view suggested by the author of a commentary on *Sefer ha-Temunah* is that even the righteous undergo up to seven *gilgulim* to reach a state of perfection.[76]

A Kabbalist of the thirteenth century argued against the contention that if a zaddik had committed some transgressions and had not succeeded in repenting, he would be punished in Gehinnom. "If so," said the Kabbalist, "there is no end to that law, and no visible end to the world, for there is 'no righteous person on earth who does good and never sins' . . . and for a single sin he committed, he would lose out on great goodness." Moreover, who can guarantee that in his return to the world he will improve himself and thus he might lose "his original reward."[77] These are reasonable questions, and engender, in R. Sheshet's eyes, "great calumny." Indeed, his work contains no answer; all we have is the solution received from one of his students that a zaddik transmigrates only for a serious transgression, like the Ten Tribes, who transmigrated to the Ten Martyrs for selling Joseph and for the pain they caused their father Jacob. This reflects the strong belief that everything happens according to the justice of Divine Providence. This declaration was often reiterated by R. Joseph ben Shalom Ashkenazi, who saw transmigration as a law applying to all of existence. A similar motion is expressed by R. Ḥayyim Vital: "There are various kinds of *gilgul*, and almost no one can escape from them,"[78] because, in his view, "Each spark of a soul must rectify all 613 of the Torah's precepts . . . in action, in speech, and in thought."[79] Thus, "They transmigrate until they reach perfection."[80] When a zaddik dies young, the reason may not be punishment but the opposite: "For he has already completed what he had to complete" and such a zaddik is happy in his death.[81]

A somewhat strange opinion is expressed by R. Sheshet concerning penitents. "Thus I say that penitents *[ba'aley teshuvah]* are not in the category [of *gilgul*], for Scripture cries out, 'But if the wicked man turn from his wickedness, and do that which is right' [after Ezek. 18:27, 33:19] . . . and reason supports this, for they have repented of their evil ways knowingly and by choice, and have no need to transmigrate."[82] This view is questionable, as the whole purpose of transmigration is, in effect, to enable repentance (although matters may be different in the case of full repentance).

The difficulty in reaching perfection, with the result that everybody must transmigrate, is expressed by R. Ḥayyim Vital: "For there is almost no one on earth who can escape those *gilgulim*."[83] The same conclusion emerges from the framework set up by various Kabbalists that links transmigration to sin. Some contend that *gilgul* began after the murder of Abel, while others hold it began in the generation of the Flood and will end only with the Resurrection of the Dead. According to R. Isaac of Acre, though, and others as well, our *shemittah* contains a few souls from the previous *shemittah*.

Some passages say that, at this stage, there are no "new souls" at all, i.e., all of them have transmigrated. The point, though, is a subject of dispute. In one view, "There will be no new souls from now until Messianic days . . . some Kabbalists, though, note that there are 'remnants' [Kabbalists] from the new ones as well, as is demonstrated in the *Zohar* . . . blessed is he who knows."[84] In other words, according to Recanati, no definitive conclusion can be reached. In any case, even if there are new souls, they are bestowed only upon an elite few.

The opportunity of transmigrating to a human body may occur only three times. If man did not succeed in that framework, he goes yet lower and transmigrates into the body of an animal. Some propose the following order of transmigration: first he transmigrates to a slave, then to a maidservant, and then to an animal.[85]

The notion that one may transmigrate to an animal is not unique to the Kabbalists, and is known among the Cathars in southern France in the twelfth century. The early Kabbalists, though, were plunged in a stormy debate concerning that question. The *Bahir* itself does not discuss such a possibility (although it appeared in an area in which the Cathar movement was active), perhaps because the connection to the question of theodicy leaves no logical room for it. But at the end of the thirteenth century, that view is often heard,[86] first as atonement for certain grave sins, but later without any distinction. A detailed list of sins and their punishment in transmigration to various sorts of animals or non-Jews is presented in Recanati's commentary in the name of "some of his contemporaries" *(keṣat me-ḥakhmey ha-kabbalah ha-aḥaronim),* the reference being, apparently, to R. Joseph of Ḥamadan. At the end of this list, Recanati states, "If it is an accepted tradition *[kabbalah],* we must also accept it."[87] Some hesitation can be detected in his words. Some affirm *gilgul* to animals,[88] while still others deny it.[89]

These contrary opinions swirl about the central question of the nature of transmigration. If it is conceived as punishment, that would explain the descent from the human level. We must remember, too, that the soul itself does not change significantly in its descent, and thus the punishment is so very severe, for that means that a human soul inhabits the body of an animal. But if the purpose of transmigration is to lead to purification, what benefit could accrue from spending time in a stone, for example? Another claim was made in the early fifteenth century by R. Shem Tov ibn Shem Tov. As he saw it, "The view of some of the Ancients that there is a transference from man to animal . . . [is wrong and] no intelligent person should imagine such a thing." There is no suggestion of it, he says, in the traditional sources. Moreover, he knows no

"Master of the Torah who was drawn to that ancient belief." In response to the reason given for transmigration in animals, i.e., punishment for serious transgressions, R. Shem Tov retorts: "Does the Holy One, blessed be He, lack Gehinnom?"[90] An interesting contrast is afforded by the dynamic conception of R. Joseph Ashkenazi in the first half of the fourteenth century. There, we find that "All inanimate, vegetative, animal and speaking [creatures]—all are subject to the mortal law of ascent and descent, all according to true justice,"[91] commensurate with the severity of the crime. He speaks extensively of descent, on one hand, and of the possibility of "rising" *('illui),* on the other, which also occurs in stages. Later, in the writings of Joseph Samuel del Medigo of Candia,[92] we find this summary of R. Ḥayyim Vital's view: "And the Holy One, blessed be He, raises them little by little from one level to the next; first he has them transmigrate into the inanimate, from the inanimate to the vegetative, from the vegetative to a nonverbal animal, and then to a verbal animal, to gentiles or to slaves, and after that to Jews." Interestingly, R. David ben Zimra mentions the view that between each transmigration to an animal, the soul returns to transmigrate into a human body, giving the soul a renewed opportunity to repair itself. If it does not succeed, it descends to a lower animal.[93]

R. Ḥayyim Vital expressed it well: "There are wicked persons whose sins are so many that, after their death, they will transmigrate to animals beneath their level; then, their sins make them equal to them, and they truly transmigrate with them. Those who are even more utterly evil transmigrate to inanimate forms."[94] In other words, the wicked person himself behaves like an animal in committing his grave deeds, and it is he who draws his own soul down to the level of subhumanness.

It should be pointed out that, according to a few Kabbalists,[95] there is no transmigration to birds. Others make no such distinction. As R. Ḥayyim Vital says: "Everything for known reasons according to their punishment."[96] As we have said, for R. Isaac Luria and his circle (perhaps under the influence of R. Joseph Ashkenazi), the framework expands to include the entire natural order:

> There are souls of the wicked that transmigrate, after their death, to all four parts of being *['asiyah]*—inanimate, vegetative, animal, and speaking . . . and there are some that transmigrate from one level to a lower one, which is an animal. And there are others that

transmigrate to the vegetative as well, and these, for their rectification, must ascend two levels. Still others transmigrate to the inanimate, and must ascend three levels. Because first [such a soul] rises from the inanimate to the vegetative, as it grows from the earth and enters the vegetative. Then an animal that eats grass consumes it, and it rises to the level of an animal; after that, people slaughter it and eat it, and it becomes, once again, part of man's own body, and then it is rectified, for man's consumption of it brings about its purification.[97]

GILGUL—COMPASSION OR PUNISHMENT?

From the beginning of Kabbalah we find two basic approaches, although the distinction between them is sometimes unclear. One sees every event as an act of divine mercy. In the words of R. Sheshet, a disciple of Naḥmanides: "*Gilgul* happens to the sinning soul that should, by rights, perish yet 'He devises means, that none of us be banished'" (2 Sam. 14:14).[98] In other words, before the soul is sentenced to Gehinnom, man is given the chance to improve his ways within the framework of a new lifetime. Thus R. Baḥya writes of a person who returns in repentance:

> And what does the Holy One, blessed be He, do in His mercy that he may merit seeing Him in the supernal light? His soul transmigrates to a body, and returns there as in the beginning . . . and when it is grown, it will beseech God and appease Him through penitence and suffering and then His justice will return to that mortal. For from the day he was born he never sinned and his suffering was because of earlier sins that should have warranted his demise. But the Holy One, blessed be He, "devises means" that he not be banished from the world to come, and then he may gaze at the supernal light.[99]

In such a case, in principle, there should be no limitation on the number of transmigrations, as we said earlier. Perhaps implicit in this view is the assumption that the soul is a divine spark, and must therefore return to its root in purity. Gehinnom, then, is a punishment with no alternative, so to speak.

The second approach sees transmigration as a form of punishment. The analogy presented in the very earliest kabbalistic work[100] already points to this perception. Let us take, as an example, a question raised by one Kabbalist at the turn of the thirteenth century: If *gilgul* increases sins and cancels previous merits, is any reward one may have gained now lost? Recanati responds to this problem: "For there are grievous sins that cannot be atoned for any other way."[101] That is to say, *gilgul* is a severe punishment for serious sins. For that reason, it takes place only three or four times. This view is reflected in the alternate term "exile" *(galut)* used to speak of transmigration (particularly in *Sefer ha-Temunah*). In effect, this conception also raises the question of the relationship between transmigration and Gehinnom. Thus there were some who held, in the thirteenth century, that *gilgul* applies solely to the wicked, while it would be better for the middling to go to Gehinnom,[102] for according to a widespread conception, Gehinnom was perceived as a refining furnace in which the soul is purified over a certain period of time. Indeed, in the view of R. Baḥya, *gilgul* occurs only after punishment has been received in Gehinnom. We must remember, as well, that these are not clear-cut, simple matters. Even the Kabbalist who claims that a totally wicked man does not transmigrate but rather receives his punishment in Gehinnom points out that there are exceptions, such as a wicked person who is the son of a righteous man, or a person who had been righteous in the past but then adopted evil ways.

The question was sometimes asked, both by followers of the Kabbalah and its opponents, of what place Gehinnom now has in light of the concept of transmigration? The underlying problem is that Gehinnom is an accepted institution, recognized for generations, and it is inconceivable that it would be undermined by some new belief. According to most of the Kabbalists, though, if a person does not succeed in utilizing *gilgul* for his own benefit, he descends to Gehinnom.

A sort of compromise position between these two central approaches may be found in the stance of R. Isaac of Acre:

> The law of *gilgul* is judgment and compassion. . . . judgment on the part of the sinner, and compassion on the part of the Holy One, blessed and extolled be He, that the soul not be destroyed in such a short time.[103]

This intermediary view, expressed here explicitly, penetrates even to the words of Kabbalists who ostensibly take a one-sided stance. Things are not determined, apparently, according to the Kabbalists' methods, but rather according to the matter at hand and its implications.

Some Kabbalists[104] contended that the *nefesh* undergoes transmigration, but not the *ru'aḥ*, and certainly not the *neshamah*, due to its superior nature. By its very essence, the *neshamah* does not sin. The opinion of most Kabbalists was that the *neshamah* may transmigrate as well. In the view of R. Abraham Azulay, in the first *gilgul* the *nefesh* is sent; in the second, the *ru'aḥ;* in the third, the *neshamah.* This, though, also depends on the severity of the sin: for what is termed *ḥet,* the *nefesh* transmigrates; for *'avon,* the *ru'aḥ;* for *pesh'a,* the *neshamah.*[105]

Another question discussed is whether it is possible to descend into the body of a non-Jew. The problem is that if transmigration is meant to rectify and complete the *miṣvot*, that possibility is annulled by the soul's very entry into a gentile, who is exempt from the commandments. Yet if transmigration is a punishment, just as it is possible to transmigrate into a stone, so it must be possible to transmigrate to a non-Jew. However, a more decisive issue is present. In the view of the Kabbalists, the soul of the gentile originates in the husks *(kelippot).* If a holy *neshamah* goes down among the nations, it will fall prisoner to *sitra aḥra* (the other side). If so, the transmigration is in vain. Indeed, Recanati makes recourse to a variety of verses—"This was the manner of attesting in Israel" (Ruth 4:7), "They shall not be in the counsel of my people" (Ezek. 13:9), and so forth—to claim that transmigration does not happen to non-Jews, and that a Jew does not transmigrate to the body of a non-Jew.[106] Some two hundred years after him, R. Yehudah Ḥayyat protests:

> And I found it necessary to treat at length the statement made by most of the Kabbalists that the soul of a wicked man, after it has completed its *gilgulim* and had not merited is put into a dog . . . this is difficult to believe. Not only animals, but even into one from the other nations—this is a hard matter.[107]

R. Isaac Luria also opposed the possibility of transmigrating into a non-Jew. Others, in contrast, saw that possibility as mandatory, among them R. Joseph Alcastiel,[108] R. Elijah ha-Kohen in chapter 18 of *Shevet Musar*, and many other Kabbalists like them. The anonymous author of *Gle Razaya* wrote (fol. 14c): "All the souls of Israel . . . [transmigrate] at the order of the supernal Court . . . and are sentenced commensurate with the transgressions they committed. Everything is done in accordance with justice. . . . The same is true of *sitra aḥra*. It, too, has its own court in which the nations of the world are judged, and they too transmigrate at the word of their own court." Different motifs thus contend with one another. The basic assumption here is that in the case of non-Jews, the seven Noahide commandments are binding to the same extent as the 613 commandments are for Jews. The difference is only quantitative, as it were, and not fundamental. This same opinion, incidentally, regarding the non-Jew is also implicit in the question whether a non-Jew who fulfills the seven Noahide commandments has a portion in the world to come. Some Kabbalists say yes, for the reason given above.[109] Another opinion is that transmigration to a non-Jew is itself the punishment of extirpation, as it is written: "That soul shall be cut off *from his people*" (Gen. 17:14).

We must take this opportunity to point out that the "*gilgul* in the hollow of a sling *[be-kaf ha-kel'a]*" referred to in 1 Sam. 25:29 does not represent a return to this world for the duration of a normal lifetime, but rather *gilgulim* and suffering of the soul in a realm beyond the terrestrial world. Similarly, the well-known term "beating of the grave"[110] *(ḥibbut ha-kever)*, which originates in the East and appears for the first time in Jewish texts in the halakhic responsum by R. Meir of Rotenburg, refers to a manner of punishment occurring after death and is unrelated to *gilgul*.

TRANSMIGRATION AND THE RESURRECTION OF THE DEAD

An important question that naturally occurs to anyone investigating the doctrine of transmigration is this: What will happen in the time of the resurrection of the dead? To what body will the soul return and reenter? In the words of R. Yehudah Ḥayyat: "This is a great and momentous question concerning those bodies—what will be with them at the Resurrection of the dead, for clearly the *neshamah* can enter only one of them, and we should know which it will be, and what will happen to the others."[111]

This question, already posed by the earliest Kabbalists, such as R. Asher ben David and others, is more than a technical one; it has moral implications as well. In the words of the *Zohar* (II, fol. 100a): "According to human reason, the first body, which died without issue, was lost because he was not worthy. In that case, it was in vain that he endeavored to keep the commandments of the Torah. Yet even if he kept only one commandment, we know that 'even the emptiest in Israel are full of good deeds as a pomegranate is full of grains.' This body, although it was not found worthy to bring forth an issue, was yet able to fulfill other commandments, and shall it all have been in vain?"

The *Zohar* assumes that *gilgul* is linked to levirate marriage, and that makes it difficult to understand how one particular commandment could tip the scales against other commandments. The ethical problem could be stated thus: If you say that the last body will be resurrected, as it was the one that succeeded in bringing the soul to completion, it may be argued that it was able to do so because of the cumulative efforts made throughout the soul's transmigrations in earlier bodies it inhabited. However, the opinion also exists that because the previous bodies did not bring about perfection, they do not merit resurrection. That, for example, is the contention in the *Zohar* (I, fol. 131a): "R. Jose answered: Those bodies which were unworthy and did not succeed [in perfecting the soul] will be regarded as though they had not been: as if they were a withered tree in this world, so will they be regarded at that time [of the resurrection]. And [only] the last that had been firmly planted and took root and prospered will come to life. . . . Regarding the part of the former body that remained fruitless . . . it is written, 'For he shall be like a tamarisk in the desert, and shall not see when good cometh . . . ' (Jer. 17:6)." It may be, though, that this view relates to extreme instances in which man did not progress in the slightest during his first stage of being.

Of great interest is the stance of Don Isaac Abravanel in his commentary on the pericope *Ki Teṣe:* "The *nefesh* will return to the first body because it was, in essence, that person, while the other bodies were only instruments to enable perfection or punishment. Thus Daniel (12:2) said, 'And many of those who sleep in the dust of the earth shall awake'—but not all." In other words, he has no moral problem, as the primary connection between the soul and the body was engendered with the first body, and together they created the "essence" of the person. The subsequent bodies do no more than assist.

In some kabbalistic texts, however, such as those of R. Asher ben David, R. Yehudah Ḥayyat, and others,[112] we find another answer, this one related to the doctrine of the sparks (or "branches" *['anafim]* in the nomenclature of R. Yehudah Ḥayyat). That is, just as a candle flickers and shines, illuminating a variety of places, so the soul—"The spirit of man is the candle of the Lord" (Prov. 20:27)—is divisible into such flashes. As R. Yehudah Ḥayyat put it: "Branches spread from the last body to the others as one candle is lit from another without being diminished in the least."[113] The last body will be resurrected, and sparks will emerge from the soul within it to illuminate all the other bodies, so that they, too, may live.

In the work of R. Ḥayyim Vital we find another solution:

> There are two kinds of *gilgulim*: the first is in the case when the first body of a certain *ru'aḥ* was among the heretics and apostates, who cannot be resurrected in the same body; then that *ru'aḥ* transmigrates alone to a second body, and in it will rise when the dead are resurrected. But if the first body is still worthy of rising when the dead are resurrected, that *ru'aḥ* cannot enter the second body alone. For afterward, at the Resurrection, one of the two bodies will have to be dead, with no spirit. Necessarily, then, *another, new ru'aḥ* must enter the second body, and the above-mentioned *ru'aḥ* that sinned transmigrates with it; thus, all the *miṣvot* performed by the new *ru'aḥ* have merit for the first as well, and when that second body dies too, when the time of the Resurrection comes, the second body will rise with its principal spirit, which is new, and that spirit that sinned and was placed in a second body returns to the first body.[114]

AGAINST *GILGUL*

Not everyone saw the belief in transmigration in a positive light. In the thirteenth century, R. Jed'aiah ha-Penini (ha-Bedersi) states, in a letter of apology to R. Solomon ben Abraham ibn Adret (RaSHBA), that the belief in transmigration may lead to carelessness in serving God under the assumption that the destiny of the present body has really already been determined by the experiences of the past, and that one may thus forgo all efforts toward appropriate behavior. A contradiction likewise exists with the belief in resurrection of the dead.[115]

In the fourteenth century, Ḥasdai Crescas argued that *gilgul* opposes the philosophical reasoning that each body is uniquely suited to a particular soul suited to it. How could it be, then, that a soul that inhabited the body appropriate for it would find its place in another body?[116]

In the debate in Candia in 1460, some of the scholars involved were fundamentally opposed to the Kabbalah in general, and some opposed to *gilgul*.[117] A number of their arguments were reiterated in the sixteenth century by R. Abraham ibn Migash in the book *Kevod Elohim* II, chapters 10–14.

The virulent criticism voiced by R. Yehudah Aryeh of Modena in the sixteenth century deserves special note. He attacked the belief in transmigration from several angles. He sought to refute Abravanel's explanation, outlined above, in the following way:

> Why is it said that the soul will be returned to another body to give it good material. . . . Yet he is still not certain he will not sin, for even with a good temperament he may sin. And if he does good, he will win little, yet if he does evil he will lose much. . . . Where, then, is the compassion and the forgiveness of our Lord to bring him once again with so many dangers?

In other words, not only is the danger of the negative as great as the chance for the positive, but the notion of *gilgul* casts the very nature of God as compassionate into question, thus multiplying the challenges posed to the soul.[118] In opposition to the Lurianic concept of *'ibbur,* he voiced this ironic critique:

> How shall I respond and what shall I say of its foolishness and impossibility, for the Rabbi, of blessed memory, was not certain about it. Therefore, he called it "the mystery of *'ibbur,*" that two or three souls come to dwell in a single living body, and that two or three forms are in force upon one body of matter at the same time. May the truth live, and may ears be saved from hearing such things from those who boast of knowing divine mystery and of standing in the covert of His sanctuary.[119]

Similarly, he scorns the belief in *gilgul* for animals. He asks how it was that Jewish thinkers knew nothing of such things for so many generations; perhaps they did not speak of them because of some fundamental objection. These and many other arguments were presented by R. Yehudah

Aryeh of Modena, both in his work *Ben David*, the source of the citations above, and in his book *Ari Nohem.*[120]

Pertinent objections are also voiced by R. Moshe Ḥefeṣ to R. Asher Lemlein. He remarks that if the Kabbalists explain the problem of "a zaddik who suffers" by saying that he was previously a wicked person, what, then, is the sin of his current body to warrant its suffering for the sins of the previous body and its pleasures?[121] It seems that the increasingly strident arguments against *gilgul* and *'ibbur* are what gave rise to the extensive defense presented by R. Manasseh ben Israel in his work *Nishmat Ḥayyim*.

EPILOGUE

In lieu of concluding statements, I would like to quote a passage written by a Kabbalist who is important and interesting from many aspects; he was exiled from his city of Acre to Spain (and perhaps first to Italy) in the wake of the Mameluk War in the Land of Israel. His name is R. Isaac of Acre, and his work *Meirat 'Eynaim* truly is as enlightening as its title, and contains some precious gems. The following passage[1] includes a certain degree of moralizing, which I do not mean to direct to my readers, and is not the focus in the present framework. The insightful reader will understand.

> And you, my brother and comrade, my intimate friend, pray be not lax in pursuing someone to teach you, for although I have arranged the table for you, and given you chains in which to imprison your evil inclination, and have opened up the source of living waters for you, that you may immerse yourself in it and strengthen your good inclination, and have given you a precious stone for the healing of your soul, and have placed in your hand a torch of fire by which you may prepare food for your sustenance, and have taken you into the cellar whence you may take spiced wine to drink as is your will, and have brought you to the orchard, to eat and enjoy the sweetness of the fruit to your heart's desire—Do not say: My house is charged with plenty and lacks nothing; I will sit and rest and eat and drink until my belly is filled with all that is in my house, and will no longer weary myself chasing after the wise. Take head, instead, of my words: I counsel you, Gird your loins like a man, and serve those who are truly wise; perhaps they will augment you with more of such things, or with one, about whom you shall say: "Many daughters have done virtuously, but thou excellest them all" [Prov. 31:29]. For as long as you pursue wisdom, you are a wise man!

NOTES

Chapter 1. Mysticism and the Kabbalah

1. This in itself does not conclusively establish whether or not there was a continuity of tradition below or above the surface. Here we are dealing with well-known and clear-cut facts. Furthermore, the way things turned out from that point onward suggests an ongoing process of exploration and crystallization.

2. True, the Jewish philosophers dealt with the reasons for the Commandments, but their concern did not carry the same weight as that in the Kabbalah. This point will be recapitulated further on.

3. I paraphrased here Isaiah Tishby's definition (*The Wisdom of the Zohar,* trans. D. Goldstein [Oxford, 1989], 1:229) of the kabbalistic teachings of the *Zohar,* as it is true of the entire world of the Kabbalah.

4. *Berakhot* 58a and parallels.

5. See also Mishnah *Sanhedrin* IV, 3, and also Maimonides, *Hilkhot De'ot,* I, 1.

6. W. R. Inge, *Christian Mysticism* (London, 1989), pp. 335–48, lists twenty-six definitions, but there are many more.

7. See Gershom Scholem, *Major Trends in Jewish Mysticism* (Jerusalem, 1941), p. 4. Hence in Christian mysticism: *gustare deo.*

8. The English version of the words of R. Menaḥem Mendel of Premyshlyany, originally translated by G. Scholem, is found in Moshe Idel, *Kabbalah* (New Haven, 1988), p. 58 and corresponding n. 160 on p. 300. See *Yosher Divrey Emet* 18c–d; *Likkutey Yekarim* 30b; *Likkutey Keter Shem Tov,* ed. B. Minz (Tel Aviv, 1961), pp. 208–9. See also Al-Ghazālī, *Ha-Podeh min ha-Te'iyah ve-ha-Ta'ut,* ed. Hava Lazarus-Yafeh (Tel Aviv, 1965), pp. 59–60. Cf. Tanya, *Sefer shel Beinonim* (Brooklyn, 1954), chap. 50, p. 140 (and see M. Ḥalamish, *Nativ la-Tanya* [Tel Aviv, 1987], p. 312) on the love of God as giving rise to the soul's raptures.

9. See Scholem, *Major Trends,* p. 353 n. 6.

10. See Isaac Guttmann, *Dat u-Madda'a* (Jerusalem, 1956), pp. 96, 273.

11. See M. M. Buber, *Be-Pardes ha-Ḥasidut* (Jerusalem, 1945), pp. 97–101, who emphasizes that mysticism obliterates the dichotomy between an "I" who knows and an object that is known. It also establishes an intimate, personal contact with God.

12. It is worth reminding that the verb *yado'a* (know), which is widespread in the Scripture, often appears in the sense of drawing a conclusion as a result of close contact. Cf. Deut. 4:39; Ps. 91:14; 1 Sam. 2:12; Judges 8:16; and Jer. 31:18. Even *yado'a* in the context of sexual intercourse (Gen. 4:1, 19:8) probably suggests a deeper, more human level of male-female relations, which in themselves are also common to other animals. Incidentally, it is probably to this biblical sense of the verb that Kabbalist

Rabbi Joseph Gikatilla referred in the opening of *Sha'arey Orah.* He emphasizes that it is said: "I will set him on high because he has known [rather than: remembered] my name" (Ps. 91:14).

13. See A. M. Haberman, *Shirey ha-Yiḥud ve-ha-Kavod* (Jerusalem, 1948), pp. 47, 51.

14. Raḥamim Nissim Isaac Palacha, *Nefesh Yafah* (Smyrna, 1883), I, 2.

15. Part of the exposition below is based on the entry "mysticism" in the *Hebrew Encyclopedia.*

16. It is noteworthy that this quality of the Kabbalist's closure raised the objection of philosopher Franz Rosenzweig: "Loved only by God, man is closed off to all the world and closes himself off. What is uncanny for every natural feeling about all mysticism, as well as objectively disastrous, is this: that it becomes such a cloak of invisibility for the mystic. His soul opens for God, but because it opens only for God, it is invisible to all the world and shut off from it. . . . This thoroughly immoral relationship to the world is thus utterly essential for the pure mystic if he wants, for the rest, to assert and preserve his pure mysticism" (*The Star of Redemption,* trans. William W. Hallo [New York/Chicago/San Francisco, 1971], pp. 207–8). See also Moshe Scwarcz's explanations in the Hebrew edition, *Kokhav ha-Ge'ulah* (Jerusalem, 1960), p. 239 nn. 2 and 3.

17. *Zohar* II, fol. 23a, as translated in Tishby, *Wisdom of the Zohar,* 1:322.

18. See Ben-Ami Scharfstein, *Ha-Ḥavayah ha-Mystit* (Tel Aviv, 1972), p. 17.

19. As to the Kabbalah, I. Tishby notes that "one of the far reaching innovations in Judaism is violating the norms of chaste language in erotic kabbalistic symbolism that refers to the divine system." See his paper in S. Pines jubilee volume, *Jerusalem Studies in Jewish Thought* 2 (1980): 467 n. 133.

20. See Tishby, *Wisdom of the Zohar,* 1:234. See, for instance, the introduction of *Sefer ha-Shem:* "And He who knows his Creator will serve him by true worship."

21. In the ancient days, the image of the thread as connecting man to God was extensively used. Hence the phrase: "The thread of his life was cut short," namely, he died. Cf. Isa. 38:12. Nonetheless, the thread is, so to speak, "external."

22. See Scharfstein, *Ha-Ḥavayah,* p. 53.

23. See also A. Epstein, *Sefer ha-Gimatriya'ot, Ha-Eshkol* 6 (1909): 207.

24. R. Isaac ha-'Azovi, "Agudat Ezov," MS Jerusalem (Mehlman), 17 (microfilm no. 31535 in the National and University Library in Jerusalem), fol. 22a.

25. The contrast between Abulafia's method and the method of symbolism is discussed at length in some of Idel's works.

26. The meaning of the Greek word *allegoria* is "to speak differently." This suggests that there is no intrinsic connection between the referent and the allegorical word that refers to it.

27. See also Gershom Scholem, *Devarim be-Go* (Tel Aviv, 1976), pp. 248–49.

28. Gershom Scholem, "Sefer Masoret ha-Berit le-R. David ben R. Abraham ha-Lavan," *Kobeṣ 'Al Yad* 11 (1936): 31.

29. Rabbi Simeon ibn Lavi, *Ketem Paz* (Djerba, 1940), fol. 1b.

30. Rabbi Shneur Zalman of Lyady, *Ma'amrey Admor ha-Zaken: Ethalekh, Liozno* (Brooklyn, 1958), p. 24.

31. Gen. 1:26. And see Job 19:26, "In my flesh I shall see God," a verse that was extensively used as support for the notion that the Kabbalist's grasp of the mystery of the Godhead results from contemplation of the innermost recesses of his soul.

32. See Scholem, *Devarim be-Go,* p. 252.

33. For more on the meanings of the symbol see Tishby, *Wisdom of the Zohar,* 1:283–90; idem, *Netivey Emunah u-Minut* (Ramat Gan, 1965), pp. 11–14.

Chapter 2. The Kabbalist and his Acquiring of the Kabbalah

1. Abraham Abulafia, "Ve-Zot Li-Yhudah," in *Ginzey Ḥokhmat ha-Kabbalah* (Leipzig, 1853), p. 15.

2. See Meir ibn Gabbay, *'Avodat ha-Kodesh* (Jerusalem, 1954), 3:18, especially concerning the discovery of the Zohar. The identity of the author of the *Zohar* and the time of its composition are controversial issues. On the whole, tradition attributes the composition of the *Zohar* to Rabbi Simeon bar Yoḥai, a tanna of the second century. However, from the end of the thirteenth century, and particularly from the end of the fifteenth century, Jewish scholars have raised various arguments and provided different proofs against this attribution. Most of these stand up in the light of modern research. In the nineteenth century attempts were made to attribute the *Zohar* to various personalities. An attempt to attribute the book to Rabbi Moses de Leon, who lived in Spain at the end of the thirteenth century, regained strength in twentieth-century research. According to this view, R. Moses de Leon composed the *Zohar* during the third quarter of the thirteenth century. A detailed clarification of the given topics is to be found in Tishby, *Wisdom of the Zohar,* 1:13–96; Gershom Scholem, *The Hebrew Encyclopaedia,* s.v. "Zohar." A. Jellinek's hypothesis, raised in the nineteenth century, that the *Zohar* was composed by a group of Kabbalists presided over by R. Moses de Leon, was repeated in various studies. See for instance, Yehudah Liebes's paper "Keiṣad Nitḥaber Sefer ha-Zohar," *Sefer ha-Zohar ve-Doro = Jerusalem Studies in Jewish Thought* 8 (1989): 1–71.

3. According to Gershom Scholem, the first Kabbalists used to quote or make statements on the basis of kabbalistic midrashim. See Scholem, "Ha-im Ḥibber R. Moshe de Leon et Sefer ha-Zohar?" *Madda'ey ha-Yahadut* 1 (1926): 23.

4. See G. Scholem, "le-Ḥeqer Kabbalat Rabbi Yitsḥak ben Ya'acov ha-Cohen," *Tarbiṣ* 5 (1934): 187.

5. In *Iggeret ha-Teshuvah,* attributed to Isaac ibn Latif, reprinted in *Kobetz 'al Yad* 1 (1885): 59.

6. *Perush ha-Aggadot le-Rabbi 'Ezra mi-Gerona,* in *Sefer Likkutey Shikheḥah u-Pe'ah* (Ferrara, 1556), fol. 8a.

7. The kabbalistic tradition of the thirteenth century tells about three or four individuals who received a revelation from Elijah and specifies their names. See A. Heschel, "'Al Ru'aḥ ha-Kodesh bi-Yemey ha-Beinaim," in *Alexander Marx Jubilee Volume,* ed. S. Lieberman (New York, 1950), pp. 190–92.

8. For instance: "Influx which is drawn to me from that supernal Plenitude, which does not descend according to my will, but only by the will of the Blessed

One, may His great, mighty and tremendous Name be blessed" (from *Sha'arey Ṣedek*). See G. Scholem, "Sha'arey Ṣedek, Ma'amarin be-Kabbalah Me-Askolat R. Abraham Abulafia," *Kiryat Sefer* 1 (1924): 127.

9. Jeremy Zwelling, ed., *Joseph of Hamadan's "Sefer Tashak"* (Ann Arbor, 1975), p. 2.

10. See Uzzi Kalkheim, *Adderet Emunah* (Jerusalem, 1975), p. 15.

11. See Gershom Scholem, "Te'udah Ḥadashah le-Toledot Reshit ha-Kabbalah," in *Sefer Bialik* (Tel Aviv, 1934), p. 144.

12. See Isaiah Tishby, *Ḥikrey Kabbalah u-Sheluḥoteha* (Jerusalem, 1982), 1:9.

13. See Gershom Scholem, "'Ikvotav shel Gabirol ba-Kabbalah," in *Me'assef Sofrey Ereṣ Yisrael* (Tel Aviv, 1940), p. 17.

14. Rabbi Todros is consistent in his approach. See, for example, his commentary on *Shabbat* 31a–b.

15. See S. O. Wilenski, *The Fourth World Congress of Jewish Studies* (Jerusalem, 1969), 2:323.

16. This epistle was published by Greenup in *Jewish Quarterly Review* 21 (1930): 375.

17. *Or ha-Yashar, 'Amud ha-Torah,* chap. 14, par. 16. For a similar formulation—"Whoever wishes to study the science of the Truth should not utter what he has not heard from a decent and reliable person"—see R. Jacob Koppel Lifshitz, *Kol Ya'akov* (Slavuta, 1894), fol. 16a.

18. See A. M. Lunṣ, *Yerushalayim* (Jerusalem, 1887), 2:147.

19. See Scholem, "Te'udah Ḥadashah le-Toledot Reshit ha-Kabbalah," p. 143.

20. See Ephraim Gottlieb, *Ha-Kabbalah be-Kitvey Rabbeynu Baḥya ben Asher* (Jerusalem, 1970), p. 26.

21. As translated in Scholem, *Major Trends,* p. 127. See also p. 379.

22. See A. Gottlieb, "Berurim be-Kitvey R. Joseph Gikatilla," *Tarbiṣ* 39 (1960): 64 n. 10.

23. *Zohar Ḥadash,* fol. 94b. Interestingly, the same image is found in Rabbi Abraham Abulafia. See Gershom Scholem, *Ha-Kabbalah shel Sefer ha-Temunah ve-shel Avraham Abulafia* (Jerusalem, 1965), p. 203.

24. See E. E. Urbach, R. J. Zvi Werblowsky, and C. H. Wirszubski, eds., *Meḥkarim ba-Kabbalah u-ve-Toledot ha-Datot,* submitted to Gershom Scholem (Jerusalem, 1968), p. 2.

25. In his commentary on Maimonides' *Guide of the Perplexed* (Venice, 1574), fol. 21b.

26. *RaMBaN (Naḥmanides), Commentary on the Torah,* ed. and trans. Charles B. Chavel (New York, 1971-76), pp. 15–16.

27. Moses de Leon, *Ha-Nefesh ha-Ḥakhamah* (Basle, 1601), par. 12

28. R. Jacob ben Sheshet, *Ha-Emunah ve-ha-Bitaḥon,* in *Kitvey ha-Ramban,* ed. H. D. Chavel (Jerusalem, 1964), 1:364. The English citation is based on R. C. Kiener's translation in J. Dan, *The Early Kabbalah* (New York, 1986), p. 122.

29. R. Jacob Ben Sheshet, *Ha-Emunah ve-ha-Bitaḥon,* p. 370.

30. R. Jacob ben Sheshet, "Sh'ar ha-Shamayim," in *Oṣar Neḥmad* (Wien, 1860), 3:154.

31. "Commentary on Sefer Yeṣirah," attributed to Rabbi Meir ibn Abu Sahulah, MS Rome/Angelica 45, fol. 70b.

32. Shabbetai Sheftel Horowitz, *Nishmat Shabbetai ha-Levi* (Podgorza, 1898), p. 15. In fact, the source is Rabbi Moses Cordovero, *Pardes Rimmonim,* I, 6. Cited in Isaiah Horowitz, *Sheney Luḥot ha-Berit* (Amsterdam, 1698), 42a.

33. Joseph Gikatilla, *Ginnat Egoz* (Hanau, 1615), fol. 3b.

34. *Commentary on the Pentateuch,* "Vayeshev," fol. 34d.

35. *Ma'arekhet ha-Elohut,* fol. 49a.

36. R. Abraham Shalom, *Neveh Shalom* (Constantinople, 1538), fol. 70a.

37. R. Isaac ha-Cohen. Cited in G. Scholem, "Le-Ḥeqer Kabbalat R. Isaac ben Jacob ha-Kohen," p. 194.

38. R. Moses Cordovero, *Shi'ur Komah* (Warsaw, 1883), fol. 17a.

39. See Gershom Scholem, *Kitvey Yad be-Kabbalah* (Jerusalem, 1930), p. 26

40. R. Isaac of Acre, *Meirat 'Eynaim,* ed. Amos Goldreich (Jerusalem, 1984), p. 245.

41. See, for instance, the Maggid's words to R. Joseph Karo: "But the secret of the case [*sa'ir ha-mishtale'aḥ,* "scapegoat"] is a mystery of mysteries *[temira de-temirin, amika da'amikin],* there is no sage in the world who knows this and it is impossible to grasp this unless it is transmitted from mouth to mouth, for this is *kabbalah* [i.e., oral tradition], and it must be received from mouth to mouth." Joseph Karo, *Maggid Meisharim* (Vilna, 1875), fol. 34b.

42. Rabbi Shem Tov ibn Shem Tov writes as follows: "As we received from our forefathers, back to the Master of prophets Moses our Rabbi, peace be with him." Published by G. Scholem, "Seridei Sifro shel R. Shem Tov ibn Gaon 'al Yesodot Torat ha-Sefirot," *Kiryat Sefer* 8 (1931–32): 400. See also R. Moses de Leon's description: "The awesome wisdom . . . is the fundamental principle of all science, and this is what is called Kabbalah, because it was transmitted *[kabbalah]* to Moses, peace be with him, from Sinai and he transmitted [it] to Joshua and Joshua to the elders and the elders to the prophets and the prophets transmitted it to the members of the Great Assembly (as the written Torah was transmitted) and they bequeathed the matter of this wisdom one to another. Indeed, the method of this science was imparted to Adam when God placed him in the Garden of Eden and disclosed to him the secret of this science and it was with him until he sinned. . . . His son Shet, who was born in his image and likeness, inherited this wisdom . . . until the last generations stood on Mount Sinai and God bequeathed it to Moses, peace be with him. . . . And from thence onwards all the successive generations received it one man from another. And in the Diaspora, because of the troubles, this science was forgotten, except for a scarcity, one of a city and two of a family. And they awakened this wisdom in every generation, and therefore this wisdom is transmission *[kabbalah],* one man from another" (Moses de Leon, *Shekel ha-Kodesh* [London, 1911], p. 22).

43. On the wisdom of Adam it is said in the *Zohar:* "'*ze sefer*' (Gen. 5:1)—Really, a book. . . . For when Adam was in the Garden of Eden, the Holy One, blessed be He, brought down to him a book by Raziel, the holy angel in charge of supernal holy secrets" (I, fol. 55b). Also: "Certainly brought down a book to Adam, by which he acquired knowledge of the supernal wisdom. And this book reached the sons of

God, the sages of the generation. And whoever merits to contemplate it, knows through it supernal wisdom" (I, fol. 37b).

44. See, for instance, R. Elijah Delmedigo, *Beḥinat ha-Dat,* ed. Jacob Ross (Tel Aviv, 1984), p. 91.

45. *Shomer Emunim,* First Debate, par. 16–17

46. *Ashmoret ha-Boker* (Venice, 1720), fol. 5a.

47. *Rav Pe'alim Responsa* (at the end), Sod Yesharim, I, 9.

48. See Shemu'el Ashkenazi, "He'arot ve-Tosafot," *Reshumot,* n.s., 4 (1947): 199.

Chapter 3. Prerequisites

1. See Scholem, *Kitvey Yad,* p. 26.

2. See also Maimonides, *Guide of the Perplexed,* pt. 1, chaps. 32–34. And see Colette Sirat, "The *Mar'ot Elohim* of Hanokh b. Solomon al-Constantini," *Eshel Be'er Sheba* 1 (1976): 123–24; G. Nigal, "De'ot R. J. Yawetz al Philosophia u-Mitpalsephim," *Eshel Be'er Sheba* 1 (1976): 285.

3. *Keter Shem Tov* by R. Shem Tov ibn Gaon, *ki Teṣe*. This treatise was published in *Ma'or va-Shemesh* (Livorno, 1839), but I used the manuscript version.

4. First introduction to *Sefer Eṣ Ḥayyim.*

5. *Or Ne'erav,* pt. 3, chap. 1.

6. *Haggida Li,* by David ben Moshe Yehudah de Medina, MS Jerusalem (Yehuda) 158, fol. 1a. Composed in Jerusalem in 1748.

7. The epistle of Rabbi 'Azriel to Burgos, published in Gershom Scholem, *Mada'ey ha-Yahadut* (Jerusalem, 1927), p. 239.

8. Yehudah Ḥayyat, *Minḥat Yehudah,* in *Ma'arekhet ha-Elohut* (Mantua, 1558), fol. 143a.

9. Ibn Gabbay, *'Avodat ha-Kodesh,* pt. 4, chap. 30.

10. *Oṣar ha-Geonim* (Jerusalem, 1931), Ḥagigah, the responsa, p. 12.[= "Question of the Rabbis of Fez," MS Oxford 1565, 6b–7a].

11. *Avot de Rabbi Nathan,* trans. Judah Goldin (New Haven, 1956), beginning of chap. 3, p. 26.

12. *Ḥagigah* 13a, ed. Soncino, p. 75.

13. *Heikhalot Rabbati,* ed. S. A. Wertheimer, in vol. 1 of *Batey Midrashot* (Jerusalem, 1950), chap. 15, p. 90.

14. See, for instance, *Seder Eliyahu Rabba,* chap. 29.

15. See, for instance, *Tikkuney Zohar,* tikkun 70, fol. 121b-134a.

16. *Zohar* II, fol. 70a–75a, and the continuation, ibid., 272b–276a, and *Zohar Ḥadash* (Warsaw, 1885), fol. 56c–60a.

17. Rabbi Jacob Ṣemaḥ, *Tif'eret Adam* (Haifa, 1982), p. 110. See also M. Idel, "Differing Conceptions of Kabbalah in the Early Seventeenth Century," in *Jewish Thought in the Seventeenth Century,* ed. I. Twersky and B. Septimus (Cambridge, 1987), p. 170 nn. 163 and 164. For an interesting description and important details see Naḥmanides, "Derashat Torat Ha-Shem Temimah," in *Kitvey ha-Ramban,* ed. Chavel, 1:161–63.

18. Pp. 13ff.

19. "Hayyei ha-Olam ha-Ba," MS Oxford 1582, fol. 34a, published in A. Jellinek, *Philosophie und Kabbala* (Leipzig, 1854), p. 44.

20. *Zohar Ḥadash,* Genesis, 6d.

21. *Or Ne'erav,* pt. 3, chap. 1.

22. Thus he accepted Maimonides' position in *Hilkhot Yesodey ha-Torah,* IV, 13. and ibid.: bread and meat. On this point see Isaiah Tishby, "Ha-'Immut ben Kabbalat ha-ARI le-vein Kabbalat ha-RaMaK . . . ," *Zion* 32 (1967): 75 n. 269. For a similar formulation of Rabbi Moses Isserles's words see also *Siftey Cohen [Shakh],* subpar. 6.

23. *Beit Yisrael be-Polin,* ed. Israel Halpern (Jerusalem, 1954), 2:276.

24. *Chasidiana,* ed. Simeon Dubnov (Jerusalem, 1962), p. 14. See also M. Piekarz, *Bi-Yemei Ṣemiḥat ha-Ḥasidut* (Jerusalem, 1978), pp. 321–23.

25. "Commentary on the Secrets of Naḥmanides" (by Rabbi Shem Tov ibn Gaon), MS Paris 790, fol. 87a.

26. Horowitz, *Sheney Luḥot ha-Berit,* Shevu'ot, fol. 182b.

27. *Or ha-Yashar,* Seder ha-Limmud ve-Hanhagato, sec. 31. See also *Or Zaddikim,* chap. 22.

28. His commentary to *Sefer Yeṣirah,* I, 2.

29. See above, n. 21.

30. Introduction to Elijah de Vidas, *Reshit Ḥokhmah* (Muncacz, 1926), fol. 5b. A very similar formulation is found in R. Joseph Ergas, *Shomer Emunim,* fol. 27b; idem, *Divrey Yoseph Responsa,* par. 25.

31. Published in A. Jellinek, *Ginzey Ḥokhmat ha-Kabbalah* (Leipzig, 1853), p. 1.

32. *Ḥemdat Yamim,* Ḥag ha-Shavu'ot (Leghorn, 1858), chap. 1, fol. 50c.

33. *Or Ne'erav,* pt. 3, chap. 2.

34. See Tishby, "Ha-'Immut," p. 74, from *Shetil Pore'aḥ,* fol. 185a.

35. See Tishby, "Ha-'Immut," p. 75, from *Shemen Mishḥat Kodesh,* 5a.

36. See Tishby, "Ha-'Immut," p. 76, from *Shemen Zayit Zakh,* 110b.

37. R. Ḥayyim Vital, *Arb'a Meot Shekel Kesef,* (Korets, 1804). See H. Liberman, "Defusei Korets," *Sinai* 70 (1972): 174.

38. *Sefer Razi'el* (Jerusalem, 1956), p. 13. See also MS Oxford 1572, fol. 1a.

39. *Ḥemdat Yamim,* Ḥag ha-Shavu'ot, chap. 1, 50d, 51a.

40. Lunṣ, *Yerushalayim,* 2:145. In another epistle he wrote, he raises, among other things, the demand "and not to angry men." Ibid., p. 147.

41. *Orḥot Zaddikim* (Leghorn, 1790), fol. 67a. The awareness of the need to distance oneself from anger spread widely, as exemplified by the prayer composed by R. Ḥayyim Joseph David Azulay. This prayer, which is to be recited as soon as one wakes up, is as follows: "I gratefully thank You, O loving King, for you have returned my soul within me with compassion—abundant is your faithfulness. Would that my heart be ready and entrusted to my hand, so that I shall neither get angry nor anger you." See *'Avodat ha-Kodesh,* Kesher Gudal, par.1, subpar. 1.

42. R. Ḥayyim Vital, *Sefer ha-Gilgulim* (Vilna, 1886), fol. 4b.

43. *Zohar* II, fol. 190b.

44. Solomon Shlumil of Dresnitz, *Shivhey ha-ARI* (Przemysl, 1869), fol. 11a.

45. R. Ḥayyim Vital, *Sha'ar ha-Kavvanot* (Jerusalem, 1902), 1b. See my paper "Gilgulav shel Minhag Kabbali," *Kiryat Sefer* 53 (1978): 534–56; Yehudah Liebes, "Ha-Mashi'aḥ shel ha-Zohar," in *Ha-Ra'ayon ha-Meshiḥi be-Israel* (Jerusalem, 1984), pp. 158–63; Ze'ev Gries, *Sifrut ha-Hanhagot* (Jerusalem, 1989), pp. 128–29 n. 96.

46. Rabbi H. Vital, *Eṣ Ha-Da'at,* Hukkat.

47. Cf. Tishby, *Wisdom of the Zohar,* 3: 1354, 1424. See also G. Nigal, "Mishnat ha-Ḥasidut ba-Sefer Ma'or Va- Shemesh," *Sinai* 75 (1974): 162.

48. According to Sheraga Weiss, *Ḥakhmey ha-Sefaradim be- Eretz Yisrael* (Jerusalem, 1976), pp. 127–28. See Meir Benayahu, *R. Ḥayyim Yoseph David Azulay* (Jerusalem, 1959), pp. 16–18. It should be noted that the circle of disciples of R. Shalom Shar'abi was named "Ahavat Shalom" (Love of Peace) for a reason. Even in the *Shetar Hitkasherut* of the disciples of R. David ibn Zimra, including ha-ARI, which was published by Barukh Dov Kahana, *Birkat ha-Areṣ* (Jerusalem, 1904), fol. 61b, it is mentioned among other things: "[A]ll of us should conduct ourselves with love and companionship." (See also Liebes, "Ha-Mashi'aḥ shel ha-Zohar," p. 158 n. 251.

49. See note in R. Kalonymus Shapira, *Sefer Ḥovat ha-Talmidim* (Warsaw, 1932), 10a: "Not only the youngest children are called *tinokot,* but also schoolboys are called *tinokot* in this context."

50. See Mikhal Oron, "Hakdamat Sefer ha-Peliah," *Kobez 'al Yad* 11, no. 2 (1989): 284.

51. R. Isaac Judah Yeḥiel Safrin, *Megillat Setarim* (Jerusalem, 1968), p. 4.

52. R. Isaac Judah Yeḥiel Safrin, *Heikhal ha-Berakhah* (Lemberg, 1869), pt. 3, fol. 291a.

53. See n. 5. See also introduction to *Pardes Rimmonim:* "When I reached the age of twenty, and blond hair sprouted [on my skin], my Maker woke me up as a man who wakes up from sleep."

54. Menaḥem 'Azariah of Fano, *Ma'amar ha-Nefesh* (Piotrkow, 1903), pt. 4, chap. 17.

55. *Or ha-Yashar, Seder ha-Limmud ve-Hanhagato,* par. 30.

56. See Gershom Scholem, "Iggeret Nathan ha-'Azzati 'al Sabbatai Ṣevi ve-Hamarato," *Kobez 'al Yad* 6, no. 2 (1966): 423.

57. Gershom Scholem, *Sabbatai Ṣevi: The Mystical Messiah* (Princeton, 1973), p. 203.

58. See Gershom Scholem, "Shetey ha-'eduyot ha-rishonot shel Ḥavurot ha-Ḥasidim ve-ha-Besht," *Tarbiṣ* 20 (1949): 230.

59. R. Ṣevi Hirsch, *Hakdamah ve-derekh le-Eṣ ha-Ḥayyim* (Lemberg, 1804), fol. 9a.

60. Introduction to R. Ḥayyim Vital, *Eṣ Ḥayyim* (Jerusalem, 1896).

61. See Sh. Ginzburg, *Iggerot ha-Ramḥal u-beney doro* (Tel Aviv, 1937), p. 19. See also p. 407.

62. See A. S. Halkin, "Ha-Ḥerem 'al Limud ha-Philosophia," *Perakim* 1 (1967–68): 35.

63. See Gershom Scholem, *Pirkey Yesod ba-Havanat ha-Kabbalah u-Semaleha* (Jerusalem, 1976), pp. 166–67. And see below.

64. In his introduction to *Eṣ Ḥayyim*.

65. And see Moshe Idel, "Toledot ha-Issur li-Lemod Kabbalah li-fney Gil Arba'im," in *AJS Review* 5 (1980): 1–20. See also David Tamar, *Meḥkarim be-Toledot ha-Yehudim be-Ereṣ Israel u-be-Arṣot ha-Mizraḥ* (Jerusalem, 1981), pp. 179–83.

66. MS Paris 790, fol. 87a.

67. *Or Ne'erav,* pt. 3, chap. 1.

68. See Tishby, "Ha-'Immut," pp. 74–77 and corresponding notes.

69. The date is not clear enough. Meir Balaban, *Le-Toledot ha-Tenu'ah ha-Frankit* (Tel Aviv, 1934), pt. 1, p. 126 n. 1, writes: 26 of the month of Sivan, 1755. The records in Halpern, ed., *Beit Yisrael Be-Polin,* p. 276, give: 26 of the month of Iyyar, 1755. Scholem, *Sabbatai Ṣevi,* p. 92, writes: the year 1757. Isaiah Tishby, "Ha-Ra'ayon Ha-Meshiḥi ve-ha-Megamot ha-Meshiḥiyot bi-Ṣemiḥat ha-Ḥasidut," *Zion* 32 (1967): 4, writes: Sivan, 1756.

70. See above, n. 23.

71. See Tishby, "Ha-Ra'ayon," p. 17 and n. 85.

72. See Scholem, *Sabbatai Ṣevi,* p. 114.

73. *Torah ve-Ḥayyim* (Salonika, 1846), fol. 19a.

74. Ibid., fol. 78a.

75. *Or Ne'erav,* pt. 3, chap. 1. With a change in order in *Ḥemdat Yamim,* fol. 51a.

76. Shem Tov ibn Gaon, *Badey Aaron u Migdal Ḥanan'el* (Jerusalem, 1978), p. 24.

77. See Tishby, "Ha-'Immut," p. 71.

78. Responsa of R. Moses Isserls, par. 7.

79. *Or Ṣaddikim,* chap. 22, par. 28–29. As to the festival of Sukkot, cf. the testimony of R. Meir ben Solomon Abi Sahula, introduction to his commentary on *Sefer Yeṣirah,* MS Rome/Angelica 45, fol. 2b: "For several years now I have consulted these things that during the Sukkot."

80. I, 5, fol. 14b. A similar idea appears in the works of Rabbi Naḥman of Bratslav. Best known is the saying that each grass has a melody of its own (*Likkutey Moharan,* Tinyyana, par. 63). On additional parallels see Idel, *Kabbalah,* p. 392.

81. The epistle of Rabbi Samson Bacchi. Cited in Gershom Scholem, "Shetar ha-hitkasherut shel talmidey ha-ARI," *Zion* 5 (1940): 150.

82. *Ḥemdat Yamim,* fol. 51a (Segullah 9).

83. Naftali Bakharakh, *'Emek ha-Melekh* (Amsterdam, 1648), fol. 10c. See also R. S. Dreznitz, *Shivḥey ha-ARI* (Przemysl, 1869), fol. 2a.

84. *Torah Or,* additions to the Book of Esther (Brooklyn, 1955), fol. 117d.

85. *Orot ha-Kodesh,* pt. 1, pp. 133–34; *Orot,* (Jerusalem, 1985), pp. 9–13.

Chapter 4. Early Preparations

1. See in particular Fischel Shneurson's wonderful book, *Ḥayyim Gravitzer,* 2d ed. (Tel Aviv, 1956).

2. See M. Idel, "ha-Hitbodedut ke-Rikkuz ba-Kabbalah ha-Ecstatit ve-Gilguleha," *Da'at* 14 (1985): 37–38.

3. Fol. 66a.

4. *Kav ha-Yashar,* I, 6.

5. See *Zohar* III, fol. 56b.

6. *Zohar Ḥadash,* Midrash ha-Ne'elam, fol. 8d.

7. *Likkutey 'Eṣot,* s.v. "hitbodedut," par. 1. And see for instance the personal description by Aaron ben Gershon Abualrabi: "For so did Moses when he brought up Joseph's Coffin, for he said: Go up, Ox. And I contemplated this in solitude and saw in it whatever I saw and it seems that what Moses did was by the power of the holy names when he brought up Joseph's coffin as is implicit in *Sefer ha-'Iggulim* by Rabbi Menaḥem Recanati and in the commentary on *Sefer Yeṣirah* by R. Joseph Sar Shalom of blessed memory. And whoever did not study either the wisdom or the knowledge of saintly men will not be able to apprehend this." Commentaries on the Torah and on Rashi, Constantinople [1522? According to Abraham Ya'ari, *Ha-Defus ha-'Ivri be-Kushta* (Jerusalem, 1967), p. 86 n. 101, it was published between 1520 and 1525], *Ki Tisa,* fol. 95c.

8. H. J. D. Azulay, *'Avodat ha-Kodesh,* Zipporen Shamir, IV, 51.

9. *Sefer Ḥaredim,* fol. 68a, as trans. in R. J. Zwi Werblowsky, *Joseph Karo: Lawyer and Mystic* (Oxford, 1962), p. 60.

10. Elijah de Vidas, *Reshit Ḥokhmah,* III, 3, fol. 133b.

11. See Tishby, *Ha-Ra'ayon,* p. 7.

12. *RaMBaN,* ed. Chavel, pp. 136–37.

13. Fol. 66a-b. Trans. based on Werblowsky, *Joseph Karo,* pp. 63–64. See also Scholem, *Devarim be-Go,* pp. 329–30.

14. Fol. 80b. Trans. in Werblowsky, *Joseph Karo,* pp. 64-65. Also cited in Elijah ha-Kohen, *Shevet Musar* (Jerusalem, 1963), chap. 19, p. 145; S. A. Horodezky, *Ha-Mystorin be-Yisrael* (Tel Aviv, 1961), 3:241; Benayahu, *Sefer Toledot,* p. 360 n. 5.

15. On this motif see M. Ḥalamish, "Be-Ṣeti Likratekha—Likrati Meṣatikha," *Bikkoret u-Parshanut* 13–14 (1979): 27–34.

16. Israel Ba'al Shem Tov, *Ṣava'at ha-RiBaSH* (Jerusalem, 1948), p. 3. Cf. *Or Torah,* fol. 105a; *Or ha-Emet* (Zhitomir, 1901), p. 162; *Likkutim Yekarim* (Lemberg, 1872), fol. 20a, 29b. See Rivka Schatz-Uffenheimer's discussion in *Hasidism as Mysticism* (Princeton, 1993), pp. 82ff. See also Baḥya ibn Pakuda, *Ḥovot ha-Levavot,* VIII, 4 and X, 6; Isaac of Acre, *Meirat 'Eynaim* (Jerusalem, 1984), p. 218.

17. Shem Tov ibn Gaon, *Badey Aaron* (Jerusalem, 1978), p. 88.

18. *Peri Eṣ,* Kedoshim. Cf. Menaḥem Mendel of Vitebsk, *Peri ha-Areṣ,* Vayeshev.

19. R. Shneur Zalman of Lyady, *Tanya, Sefer shel Benonim* (Brooklyn, N.Y., 1954), chap. 49, pp. 137, 139.

20. I have discussed this in a lecture subsequently published in Mosheh Ḥalamish and Asa Kasher, eds., *Dat ve-Safa* (Tel Aviv, 1982), pp. 79-89.

21. R. Ḥayyim Vital, *Sha'ar Ru'aḥ ha-Kodesh* (Jerusalem, 1912), fols. 11b–12a.

22. Vital, *Eṣ Ḥayyim,* introduction, fol. 4c.

23. See Ephraim Gottlieb, *Meḥkarim be-Sifrut ha-Kabbalah* (Tel Aviv, 1976), pp. 242–43.

24. *Orot ha-Kodesh* (Jerusalem, 1964), pt. 3, p. 270.

25. *Ha-Torah ve-ha-Ḥayyim be'Arṣot ha-Ma'arav bi-yemey ha-Beinayim* (Warsaw, 1897), pt. 1, p. 80.

26. Ben-Zion Dinur, *Toledot Yisrael—Yisrael ba-Golah* 2, no. 3 (1968): 338. See also Gershom Scholem, *Reishit ha-Kabbalah* (Jerusalem and Tel Aviv, 1948), pp. 70–87.

27. See G. Scholem, "Le-Ḥeqer Kabbalat R. Isaac ben Jacob ha-Cohen," p. 194.

28. Elijah de Vidas, *Reshit Ḥokhmah,* IV, 6, fol. 141a–b.

29. Ibid., II, 3, fol. 59a.

30. Something of the same sort was said by the sages about the world to come. See *Berakhot* 17a.

31. Vidas, *Reshit Ḥokhmah,* III, 4, fol. 114d.

32. *Zohar* I, fol. 4a. Though there is also a seven-day fast (*Sefer ha-Peliah* [Przemysl, 1884], pt. 2, fol. 11c) and a seventy-day fast (See G. Scholem, "Mekorotav shel Ma'aseh R. Gadiel ha-Tinok be-Sifrut ha-Kabbalah," in *Le-'Agnon Shay* (Jerusalem, 1959), p. 302.

33. See Tishby, *Wisdom of the Zohar,* 3:993 and corresponding notes.

34. See Naftali Wieder, "Hashpa'ot Islamiyot 'al ha-Pulḥan ha-Yehudi," *Melilah* 2 (1946): 68–69.

35. As quoted at length in Vidas, *Reshit Ḥokhmah,* IV, 6, fols. 140d–141a.

36. See Scholem, *Sabbatai Ṣevi,* p. 185.

37. See *Commentary on Sefer Yeṣirah* by Rabbi Joseph ben Shalom Ashkenazi (in the printed versions, it is mistakenly attributed to RABaD), fol. 52c. See also introduction to Vidas, *Reshit Ḥokhmah,* fol. 4b.

38. See Scholem, *Reishit ha-Kabbalah,* p. 57. Idem, *Reishit ha-Kabbalah ve-Sefer ha-Bahir* (Jerusalem, 1962), p. 247. See also Ben-Zion Dinur. *Toledot Yisrael—Yisrael ba-Golah* 2, no. 3 (1968): 161.

39. See for instance Mikhal Oron, introduction to *Sefer ha-Peliah,* in *Kobez 'al Yad* 11, no. 2 (1989): 278–84; Scholem, *Sabbatai Ṣevi,* p. 185.

40. See Oron, introduction, p. 284. See also *Sefer ha-Kanah* (Cracow, 1894), fol. 58b. See also the wording as cited in Mikhal Oron, "Ha-Peliah ve-ha-Kanah . . ." (doctoral diss., Hebrew University, Jerusalem, 1980), p. 61. Note also the phrase "neṣe ha-sadeh" [Let us go forth unto the field] in *Sefer ha-Peliah* (Korets, 1784), fol. 59b.

41. As transmitted "by my teacher, God bless him." See *Perush Talmidey Rabbenu Yonah,* Berakhot, chap. 5.

42. Vidas, *Reshit Ḥokhmah,* II, 4, fol. 63a.

43. Also cited by R. Ḥayyim Joseph David Azulay, *Petaḥ 'Eynaim* on *Avot* VI, 4.

44. See Vidas, *Reshit Ḥokhmah,* II, 4, fol. 63a.

45. Ibid., fol. 61a.

46. Cited in ibid., IV, 6, fol. 141a.

47. *Ḥemdat Yamim, Mo'adim, Hag ha-Shavu'ot,* chap. 1, *Segulot le-Hasagat ha-Ḥokhmah,* segulah 1.

48. *Avot* VI, 5. See also *Avot* VI,1.

49. According to Scharfstein, *Ha-Ḥavayah,* pp. 18–19.

50. Ibid., p. 175.

51. Gershom Scholem, "Te'udah Ḥadashah le-Toledot Reishit ha-Kabbalah," *Sefer Bialik,* 1934, 159.

52. His commentary on Lev. 19:19 (translated in *RaMBaN,* ed. Chavel, p. 296 as "colleagues").

53. See also Scholem, *Reishit,* p. 239.

54. *Livnat ha-Sappir* (Jerusalem, 1913), fol. 34d.

55. In contrast to Tishby's explanation (*Wisdom of the Zohar,* 3:1170 n. 69) that "the companions who dwell in the South" is a veiled reference to a Spanish circle of kabbalists. In my opinion, this is a generic term that transcends place, thus referring to the Kabbalists in general.

56. *Zohar* II, fol. 190b, in *Zohar,* trans. Sperling, Simon, and Levertoff (London, 1933), 4:142.

57. *Zohar* III, fol. 163a.

58. Lunz, *Yerushalayim,* 1:145.

59. See, e.g., Benayahu, *Sefer Toledot ha-ARI,* p. 176 n. 2.

60. And see Y. Liebes's clarification in *Ha-Ra'ayon ha-Meshiḥi Be-Yisrael* (Jerusalem, 1982), pp. 93–94.

61. "Or Zaru'a," MS London 771, fol. 22a.

62. Rabbi Ḥayyim Vital, *Sefer ha-Ḥezyonot,* ed. A. Z. Aescoly (Jerusalem, 1954), p. 153. Also consult Meir Benayahu, "Hanhagot Mekublei Ṣefat be-Miron," *Ṣefunot* 6 (1962): 17–18.

63. *Likkutey Amarim* (Lemberg, 1911), pt. 2, letter no. 5, fol. 5a–b.

64. See R. Ḥayyim Vital, *Sha'ar ha-Miṣvot,* beginning of *Ki Teṣe; Peri 'Eṣ Ḥayyim,* fol. 78a.

65. *Peri 'Eṣ Ḥayyim,* fol. 78a; *Orḥot Ṣaddikim* in *Likkutey Shas* (Livorno, 1790), fol. 62a.

66. *Ma'avar Yabbok,* Imrey Noam, chap. 18.

67. See Scholem, *Sabbatai Ṣevi,* p. 123.

68. See Benayahu, *Sefer Toledot ha-ARI,* p. 257. See also p. 163 and corresponding notes.

69. Todros Abulafia, *Sha'ar ha-Razim,* ed. Mikhal Oron (Jerusalem, 1989), p. 44.

70. *Ḥemdat Yamim,* Ḥag ha-Shavu'ot, chap. 1, segulah 10. The source is *Seder ha-Yom,* fol. 13c (in the end).

71. See *Orḥot Ṣaddikim.* Also Vital, *Sefer ha-Gilgulim,* Likkutim, p. 128. It is said that he used to pick up the *Zohar* and "consult it with great care." See Benayahu, *Sefer Toledot ha-ARI,* p. 154. See also Bakharakh, *'Emek ha-Melekh,* Third Introduction.

72. Introduction to the commentary of R. Elijah, the Gaon of Vilna, on *Sifra De-Ṣeni'uta.*

73. Such as in *Sefer Seder ha-Yom; Ḥemdat Yamim,* fol. 51a; and *Migdal 'Oz* by R. Moses Ḥayyim Luzzatto.

74. *Zohar* II, fol. 97b, as translated in Tishby, *Wisdom of the Zohar,* 1:196–97.

75. R. Joseph Gikatilla, *Sod ha-Ḥashmal,* in *Arzey Levanon* (Venice, 1601).

76. See Scholem, *Kitvey Yad,* pp. 227–29.

Chapter 5. Mystical Inquiry and its Dangers

1. See the beginning of chapter 8, below.

2. Gershom Scholem, Responsa attributed to Gikatilla, section 9, in *Emet le-Ya'akov: Jacob Freimann Jubilee Volume* (Berlin, 1937).

3. Rabbi Moses de Leon, *Shushan 'Edut.* Cited in Alexander Altmann, "Sefer Or Zaru'a Le-R. Moshe de-Leon," *Kobez 'al Yad* 9 (1980): 272.

4. As translated in Peter Schäfer, *The Hidden and Manifest God: Some Major Themes in Early Jewish Mysticism,* trans. A. Pomerance (Albany, N.Y., 1992), p. 14 n. 11

5. *Ḥet'o shel Elisha* (Jerusalem, 1986).

6. *Avot de Rabbi Nathan,* ed. Solomon Schechter (New York, 1997) version B, chap. 33, p. 72 (= J. Saldarini, *The Fathers According to Rabbi Nathan, High Wycombe* [Ann Arbor, Mich. c. 1972], p. 195).

7. Rachel Elior, ed., *Heikhalot Zutarti* (Jerusalem 1982), p. 22. Trans. into English in Schaefer, *Hidden and Manifest God,* p. 70.

8. Recanati, *Genesis,* fol. 16c. Also Isaac of Acre, *Meirat 'Eynaim,* p. 32.

9. Vital, *Sha'ar ha-Miṣvot,* 'Ekev.

10. *Ḥagigah* 13a, trans. I. Epstein (London, 1938), p. 77.

11. In Eliezer Ashkenazi, *Ta'am Zekenim* (Frankfurt am Main, 1855), pp. 54–58.

12. See Scholem, *Temunah,* pp. 203–4.

13. Ibid., p. 204.

14. *Pirkey Heikhalot Rabbati,* ed. S. A. Wertheimer (Jerusalem, 1950), pp. 99–100.

15. Beginning of *Sod Ha-Ḥashmal* by R. J. Gikatilla, in *Erez ba-Levanon* (Vilna, 1899), fol. 13a–c.

16. *Sefer ha-Temunah* (Lemberg, 1892), fol. 26b.

17. *Sefer ha-Ḥezyonot* (Jerusalem, 1954), p. 237. Moreover, the ARI's son died in his youth because he had revealed a certain secret. See Benayahu, *Sefer Toledot ha-ARI,* p. 198. See also S. Ginzberg, *Iggerot Ramḥal [R. Moses Ḥayyim Luzzatto]* (1937), 1:30.

18. See his paper, "Ereṣ Yisrael ve-ha-Kabbalah ba-Me'a ha-Shlosh-Esre," *Shalem* 3 (1981): 122.

19. *Oṣar ha-Geonim,* Ḥagigah, the responsa section, pp. 14–15.

Chapter 6. Techniques of Exploring Mysteries

1. *Oṣar ha-Geonim,* Ḥagigah, the responsa section, p. 14 (the translation of the excerpt is based on Scholem, *Major Trends,* p. 49). Also cited in *Ma'avar Yabbok, Imrey Noam,* chap. 20. On the rejection of special means to gain attainment in Christian

mysticism, according to St. John of the Cross, see Zwi Werblowsky, "'Al ha-Deḥiyya ha-Mystit shel He'arot ve-Gilluyei Razim," *'Iyyun* 14–15 (1964): 205–12.

2. See Scholem, *Kitvey Yad,* p. 90.

3. Mentioned in n. 1, above.

4. *Or Ne'erav,* pt. 3, chap. 2.

5. *Oṣar ha-Geonim,* Ḥagigah, the commentaries section, p. 61.

6. *Ketav Tamim,* in *Oṣar Neḥmad* (Wien, 1860), 3:84. Also cited in A. Heschel, "'Al Ru'aḥ ha-Kodesh bi-Yemei ha-Beinaim," in Lieberman, ed., *Alexander Marx Jubilee Volume,* p. 187.

7. *Mesillat Yesharim,* chap. 26.

8. See Ithamar Gruenwald, "Keta'im Ḥadashim mi-Sifrut ha-Heikhalot," *Tarbiṣ* 38 (1969): 372.

9. 1 Kings 19:13, 19:19; 2 Kings 2:8, 2:13, 2:14.

10. See Gruenwald, "Keta'im Ḥadashim mi-Sifrut ha-Heikhalot," from MS Oxford.

11. See Scholem, *Temunah,* p. 210. See also Al-Butini's book, cited by Scholem, *Kitvey Yad,* p. 227.

12. See also *Avot* I, 11.

13. See 2 Kings 3:11.

14. See E. E. Urbach, "Ha Masorot 'al Torat ha-Sod bi-Tekuphat ha-Tannaim," in *Meḥkarim ba-Kabbalah u-be-Toledot ha-Datot,* presented to Gershom Scholem (Jerusalem, 1968), p. 17 n. 73.

15. The story was cited in Gottlieb, *Meḥkarim,* pp. 573–74.

16. See Benayahu, *Sefer Toledot ha-ARI,* p. 257.

17. As translated by R. Manheim in Gershom Scholem, *On the Kabbalah and Its Symbolism* (New York, 1965), p. 136. See also ibid., pp. 136–37 on the theurgic ritual.

18. Commentary on Lev. 16: 30, in *RaMBaN,* ed. Chavel, 2:505.

19. Ezek. 1:6; Dan. 8:2, 10:4–5.

20. 1 Apocalypse of Baruch I [= Barukh the Syrian] 21:1–3. See also 2 Apocalypse of Baruch [= Barukh the Greek] 2:1. See also Urbach, "Ha Masorot"; I. Gruenwald, *Ha-Aspaklaria ve-ha-Technika shel he-Ḥazon ha-Nevu'i, Beit Mikra* (Jerusalem, 1960), pp. 95–97.

21. The text was published in *Temirin* 1 (1972): 112, 114.

22. On the metamorphoses of this technique and its significance for the Kabbalists see Idel, "Le-Gilguleha shel Technika Kedumah," *Sinai* 86 (1980): 1–7.

23. The words of Rabbi Joseph Ibn Tabul. See Gershom Scholem, "Shetar Hitkasherut shel Talmidey ha-ARI," *Zion* 5 (1900): 152.

24. See Abraham Ya'ari, *Iggerot Ereṣ Yisrael* (Tel Aviv, 1943), p. 218.

25. Responsa *Yabi'a Omer,* vol. 4, *Yore De'a,* par. 35. According to Responsa Sedeh ha-Areṣ, vol. 3, *Eben ha-'Ezer,* par. 11, fol. 57c.

26. In the introduction to Vidas, *Reshit Ḥokhmah.*

27. See Scholem, *Sabbatai Ṣevi,* p. 123.

28. *Or Ne'erav,* pt. 5, chap. 2 (as translated in Werblowsky, *Joseph Karo,* p. 54).

29. Sefer Gerushin, par. 4 (as translated in Werblowsky, *Joseph Karo,* p. 54).

30. Ibid., end of par. 17 (as translated in Werblowsky, *Joseph Karo,* p. 53) and beginning of par. 18.

31. Ibid., par. 10.

32. Ibid., end of par. 33.

33. "If one rises early and a scriptural verse comes to his mouth, this is a kind of minor prophecy" (*Berakhot* 55b).

34. See also Gershom Scholem, "Sefer Gerushin Mahu?" *Kiryat Sefer* 1 (1924): 164.

35. See Scholem, *Reshit ha-Kabbalah,* pp. 92–93.

36. Concerning these aspects see Idel, *Mystical Experience in Abraham Abulafia* (New York, 1988).

37. From the Besht's letter to his brother-in-law, in B. Minz, *Shivḥey ha-Ba'al-Shem-Tov* (Tel Aviv, 1961), p. 167. The translation is that of Idel, *Kabbalah,* p. 94.

Chapter 7. Evolution of the Kabbalah

1. *Zohar* II, fol. 23a; trans. Tishby, 1:322.

2. R. Yehudah ben Barzilai ha-Barṣeloni, *Perush Sefer Yeṣirah* (Berlin, 1885), p. 65.

3. Ibid., p. 77.

4. Ibid., p. 189.

5. See Moses de Leon, *Shekel ha-Kodesh,* p. 22.

6. A poem by Gikatilla. See Gruenwald, "Shnei Shirim shel ha-Mekubal Yosef Gikatilla," *Tarbiṣ* 36 (1967): 87. But see also A. Kuppfer's note in the latter, pp. 205–6.

7. Joseph Gikatilla, *Sha'arey Orah* (Warsaw, 1883), fol. 7a.

8. Introduction to Vidas, *Reshit Ḥokhmah,* fol. 5b.

9. See Scholem, *Mada'ey ha-Yahadut,* p. 289.

10. See Scholem, "Le-Ḥeqer Kabbalat Rabbi Yitṣḥak ben Ya'acov ha-Cohen," p. 51. Saul Lieberman, *Sheki'in* (Jerusalem, 1970), p. 13, writes that "the Rishonim call the books of the Kabbalah *Yerushalmi.*"

11. See Scholem, "Sheney Kuntresim Le-Rabbi Moshe de Leon," *Kobez 'al Yad* 8, no. 18 (1976): 370.

12. See Gershom Scholem, *Ha-Kabbalah be-Gerona* (Jerusalem, 1964), p. 127.

13. See Tishby, *Wisdom of the Zohar,* 1:230–31, 3:1087.

14. *Adir ba-Marom,* fol. 15a.

15. Ibid., fol. 13a.

16. Several times in *Sefer Ṣioni.* And see Meir ibn Gabbay, *'Avodat ha-Kodesh,* II, 1; R. David ben Zimra (RaDBaZ), *Meṣudat David* (Zolkiew, 1862), fol. 35d; Rabbi Abraham ibn Migash, *Kevod Elohim* (1585; photoprint, Jerusalem 1977), chap. 15.

17. See Tishby's paper in Kiryat Sefer 19 (1942): 56.

18. Menaḥem Mendel, *Peri ha-Areṣ,* Vayyiggash.

19. Moses de Leon, *Ha-Nefesh ha-Ḥakhamah,* par. 13, fol. 31b.

20. See Tishby, "Ha-'Immut," pp. 24, 43.

21. Moses de Leon, *Shekel ha-Kodesh,* p. 5; Tanya, *Iggeret ha-Kodesh,* par. 23, p. 271.

22. Moses de Leon, *Shekel ha-Kodesh,* p. 108; idem, *Ha-Nefesh ha-Ḥakhamah,* fol. 14c.

23. See Gottlieb, *Meḥkarim,* e.g. pp. 384, 391.

24. R. Moses Isserles, *Torat ha-'Olah,* part 2, chap. 1.

25. *Derekh Emunah,* fol. 16a. Cf. R. Shneur Zalman of Lyady, *Likkutey Torah* (Brooklyn, 1965), Pekudey, p. 4b.

26. Vidas, *Reshit Ḥokhmah,* fol. 5b.

27. R. Moses Botarel, commentary on *Sefer Yeṣirah,* I, 2.

28. Isserles, *Torat ha-'Olah,* pt. 3, chap. 4.

29. *Ṣava'at R. Sheftel Horowitz* (d. 1660), published in Simḥah Asaf, *Mekorot le-Toledot ha-Ḥinukh be-Yisrael* (Tel Aviv, 1954), pt. 1, p. 69.

30. Responsa *Bayyit Ḥadash,* par. 5

31. Horowitz, *Sheney Luḥot ha-Berit,* Shevu'ot, 182b.

32. See Scholem, "R. Moshe mi-Burgos," *Tarbiṣ* 3 (1932): 266–67.

33. It originates in Joel 3:5. But see also Maimonides, *Guide of the Perplexed,* pt. 1, chap. 34. Rabbi Abraham, son of Maimonides, also used this phrase. See Naftali Wieder, "Haspa'ot Islamiyot 'al ha-Pulḥan ha-Yehudi," *Melilah* 2 (1946): 72 n. 168. See also Y. Liebes, "Ha-Mashi'aḥ shel ha-Zohar," *Ha-Ra'ayon ha-Meshiḥi be-Yisrael* (1982): 210 n. 16.

34. See Tishby, *Wisdom of the Zohar,* 3:1086–89.

35. Fols. 65b–66a.

36. S. Mussaieff, ed., *Merkavah Shelemah,* fol. 34b. See also the excerpt from the responsum of R. Hai Gaon, quoted by Moshe Idel, *Ha-Ḥavayah ha-Mystit ezel Abraham Abulafia* (Jerusalem, 1989), p. 16 (= *Mystical Experience in Abraham Abulafia,* p. 15).

37. *Ra'aya Mehemna,* in *Zohar* III, fol. 124b.

38. See citation from *Or Ha-Ḥamah* in Scholem, *Major Trends,* p. 408 n. 13.

39. R. Moses Cordovero, *Hanhagot,* section 33, in Schechter, *Studies in Judaism,* 2d ser. (Philadelphia, 1928), p. 294. Cf below, n. 41.

40. See Ronit Meroz, "Ḥavurat R. Moshe ben Makhir ve-Takanoteha," *Pe'amim* 31 (1987): 47, esp. n. 27.

41. R. Meir Poppers, *Or ha-Yashar, "Seder ha-Limmud ve- Hanhagato,"* sec. 24. Cf. above, n. 39.

42. Ibid., secs. 28–29.

43. See Tishby, *Wisdom of the Zohar,* 1:29. It should be added that the phrase *ha-lashon mesugalah la-neshama* (the language is precious for the soul) became a fixed idiom for many people who have read the *Zohar* without understanding its exact meaning. See also A. Stahl, "Keriah Pulḥanit shel Sefer ha-Zohar," *Pe'amim* 5 (1980): 77–86.

44. Korets, 1804.

45. *Moreh ba-Etzb'a,* par. 2, subpar. 44.

46. *Midrash Talpiyyot,* 'anaf din.

47. See, e.g., *Hanhagot Adam* by Rabbi Elimelekh of Lyzhansk, par. 5

48. *Simḥat Yisrael* (Pietrekov, 1910), fol. 62b. The citation is according to Idel, *Kabbalah,* p. 301.

49. See Tishby, *Wisdom of the Zohar,* 1:38.

50. *Shi'ur Komah,* published in Mussaieff, ed., *Merkavah Shelemah,* fol. 38b; as translated in David Meltzer, ed., *The Secret Garden* (New York, 1976), p. 32.

51. See Joseph Dan, "Sefer ha-Navon Le-Eḥad me-Ḥasidei Ashkenaz," *Kobez 'al Yad* 16, no. 1 (1966): 223.

52. *Sefer ha-Temunah,* fol. 46b. See also ibid., fol. 45a: "And those are hinted in a marvelous secret, and he who knows it and mentions it in fear and awe."

53. See Joseph Dan, *Torat ha-Sod shel Ḥasidut Ashkenaz* (Jerusalem, 1968), p. 35.

54. R. Shalom Dober Schneersohn, *Eṣ ha-Ḥayyim* (Brooklyn, 1973), p. 42.

55. *Orot ha-Kodesh,* pt. 1, p. 141.

56. *Pardes Rimmonin,* I, 9.

57. Horowitz, *Sheney Luḥot ha-Berit,* "Shevu'ot," 182b.

58. *Pele Yo'eṣ,* s.v. "Limmud."

59. Tishby, *Wisdom of the Zohar,* 3:953–54.

60. Though there are still some sages who euphemistically express wonder at the great masters of Halakha who deal with the Kabbalah. For instance, see the responsa of the RIBaSh, par. 157, on R. Pereṣ's surprise at Naḥmanides, who "stuck" himelf in this wisdom.

61. See for instance I. Tishby, "Ha-Pulmus 'al hadpasat Sefer ha-Zohar," *Perakim* 1 (1967–68): 131–82.

62. His ruling was published by R. Simḥah Asaf in *Sinai* 5 (1939–40): 360–68.

63. Vol. 1 (Mantua, 1558).

64. *Ari Nohem* (Jerusalem, 1971), par. 55. See his beautiful language at the end of p. 77. This prohibition was also discussed by R. Y. Finzi, who is mentioned above. R. Moses Botarel, in his commentary on *Sefer Yeṣirah* I, 2, writes: "I highly praise the kabbalist sages who did not wish to study this magnificent science in public, but rather strove to conceal it."

65. See Tishby, *Wisdom of the Zohar,* 1:35. See also Scholem, *Reishit Ha-Kabbalah ve-Sefer ha-Bahir,* p. 4.

66. See Tishby, "Ha-Pulmus," pp. 179–82

67. Bakharakh, *'Emek ha-Melekh,* Second Introduction, fol. 7a ff.

68. Responsa of the RiBaSh, par. 157. Cited also in Ibn Gabbay, *'Avodat ha-Kodesh,* pt. 2, chap. 13. See Adolff Jellinek, *Ginzey Ḥokhmat ha-Kabbalah* (Leipzig, 1853), p. 19; Scholem, *Reshit ha-Kabbalah,* pp. 173–75; See, e.g., *Ketem Paz,* vol. 1, fol. 23c: "This is a sufficient response to those who take issue with us, the fools amongst our coreligionists, who in their confusion say that the masters of the Kabbalah multiply God by establishing ten [Sefirot]. Alas to their souls for they were badly treated. For this plurality is in honor of the Holy One, blessed be He, not in His essence, heavens forbid, only in the created entities, which His Wisdom required that through them everything will come into being."

69. According to Idel, "Differing Conceptions of Kabbalah in the Early Seventeenth Century," in *Jewish Thought in the Seventeenth Century*, ed. I. Twersky and B. Septimus (Cambridge, Mass., 1986), p. 163.

70. R. Elijah del Medigo, *Beḥinat ha-Dat* (Vienna, 1833), p. 69.

71. On all of this see Tishby, *Wisdom of the Zohar,* 1:30–96.

72. E.g., in his letter to S. D. Luzzatto, S. Y. Rappoport writes: "To tell the truth, I am so much confused about the books of Kabbalah and their writers that I am tired of reflecting on them. Their beginning is *tohu va-vohu* and darkness on the face of the deep [cf. Gen. 1:2], which is not further redeemed by the utterance 'Let there be light . . .' There is no gratification in reading and investigating them." See S. A. Graber, *Iggerot Shyr el Shadal* (Przemysl, 1885–86), 3:211.

73. *Torat ha-'Olah,* pt. 3, chap. 4. In the following generation by MaHaRSHA, *Ḥiddushey Aggadot,* Ḥagigah 13a–b and Kiddushin 71a. Later on, in the beginning of the eighteenth century, by Rabbi Moshe Ḥaggiz. Also the "Nod'a bi-Yehudah," *Yore De'ah,* par. 74. See also Tishby, *Wisdom of the Zohar,* 1:38; Scholem, *Sabbatai Ṣevi,* p. 78; S. A. Horodezky, *Shelosh Me'ot Shanah shel Yahadut Polin* (Tel Aviv, 1946), pp. 24–29.

74. Responsa *Ḥayyim Sha'al,* part 2, par. 10.

75. Rabbi Joseph Ergas, Responsa *Divrey Yoseph* (Livorno, 1742), fol. 45c–d. See also the words of a Moroccan Kabbalist, Rabbi Repha'el Ya'akov ben Simḥon, in his introduction to *Sover ha-Razim,* published at the end of *Bat Rabbim.*

76. *Darkhey No'am* (Königsberg, 1764), 97a.

77. Responsa *Bayyit Ḥadash,* par. 4.

Chapter 8. The Sources of the Revelations

1. See Tishby, *Wisdom of the Zohar,* 2:845–46. The Tosafists (*'Avodah Zarah* 18a) make the following observation on the question "What do you see?" asked of Rabbi Ḥanina ben Teradyon, one of the Ten Martyrs: "It seemed to them that he must have seen something, whether angels or something else."

2. Commentary on *Sefer Yeṣirah* by Rabbi Joseph ben Shalom Ashkenazi (Jerusalem, 1965), fol. 27a. Erroneously attributed to R. Abraham b. David of Posquières.

3. Cf. Menaḥem Ṣioni, *Perush 'al ha-Torah* (Lemberg, 1872), fol. 17d.

4. Maimonides, too, in *Guide of the Perplexed,* I, 4, refers to the eye as an instrument of mental vision.

5. See Exod. 23:33; Benayahu, *Sefer Toledot ha-ARI,* pp. 231–32.

6. The motif of tremor or trembling appears also in later sources and it expresses the sublimity that a mortal human being must confront. See also above, pp. 51–52. Cf. what is told about the Besht, who in his prayer used to reach the state of trembling; sometimes "he was trembling for a long time and his followers had to wait till he rested from his worship." See *Shivḥey ha-Ba'al Shem Tov,* ed. B. Minz (Tel Aviv, 1961), p. 61.

7. *Heikhalot Rabbati,* ed. Wertheimer, p. 77.

8. See, e.g., R. Yishmael's prayer in A. Jellinek, *Bet ha-Midrasch* (Leipzig, 1855), 5:170–71.

9. R. Isaac of Acre, *Meirat 'Eynaim (Va-Yishlaḥ)*, p. 56. See Scholem, "Le-Ḥeqer Kabbalat Rabbi Yitsḥak ben Ya'akov ha-Cohen," p. 318. Consult Hava Lazarus-Yafeh, *"Ha- Podeh min ha-Te'iyah ve-ha-Ta'ut" by Al-Ghazālī* (Tel Aviv, 1965), pp. 61–64.

10. Benayahu, *Sefer Toledot ha-ARI,* p. 155. The English translation is based on Idel, *Kabbalah,* p. 92.

11. Benayahu, *Sefer Toledat ha-ARI,* p. 218.

12. See G. Scholem, "'Ikvotav shel ibn Gabirol be-Sifrut ha-Kabbalah," in *Me'assef Sofrey Erez Yisrael,* ed. A. Kabak and A. Steinman (Tel Aviv, 1940), p. 176.

13. Naḥmanides, end of the introduction to his commentary on the Torah, as translated in *RaMBaN,* ed. Chavel, p. 15.

14. Naḥmanides, "Derashah 'al Kohelet," in part 1 of *Kitvey ha-Ramban*, ed. Chavel, p. 190.

15. Shem Tov ibn Gaon, *Badey Aaron,* p. 27.

16. See G. Scholem, "Sidrei de-Shimusha Rabbah," *Tarbiṣ* 16 (1945): 205.

17. See Scholem, *Reshit ha-Kabbalah,* pp. 71–72; A. Y. Heschel, "'Al Ru'aḥ ha-Kodesh bi-Ymey ha-Beinaim," in Lieberman, ed., *Alexander Marx Jubilee Volume,* pp. 192–95.

18. *Pardes Rimmonim,* XXVIII, 5.

19. See G. Scholem's article in *Kiryat Sefer* 11 (1934–35): 188–89.

20. See A. Jellinek, *Bet ha-Midrasch,* pt. 3, p. xlii.

21. In the Talmud, *Berakhot* 57b, a dream is considered one sixtieth of prophecy. On the difference between a dream and a prophecy, see *Zohar* I, fol. 183a.

22. *She'elot u-Teshuvot min ha-Shamayim,* ed. Rabbi Reuben Margaliot (Jerusalem, 1957).

23. See, e.g., *Sefer Ḥasidim,* pp. 116–17, par. 382. See Joseph Dan, "Le-Torat ha-Ḥalom shel Ḥasidei Ashkenaz," *Sinai* 68 (1971): 290–2.

24. See Tishby, *Perush ha-Aggadot le-Rabbi 'Azriel* (Jerusalem, 1945), p. 76.

25. See Moshe Idel, "'Iyyunim be-Shitato shel ba'al Sefer ha-Meshiv," *Ṣefunot* 17 (1983): 210. This paper presents a lengthy and important discussion of this phenomenon. On its emergence in the thirteenth century see Scholem, *Mada'ey ha-Yahadut,* p. 192 in par. 5, and pp. 247, 263. See also idem, comments in *Kiryat Sefer* 11 (1934–35).

26. As stated by Gershom Scholem, "Ha-Mekubal Rabbi Abraham ben Eli'ezer Ha-Levi," *Kiryat Sefer* 2 (1925–26): 123. The book was originally published in Mohilev, 1912. See also its recent edition, ed. Rachel Elior (Jerusalem, 1981). See also M. Ḥalamish, *Ohel Ḥayyim* (Jerusalem, 1988), pp. 45–47.

27. Scholem, *Sabbatai Ṣevi,* p. 209.

28. See Werblowsky, *Joseph Karo*. On the sources of the revelations see particularly his chap. 4.

29. According to the testimony of his disciple, Rabbi Yekuthiel Gordon of Vilna, he was twenty years old when "A certain *maggid,* a great and awesome angel, was revealed to him, and the man Moses [Luzzatto] was very meek and hid his face and

did not tell about this revelation even to his father and mother, only to some friends who hearken to his voice and attend his eminent yeshivah." See Simeon Ginzburg, *Iggerot ha-Ramḥal u-beney Doro* (Tel Aviv, 1937), p. 407.

30. See Werblowsky, *Joseph Karo*, app. F. See also n. 25.

31. See Karo, "musar she-hayah meyasser oto ke-av le-ben," introduction to *Maggid Meisharim,* fol. 3c.

32. Ibid.

33. Horowitz, *Sheney Luḥot ha-Berit,* Shevu'ot, fol. 180a.

34. R. Nathan Net'a Hannover, *Yeven Meṣulah* (Tel Aviv, 1966), p. 46.

35. See Ḥayyim Hillel Ben-Sason, "Ishiyyuto shel Ha-GRA ve-hashpa'ato ha-historit," *Zion* 31 (1966): 45.

36. See end of chapter 7.

37. *Or Ne'erav,* pt. 5, as trans. in Werblowsky, *Joseph Karo,* p. 54.

38. *Sefer Gerushin,* end of par. 5, as trans. in Werblowsky, *Joseph Karo,* p. 53.

39. Ibid., par. 13, as trans. in Werblowsky, *Joseph Karo,* p. 53.

40. I, fol. 218a, as trans. in Tishby, *Wisdom of the Zohar,* 1:137.

41. Tishby, *R. 'Azriel,* p. 40; Recanati, *Vayeḥi,* fol. 37d. Quoted, for instance, in *Minḥat Yehudah,* fol. 143a et seq. Also translated into Latin and used by Giovanni Pico della Mirandola. See Chaim Wirszubski, *Sheloshah Perakim be-Toledot ha-Kabbalah ha-Noṣrit* (Jerusalem, 1975), pp. 14–20. Incidentally, in his *Niṣoṣey Zohar,* R. Margaliot called attention to a parallel in Talmud Yerushalmi, *Shabbat* V,1, to the words of the *Zohar* quoted above.

42. On the role of weeping among the Sufi ascetics see Wieder, "Hashpa'ot Islamiyot 'al ha-Pulḥan ha-Yehudi," pp. 73–74. See also Idel, *Kabbalah,* pp. 75–88.

43. See, e.g., *Zohar* I, fol. 4a: "Rabbi Ḥiyya prostrated," etc.

44. III, fol. 75a, as trans. in Tishby, *Wisdom of the Zohar,* 1:420.

45. II, fol. 102a, as trans. in *Zohar,* ed. Sperling, Simon, and Levertoff, 3:311.

46. II, fol. 96a, as trans. in Tishby, *Wisdom of the Zohar,* 1:183.

47. III, fol. 79a, as trans. in Tishby, *Wisdom of the Zohar,* 1:150.

48. Vital, *Sha'ar Ru'aḥ ha-Kodesh* (Jerusalem, 1912), fol. 11b.

49. On the role of prostration among the Muslims see Weider, "Hashpa'ot Islamiyot 'al ha-Pulḥan ha-Yehudi," p. 73 and corresponding notes.

50. *Zohar* II, fol. 98a, as trans. in Tishby, *Wisdom of the Zohar,* 1:191.

51. *Zohar* II, fol. 190b, as trans. in *Zohar,* ed. Sperling, Simon, and Levertoff, 4:143.

52. *Zohar* I, fol. 11b, as trans. in Tishby, *Wisdom of the Zohar,* 3:1065. Incidentally, already in the Talmud (BB 89b) there appears the idiom, "Woe to me, if I should speak; woe to me if I should not speak." See also *Zohar* II, fol. 257b; III, fol. 127b.

53. See Gottlieb, *Meḥkarim,* p. 100.

54. *Gle Razaya* (Mohilev, 1812), fol. 33a.

55. Elijah Ḥayyim of Ginazano, *Iggeret Ḥamudot* (London, 1912), p. 3.

56. As trans. in *RaMBaN,* ed. Chavel, pp. 15, 16. See Gottlieb, *Meḥkarim,* p. 90.

57. See David ben Yehudah he-Ḥasid, *Sefer Mar'ot ha-Zove'ot,* translated as

The Book of Mirrors, ed. Daniel Chanan Matt (Chico, Calif., 1982), introduction, p. 118.

58. R. Shneur Zalman of Lyady, *Iggeret ha-Kodesh,* par. 21 (in the end), pp. 282–83.

59. See, e.g., the parable of the music players and the deaf man, cited in R. Moses Ḥayyim Ephraim of Sudylkow, *Degel Maḥaneh Ephraim,* Yitro. On the turnabout in Rabbi Naḥman of Bratslav, see Arthur Green, *The Tormented Master* (University, Ala., 1979), pp. 141ff.

60. *Zohar* III, fol. 79b, trans. in Tishby, *Wisdom of the Zohar,* 1:151).

61. Benayahu, *Sefer Toledot ha-ARI,* p. 180.

62. Bakharakh, *'Emek ha-Melekh,* fol. 10.

63. Consult Scholem, *Kitvey Yad,* p. 247.

64. Rabbi Aaron Berakhia of Modena. See Tishby, "Ha-'Immut," pp. 64–65.

65. *Zohar* I, fol. 79a.

66. Ṣioni, *Perush 'al ha-Torah,* fol. 10c.

67. See Heschel, "'Al Ru'aḥ ha-Kodesh bi-Ymey ha-Beinaim," p. 186. See also ibid., n. 71.

68. See A. Z. Aescoly, *Ha-Tenu'ot ha-Meshiḥiyyot be-Yisrael* (Jerusalem, 1988), p. 306.

69. *Mishnat Ḥasidim* (Amsterdam, 1727), fol. 32a, par. 9.

70. Recanati, *Vayeḥi,* fol. 38b. The English translation of the quotation is based on Idel, *Kabbalah,* pp. 43–44. See also the definition of R. 'Ezra in his commentary on the Song of Songs 1:2 (*Kitvey RaMBaN,* ed. Chavel, p. 485): "The kiss is a parable of the joy of the communion of the souls in the source of life and the addition of the Holy Spirit." (In this context, the reference is certainly not to death). See also *Or Ne'erav,* pt. 4, chap. 1. See also Idel, *Mystical Experience in Abraham Abulafia,* pp. 780–84.

71. The same is true of Vital, *Sefer ha-Gilgulim,* chap. 4, fol. 7a (as trans. by Yehuda Shamir in Meltzer, *Secret Garden,* p. 193): "There are righteous people who die in their youth . . . because he had already completed what he needed to complete . . . therefore he died in his youth." In fact this matter is already discussed by (the second) Rabbi Isaac Abuhav (of the fifteenth century), *Nehar Pishon* (Zolkiew, 1806), fol. 7d: "We have found out that when a boy is good and knows a great deal of Torah he dies in the midst of his life. The reason is that he has already completed what he needed to complete in Torah and its Commandments. . . . This is analogous to a man who worked fast and did what he was supposed to do soon enough and therefore he died in the midst of his life."

Chapter 9. The Doctrine of the Sefirot

1. After Ps. 145:18. The view of the Philosopher presented at the beginning of the *Kuzari* (by R. Yehudah ha-Levi), for instance, clearly exemplifies the problem of a completely impersonal relationship between God and man.

2. *Midrasch Tannaim zum Deuteronomium*, ed. D. Hoffmann (Berlin 1909), p. 25.

3. See also Scholem, *Major Trends*, pp.10–14. It should be pointed out that even the Ashkenazic Hasidim distinguished between concealed and revealed instances of the Divine. Concealed, God has no image but is called "Creator." Revealed, he is called *kavod* (glory), Shekhinah, *keruv* (cherub), etc. See Dan's discussion, *Torat ha-Sod*, p. 27.

4. "That which thought cannot grasp"—this was the phrase for 'Eiyn Sof used by R. Isaac the Blind in his commentary on *Sefer Yeṣirah* and by his followers. Other appellations popular in the thirteenth century in Gerona and the literature of the Iyyun circle included "the disappearing light" and "the indifferent unity." The phrase coined in *Tikkuney Zohar*, "You are altogether beyond the reach of thought," is recognized in *Shomer Emunim*, argument B, 35, as an "authoritative preface," i.e., a postulate beyond dispute.

5. A few of the Geronese Kabbalists, among them R. Asher ben David, added praises to that appellation, such as "blessed be He," after the model of the personal God common in rabbinic sources. The system of some authors, such as R. 'Azriel, opposed even that. In contrast, beginning with Lurianic teaching, Kabbalists went much further, indicating various aspects of 'Eiyn Sof, in forms such as "Malkhut of 'Eiyn Sof," etc.

6. A commentary on *Sefer ha-Komah*. See Scholem, *Reshit ha-Kabbalah*, p. 212. In this early work God is still presented as identical with 'Eiyn Sof, or the Cause of Causes as He is called there. This subject will be discussed below.

7. See, for example, *Zohar* I, fol. 2a: "The Holy One blessed be He had a deep secret which He at length revealed at the celestial Academy. It is this. When the most Mysterious wished to reveal Himself . . ." (trans. Sperling, Simon, and Levertoff, p. 6).

8. *Ma'arekhet ha-Elohut*, fol. 22b. This statement is cited in other kabbalistic works as well, such as *'Avodat ha-Kodesh* I, 9.

9. See, for instance, *Ma'arekhet ha-Elohut,* fol. 7b, 112b; *'Avodat ha-Kodesh* I, 12; *Ketem Paz* I, fols. 23d, 34d ff., etc.

10. In kabbalistic sources, symbols are termed *meshalim* (analogies), *shemot* (names); *kinnuyim* (appellations), etc.

11. For more extensive discussion of the subject, see chapter 1 above.

12. Naḥmanides states that notion expressly at the end of the introduction to his *Commentary on the Pentateuch*. See below, chap. 12.

13. *Ma'arekhet ha-Elohut,* fol. 49a.

14. *Pardes Rimmonim* I, 8. See also Tishby, *Wisdom of the Zohar,* 1:252 n. 20.

15. See below, chap. 12.

16. G. Scholem (for example, in *Reshit ha-Kabbalah*, pp. 63, 104–7) holds that the Kabbalists first used that name as an adverb, and that it gradually became a noun. On the possibility that the substantial meaning of the term is already present in the poetry of R. Solomon ibn Gabirol, see Idel's discussion in *Tarbiṣ* 51 (1982) p. 278, n. 2. A different use of the concept "'Eiyn Sof" is found in the *Zohar* I, fol. 65a; in Tishby, *Wisdom of the Zohar,* 1:324–25.

17. In some works, these terms are used interchangeably. Some do not employ

the term "'Eiyn Sof" at all, but rather "the Root of all Roots" common in Neoplatonism. This is the case, for instance, in the writings of the Iyyun circle, and in an responsum attributed to R. Hai Gaon, which apparently is also associated with that circle.

18. The origin of the term is Aristotelian. Aside from "'Eiyn Sof," it is the most commonly used expression; compare the description presented above, n. 6. In later generations, the expression became very popular due to *Pataḥ Eliyahu* (*Tikkuney Zohar*, introduction, fol. 19a), which opens thus: "You are Master of the Worlds, the Cause of Causes." This formula is found in many prayer books and appears in varied contexts. Moreover, the meaning of the term in *Tikkuney Zohar* is not always identical to its usage in the *Zohar*. See Tishby, *Wisdom of the Zohar,* 1:246–47.

19. See below, n. 120. Thus: "The sun bleaches clothes and browns the face of the launderer, melts wax and congeals mud" (Samuel ibn Ṣarṣa, *Mekor Ḥayyim* [Mantua, 1559], fol. 126a). See also *Meirat 'Eynaim*, p. 394.

20. This was already true in the thought of R. Abraham ben David and his son, R. Isaac the Blind; see Gershom Scholem, *Origins of the Kabbalah* (Philadelphia, 1987), p. 219 and the writings of R. Joseph Gikatilla (see Scholem, *Kitvey Yad*, pp. 219–25) and later in *Tomer Devorah* by R. Moses Cordovero, as mentioned below.

21. See R. Joseph Gikatilla, *Sha'arey Orah*, ed. J. Ben-Shelomo (Jerusalem, 1970), 2:107.

22. See Tishby, *Wisdom of the Zohar,* 1:269.

23. See Idel's discussion in *Tarbiṣ* 51 (1980): 246 n. 41.

24. Compare Scholem, *Reshit ha-Kabbalah*, p. 164.

25. See, for example, *Ma'arekhet ha-Elohut*, fol. 8a: "For the basis of all definite entities is the number ten; the hundreds, thousands, myriads, and all numbers are defined by ten, as mathematicians well know." Compare n. 32 below.

26. Section 125.

27. Additional interpretations and further development of the idea may be found in R. Moses Cordovero's *Shi'ur Komah* s.2, fol. 4.

28. See *Avot* 5:1. On the number ten, see M. M. Kasher, *Torah Shelemah* Genesis 1:9, s. 40.

29. As, for instance, the contention made by Rav in *Ḥagigah* 12a that the world was created with ten utterances.

30. In any case, R. Moses Cordovero (*Pardes Rimmonim* I, 1) writes: "It is common knowledge that, regarding the number of the Sefirot, all who occupy themselves with that esoteric wisdom *have unanimously agreed* they are ten, and the matter is undisputed."

31. In his commentary on *Sefer Yeṣirah* I, 4; see also R. 'Azriel, *Sha'ar ha-Sho'el* 4, fol. 2c, in *Derekh Emunah* (Warsaw, 1890).

32. Fols. 192b–193a. Opposition to this view is expressed in Ḥayyat, *Minḥat Yehudah*, fol. 193a. Compare n. 25 above.

33. For English translation, see Tishby, *Wisdom of the Zohar,* 1:273–74.

34. R. Shem Tov, in the fragments of his work on the doctrine of the Sefirot, presents three alternative formations of the ten Sefirot. The difference among them, though, remains only in the placement of the first three:

Keter Ḥokhmah Binah	Keter Ḥokhmah Binah	Keter Ḥokhmah Binah

See Scholem's discussion in *Kiryat Sefer* 8 (1931–32): 534. The first view, of "one above the other" is expressed in *Ma'arekhet ha-Elohut*, fol. 85b. The second view is founded on a triad, in which the third Sefirah is placed in the center. An interesting result of this conception concerns the possibility of Ḥokhmah being the source of stern judgment *(din)*. Some contexts in which this view is voiced are: a commentary on the Tetragrammaton by R. Asher ben David (published in *Ha-Segullah* 7 [1932]: 6); by Todros Abulafia in *Oṣar ha-Kavod* (Novidvor, 1808), fol. 30b; in *Ma'arekhet ha-Elohut*, fol. 164b. The third view is the most common among the Kabbalists. See Tishby, *R. 'Azriel*, pp. 90–91 n. 25; M. Oron in her discussion in *Kiryat Sefer* 51 (1976): 697–98. Compare *Heikhal ha-Shem*, fol. 5b.

35. R. Eleazar of Worms does refer to "Keter 'Eliyon" as one of the divine names, yet not as a Sefirah. See Scholem, *Reshit ha-Kabbalah*, p. 60 n. 2; idem, *Origins of the Kabbalah*, p. 125.

36. See, for example, Menaḥem 'Azariah de Fano at the beginning of *Kanfey Yonah* and the opening pages of *Sheney Luḥot ha-Berit.*

37. This was the case in early kabbalistic thought. For some of the Geronese Kabbalists, the term "thought" *(maḥashavah)* became a symbol of the second Sefirah, Ḥokhmah, and that trend gained momentum in successive generations. On the origin of the expression "pure thought" and its use by the Kabbalists, see Scholem, *Reshit ha-Kabbalah*, p. 60, and Idel's discussion in *Tarbiṣ* 51 (1982): 244. The notion of Keter as *mezimah* (in the positive sense of "intention," "device"), parallel to thought, appeared in the works of R. Isaac ha-Kohen and a few other Kabbalists; see J. Dan, "Iggeret Vermaisa . . . ," in *Meḥkarim be-Kabbalah, be-Philosophia Yehudit u-ve-Sifrut ha-Musar ve-he-Hagut, Mugashim le-Yeshayahu Tishby*, ed. J. Dan and J. Hacker (Jerusalem, 1986), p. 133 and n. 55.

38. On Keter as the cessation of all thought see Tishby, *Perush ha-Aggadot le-Rabbi 'Azriel*, p. 116; also in *Shoshan 'Edut* by R. Moses de Leon. See Scholem, "Sheney Kuntresim Le-Rabbi Moshe de Leon," p. 334.

39. Cordovero, *Pardes Rimmonim*, XXIII, s.v. "Ayin."

40. Gikatilla, *Sha'arey Orah*, X (ed. Ben-Shelomo, 2:118). Compare *'Eṣ Ḥayyim*, VI, 3.

41. R. David ben Abraham ha-Lavan, *Masoret ha-Berit*, published by Gershom Scholem, *Kobeṣ 'Al Yad* 1 (1936): 31.

42. The origin of the term in the writings of John the Scot, called Scotus Erigena, who also recognized darkness as *causae primordiales*, is discussed by Scholem, *Origins of the Kabbalah*, p. 428 and n. 149, also pp. 313–14. Compare Idel's essay in *Tarbiṣ* 51 (1982), p. 242, n. 17, and p. 267.

43. In the responsum of R. Hai Gaon. See Scholem, *Origins of the Kabbalah*, p. 357.

44. *Ḥoker u-Mekubal*, chap. 6.

45. Regarding a possible Ismailian source, see A. Goldreich, "Mi-Mishnat Ḥug ha-'Iyyun," *Jerusalem Studies in Jewish Thought* 6, nos. 3–4 (1987): 143–56.

46. This according to Israel Efrat, *Massot Ketanot* (Tel Aviv, 1976) p. 325.

47. See Yehudah Liebes, *Perakim be-Millon Sefer ha-Zohar* (Jerusalem, 1977), pp. 38–39, pars. 55, 59.

48. After Rashi's commentary on Gen. 2:24.

49. The term already appears in *Sefer ha-Bahir*, par. 2. See Scholem, *Reshit ha-Kabbalah*, p. 25.

50. In the view of Isaac and Jacob ha-Kohen, evil originates in this Sefirah.

51. See Louis Jacobs, *Tract on Ecstasy* (London, 1963), p. 37 and note 17.

52. Recanati, for example, stresses: "The first three are intellectual and are not called 'attributes.'" See the citation in *Minḥat Yehudah*, fol. 34b.

53. In his commentary on *Sefer Yeṣirah*, III, 1. On the categorization of "primordial" and "renewed," see R. 'Azriel, *Sha'ar ha-Sho'el*, fol. 4b; M. Ḥalamish, *Perush* (Jerusalem, 1985), p. 47 n. 8.

54. *Genesis Rabbah* 12.

55. *Bahir*, par. 11.

56. For a clarification of these concepts, see Tishby, *Wisdom of the Zohar,* 1:244–46, 295–98.

57. Gikatilla, *Sha'arey Orah*, III-IV, fol. 39a. On the internal order of Nezah and Hod see also Scholem, "Ha'im Ḥiber Rabbi Moshe de Leon et Sefer ha-Shem?" *Kiryat Sefer* 1 (1924): 47.

58. Note that in the *Bahir*, as well as a few kabbalistic works from the early thirteenth century, Yesod is numbered as the seventh Sefirah, and only from the period of the Geronese Kabbalists onward was its place fixed as the ninth Sefirah.

59. See *Ḥagigah* 12b. The moral and theurgic aspects of this appellation will be considered later in our discussion.

60. At times, the similarity between *Yesod* and *Malkhut* becomes apparent through common qualities and tendencies. For instance, *kol* (all) is usually used in the writings of R. Moses de Leon to designate Yesod (see also Scholem, "Sheney Kuntresim le-Rabbi Moshe de Leon," pp. 338, 339), but in the *Bahir* (par. 78) it designates the Shekhinah.

61. See Scholem, *Reshit ha-Kabbalah*, p. 34.

62. Scholem distinguishes an influence from the Kuzari. See ibid., pp. 83–84.

63. In talmudic literature, this appellation is identical with God, although in later midrashim the Shekhinah designates a specific and separate aspect, as it were (see ibid., pp. 50–51). This facilitated the transition in kabbalistic thought to a single Sefirah, in this case the lowest.

64. At times she is called "Rachel," after that figure's warm, maternal relationship to the Assembly of Israel described in Jeremiah 31 and midrashim concerning those verses. Following this logic, Binah would be called "Leah."

65. R. Moses Cordovero, *Shi'ur Komah*, sec. 27, fol. 42b. Compare R. Joseph Gikatilla, *Sha'arey Ṣedek*, fol. 9b: "Know that it has many names corresponding with its many qualities."

66. Fol. 193b. In his work *Meirat 'Eynaim*, p. 136, R. Isaac of Acre discusses five spiritual and five material Sefirot. Compare Tishby, *R. 'Azriel*, p. 7 and n. 8.

67. These are the intermediary stages through which the supernal influence passes after leaving its source in the "One," the absolute and supreme essence, and expanding through the cosmos.

68. See Scholem, *Reshit ha-Kabbalah,* p. 54; M. Ḥalamish, "Le-Verur Hashpa'at Sefer ha-Bahir 'al Rabbi Yosef ben Shalom Ashkenazi," *Bar-Ilan Yearbook* 7–8 (1970): 215.

69. For example, Salmon ben Yeruhim in his work *Milḥamot ha-Shem* (New York, 1934).

70. For instance, *Minḥat Yehudah* fol. 64a, 123a ff. Also worthy of mention is R. Moses Cordovero. Maimonides had decided to preface the first part of his *Guide to the Perplexed* with an explanation of biblical anthropomorphism. Cordovero devoted a separate composition, entitled *Shi'ur Komah,* to an explanation, arranged in alphabetical order, of blatantly anthropomorphic terms.

71. This tendency is particularly pronounced in the *'Idra Rabbah* of the *Zohar* and the writings of R. Isaac Luria. One work in contrast with these is R. Moses Cordovero's *Shi'ur Komah*. See above, n. 70.

72. "The Sefirot take human form because man is a microcosm ['*olam katan*], in the sense of 'Let us make mankind in our image, after our likeness' (Gen. 1:26)" (*Sefer ha-Temunah* fol. 25a). Similar expressions include *Adam kadmon* (primordial man) or *Adam de-le'eyla* (supernal man). It is important to remember that the Kabbalists portrayed man's performance of the commandments by means of his bodily limbs as thereby connecting to the "limbs" of that higher image; this was a further development of the concept of having been created in God's image, which gives man special status.

73. For example, in the *Bahir* (secs. 63, 97, 98, 106, 159), Naḥmanides' thought, and in Cordovero's *Pardes Rimmonim*, XXIII, it is Malkhut. In the *Zohar*, the writings of R. Joseph ben Shalom Ashkenazi, and other sources, in contrast—as Tiferet. See Ḥalamish, "Le-Verur Hashpa'at Sefer ha-Bahir 'al Rabbi Yosef ben Shalom Ashkenazi," pp. 219–20.

74. See Tishby, *Wisdom of the Zohar,* 1:244–46. Concerning R. Joseph of Ḥamadan, see Altmann, "Li-She'elat ba'aluto shel Sefer Ta'amei ha-Miṣvot," *Kiryat Sefer* 40 (1965): 274–75, 410.

75. Gikatilla, *Sha'arey Orah*, introduction, fol. 2b, translated in Tishby, *Wisdom of the Zohar,* 1:286. Many authors subsequently used the example given by Gikatilla of the name Reuben ben Jacob.

76. This idiomatic form of benediction is common in kabbalistic sources, such as Recanati. See also below at the end of chapter 11.

77. See Ḥ. Pedaya, "Pegam ve-Tikkun shel ha-Elohut be-Kabbalat Rabbi Yiṣḥak Sagi Nahor," *Jerusalem Studies in Jewish Thought* 6, nos. 3–4 (1987): 157–269.

78. The graphic form of the letter *vav* explains its role as a central axis connecting beginning to end, and as the trunk of a tree. The *gematria* of *vav* is also 6, an allusion to the six extremities—i.e., the six Sefirot from Ḥesed to Yesod, as mentioned above.

79. In the words of the commentary printed with *Sefer ha-Temunah*, fol. 10a, "In the sense that the unique Name [the Tetragrammaton] alludes to it . . . for all the Sefirot are embodied in Tiferet, and it is the root *['ikkar]* of all."

80. For a summary of this halakhic ruling, see Maimonides, *Hilkhot Yesodey ha-Torah*, chap. 6.

81. For the reader seeking to learn more on the subject, I would suggest studying Gikatilla, *Sha'arey Orah*, V.

82. Exod. 3:14. Perhaps Hos. 1:9, as well, according to certain interpretations, such as that of Buber.

83. R. Joseph Ashkenazi, for example. See Ḥalamish, *Perush*, p. 47 n. 9. See also Scholem, *Kitvey Yad*, p. 45.

84. Compare, for instance, Exodus 1:10. The plural form of *tikrena* (instead of the grammatically more correct *tikre,* "and it come to pass") emphasizes the potential intensity of the dreaded war to which the verb refers.

85. In his commentary on Gen. 1:1 (*RaMBaN,* ed. Chavel, p. 25). Compare R. Joseph Karo, *Shulhan 'Arukh, Oraḥ Ḥayyim*, end of sec. 5.

86. See, for instance, Ps. 7:14 and compare Ps. 82:1.

87. *Ḥagigah* 12a. Compare *Zohar* III, fol. 251b.

88. What follows is a very brief discussion of the correlation between the colors and the symbolism of the Sefirot. A more extensive examination of a wide spectrum of colors can be found in Cordovero, *Pardes Rimmonim*, "Sha'ar ha-Gevanim."

89. This symbolism is also related to comments on the primeval waste and void *(tohu va-vohu)* found in *Ḥagigah* 12a, and in *Sefer Yeṣirah* I, 11. The identification of *tohu* with Ḥokhmah and *bohu* with Binah had already been made in the earliest period of kabbalistic thought. We may add that in Muslim symbolism, green designates the Garden of Eden (see Scholem, *Sabbatai Ṣevi*, pp. 242–43), and in the Kabbalah, the Garden of Eden symbolizes Binah. While this association may be no more than coincidence, there may be something to it.

90. R. Isaac of Acre, *Meirat 'Eynaim*, p. 47.

91. *Pirkey de Rabbi Eliezer*, chap. 49. See *Zohar* I, fol. 55a, 91b.

92. Compare our discussion below, the end of chap. 12.

93. R. Isaac of Acre, *Meirat 'Eynaim,* p. 158.

94. See Tishby, *Netivey Emunah u-Minut*, chap. 2.

95. This list of works was compiled by Gershom Scholem in "Mafte'aḥ Le-Perushim 'al 'Eser Sefirot," *Kiryat Sefer* 10 (1933): 498–515. Scholars have discovered additional sources since then, and Scholem's list may be expanded.

96. As early as the sixteenth century, R. Yehudah Ḥayyat suggested: "Whoever would like to know the meanings [of the names of the Sefirot] should consult *Sha'arey Orah* or *Sha'arey Ṣedek*, and there he will find them" (*Minḥat Yehudah,* fol. 49c). Even in later periods it was common practice to teach beginners using *Sha'arey Orah*. See, for example, R. Mattathias Delacrut, at the end of the preface to his commentary on *Sha'arey Orah*; *Likkutim Yekarim*, fol. 35b; R. Ḥayyim Eleazar Shapira, *Minḥat Eleazar,* I, response 50; Shelomo Maimon, *Hayey Shelomo Maimon* (Tel Aviv, 1942), p. 113. Compare S. Assaf, *Mekorot le-Toledot ha-Ḥinukh be-Yisrael* (Tel Aviv, 1954), 1:42.

97. *Midrash Talpiyyot* (Czernowitz, 1860), fol. 233a–237a.

98. See Scholem, "Mafte'aḥ Le-Perushim," p. 511 n. 119.

99. M. Ḥalamish, *Ohel Ḥayyim* I, (Jerusalem, 1988), 1:181–83, 288–89.

100. This seems to be Naḥmanides' motive in stating (in his commentary on *Sefer Yeṣirah*) that, "What is above it [Keter] is utterly concealed, beyond thought and beyond expression, uncountable." See Scholem, "Perusho ha-Amiti shel ha-Ramban le-Sefer Yeṣirah," *Kiryat Sefer* 6 (1929): 406–7.

101. At the beginning of his commentary on Prov. 8:30.

102. Shem Tov ibn Shem Tov, *Sefer ha-Emunot* (Ferrara, 1556), IV, 10, fol. 36a. See also R. Abraham of Köln, *Keter Shem Tov,* in Jellinek, *Ginzey Ḥokhmat ha-Kabbalah*, p. 41.

103. *'Avodat ha-Kodesh* I, 3, fol. 9b.

104. See, for example, Cordovero, *Pardes Rimmonim*, III, 3, fol. 14b.

105. Tishby, *Wisdom of the Zohar,* 1:244. See also pp. 242–44; Scholem, *Reshit ha-Kabbalah*, pp. 109–10.

106. See *Sha'ar ha-Hakdamot* (Jerusalem, 1905), fol. 60c; *'Eṣ Ḥayyim*, XXIII, 2,5,8; XXV, sec. 6; XLII, 1. Other opinions may be found as well. See, for instance, *'Eṣ Ḥayyim*, XXIII, 5, sec. 4; *Sha'ar ha-Kavvanot* (Jerusalem, 1901), fol. 14d.

107. See Joseph Ben-Shelomo, *Torat ha-Elohut shel Rabbi Moshe Cordovero* (Jerusalem, 1965), pp. 54–55, 224–30.

108. See Ben-Shelomo in his preface to *Sha'arey Orah* (Jerusalem, 1971), 1:30–33.

109. *Minḥat Yehudah*, fol. 42a–b.

110. *Ketem Paz* I, fol. 56b–c, also 43d, 44d, etc.

111. This is the case in *Shoshan 'Edut*, in *Kobeṣ 'Al Yad* 8, no. 18 (1976): 337; *Shekel ha-Kodesh*, p. 6.

112. *The Book of the Pomegranate*, ed. Elliot R. Wolfson (Atlanta, 1988), p. 62.

113. See Idel, "Demut ha-Adam she-me-'al ha-Sefirot," *Da'at* 4 (1980): 41–55.

114. See Tishby, *Wisdom of the Zohar,* 1:245. On the question of multiplicity itself, see above, chap. 7, nn. 68–69.

115. *Kelaley Ḥokhmat ha-Emet*, *Kelalim Rishonim*, (Jerusalem, 1961), fol. 17a.

116. See, for example, Scholem's discussion in *Kiryat Sefer* 1 (1924): 48; Tishby, *Wisdom of the Zohar,* 1:290; Ben-Shelomo, *Moses Cordovero*, pp. 248–50.

117. The image is drawn from *Sefer Yeṣirah* I, 7. See his explication in *Ma'arekhet ha-Elohut*, fol. 36b. Compare Tishby, *Wisdom of the Zohar,* 1:238–39; Gottlieb, *Meḥkarim*, p. 294.

118. *Ketem Paz* I, fol. 35a.

119. *Sha'ar ha-Sho'el*, par.9.

120. *More Nevukhim* I, chap. 53.

121. *Sefer ha-Bahir*, par. 119.

122. This term was put to varied uses. Some saw it as a description of the Divinity itself. Others, such as R. Sa'adya Gaon and Ashkenazic Hasidim in his wake, perceived it as referring to "the created glory *[kavod nivra]* of the angels." According to *Ma'arekhet ha-Elohut*, fol. 134b, it designates the seven lower Sefirot. In *Ma'avar Yabok* by R. Aaron Berakhiah of Modena it is the six Sefirot. *Meirat 'Eynaim*,

p. 39, saw it as Yesod and Malkhut in the aspects of male and female. Other views exist there as well: on p. 40 it is 'Atarah or, alternatively, Metatron. Some traditions indicate the angelic order modeled after the human form. See Scholem, *Pirkey Yesod*, pp. 153–86; Idel, "The World of Angels in Human Shape," in Dan and Hacker, eds., *Meḥkarim be-Kabbalah*, pp. 1–66.

123. The source from which Naḥmanides drew his interpretation seems to have been Onkelos's Aramaic translation of Gen. 27:36, *shvakta*, which he uses as a synonym for *aṣl*. Following his understanding, additional blessings remained with Isaac (in the case of Esau). However, Onkelos translates the root *AṢL* in Num. 11:17 as *vearbi* (I will increase). This interpretation is drawn from the midrash in *Numbers Rabbah*: when one candle is kindled from another, light is increased. The two interpretations are, in fact, similar; the first puts more emphasis on the position of the giver, while the second focuses on the receiver.

124. See, for instance, the commentary by R. 'Ezra on Song of Songs 3:9.

125. See *Pesikta de-Rav Kahana* XXII, 5 and *Song of Songs Rabbah* IV, 21. Both are mentioned by Menaḥem Recanati, *Perush 'al ha-Torah* (Lemberg, 1880), fol. 3c.

126. The expression originates in *Genesis Rabbah* XXI, 5 (ed. Theodor-Albeck, p. 201). See Scholem, *Gerona*, p. 276; M. Oron, "Ha-Peliah ve-ha-Kanah, etc." (diss., Hebrew University, 1980), pp. 201, 223 n. 167.

127. See *Guide to the Perplexed*, end of introduction (ed. Pines, pp. 10–12).

128. This image was engendered by the Gerona school. R. 'Ezra, for example, says: "The Holy One blessed be He reveals Himself in the world and disappears; His trace may be recognized through His attributes, in the same way that the soul manifests itself through the body." See his commentary on Song of Songs, p. 507. Compare *Zohar* I, fol. 103b; Recanati, *Perush 'al ha-Torah,* fol. 3c. And consider Scholem, *Gerona*, p. 276. On the metamorphoses of this analogy, see Idel, "Bein Tefisat ha-'Aṣmut li-tefisat ha-Kelim," *Italia* 3 (1982): 102–11.

129. See Ben-Shelomo, *Moses Cordovero*, pp. 72–80, 100–169; Gottlieb, *Meḥkarim*, pp. 293–315, 418–22.

130. In his discussion of the teaching of Ibn Gabbay, Gottlieb writes (*Meḥkarim*, p. 413) that the Kabbalist described things incompletely because he sensed that kabbalistic views on the matter were not wholly logical, and he preferred not to magnify "fissures in kabbalistic thought."

131. His comments are quoted more fully in *Minḥat Yehudah*, fol. 28a ff.

132. He lived in the Balkans. See Ḥava Tirosh-Goldschmidt, "Sefirot as the Essence of God in the Writings of David Messer Leon," *AJS Review* 7–8 (1982–83): 489.

133. See Scholem, *Kitvey Yad*, p. 206.

134. The use of the term *kelim* itself, though, to speak of the six or seven lower Sefirot is found even earlier, as in *Sefer ha-Bahir*, par. 57.

135. His comments in *Sefer ha-Yiḥud,* were published by R. Ḥasidah in *Ha-Segullah* 7 (1934–35).

136. *Ma'arekhet ha-Elohut*, 30b.

137. For more extensive treatment of the subject, see Tishby, *Wisdom of the Zohar,* 1:246–49, 265–66. On the latter pages, Tishby presents the text from *Ra'ya Meheimna*,

which appears in *Zohar* II, fol. 42b–43a. Compare the famous "Petiḥat Eliyahu" (the introduction to *Tikkuney Zohar*, fol. 17a ff).

138. See Ben-Shelomo, *Moses Cordovero*, pp. 100–101; Gottlieb, *Meḥkarim*, pp. 308–15.

139. Who writes: "And he made measures and vessels, limited and bounded in nature." See his commentary on Song of Songs, p. 482. See also Scholem, *Gerona*, pp. 276–77; Idel,"Bein Tefisat ha-'Aṣmut li-tefisat ha-Kelim," pp. 102–3.

140. See Gottlieb, *Meḥkarim*, pp. 303–5.

141. *Minḥat Yehudah*, fol. 30a–35a.

142. *Ma'arekhet ha-Elohut*, fol. 36b.

143. Ibid., fol. 8a. See also 36b.

144. Compare Tishby, *Wisdom of the Zohar,* 1:282–83.

145. See his epistle, published in *JQR*, n.s., 21 (1930–31): 365–75.

146. See Tishby, *Wisdom of the Zohar,* 1:250–51.

147. Gottlieb, *Meḥkarim*, p. 297.

148. *'Avodat ha-Kodesh* I, especially chaps. 3–6.

149. *Ketem Paz* II, fol. 414a.

150. *Vikku'ah 'al Ḥokhmat ha-Kabbalah* (Gorizia, 1852), pp. 33–48.

151. The subject will be treated in greater depth in the following chapter.

Chapter 10. Good and Evil

1. See Isaiah Tishby, *Torat ha-R'a ve-ha-Kelippah be-Kabbalat ha-ARI* (Jerusalem, 1942), p. 17.

2. See M. Ḥalamish, "Leqet Pitgamim," *Sinai* 80 (1977): 278; idem, "Leqet Pitgamim (2)," *Sinai* 85 (1979): 264.

3. See Tishby, *Wisdom of the Zohar,* 2:447.

4. *Moreh Nevukhim* III, 10.

5. *Ma'arekhet ha-Elohut*, fol.6b. On the metamorphoses of the midrashic statement "Nothing evil comes from above [or: from Heaven]," see Ḥalamish, "Leqet Pitgamim," n. 2. On its various interpretations, see J. Dan, "Samael, Lilith, and the Concept of Evil," *AJS Review* 5 (1980): 17–40. In any case, according to the simplest understanding of the phrase, responsibility for the existence of evil and suffering is placed upon man himself.

6. According to Gottlieb, *Meḥkarim*, p. 342.

7. Secs. 162–63. Shulamit Shaḥar, "Ha-Katharism ve-Reshit ha-Kabbalah be-Languedoc," *Tarbiṣ* 40 (1971) sought to isolate similarities between the *Sefer Bahir* and the Cathar movement in Provence; one of them concerns the question of Satan. Yet even if both do consider the question, that would only testify to a dilemma that gives thinkers no rest. What is important is the radically different answers given. On the position taken by Ashkenazic Hasidism, see Dan, *Torat ha-Sod*, pp. 99, 199–202.

8. Compare Scholem, *Reshit ha-Kabbalah*, pp. 55–56.

9. In another context in *Ma'arekhet ha-Elohut*, fol. 164b, it is said that *din* is rooted in the Sefirah of Ḥokhmah. Generally, though, the author seems to hold that

its source is in Gevurah. Compare, for example, *Ma'arekhet ha-Elohut,* fol. 88b. See Gottlieb, *Meḥkarim*, pp. 339–43. And see n. 16 below.

10. See Ḥavivah Pedaya, "Pegam ve-Tikkun," *Jerusalem Studies in Jewish Thought* 6, nos. 3-4 (1987): 212–15.

11. See *Kelaḥ Pitḥei Ḥokhmah*, secs. 46–49. Compare R. Shneur Zalman of Lyady's *Sefer shel Benonim*, chap. 29: "As for the holy and divine soul in man, the Holy One blessed be He has granted it the permission and ability to raise itself against [evil], that man may arouse himself to overcoming it." (See Ḥalamish, *Nativ*, p. 177).

12. See Scholem, *Mada'ey ha-Yahadut*, pp. 244–64.

13. That is the formulation in the Talmud, *Ḥagigah* 13b.

14. *Genesis Rabbah* 1:9.

15. See Scholem, *Mada'ey ha-Yahadut*, p. 250.

16. R. Moses of Burgos, though, a disciple of R. Jacob ha-Kohen, named Gevurah as the source of evil. Others even speak of the lowest point in the chain of emanation, i.e., Malkhut, as the source of evil. See n. 9 above.

17. See loc.cit., n. 12, p. 251.

18. *Minḥat Yehudah*, fol. 139a. The meaning of the term *kelippot* will be discussed below.

19. Cordovero, *Pardes Rimmonim*, fol. 32d.

20. The difference should be pointed out, though, that while the Castilian Kabbalists exaggerated in their personification of the powers of evil, even giving them individual names, the author of the *Zohar* tends to speak in more general categories. The given names are those of Samael and Lilith. Other forces are designated by symbols, such as donkey, dog, snake, bull, crocodile *(tannin),* etc. But note *Zohar* II, fols. 262–69, in which the "Chambers of Impurity" *(heikhalot ha-tum'ah)* are described in great detail.

21. In the fourteenth century, the parallels in structure become more extensive. For instance, R. Joseph Ashkenazi and R. David ben Yehuda he-Ḥasid speak of "wheels of Sefirot" *(galgallei Sefirot)*, "opposites" *(temurot)*, etc. Later Kabbalists, such as R. Isaac Luria, went even further, contending that even in the realm of evil, 'Eiyn Sof exists.

22. David ben Yehudah he Hasid, *Sefer Mar'ot ha-Ṣove'ot*, pp. 65–67.

23. *Zohar* II, fol. 163a. See also Tishby, *Wisdom of the Zohar,* 2: 456.

24. Deut. 30:15, 30:19.

25. Such an idea is expressed in Isa. 10:5–7.

26. *Zohar* II, fol. 148b. See also *Zohar* III, fol. 189a. In the midrash *Ecclesiastes Rabbah* it is also said that the evil inclination is implanted in man from birth, while the good inclination becomes a part of him only from the age of thirteen, when he is mature enough to activate the force of good.

27. The primary source is R. 'Azriel of Gerona. See Altmann, "The Motif of 'Shells' (Qelipoth) in 'Azriel of Gerona," *JJS* 9 (1958): 73–80.

28. *Zohar* II, fol. 108b; Goldstein's translation in Tishby, *Wisdom of the Zohar,* 2:496.

29. Called *sitra aḥra* (the other side) a name that points to no positive content whatsoever. Some Kabbalists called it "external tree" *(ilan ḥiṣon).*

30. *Megillah* 6a. Compare Rashi's commentary on Gen. 25:23: "When one [Esau] prevails, the other [Jacob] falls."

31. *Ta'anit* 5a. Compare *Zohar* III fol. 15b, and other places.

32. We mentioned earlier the practice of the *gerushim* in Safed in the writings of R. Moses Cordovero, and said that in certain cases they, too, walked barefoot for the same reason.

33. See Schechter, *Studies in Judaism,* pp. 293, 296; Benayahu, *Sefer Toledot ha-ARI,* p. 309.

34. It should be noted that even a sworn opponent like R. Abraham Berliner saw this custom as a "pretty flower." See Ḥalamish, "Gilgulav shel Minhag Kabbali," p. 534.

35. His commentary on Deut. 30:6. Other Kabbalists in his wake upheld the same position.

36. *Nidah* 61b.

37. See "*Sod ha-Naḥash u-Mishpato,*" quoted by Scholem, *Major Trends*, pp. 405–6.

38. *'Arfilley Tohar*, Jerusalem 1983, p. 39.

39. See Tishby, *Torat ha-R'a*, pp. 134–43. In our discussion in this chapter, we have not considered R. Isaac Luria's doctrine of evil. Consult this work by Tishby, which is the only monograph that has been devoted to the subject.

40. R. Moses Ḥayyim Luzzatto, *Kelaḥ Pitḥey Ḥokhmah*, secs. 48–49.

41. See Scholem, *Sabbatai Ṣevi*, and Yehuda Liebes, "Yaḥaso shel Sabbatai Ṣevi la-Hamarat Dato," *Ṣefunot* 17 (1983): 267–307.

42. Even declaring: "Ninety-nine [die] of the evil eye, and one dies a natural death"—*Baba Mezi'a* 107b.

43. See M. Guedemann, *Ha-Torah ve-ha-Ḥayyim be-Arṣot ha-Ma'arav* (Warsaw, 1897), chap. 7.

44. For more on the subject, see Shalom Rosenberg's work, *Tov va-R'a be-Hagut ha-Yehudit* (Tel Aviv, 1985), pp. 53–73.

Chapter 11. The Doctrine of Creation

1. *Tikkuney Zohar*, par. 57, fol. 91b. Also par. 70, fol. 122b.

2. In A. M. Haberman, *Shirey ha-Yiḥud ve-ha-Kavod* (Jerusalem, 1948).

3. *The Penguin Book of Hebrew Verse*, ed. and trans. T. Carmi (New York, 1981), p. 338.

4. Commentary on Gen. 1:6.

5. Commentary on Exod. 23:21.

6. *Sha'arey ha-Sod*, in *Kokhvey Yizḥak* 27 (1862): 9. Also cited by Naḥmanides in his Epistle. See *Kitvey ha-Ramban*, ed. Chavel, 1:347.

7. See Ḥalamish, "Leqet Pitgamim," pp. 265–66.

8. R. Jacob Joseph of Polonnoye, *Toledot Ya'akov Yoseph* (Jerusalem, 1962), fol. 17a, introduction.

9. Compare R. 'Azriel's formulation: "All comes from 'Eiyn Sof; beside Him there is nothing." See *Sha'ar ha-Sho'el*, fol. 2c, and many other places as well.

10. See *Rosh ha-Shanah* 32a.

11. And see E. E. Urbach, *The Sages* (Jerusalem, 1975), 1:196–97.

12. Variants include: "regard" *(mistakel);* in the midrash *Tanḥuma:* "take council" *(nitia'eṣ).*

13. *Berakhot* 55a. See also Gikatilla, *Sha'arey Orah*, chap. 5, fol. 68b–69a.

14. It should be noted that certain rabbis may have expressed their opposition to this stance by stressing that the world was created by one letter alone. Consider, for example, *Genesis Rabbah* 12:9. And see Urbach, *Sages*, pp. 197–99. The idea also appears in the *Heikhalot* literature along with the other statements: "The single letter with which heaven and earth were created." See Peter Schaefer, *Synopse zur Hekhalot-Literatur* (Tübingen, 1981), 389.

15. Schaefer, *Synopse,* 16.

16. Ibid., 651.

17. Ibid., 79.

18. The other chapters contain a "linguistic theory" that, according to Neḥemiah Aloni, could not have been composed before exposure to Arabic, i.e., in the sixth century at least. His view has been challenged. Our interest, though, lies in the first chapter, and its date of composition is generally agreed upon in modern scholarship.

19. See Scholem, *Reshit ha-Kabbalah, ve-Sefer ha-Bahir,* 23–24.

20. On the rabbinic view of Creation, see Urbach, *Sages*, pp. 184–213. See also Elias Lipiner, *Ḥazon ha-Otiot* (Jerusalem, 1989).

21. It is not my intent to investigate the roots of this teaching in Eastern or Indian thought, nor to analyze variations of it, but rather to present the method in general terms.

22. Other metaphors also appear: the outflow of a teacher's understanding to his pupil, leaving his own store of wisdom undiminished, etc.

23. See Scholem, *Gerona*, pp. 262–63.

24. Fol. 193a.

25. After the midrash in *Genesis Rabbah* 56 and *Ḥagigah* 12a. The contention is even made in *Ketem Paz* (I, fol. 67a) that such a view is "a tradition handed down to us from the Sages and their works."

26. The word *parsah* appears in Onkelos's Aramaic translation of the Bible for the Hebrew *masakh.* See Exod. 26:36.

27. R. Moses Cordovero, *Eilimah* (Jerusalem, 1966), p. 24.

28. Thus, for example, in *Nefesh ha-Ḥayyim*, II, 2: "God, blessed be He, joins Himself to the world to create and sustain them every moment." Note that the Neoplatonist Solomon ibn Gabirol also tended to consider divine free will as a dominant factor.

29. *Kedushat Levi*, beginning of his commentary on Genesis.

30. See Scholem, *Perakim*, p. 103; idem, *Gerona*, pp. 286–89.

31. See Scholem, *Gerona*, p. 289; idem, *Major Trends*, p. 410, n. 42. Compare his article "L'idi'at ha-Kabbalah bi-Sefarad 'erev ha-Gerush," in *Tarbiṣ* 24 (1955): 173.

32. Scholem, *Gerona*, p. 291.

33. On the relationship to the Christian trinity, see Scholem, *Reshit ha-Kabbalah*, pp. 172–75.

34. R. Sa'adya Gaon, *Emunot ve-De'ot*, beginning of pt. 4, in *The Book of Beliefs and Opinions*, trans. Samuel Rosenblatt, (New Haven, 1948), p. 180.

35. R. Moses Ḥayyim Luzzatto, *Derekh ha-Shem*, I, beginning of chap. 2.

36. Ibid. Similarly, "The light of His countenance and His proximity is the root and cause of all completeness."

37. See Ben-Shelomo, *Moses Cordovero*, pp. 88–89.

38. Gate 1, *Sha'ar ha-Kelalim*, beginning of chap. 1.

39. See Scholem, *Sabbatai Ṣevi*, p. 26.

40. Ibid., p. 29.

41. *Mevo She'arim*, beginning.

42. See Tishby, *Torat ha-R'a*, p. 22.

43. *Tanḥuma*, *Va-yakhel* 7.

44. *'Eṣ Ḥayyim*, VIII, 2. See Tishby, *Torat ha-R'a*, p. 18.

45. Tishby, *Torat ha-R'a*, p. 24.

46. See Chaim Wirszubski's review of *Torat ha-R'a,* by Isaiah Tishby, *Kiryat Sefer* 19 (1942): 241.

47. *Shef'a Tal* (Amsterdam, 1786) pp. 65–66.

48. *Mitpaḥat Sefarim* (Lemberg, 1871), p. 111.

49. *Shomer Emunim*, second argument, sec. 35 (and 46). According to Nissim Yosha, *Mythos u-Metafora* (Jerusalem, 1994), 15–16, 190, Abraham Herrera was the first to express the metaphoric *ṣimṣum.*

50. *Kelaḥ Pitḥey Ḥokhmah*, sec. 24.

51. *Nefesh ha-Ḥayyim*, III, 7.

52. For more on the idea of *ṣimṣum*, see M. Ḥalamish, "Mishnato ha-'Iyunit shel R. Shneur Zalman mi-Liady ve-Yaḥasa le-Torat ha-Kabbalah u-le-Reshit ha-Ḥasidut" (diss., Hebrew University, Jerusalem, 1976), pp. 95–106; Tamar Ross, "Shney Perushim le-Torat ha-Ṣimṣum," *Jerusalem Studies in Jewish Thought* 2 (1982): 153–69.

53. See Scholem, *Reshit ha-Kabbalah*, pp. 177–79; idem, *Temunah*, pp. 31–84; I. Weinstock, *Be-Ma'agley ha-Nigle ve-ha-Nistar* (Jerusalem, 1970), pp. 151–241; Gottlieb, *Meḥkarim*, pp. 332–39; Scholem, *Pirkey Yesod*, pp. 77–85.

54. Naḥmanides, commentary on Lev. 25:2.

55. Abraham bar Ḥiyya, *Megillat ha-Megalleh* (Berlin 1924), pp. 10–11.

56. Scholem, *Temunah*, p. 26.

57. Fol. 6a, col.2.

58. See *Shi'ur Komah*, sec. 83. Also, Berakhah Zak, "Sheloshet Zemanei Geullah," in *Messianism and Eschatology: A Collection of Essays* (in Hebrew), ed. Ṣevi Baras (Jerusalem, 1984), pp. 281–84.

59. *Sha'ar Ma'amrei RaShBI* on *Zohar* II, 135a.

60. See Scholem, *Sabbatai Ṣevi*, pp. 312–14, 811–14.

61. See Tishby, *Netivey Emunah u-Minut*, p. 217.

62. For instance, *Ma'arekhet ha-Elohut*, fol. 187a ff.; *Sefer ha-Peliah*, fol.18d.

63. *Sanhedrin* 97a.

64. See Lev. 25.

65. See Gottlieb, *Meḥkarim*, p. 333. Compare ibn Sahulah's commentary on the Pentateuch, *Behar*; *Ma'arekhet ha-Elohut*, 192b. Some presented the interpretation without attributing it to R. Solomon ben Abraham Adret, among them Recanati; *Keter Shem Tov*, *Behar*.

66. See Gottlieb, *Meḥkarim*, pp. 335, 337.

67. Interestingly, Abraham bar Ḥiyya presents the opinion of philosophers that the universe will exist throughout the reign of the seven planets, i.e., forty-nine thousand years; in the fiftieth millennium it will revert to chaos [*tohu va-vohu*], and then be created anew.

68. See also *Ma'arekhet ha-Elohut*, fol. 190b; David ben Yehudah he Ḥasid, *Sefer Mar'ot ha-Ṣove'ot*, p. 106; *Ketem Paz* II, fol. 445b.

69. David ben Yehudah he Ḥasid, *Sefer Mar'ot ha-Ṣove'ot*, p. 224.

70. See Gottlieb, *Meḥkarim*, p. 337.

71. See A. Altmann, "Li-She'elat ba'aluto shel Sefer Ta'amei ha-Miṣvot," pp. 268–69.

72. For example, Commentary to *Sefer ha-Temunah*, fol. 36a.

73. See Zak, "Sheloshet Zemanei Geullah," p. 281.

74. See Gottlieb, *Meḥkarim*, pp. 332–38.

75. Above, n. 53.

76. See Scholem, *Temunah*, pp. 51–62; Scholem, *Pirkey Yesod*, pp. 78–79.

77. Cracow 1894, fol. 31a.

78. *Livnat ha-Sappir* (Jerusalem, 1971), fol. 1a ff.

79. See *Or Yakar*, 7:66. Compare Zak, "Sheloshet Zemanei Geullah," pp. 281–84.

80. See Tishby, *Netivey Emunah u-Minut*, p. 336, n. 84.

81. Recanati's commentary on *Yetro*, fol. 45d.

82. Compare the view in Greek mythology that the period preceding the present one was a "golden age."

83. *Ma'arekhet ha-Elohut*, fol. 189b–190a.

84. R. Jacob ben Sheshet, *Meshiv Devarim Nekhoḥim* (Jerusalem, 1969), p. 94.

85. Warsaw, 1887, p. 196.

Chapter 12. The Torah

1. Indeed, the letter *resh* is counted as one of the letters receiving a *dagesh*, as it did in ancient times. See S. Morag's discussion in the jubilee volume of *Tur Sinai*, Jerusalem 1960, pp. 207–42. See also, more recently, the essay by Y. Liebes, "Shev'a Kefulot Begad Kafrat," *Tarbiṣ* 61 (1992): 237–48.

2. *Moreh Nevukhim*, III, 8.

3. Naḥmanides on Exod. 30:13.

4. See, for example, R. Joseph ben Shalom Ashkenazi, *Sefer Yeṣirah* I, 3, fol. 22b. Various proverbs were coined reflecting this idea, such as "language is the pen of the intellect."

5. *Zohar* III, 149a–152a; translated in Tishby, *Wisdom of the Zohar*, 3:1124–27. Similarly, R. Isaac of Acre wrote: "The verses, i.e., the words and letters one sees are like the garments covering man's body; the literal sense and interpretations are the body, while the true Kabbalah, the forces and the great and wondrous secrets emerging from the Torah are the soul" (*Yetro*, p. 110).

6. See *Sotah* 35a.

7. *Ṣidkat ha-Ṣaddik*, par. 216.

8. *Nefesh ha-Ḥayyim*, IV, 11.

9. "Sod Ta'amey ha-Torah," in *Likkutei Shikheḥah u-Peah* (Ferrara, 1556), fol. 25b–26a.

10. *Likkutey Torah* (Brooklyn, 1965), Vayikra, fol. 5b.

11. Compare R. Ḥayyim Joseph David Azulai, *Moreh ba-Eṣb'a*, II, 44; R. Moses Ḥayyim Luzzato, introduction to *Kelaḥ Pitḥey Ḥokhmah* (quoted by Tishby in *Wisdom of the Zohar,* 1:29 n. 137).

12. *Torah ve-Ḥayyim* (Salonica, 1846), fol. 78a. See also above, pp. 92–96.

13. *Iggeret Ḥamuddot* (London, 1912), p. 4.

14. *Yosher Divrey Emet*, fol. 12c.

15. Relevant here is a source from kabbalistic liturgy. A work entitled *Hillula Rabba* (Leghorn, 1877), begins with a "Seder Limmud for Lag ba-'Omer" and in one of the first paragraphs it says: "We also believe in full and complete faith that the holy Torah contains a literal meaning, which is the body of the Torah, and a secret meaning, which is the soul, and the holy Torah may be interpreted in various ways."

16. *Or Zaru'a*, ed. A. Altmann, in "Sefer Or Zaru'a Le-Rabbi Moshe de Leon," *Kobeṣ 'Al Yad* 9, no. 19 (1980): 248.

17. See *Zohar* II, 98b, in Tishby, *Wisdom of the Zohar*, 1:196. Compare Maimonides' introduction to the *Guide* and his description of the light that "flashes and is hidden again" (trans. Pines, p. 7]. See also Tishby, *Wisdom of the Zohar*, 3:1084–86.

18. *Or Ne'erav*, IV, 1–2.

19. See *Zohar* III, fol. 202a.

20. *Zohar Ḥadash*, Midrash Ruth, fol. 83a.

21. *Zohar* III, fol. 110a, and also *Zohar Ḥadash*, Tikkunim, fol. 102d. According to Gershom Scholem, *On the Kabbalah and its Symbolism* (New York, 1965), p. 58, it should be read *re'iyah*. According to Tishby, *Wisdom of the Zohar*, 3:1090, it should be read *re'ayah*.

22. See Scholem, *On the Kabbalah,* p. 62 n. 1. Scholem speaks of a Christian influence. Moshe Idel (in an unpublished statement) indicates an early Muslim influence.

23. See Idel, "'Al Rabbi Moshe Cordovero ve-Rabbi Abraham Abulafia," *Da'at* 15 (1985): 120, near n. 31.

24. See above, n. 5.

25. R. Joseph Gikatilla, *Sha'arey Zedek*. See Gottlieb, *Meḥkarim*, p. 154.

26. *Zohar* II, fol. 99a–b. We have quoted Goldstein's translation in Tishby, *Wisdom of the Zohar,* 1:196–97.

27. See F. Lahover, *'Al Gevul ha-Yashan ve-he-Hadash* (Jerusalem, 1951), pp. 40ff.

28. JT *Shekalim* VI, 1.

29. *Zohar* III, fol. 215b. (*Ra'aya Meheimna*).

30. *Tikkuney Zohar*, par. 69.

31. Ibid., par. 43, fol. 82a.

32. R. Abraham ibn Migash, *Kevod Elohim* (Constantinople, 1585), end of chap. 26. See the introduction by H. H. Ben-Sasson, photocopy edition (Jerusalem, 1977), p. 26.

33. *Perush Shir ha-Shirim*, in *Kitvey ha-Ramban,* ed. Chavel, 2:479. Perhaps this is characteristic of his approach as a whole, and the importance in it of the spiritual element.

34. *Siddur ha-Tefillah*, "Sha'ar ha-Hanukkah" (Brooklyn, 1965), 275a. See also R. Shneur Zalman, *Hilkhot Talmud Torah* II, 2.

35. *Siddur ha-Tefillah*, "Derushim le-Hanukkah," beginning, 128b.

36. Midrash *Shoher Tov* III, 1.

37. *Perush ha-Aggadot*, MS Vatican 294, fol. 34a. See also Tishby, *R. 'Azriel*, p. 76.

38. See also *Nisosey Zohar*, III, fol. 36a, n. 2.

39. Tishby, *R. 'Azriel*, pp. 37–38.

40. *She'elot u-Teshuvot le-R. Moshe de Leon*, published by Tishby in "She'elot u-Teshuvot le-R. Moshe de Leon," *Kobes 'al Yad,* 1951, 30–31.

41. *Pesahim* 54b; *Genesis Rabbah* VIII, 2 (ed. Theodor-Albeck, p. 57).

42. Gikatilla, *Sha'arey Orah*, fol. 47b.

43. Ibid., fol. 2a.

44. Indeed, in the Renaissance it was translated to Latin, and Jews entering study of Kabbalah would begin with it.

45. *Meshiv Devarim Nekhohim* (Jerusalem, 1969), pp. 107–8. Translated in Tishby, *Wisdom of the Zohar*, 3:1081. See R. Bahya's commentary on Num. 11:15.

46. Tishby. *R. 'Azriel*, p. 37.

47. Ibid. p. 38.

48. *Sefer Tashak*, fol. 1b (ed. Zwelling, p. 6).

49. R. 'Ezra, *Perush Shir ha-Shirim*, p. 548.

50. *Tikkun ha-De'ot* (Jerusalem, 1973), p. 38.

51. On other possibilities offered in early Kabbalah, see Tishby, *R. 'Azriel*, p. 77.

52. See Tishby, *Kiryat Sefer* 50 (1975): 480–92, 668–74.

53. Compare, for example, *Zohar* II, fol. 234a.

54. *Ma'arekhet ha-Elohut*, fol. 4b.

55. R. 'Azriel, *Derekh ha-Emunah ve-Derekh ha-Kefirah*, in G. Scholem, "Sridim Hadashim mi-Kitvey Rabbi 'Azriel mi-Geronah," in *Sefer Zikkaron le-A. Gulak ve-S. Klein*, ed. S. Asaf and G. Scholem (Jerusalem, 1942), p. 208.

56. *Moreh Nevukhim* III, 26 (trans. Pines, pp. 508–9).

57. Consider the comments about him made by R. Ṣaddok ha-Kohen in *Sefer ha-Zikhronot* (Benei-Berak, 1967), fol. 29d: "He should not have included knowledge of such matters in his *Hilkhot Yesodey Torah* at all, for no one faithful to the Torah has need of them, all the more so that much of what he says is untrue according to the contemporary views of their [non-Jewish] sages."

58. Ibn Gabbay, *'Avodat ha-Kodesh*, II, 3.

59. See, for instance, Abba Mari, *Minḥat Kena'ot* (Pressburgh, 1838), p. 60; R. Isaac 'Arama, *Ḥazut Kashah*, VIII; and R. Joseph Yabez, *Or ha-Ḥayyim* (Lublin, 1912), p. 55.

60. *Sefer Miṣvot Gadol*, positive commandments, end of no. 3.

61. *Tur*, *Oraḥ Ḥayyim*, par. 585.

62. R. Jacob ben Sheshet, *Sha'ar ha-Shamayim*, in *Oṣar Neḥmad* 3 (1920): 163–64.

63. R. Moses de Leon, *Sefer ha-Rimmon*. See Scholem, *Major Trends*, pp. 397–98.

64. The idea, though, that a new Torah will make its appearance in the messianic era is expressed in the midrashic literature (and in Christianity as well), e.g., *Ecclesiastes Rabbah* on Eccles. 11:8; S. A. Wertheimer, *Batey Midrashot*, (Jerusalem, 1955), 2:368. See Y. Rosenthal's discussion in the jubilee volume for Meir Waxman, *Ra 'ayon Bittul ha-Miṣvot be-Escatologia ha-Yehudit* (Jerusalem, 1967), pp. 217ff. In Sabbatianism, this idea became actual and radically relevant. (See also ibid., p. 231 n. 66a.)

65. *Peri ha-Areṣ*, Vayeshev.

66. *Likkutey Shikheḥah u-Peah*, fol. 7b–8a.

67. R. 'Ezra, *Perush le-Shir ha-Shirim*, p. 528. See also Tishby, *Netivey Emunah u-Minut*, pp. 18–21.

68. R. Joseph Gikatilla, *Sod Re'uyah Hayetah Bat Shev'a le-David*, in *Erez ba-Levanon* (Vilna, 1899), p. 31.

69. Gen. 9:9. In *Sefer ha-Bahir*, par. 82, the seven limbs parallel the seven lower Sefirot, yet in later kabbalistic thought, parallels to all ten Sefirot were made.

70. See Scholem, *On the Kabbalah*, p. 123.

71. Tishby, *R. 'Azriel*, p. 38.

72. Recanati, introduction to *Ta'amey Miṣvot* (Basel, 1581), fol. 3a; translated in Tishby, *Wisdom of the Zohar,* 1:284.

73. Recanati, introduction to *Ta'amey Miṣvot,* fol. 5c; translated in Idel, *Kabbalah*, p. 188. See also *Zohar* III, fol. 118a, 122a.

74. Acccording to Tishby, *Wisdom of the Zohar,* 3:1086.

75. Introduction to *Sefer ha-Peliah*. See Michal Oron, "Ha-Peliah ve-ha-Kanah etc." (diss., Hebrew University, Jerusalem, 1980), p. 66.

76. See Tishby, *R. 'Azriel*, pp. 38–39.

77. *Zohar* II, 162b. See Tishby, *Wisdom of the Zohar,* 1:284 nn. 68, 69. Also 3:1158.

78. Ibid., 3:1160.

79. Thus, for example, R. Jacob Joseph of Polonnoye, disciple of the Ba'al Shem Tov, explains, on the basis of kabbalistic writings, that the word *miṣvah* is

divisible in two: the first two letters, *mem, ṣadik* equal the letters *yod, heh* according to the rule of *at-bash*. Thus the word *miṣvah* in its entirety contains the Tetragrammaton. R. Jacob Joseph adds that the present combination in the word *miṣvah* itself testifies to a combination of concealedness (reflected in the letters *mem, ṣadik*, representing the divine name *yod, heh*), and revelation (in the name *vav, heh*). This implies that the true meaning of *miṣvah* is the combination within it of literal and mystical meaning. (Introduction to *Toledot Ya'akov Yosef*).

80. *Sha'arey Ṣedek* (Cracow, 1881), fol. 13b–14a.

81. Ibid., fol. 12b. See also Recanati, *Teṣaveh; 'Avodat ha-Kodesh* III, 18. And see Gottlieb, *Meḥkarim*, p. 37.

82. David ben Yehudah he Ḥasid, *Sefer Mar'ot ha-Ṣove'ot*, p. 50.

83. *Ma'arekhet ha-Elohut*, fol. 159a–b.

84. *Ṣava'at ha-Ribash* (Jerusalem, 1948), p. 17; the reasoning given is particularly interesting. There are parallels to this statement, as for instance in *Or ha-Emet*, p. 65; *Likkutey Yakarim*, fol. 6b, 22b, 45a. See also R. Schatz-Uffenheimer, *Hasidism as Mysticism*, trans. J. Chipman (Princeton, 1993), pp. 148 n. 10, 164 n. 54.

85. In many places. An interesting parallel to this idea may be found in utterances such as "He said to him: Yishma'el, my son, bless me" (*Berakhot* 7a).

86. R. Baḥya was apparently influenced by him in *Shulḥan Shel Arb'a*, pp. 488–89. The latter's influence on Ibn Shu'eib, beginning of *Emor*, has been discussed by S. Abramson, *'Inyanot be-Sifrut ha-Geonim* (Jerusalem, 1974), pp. 158–59.

87. *'Avodat ha-Kodesh*, introduction, fol. 3d.

88. Ibid., II, 3, fol. 27a.

89. The author there uses the words *shituf ha-shem*, which is a talmudic legal term used to indicate an attempt at dualistic faith. See Maimonides, *Hilkhot Shevu'ot*, XI, 2.

90. Ibid., VI, 29b.

91. Fol. 4a.

92. *'Avodat ha-Kodesh*, II, 16, fol. 36a.

93. *Devarim Be-go*, p. 253.

94. *Sha'arey Orah*, IX, fol. 95a. See also Gottlieb, *Meḥkarim*, p. 36; *Likkutey Moharan*, fol. 58c; *Peri ha-Areṣ*, *'Ekev*, etc.

95. See n. 49 above.

96. *Nefesh ha-Ḥayyim*, II, 4.

97. On a similar problem in Islam, see Ḥava Lazarus-Yafe, "Ha-Mystica ha-Muslemit ve-Yaḥasa la-Miṣvot," *Molad* 18 (1960): 485–88.

98. See Tishby, *Wisdom of the Zohar*, 3:1171 n. 113.

99. *Ṣava'at ha-Ribash*, p. 12. Compare *Midrash Pinḥas* (Bilguray, 1929), p. 64: "He often said to me: You must follow the path set out in *Ṣava'at me-Ribash* [!], do not be excessive with details, etc., see there. That strengthened me in my childhood." Similar statements appear in other Hasidic texts as well. This is one of the central elements in Hasidism. See R. Ḥayyim Vital, *Sha'arey Kedushah*, II, 4 (Benei Berak, 1967), p. 55.

100. See *Maggid Devarav le-Ya'akov*, ed. R. Schatz (Jerusalem, 1976), par. 97. Compare par. 51, and many other instances.

101. Compare *Or ha-Emet*, fol. 75d–76a.

102. *Ṣava'at ha-Ribash*, p. 5. Also *Maggid Devarav le-Ya'akov*, p. 282: "'Know the God of thy father' [1 Chron. 28:9]—meaning, join with and cleave to the God of your father continually *in all your acts.*"

103. See I. Shoḥat, "'Al ha-Simḥa ba-Ḥasidut," *Zion* 16 (1951).

104. Eleazar Azikri, *Sefer Ḥaredim* (Venice, 1601), fol. 6a.

105. *Reshit Ḥokhmah* (Amsterdam, 1708), fol. 95b; II, 10, fol. 47a.

106. Elijah ha-Kohen, *Shevet Musar*, chap. 14.

107. *Mesillat Yesharim*, chap. 19.

108. *Sefer ha-Middot, Simḥah.* See also Maharal, *Ḥiddushey Aggadot, Yebamot* 62b.

109. P. 188.

110. R. Baḥya, commentary on Deut. 15:10.

111. Ibid., on Gen. 1:28. Compare above, chap. 9, n. 92.

Chapter 13. The Soul

1. Philo, *On Dreams* I, 54–57, trans. Colson and Whitaker (London, 1934), 5:324–25.

2. See *Lamentations Rabbah*, ed. Solomon Buber (Vilna, 1899), p. 70 n. 301.

3. *Pesikta de-Rab Kahana*, chap. 26, trans. Braude and Kaplan (New York, 1975), p. 387; *Yalkut Shimoni*, par. 945, and parallels.

4. *'Avodat ha-Kodesh*, II, 3.

5. *Ma'amar Massoret ha-Ḥokhmah* by R. Abraham ha-Levi. See Scholem, *Perakim*, p. 149.

6. See A. Altmann, "Li-She'elat ba'aluto shel Sefer Ta 'amei ha Miṣvot," p. 275. See also Ḥalamish, "Leqet Pitgamim," p. 277; and idem, "Leqet Pitgamim (2)," p. 263. Many other examples could be added. Among them: Recanati, *Perush 'al ha-Torah,* fol. 51c; *Heikhal ha-Shem*, fol. 18a; *SHeLaH*, fol. 209a; Elish'a Galiko, *Be'ur le-Sefer Kohelet* (Venice, 1578), fol. 16b; *Seder ha-Yiḥud* by R. Mordekhay Hasib'oni, MS NY/JTS 1848, fol. 1b, etc.

7. *Zohar Ḥadash*, Midrash Ruth, fol. 78c.

8. See Commentary *P"Z*, quoted in Ḥayyat, *Minḥat Yehudah*, fol. 138a.

9. This distinction is famed for the names assigned in it to man and the angel. Man is called "walking" *(mehalekh),* and the angel—"standing" *('omed)* (after Zech. 3:7). R. Meir ibn Gabbay stated that "The truth, traditionally upheld in our nation, is that the source and level of the soul *[neshamah]* is higher than that of the ministering angels, and that it therefore has dominion over everything that is below it" (*'Avodat ha-Kodesh*, III, 5. See also Tishby, *Wisdom of the Zohar*, 2:679.

10. The source of this expression is in midrash *Tanḥuma, Pekudey* 3. See Urbach, *Sages*, 1:232–33; Ḥalamish, "Leqet Pitgamim (2)," p. 270; and many more.

11. Dov Baer, *Maggid Devarav le-Ya'akov*, fol. 4a, ed. Schatz-Uffenheimer (Jerusalem, 1976), par. 24, p. 38). See also Schatz-Uffenheimer, *Hasidism as Mysticism,* p. 213.

12. See above, chap. 3.

13. I hope to discuss this matter in greater depth in another context. Some comments on the subject appear above, chap. 4. See also S. Sperber, "'Al Yesod ha-Ḥiddush," *Da'at* 18 (1987): 111–14.

14. See *Tanya* (*Sefer shel Beinonim*), chap. 15. And see Ḥalamish, *Nativ*, pp. 100–102.

15. Ibn Gabbay, *'Avodat ha-Kodesh*, III, 1.

16. See Ḥalamish, "Li-Mekoro shel Pitgam be-Sifrut ha-Kabbalah," *Bar Ilan* 13 (1976): 211–23.

17. For example, R. Ḥayyim Vital formulated it thus in the beginning of *Sha'arey Kedushah*: "As men of science know, a man's body is not the man. Rather, it is a certain garment, in which the intellectual soul is clothed; [the latter] is the man himself." Compare the work *Torot ha-Nefesh*, attributed to Bahya ibn Pakuda (Paris, 1896), p. 24: "Know that, in truth, the soul *[nefesh]* is the man, and he is nothing without it." (On that work, see M. Plussner, "Kavanato shel Kitab Ma'ani al-Nafs," *Kiryat Sefer* 48 [1973]: pp. 491–98.) See also *Zohar* II, fol. 76a; de Leon, *Shekel ha-Kodesh*, p. 33; idem, *Ha-Nefesh ha-Ḥakhamah*, III, fol. 2a; Recanati, *Perush 'al ha-Torah,* fol. 3d–4a; Ibn Gabbay, *'Avodat ha-Kodesh* II, end of chap. 20; R. Menaḥem 'Azariah de Fano, *Ma'amar ha-Nefesh* IV, 4. Manasseh ben-Israel writes in *Nishmat Ḥayyim*, I, 1: "In the end, [R. Yehudah] ha-Ḥayyat, ha-Ṣioni, and Recanati decided that it is not the flesh that is called man but the soul."

18. *Zohar Ḥadash*, Bereshit, fol. 28b. Translated in Tishby, *Wisdom of the Zohar,* 2:782.

19. See Idel, "Sarid mi-Perush Rabbi Meshulam ben Asher mi-Lunel," *Kobeṣ 'al Yad* 11, no. 21 (1985): 88.

20. On its usage in Jewish philosophy, see Aviezer Ravizky, "Ha-Torah ha-Antropologit shel ha-Nes," *Jerusalem Studies in Jewish Thought* 2, no. 3 (1983): 331–36.

21. See *Tanya*, chap. 19. And see Ḥalamish, *Nativ*, pp. 116–17. It should be pointed out that R. Shneur Zalman interpreted the precept of repentance as the climax of man's success in returning his soul to its origin (See, for instance, *Torah Or*, beginning of *Vayeḥi*). That is to say, it is incumbent upon every individual to repent, including the zaddik, and not only in the case of sin.

22. *Tanya*, chap. 22. See Ḥalamish, *Nativ*, pp. 132–34.

23. *Zohar* II, fol. 96b. The translation appears in Tishby, *Wisdom of the Zohar,* 2:752–53.

24. Ibid. 2:754.

25. I, fol. 59b–60a, etc.

26. *Tikkun* 22, fol. 65b.

27. See Tishby, *Wisdom of the Zohar,* 2:751–52.

28. Ibid., 2:752

29. On the reasons for the soul's descent in Greek philosophy, see ibid. 2:774 n. 44.

30. De Leon, *Shekel ha-Kodesh*, p. 5.

31. On the separation between body and soul, see Ezekiel Kaufmann, *Toledot*

ha-Emunah ha-Israelit (Jerusalem, 1960), pp. 245–47; Z. Hirsch, *Ha-Psychologia be-Sifruteynu ha-'Atika* (Tel Aviv, 1957), pp. 108–51; Urbach, *Sages,* 1:214–23.

32. *Sheney Luḥot ha-Berit*, Rosh ha-Shanah, fol. 221b.

33. See, for example, *Ḥovot ha-Levavot, Sha'ar Ḥeshbon ha-Nefesh* [On self-reckoning for God's sake], chap. 4.

34. See Berakhah Zak, "Ha-Adam Ke-Mar'ah," *Da'at* 12 (1984): 37–45.

35. R. Moses Cordovero, *Sefer Gerushin* (Jerusalem, 1962), p. 70. See also Zak, "Ha-Adam Ke-Mar'ah," pp. 40–41.

36. Schatz-Uffenheimer, *Maggid Devarav le-Ya'akov*, p. 275.

37. De Leon, *Ha-Nefesh ha-Ḥakhamah*, pt. 2. See Tishby, *Wisdom of the Zohar*, 2:680.

38. *Be'ur 'al Moreh Nevukhim* (Venice, 1574), fol. 24b.

39. This image is ancient. Note, for example, the Hebrew expression *ṣippor ha-nefesh* (the bird of the soul) or the figure in verses such as "As a bird that wanders from her nest, so is a man who wanders from his place" (Prov. 27:8), or "Our soul is like a bird escaped out of the snare of the fowlers" (Ps. 124:7). See also A. Aptovizer, "Die Seele als Vogel," *MGWJ* 69 (1925): 150–69. In the phrase of the *Zohar* III, fol. 228a: "The twittering of birds, which are the souls *[neshamot]* dwelling within the limbs."

40. *Sefer ha-Bahir*, par. 22; *Ma'arekhet ha-Elohut*, fol. 183b.

41. Naḥmanides on Gen. 2:7.

42. Hos. 14:9. See the commentary by R. 'Ezra on Song of Songs 2:3; 5:15 (*Perush Shir ha-Shirim,* pp. 489, 504). See also de Leon, *Shekel ha-Kodesh*, p. 69; Cordovero, *Sefer Gerushin*, par. 24; *Ḥemdat Yamim*, III, fol. 48d; and more.

43. Fol. 149b–151a.

44. Ibid., fol. 51b.

45. Abulafia, *Sha'ar ha-Razim*, p. 104. See also ibid., note 331.

46. *Genesis Rabbah,* XIV, 9.

47. De Leon, *Ha-Nefesh ha-Ḥakhamah* II, fol. 4a.

48. For instance, Gikatilla, *Sha'arey Orah,* I (ed. Ben-Shelomo, p. 89) and VIII (ed. Ben-Shelomo, p. 60).

49. See Tishby, *Wisdom of the Zohar,* 2:680–84.

50. Ibid. 2:705–8.

51. For example, the Commentary *P"Z* on *Ma'arekhet ha-Elohut*, fol. 51a.

52. Gikatilla, *Sha'arey Orah* VIII (ed. Ben-Shelomo, p. 60).

53. *Berit ha-Levi* (Lemberg, 1863), fol. 10b.

54. According to *Zohar Ḥadash*, Ruth. See Tishby, *Wisdom of the Zohar*, 2:730.

55. *Ecclesiastes Rabbah* had said that upon man's birth he is given the evil inclination, and only at the age of thirteen does the good inclination enter him. That is to say, at that point he is given the possibility of realizing the commandments. What is important here is the principle that man's life entails progress.

56. Similarly, Plato's theory of cognition is based on the soul's recollection of what it received above before birth. A renowned aggadah (*Niddah* 30b) says an angel teaches the fetus in utero, and upon his emergence into the world, hits his cheek, causing him to forget all he has learned. See L. Ginzburg, *The Legends of the Jews* (Philadelphia, 1942), 5:76–78; Tishby, *Wisdom of the Zohar,* 2:698.

57. *Zohar* I, fol. 224b.

58. Urbach, *Sages,* 1:232–50.

59. Tishby, *Wisdom of the Zohar,* 2:698–703.

60. See, for example, *Tur*, *Oraḥ Ḥayyim*, par. 46. Compare the end of the well-known liturgical poem, *Adon 'Olam*.

61. *Hanhagot RaMaK*, par. 29. See also Schechter, *Studies in Judaism,* pp. 293, 297, 298. Such practices were exceedingly common. See also *Yesod ha-Teshuvah* by R. Yonah Gerondi.

62. See Tishby's adept analysis in *The Wisdom of the Zohar,* 2:754–61.

63. *Zohar* II, fol. 95b.

64. Morning benedictions. The version that omits the word *hi* is preferable ("Neshamah . . . tehora").

65. See, for instance, *Iggeret ha-Kodesh*, attributed to Naḥmanides (*Kitvey ha-Ramban*, ed. Chavel, p. 328):

> It is well known that a man born from a cold drop will always be a foolish simpleton, and one born from a hot drop will be irascible and hot-tempered and easily angered, but he who is born of a drop tempered between hot and cold will always be wise and reasonable, noble and a man of intelligence, and will, by nature, be involved with his fellow men.

And further on (p. 331):

> When a man conjoins with his wife, if his imagination and his thoughts are occupied with matters of wisdom and understanding, and with worthy and respectable attributes, he has the power to invest the image in his thoughts within the drop of seed, just as he perceives it in the moment of union, and this is beyond all doubt. . . . And do not be surprised that it is so, for nature is simple even in the eyes of philosophers—commensurate with the thoughts and meditations that pass over the heart of a man and his wife as they unite, so will their offspring be formed, either good or evil [in a moral sense].

See also Recanati, *Perush 'al ha-Torah,* end of *Ki Teṣe*.

66. R. Abraham ben R. 'Azriel, *'Arugat ha-Bosem*, ed. E. E. Urbach (Jerusalem, 1963), p. 180; see also p. 112.

67. *Shef'a Tal* (Brooklyn, 1960), fol. 1a–4c.

68. Solomon Molkho, *Sefer ha-Mefo'ar* (Warsaw, 1884), fol. 13b.

69. R. Isaac of Acre, *Meirat 'Eynaim*, p. 31.

70. R. Meir ibn Gabbay, *Tola'at Ya'akov* (Jerusalem, 1967), fol. 45d.

71. See R. 'Azariah, *Ma'amar ha-Nefesh*, II, 10, fol. 19b. An extreme view is expressed by R. Joseph of Ḥamadan: "That is the mystical meaning of 'the righteous gentiles of the world have a share in the world to come'—because they come from an attribute of Israel [Tiferet!]." See *Ta'amey ha-Mizvot*, no. 80. An opposite view is presented in de Leon, *Shekel ha-Kodesh*, p. 66.

72. Vistinezky edition, par. 1021.

73. Ḥayyat, *Minḥat Yehudah*, 151a. See also *Zohar* I, fol. 216a.

74. See Scholem, *Von der Mystischen Gestalt der Gottheit* (Zurich, 1962), p. 235. Hebrew translation in idem, *Pirkey Yesod*, p. 346.

75. *SheLaH*, fol. 161b.

76. See Gottlieb, *Ha-Kabbalah*, p. 211 and n. 33.

77. *Sha'arey Kedushah* I, 5. Compare II, 4, on *sina'h*.

78. *Sefer ha-Peliah* (Przemysl, 1884), fol. 23b. The same direction, with no explanation, also appears in R. Meir Poppers's book, *Or Ṣaddikim*, *Tefillah*, sec. 24, par. 29.

79. See also M. Ḥalamish, "Aspektim Aḥadim . . . ," in *Philosophia Israelit*, ed. M. Ḥalamish and A. Kasher (Tel Aviv, 1983), pp. 49–71.

80. See Benjamin Minz, *Sefer ha-Histalkut* (Tel Aviv, 1930).

81. See Yissahar Ben-'Ami, *Ha'araṣat ha-Kedoshim be-Kerev Yehudey Morocco* (Jerusalem, 1984).

82. See *Zohar*, Vayeḥi. Also *Ma'avar Yabbok* by R. Aaron Berakhiah of Modena.

83. See Tishby, *Wisdom of the Zohar*, 2:834.

84. Some of them are described in *Ma'avar Yabbok*, and some in Meir Benayahu's work, *Ma'amadot u-Moshavot* (in memory of R. Isaac Nissim) vol. 6 (Jerusalem, 1985), which contains an extensive bibliography.

85. See Tishby, *Wisdom of the Zohar*, 2:845–46.

86. See, for example, Naḥmanides on Gen. 3:22. See also Ibn Gabbay, *'Avodat ha-Kodesh* II, chaps. 26-28.

87. R. Isaac of Acre, *Meirat 'Eynaim*, pp. 248–49.

88. See S. Assaf, "Iggerot mi-Ṣefat," *Kobeṣ 'al Yad* 3, no. 13 (1940): 123–24.

89. *Oṣar ha-Kavod*, on *Shabbat*, fol. 107. Compare, during the same period, the position of other thinkers, such as Maimonides, *Hilkhot Teshuvah* V, 4; R. Yehudah ben R. Asher [ha-RoSH], Responsa *Zikheron Yehudah*, par. 91, etc.

90. Consider the extensive discussions by Tishby, *Wisdom of the Zohar*, 2:770–73; Scholem, *Von der Mystischen Gestalt*, pp. 249–71. In Hebrew translation: idem, *Pirkey Yesod*, pp. 358–80.

91. *Livnat ha-Sappir* (Jerusalem, 1914), fol. 6d. See also *'Eṣ Ḥayyim*, XXVI, 1.

92. See Tishby, *Wisdom of the Zohar*, 2:787–89.

93. Vital, *Sefer ha-Gilgulim* (Przemyshl, 1875), chap. 64, fol. 85c.

94. Lurianic Kabbalah went even further, teaching that each part of the tripartite soul *(nefesh-ru'ah-neshamah)* had a separate *ṣelem*. Were that not so, the meeting between the soul and the body would have been exceedingly destructive due to the great disparity between them.

95. *Zohar* II, fol. 142b. According to R. Joseph Angelino (*Livnat ha-Sappir*, fol. 6d), though, "It will not be stripped naked," that is, the body will remain clothed.

96. *Keter Shem Tov*, in *Ma'or va-Shemesh* (Leghorn, 1839), fol. 39a, but with errors. Our citation here is according to MS Munich 17, fol. 37a.

97. See Naḥmanides on Numbers 14:9.

98. On this idea in greater depth, see the discussion by Y. D. Wilhelm, *'Aley 'AYiN* (Jerusalem, 1948–52), pp. 130–43.

99. *Keter Shem Tov*, *Ki Teṣe*, according to MS Munich 17, fol. 282a. Recanati,

though, *Vayeshev*, fol. 34a writes: "He could tell according to a person's face whether he was among the new or the old."

100. Benayahu, *Sefer Toledot ha-ARI,* p. 157.

101. *'Ad Hena* (Jerusalem, 1960), pp. 305–20.

102. See Scholem, *Sabbatai Ṣevi,* pp. 39–41.

103. Ibid, p. 41.

104. *Tanya* (*Sefer Shel Beinonim*), chap. 51, trans. N. Mindel (New York, 1962). See Ḥalamish, *Nativ*, pp. 316–17.

Chapter 14. The Doctrine of Transmigration

1. In his commentary to Deut. 29:17, Naḥmanides writes: "For the matter is true, there being a great secret therein which I cannot explain." (*RaMBaN*, ed. Chavel, 5:334.)

2. Shem Tov ibn Shem Tov, *Sefer ha-Emunot* VII, chap. 4, 8.

3. Though, according to the midrash (*Genesis Rabbah* 28.3, and see also Tosafot to *Babba Kama* 15b), there is a bone in the spine called *luz* which is not consumed in the grave.

4. Shem Tov ibn Shem Tov, *Sefer ha-Emunot* VII, end of chap. 1.

5. See Scholem, *Pirkey Yesod*, p. 310.

6. Naḥmanides, *Sha'ar ha-Gemul*, in *Kitvey ha-Ramban,* ed. Chavel, 2:279.

7. For example, in a poem by R. Joseph Gikatilla, in which he devotes but a single line to it, writing: "And there is punishment at man's end and recompense in hidden mystery." See Gruenwald, "Shney Shirim shel ha-Mekubal Yosef Gikatilla," *Tarbiṣ* 36 (1967): 88. Consider also Shem Tov ibn Shem Tov, *Sefer ha-Emunot* fol. 76a.

8. Recanati, for instance, remarks on a few occasions: "Yet if it is a received tradition *[kabbalah],* let us accept it" (e.g., end of *Kedoshim*, fol. 65b). This would imply he is not completely at ease with the idea.

9. *'Avodat ha-Kodesh*, II, chap. 33.

10. Fol. 35d.

11. Vital, *Sefer ha-Gilgulim,* p. 42.

12. See Tishby, *Ha-Ra'ayon*, p. 17.

13. "Kobeṣ Likkutim Teimani," MS Jerusalem 4°657, p. 77.

14. *Sava de-Mishpatim*, fol. 99b. Translation from *Zohar,* trans. Sperling, Simon, and Levertoff, 3:302. On the complexity of the doctrine of transmigration in Lurianic teaching, see, for example, Vital, *Sefer ha-Gilgulim*, chap. 4.

15. For instance: Gen. 38:18; Exod. 34:4; Deut. 3:26; 33:6; 2 Sam. 14:14; Amos 2:4; Job 33 (in particular); Eccles. 1:4; 1:9; 4:2; 8:10; 8:14; and many others. See also *Sefer ha-Bahir*, par. 121; Recanati, *Perush 'al ha-Torah,* fol. 34b–c; Ṣioni, *Perush 'al ha-Torah,* fol. 17d, etc. In R. Isaac of Acre, *Meirat 'Eynaim*, pp. 29–30, numerous verses are mentioned.

16. See, for example, Recanati, *Perush 'al ha-Torah,* fol. 16a–c; R. Isaac of Acre, *Meirat 'Eynaim*, pp. 31–32.

17. See Naḥmanides' commentary on Job, and *Kad ha-Kemaḥ*, entry "*hash-gaḥah.*"

18. *Sefer ha-Bahir*, par. 195. And see also *Zohar Ḥadash*, Midrash ha-Ne'elam, Teṣe, fol. 59a, and other sources from the Geronese circle.

19. Its resolution of that essential problem is what convinced a foremost halakhic scholar, R. Levi ben-Ḥabib (who lived in the sixteenth century; see RaLBaḤ Responsa, par. 8) to adopt the belief in transmigration, despite his inadequate understanding of it due to the veil of secrecy in which the Kabbalists had concealed it.

20. *Ma'arekhet ha-Elohut*, Commentary *P"Z*, fol. 7d. Also cited in *Segulot*, chap. 2. See M. Ḥalamish, *Le-Toledot ha-Kabbalah be-Teiman* (Jerusalem, 1984), p. 42.

21. Par. 195. Incidentally, this explanation offered by *Sefer ha-Bahir* in response to the question of theodicy was even used by Naḥmanides in his interpretation of Job's suffering.

22. For another answer in the *Zohar*, see Tishby, *Wisdom of the Zohar,* 2: 852–54.

23. Hasidic lore tells of a man who bought a young, healthy horse, and made his livelihood from it. One day, the horse refused to move. In despair, the Hasid turned to his teacher, the zaddik, who "explained" to him that a certain person who had been his debtor had died before he had managed to pay off his debt, and in order to pay it off had transmigrated to the horse. Once the debt had been paid, the horse died.

24. Ibn Shem Tov, *Sefer ha-Emunot*, VII, chap. 2.

25. See Ṣioni, *Perush 'al ha-Torah,* fol. 17d.

26. The first to do so was R. Joseph of Ḥamadan, in his book *Ta'amey ha-Miṣvot*; he explained ritual sacrifices, ritual slaughter, and the prohibition against inflicting animals with needless suffering, for example, on the basis of transmigration. See Scholem, *Pirkey Yesod*, p. 335.

27. See the discussion by Recanati, *Perush 'al ha-Torah,* fol. 34d.

28. See Commentary *P"Z* of *Ma'arekhet ha-Elohut*, fol. 127.

29. See, for instance, *Sefer ha-Peliah*, fol. 12a–b; *Sefer ha-Kanah*, *Sod ha-Sheḥitah*, fol. 130a. See also Elijah ha-Kohen, *Shevet Musar*, chap. 36.

30. Abraham Azulay, *Ḥesed le-Avraham* (Vilna, 1877), V, 17. It originates in Vital, *Sha'ar ha-Miṣvot*, '*Ekev*, where various and detailed discussions about eating may be found.

31. This was aptly described by Ḥ. Shmeruk in his essay "Mashma'utah ha-Ḥevratit shel ha-Sheḥitah ha-Ḥasidit," *Zion* 20 (1955): 47–72.

32. Vital, *Sha'ar ha-Miṣvot*, *Kedoshim*, fol. 24b.

33. Vital, *Sefer ha-Gilgulim*, IV.

34. *Tikkun* 69, fol. 112a. See also fol. 114a.

35. This follows from the context. Refer to the passage itself. Some Kabbalists, however, did not interpret in that way. See Scholem, *Pirkey Yesod*, p. 330 n. 54.

36. *Tikkun* 70, fol. 133a. Similarly, in David ben Yehudah he-Ḥasid, *Sefer Mar'ot ha-Ṣove'ot*, p. 135: "The soul of a male sucks from the soul of a male, and the soul of a female sucks from the soul of a female. Hence [the benediction] 'For not creating

me a woman,' for sometimes the souls are exchanged, and for that reason barren women came into the world, their souls stemming from the male." Interestingly, in many prayer books, as early as the Middle Ages, that explanation was added in a marginal note. This seems to ring of apologetics.

37. R. Isaac of Acre, *Me'irat 'Eynaim*, p. 35.

38. Such as R. Sheshet of Desmercadil, student of Naḥmanides. See Scholem, *Pirkey Yesod*, pp. 31, 318; Recanati, *Vayeshev*, fol. 34b; R. David ben Zimra, *Ta'amey ha-Miṣvot* (Zolkiew, 1862), fol. 27d.

39. R. 'Ezra of Gerona, *Perush le-Shir ha-Shirim,* in vol. 2 of *Kitvey ha-Ramban,* ed. H. D. Chavel (Jerusalem, 1964), p. 511.

40. *Emunot ve-De'ot* VI, chap. 7. See also Ibn Daud, *Ha-Emunah ha-Ramah*, p. 39; Abraham bar Ḥiyya, *Megillat ha-Megalleh*, p. 51. The same is true in Arabic. On the sources of this idea, see Scholem, *Pirkey Yesod*, p. 318 n. 23.

41. *Ta'amey ha-Miṣvot* (Basle, 1581), fol. 16a. See also Ibn Shem Tov, *Sefer ha-Emunot*, VII, end of chap. 1, fol. 76a (the page numbering there is distorted).

42. And see Scholem, *Pirkey Yesod*, pp. 317 n. 19, 331 n. 56. Compare Scholem's discussion on R. Joseph Taitazak, "Ha-Hagid shel R. Joseph Taitaṣak," in *Ṣefunot* 11 (1971–78): 71.

43. Vital, *Sefer ha-Gilgulim*, V, fol. 8b.

44. Yeḥiel Ashkenazi, *Heikhal ha-Shem* (Venice, [1605?]), fol. 37a.

45. Vital, *Sha'ar ha-Miṣvot*, Teṣe, fol. 54b.

46. Quoted by Benayahu, *Sefer Toledot ha-ARI*, pp. 175–77.

47. Vital, *Sefer ha-Gilgulim*, fol. 8b.

48. Ibid, fol. 9b. See also Azulay, *Ḥesed le-Avraham*, V, end of *Nahar* 17, etc.

49. *Responsa ha-RaDBaZ*, III, sec. 910 (= Part VI, 2088).

50. See above, note 44.

51. See the account in *Nishmat Ḥayyim* by R. Manasseh ben Israel, III, chap. 10 (Israel, 1968), fol. 47c–48d. Also Benayahu, *Sefer Toledot ha-ARI*, pp. 252–56.

52. Scholem, *Pirkey Yesod*, p. 332. On the phenomenon of the *dibbuk*, its evolution and related details, see the work by Gedaliyah Nigal, *Sippurey Dibbuk* (Jerusalem, 1983).

53. *Sha'ar ha-Miṣvot, 'Ekev*, fol. 43b.

54. Azulay, *Ḥesed le-Avraham*, V, 25, fol. 46c. On the tale of the spirit, see above, n. 51.

55. "Perush Ma'aseh Bereshit," MS Paris 823, fol. 181a.

56. *Sefer ha-Peliah*, fol. 27b.

57. Commentary *P"Z* to *Ma'arekhet ha-Elohut*, fol. 127a.

58. Ibn Gabbay, *'Avodat ha-Kodesh*, fol. 49b.

59. He may have been preceded by a Kabbalist by the name of ben Belimah. See Scholem, *Reshit ha-Kabbalah*, p. 242.

60. Ibn Gabbay, *'Avodat ha-Kodesh*, II, chap. 35, fol. 52a.

61. See *Zohar Ḥadash*, Midrash ha-Ne'elam on Ruth, fol. 89a. See also Recanati, *Perush 'al ha-Torah,* fol. 34c–d.

62. This view is voiced by R. Joseph Ḥamadan. See Scholem, *Pirkey Yesod*, p. 319 n. 26.

63. See Gottlieb, *Meḥkarim*, pp. 370–96.

64. *Sod ha-Yibbum*, fol. 114a. See also fol. 112a ff. of that work.

65. For some sources, see Scholem, *Mada'ey ha-Yahadut*, pp. 286–87.

66. Ṣioni, *Perush 'al ha-Torah,* fol. 36b. And see note 76 below.

67. This is said, for instance, by R. Baḥya on Deut. 33:6 (ed. Chavel, p. 480); R. Yosef Alcastiel (see Scholem, "li-idi'at ha-Kabbalah bi-Sefarad 'erev ha-Gerush," *Tarbiṣ* 24 [1955]: 194). It may be understood from "The Story of a Widow." See Manasseh ben-Israel, *Nishmat Ḥayyim*, fol. 72b ff.

68. Azulay, *Ḥesed le-Avraham*, 5:19.

69. See, for example, *Tikkuney Zohar*, Tikkun 70, fol. 126a.

70. *Minḥat Yehudah*, fol. 150a–151b.

71. RaDBaZ, *Magen David* (Lemberg, 1883), fol. 30a.

72. Recanati, *Perush 'al ha-Torah,* fol. 35b.

73. R. Avraham ha-Levi, *Ma'amar Masoret ha-Ḥokhmah*. See Scholem, *Perakim*, p. 151.

74. Commentary *P"Z* to *Ma'arekhet ha-Elohut*, fol. 127a.

75. Fol. 16a.

76. See Scholem, *Temunah*, p. 60. And compare above, n. 66.

77. R. Sheshet Desmercadil. See Scholem, "Le-Ḥeqer Torat ha-Gilgul ba-Kabbalah ba-Me'ah ha-Slosh-'Esreh," *Tarbiṣ* 16 (1945): 144.

78. Vital, *Sefer ha-Gilgulim*, Likkutim, fol. 75b. Also, *Sha'ar ha-Gilgulim*, Hakdamah 22.

79. Vital, *Sefer ha Gilgulim*, IV, fol. 6b.

80. Ibid., XIII, fol, 21b.

81. Ibid., IV, fol. 7a. See also above, chap 8, n. 63.

82. Scholem, "Le-Ḥeqer Torat ha-Gilgul," pp. 145–49.

83. Vital, *Sha'ar ha-Gilgulim*, Hakdamah 22.

84. Recanati, *Vayeshev*, fol. 34a. Compare Commentary *P"Z* of *Ma'arekhet ha-Elohut*, fol. 184b.

85. This is the view of R. Joseph Ḥamadan. See Gottlieb, *Meḥkarim*, p. 254 n. 30.

86. See, for example, *Tikkuney Zohar*, Tikkun 70, fol. 133a.

87. See Recanati, *Kedoshim*, fols. 65b, 64c, 61c.

88. Such as R. David ben Abraham Halavan, in *Sefer Masoret ha-Berit; Sefer ha-Temunah; Sefer ha-Peliah*, fol. 31c.

89. Such as Ibn Shem Tov, *Sefer ha-Emunot; Sefer Iggeret Hamudot; Minḥat Yehudah*, fol. 150b.

90. Ibn Shem Tov, *Sefer ha-Emunot*, VII, 8. Consider the wider context there. See also *Nishmat Ḥayyim* by Manasseh ben-Israel, fol. 71d.

91. *Perush le-Sefer Yeṣirah*, Hakdamah, 8b–c.

92. *Novelot Ḥokhmah* (Basle, 1631), fol. 186a.

93. *Migdal David*, fol. 30c.

94. *Sha'ar ha-Miṣvot*, *'Ekev*, fol. 41b–42a.

95. Such as R. Joseph Ḥamadan, *Miṣvah* 74. See Gottlieb, *Meḥkarim*, p. 252.

96. Vital, *Sha'ar Ru'aḥ ha-Kodesh*, fol. 6a. And see, for example, Azikri, *Sefer Ḥaredim*, fol. 41b.

97. Vital, *Sha'ar ha-Mişvot*, 'Ekev, fol. 42b.
98. See Scholem, "Le-Ḥeqer Torat ha-Gilgul," 145.
99. *Kad ha-Kemah*, fol. 151.
100. *Sefer ha-Bahir*, par. 195. See above, p. 284 and n. 18.
101. Fol. 33a.
102. Scholem, "Le-Ḥeqer Torat ha-Gilgul," p. 145.
103. Recanati, *Vayeshev*, pp. 65, 34.
104. Like the *Zohar*, and Azulay, *Ḥesed le-Avraham* II, 47.
105. Azulay, *Ḥesed le-Avraham*, V, 16.
106. Recanati, *Perush 'al ha Torah,* fol. 35b; 63c, end of *Aḥarey*. See also Ṣioni, *Perush 'al ha Torah,* fol. 17d.
107. Ḥayyat, *Minḥat Yehudah*, fol. 150b.
108. See Scholem, "li-idi 'at ha Kabbalah bi-Sefarad 'erev ha-Gerush," p. 194.
109. On this in greater detail, see M. Ḥalamish, "Aspektim Aḥadim be-She'elat Yaḥasam shel ha-Mekubbalim le-Umot ha-'Olam," in *Philosophia Israelit,* ed. M. Ḥalamish and A. Kasher (Tel Aviv, 1982), pp. 49–71.
110. *Massekhet Ḥibbut ha-Kever*, in A. Jellinek, *Bet ha-Midrasch*, Heder 1, pp. 150–52. See also his introduction. And see Vidas, *Reshit Ḥokhmah*, I, 12; Vital, *Sha'ar ha-Gilgulim* (Przemysl, 1875), chap. 20.
111. Ḥayyat, *Minḥat Yehudah*, fol. 150b.
112. See, for example, R. Isaac of Acre, *Meirat 'Eynaim*, pp. 32–35.
113. Fol. 150b. Compare Scholem, *Pirkey Yesod*, pp. 325–27.
114. *'Eṣ ha-Da'at*, Mishpatim.
115. *Responsa RaShBA* (Benei Berak, 1958), par. 418, pp. 164–65.
116. *Or ha-Shem*, IV, 7.
117. See Gottlieb's discussion in *Meḥkarim*, pp. 370–96, and pp. 385–91 in particular.
118. *Sefer ben David*, in *Ta'am Zekenim* (Frankfort-am-Main, 1854), fol. 62a.
119. Ibid., fol. 63a.
120. *Ari Nohem,* pp. 36–47.
121. See *Kobeṣ 'al Yad* 8, no. 18 (1976): 408ff.

Epilogue

1. R. Isaac of Acre, *Meirat 'Eynaim,* p. 212.

BIBLIOGRAPHY

Abulafia, Todros. *Sha'ar ha-Razim*. Edited by Mikhal Oron. Jerusalem, 1989.

Ashkenazi, Yeḥiel. *Heikhal ha-Shem*. Venice [1605?].

Azikri, Eleazar. *Sefer Ḥaredim*. Venice, 1601.

Azulay, Abraham. *Ḥesed le-Avraham*. Vilna, 1877.

Baḥya ben Asher. *Shulḥan shel Arb'a*. Edited by H. D. Chavel. In vol. 4 of *Kitvey Rabbeynu Baḥya*. Jerusalem, 1964.

Bakharakh, Naftali. *'Emek ha-Melekh*. Amsterdam, 1648.

Benayahu, M. *Sefer Toledot ha-ARI*. Jerusalem, 1967.

Ben-Shelomo, Joseph. *Torat ha-Elohut shel Rabbi Moshe Cordovero*. Jerusalem, 1965.

Cordovero, Moses. *Eilimah*. Jerusalem, 1966. Photocopy edition.

———. *Sefer Gerushin*. Jerusalem, 1962.

Dan, Joseph. *Torat ha-Sod shel Ḥasidut Ashkenaz*. Jerusalem, 1968.

David ben Yehudah he-Ḥasid. *Sefer Mar'ot ha-Zove'ot*. In *The Book of Mirrors*, edited by Daniel Chanan Matt. Chico, Calif., 1982.

Dov Baer, the Maggid of Mezhirech. *Maggid Devarav le-Ya'akov*. Edited by R. Schatz. Jerusalem, 1976.

Elijah ha-Kohen. *Shevet Musar*. References according to chapters.

'Ezra of Gerona. *Perush le-Shir ha-Shirim*. In vol. 2 of *Kitvey ha-Ramban*, edited by H. D. Chavel. Jerusalem, 1964.

Gikatilla, Joseph. *Sha'arey Orah*. Warsaw, 1883.

Gottlieb, Ephraim. *Ha-Kabbalah be-Kitvey Rabbeynu Baḥya ben Asher*. Jerusalem, 1970.

———. *Meḥkarim be-Sifrut ha-Kabbalah*. Tel Aviv, 1976.

Ḥallamish, Moshe. *Nativ la-Tanya*. Tel Aviv, 1987.

Ḥayyat, Yehudah. *Minḥat Yehudah*. In *Ma'arekhet ha-Elohut*. Mantua, 1558.

Heikhalot Rabbati. Edited by S. A. Wertheimer. In vol. 1 of *Batey Midrashot*. Jerusalem, 1950.

Horowitz, Isaiah. *Sheney Luḥot ha-Berit* (*ShLaH*). Amsterdam, 1698.

Horowitz, Shabbetai Sheftel. *Nishmat Shabbetai ha-Levi*. Podgorza, 1898.

ibn Gabbay, Meir. *'Avodat ha-Kodesh*. Jerusalem, 1954.

ibn Gaon, Shem Tov. *Badey Aaron u-Migdal Ḥanan'el*. Jerusalem, 1978.

ibn Lavi, Simeon. *Ketem Paz*. Djerba, 1940.

ibn Shem Tov, Shem Tov. *Sefer ha-Emunot*. Ferrara, 1556.

Idel, Moshe. *Kabbalah*. New Haven, 1988.

Isaac of Acre. *Meirat 'Eynaim*. Edited by Amos Goldreich. Jerusalem, 1984.

Israel Ba'al Shem Tov. *Ṣava'at ha-RiBaSH*. Jerusalem, 1948.

Jacob ben Sheshet. *Ha-Emunah ve-ha-Bitaḥon*. In vol. 1 of *Kitvey ha-Ramban*. Jerusalem, 1964.

Jellinek, Adolff. *Ginzey Ḥokhmat ha-Kabbalah*. Leipzig, 1853.

Karo, Joseph. *Maggid Meisharim*. Vilna, 1875.

Likkutim Yekarim. Lemberg, 1872.

Ma'arekhet ha-Elohut. Mantua, 1558.

Manasseh ben Israel. *Nishmat Ḥayyim*. Jerusalem, 1968. Photocopy edition.

Menaḥem 'Azariah of Fano. *Ma'amar ha-Nefesh*. Piotrkow, 1903.

Menaḥem Mendel of Vitebsk. *Peri ha-Areṣ*. References according to the pericope.

Merkavah Shelemah. Edited by S. Mussaieff. Jerusalem, 1921.

Meshullam Phoebus of Zbarazh. *Yosher Divrei Emet*. Muncacz, 1905.

Moses de Leon. *Ha-Nefesh ha-Ḥakhamah*. Basle, 1601.

———. *Shekel ha-Kodesh*. London, 1911.

Naḥmanides. *RaMBaN (Naḥmanides), Commentary on the Torah*. Translated and annotated by Charles B. Chavel. New York, 1971–76.

———. *Sha'ar ha-Gemul*. In vol. 2 of *Kitvey ha-Ramban*, edited by H. D. Chavel. Jerusalem, 1964.

Or ha-Emet. Zhitomir, 1901.

Or Torah. Jerusalem, 1968.

Recanati, Menaḥem. *Perush 'al ha-Torah*. Lemberg, 1880.

Schaefer, Peter. *Synopse zur Hekhalot-Literatur*. Tübingen, 1981.

Scharfstein, Ben-Ami. *Ha-Ḥavayah ha-Mystit*. Tel Aviv, 1972.

Schatz-Uffenheimer, Rivka. *Hasidism as Mysticism*. Translated by J. Chipman. Princeton, 1993. Originally published in Hebrew in 1968.

Schechter, Solomon. *Studies in Judaism*. 2d ser. Philadelphia, 1928.

Scholem, Gershom. *Devarim be-Go*. Tel Aviv, 1976.

———. *Ha-Kabbalah be-Gerona*. Jerusalem, 1964.

———. *Ha-Kabbalah be-Provence*. Jerusalem, 1963.

———. *Ha-Kabbalah shel Sefer ha-Temunah ve-shel Avraham Abulafia*, Jerusalem, 1965.

———. "Kitvey Rabbi Ya'akov ve-Rabbi Yizhak beney Ya'akov ha-Kohen." In vol. 2 of *Mada'ey ha-Yahadut*. Jerusalem, 1927.

———. *Kitvey Yad be-Kabbalah*. Jerusalem, 1930.

———. *Major Trends in Jewish Mysticism*. Jerusalem, 1941.

———. *The Origins of the Kabbalah*. Philadelphia, 1987.

———. *Perakim le-Toledot Sifrut ha-Kabbalah*. Jerusalem, 1931.

———. *Pirkey Yesod ba-Havanat ha-Kabbalah u-Semaleha*. Jerusalem, 1976.

———. *Reshit ha-Kabbalah*. Jerusalem and Tel Aviv, 1948.

———. *Reshit ha-Kabbalah ve-Sefer ha-Bahir*. Jerusalem, 1962.

———. *Sabbatai Ṣevi: The Mystical Messiah*. Translated from Hebrew by R. J. Zwi Werblowsky. Princeton, 1973. Originally published in Hebrew in 1957.

Sefer ha-Bahir. Edited by R. Margaliot. Jerusalem, 1951.

Sefer ha-Kanah. Cracow, 1894.

Sefer ha-Peliah. Przemysl, 1884.

Sefer ha-Temunah. Lemberg, 1892.

Sha'ar ha-Sho'el (also entitled *Perush le-'Eser Sefirot le-Rabbi 'Azriel* [of Gerona]). In *Derekh Emunah*. Warsaw, 1890.

Solomon Shlumil of Dresnitz, *Shivḥey ha-ARI*. Przemysl, 1869.

Tishby, Isaiah. "Ha-'Immut bein Kabbalat ha-ARI le-vein Kabbalat ha-RaMaK, etc." *Zion* 39 (1974): 8–85.

———. "Ha-Ra'ayon ha-Meshiḥi ve-ha-Meggamot ha-Meshiḥiot be-Ṣemihat ha-Ḥasidut." *Zion* 32 (1967): 1–45.

———. *Ḥikrey Kabbalah u-Sheluḥoteha*. Vol. 1. Jerusalem, 1982.

———. *Netivey Emunah u-Minut*. Ramat Gan, 1965.

———. *Perush ha-Aggadot le-Rabbi 'Azriel*. Jerusalem, 1945.

———. *Torat ha-R'a ve-ha-Kelippah be-Kabbalat ha-ARI*. Jerusalem, 1942.

———. *The Wisdom of the Zohar*. Translated by D. Goldstein. Oxford, 1989. Originally published in Hebrew in 1957 and 1959.

Urbach, E. E. *The Sages*. Jerusalem, 1975. Originally published in 1969.

Vidas, Elijah de. *Reshit Ḥokhmah*. Muncacz, 1926.

Vital, Ḥayyim. *'Eṣ Ḥayyim*. Jerusalem, 1896.

———. *Sefer ha-Gilgulim*, Vilna, 1886.

———. *Sha'ar ha-Kavvanot*, Jerusalem, 1902.

———. *Sha'ar ha-Miṣvot*. Jerusalem, 1905.

———. *Sha'ar Ru'aḥ ha-Kodesh*. Jerusalem, 1912.

Werblowsky, R. J. Zwi. *Joseph Karo: Lawyer and Mystic*. Oxford, 1962.

Ṣioni, Menaḥem. *Perush 'al ha-Torah*. Lemberg, 1872.

The Zohar. Translated by H. Sperling, Maurice Simon, and Paul Levertoff. 5 vols. London, 1933.

Zohar Ḥadash. Warsaw, 1885.

INDEX OF PERSONS

INDEX OF TITLES